D0606915

U·X·L ENCYCLOPEDIA OF
NATIVE AMERICAN TRIBES

U·X·L ENCYCLOPEDIA OF NATIVE AMERICAN TRIBES

VOLUME

2

The Great Basin
Southwest

Sharon Malinowski, Anna Sheets
& Linda Schmittroth, *Editors*

AN IMPRINT OF THE GALE GROUP

DETROIT · SAN FRANCISCO · LONDON
BOSTON · WOODBRIDGE, CT

U•X•L Encyclopedia of Native American Tribes

Sharon Malinowski, Anna Sheets, and Linda Schmittroth, *Editors*

Staff

Sonia Benson, *U•X•L Senior Editor*
Carol DeKane Nagel, *U•X•L Managing Editor*
Thomas L. Romig, *U•X•L Publisher*
Jeffrey Lehman, *Editor*
Melissa Walsh Doig, *Editor*
Dorothy Maki, *Manufacturing Manager*
Evi Seoud, *Assistant Production Manager*
Rita Wimberley, *Senior Buyer*
Cynthia Baldwin, *Product Design Manager*
Barbara Yarrow, *Graphic Services Director*
Michelle DiMercurio, *Senior Art Director*
Keasha Jack-Lyles, *Permissions Associate*
LM Design, *Typesetter*

Library of Congress Cataloging-in-Publication Data

U•X•L Encyclopedia of Native American Tribes / Sharon Malinowski, Anna Sheets, and Linda Schmittroth, editors

p. cm.

Includes bibliographical references.

Contents: v. 1. The Northeast and Southeast – v. 2. The Great Basin and Southwest – v. 3. The Arctic, Subarctic, Great Plains, and Plateau – v. 4. California and the Pacific Northwest.

ISBN 0-7876-2838-7 (set).

ISBN 0-7876-2839-5 (volume 1)   ISBN 0-7876-2841-7 (volume 3)

ISBN 0-7876-2840-9 (volume 2)   ISBN 0-7876-2842-5 (volume 4)

1. Indians of North America – Encyclopedias, Juvenile. [1. Indians of North America – Encyclopedias.] I. Malinowski, Sharon. II. Sheets, Anna J. (Anna Jean), 1970– . III. Schmittroth, Linda. IV. Title: Encyclopedia of Native American tribes.

E76.2.U85 1999

970'.003—dc21

98-54353

CIP
AC

Contents

VOLUME 2

The Great Basin

Southwest

VOLUME 3

VOLUME 4

Tribes Alphabetically

First numeral signifies volume number. The numeral after the colon signifies page number. For example, **3:871** means Volume 3, page 871.

Reader's Guide

Long before the Vikings, Spaniards, and Portuguese made land-fall on North American shores, the continent already had a rich history of human settlement. The *U•X•L Encyclopedia of Native American Tribes* opens up for students the array of tribal ways in the United States and Canada past and present. Included in these volumes, readers will find the stories of:

- the well-known nineteenth century Lakota hunting the buffalo on the Great Plains

- the contemporary Inuit of the Arctic, who have recently won their battle for Nunavut, a vast, self-governing territory in Canada

- the Seminole in Florida, drawing tourists with their alligator wrestling shows

- the Haida of the Pacific Northwest, whose totem poles have become a familiar adornment of the landscape

- the Anasazi in the Southwest, who were building spectacular cities long before Europeans arrived

- the Mohawk men in the Northeast who made such a name for themselves as ironworkers on skyscrapers and bridges that they have long been in demand for such projects as the World Trade Center and the Golden Gate Bridge

- the Yahi of California, who became extinct when their last member Ishi died in 1916.

The *U•X•L Encyclopedia of Native American Tribes* presents eighty tribes, confederacies, and Native American groups. Among the tribes included are large and well-known nations, smaller communities with their own fascinating stories, and prehistoric peoples. The tribes are grouped in the ten major geographical/cultural areas of North America in which tribes shared environmental and cultural connections. The ten sections, each beginning with an introductory essay on the geographical area and the shared history and culture within it, are arranged in the volumes as follows:

- Volume 1: Northeast and Southeast
- Volume 2: The Great Basin and Southwest
- Volume 3: Arctic, Subarctic, Great Plains, and Plateau
- Volume 4: California and Pacific Northwest

The *U•X•L Encyclopedia of Native American Tribes* provides the history of each of the tribes featured and a fascinating look at their ways of life: how families lived in centuries past and today, what people ate and wore, what their homes were like, how they worshiped, celebrated, governed themselves, and much more. A student can learn in depth about one tribe or compare aspects of many tribes. Each detailed entry is presented in consistent rubrics that allow for easy access and comparison, as follows:

- History
- Religion
- Language
- Government
- Economy
- Daily Life
- Arts
- Customs
- Current Tribal Issues
- Notable People

Each entry begins with vital data on the tribe: name, location, population, language family, origins and group affiliations. A locator map follows, showing the traditional homelands and contemporary communities of the group; regional and migration maps throughout aid in locating the many groups and at different times in history. Brief timelines in each entry chronicle important dates of the tribe's history, while an overall timeline at the beginning of all the volumes outlines key events in history pertinent to all Native Americans. Other sidebars present recipes, oral literature or stories, population statistics, language keys, and background material on the tribe. Black-and-white photographs and illustrations, further reading sections, a thorough subject index, and a glossary are special features that make the volumes easy, fun, and informative to use.

A note on terminology

Throughout the *U•X•L Encyclopedia of Native American Tribes* various terms are used for Native North Americans, such as *Indian, American Indian, Native,* and *aboriginal.* The Native peoples of the Americas have the unfortunate distinction of having been given the wrong name by the Europeans who first arrived on the continent, mistakenly thinking they had arrived in India. The search for a single name, however, has never been entirely successful. The best way to characterize Native North Americans is by recognizing their specific tribal or community identities. In compiling this book, every effort has been made to keep Native tribal and community identities distinct, but by necessity, inclusive terminology is often used. We do not wish to offend anyone, but rather than favor one term for Native North American people, the editors have used a variety of terminology, trying always to use the most appropriate term in the particular context.

Europeans also had a hand in giving names to tribes, often misunderstanding their languages and the relations between different Native communities. Most tribes have their own names for themselves, and many have succeeded in gaining public acceptance of traditional names. The Inuit, for example, objected to the name Eskimo, which means "eaters of raw meat," and in time their name for themselves was accepted. In the interest of clarity the editors of this book have used the currently accepted terms, while acknowledging the traditional ones or the outmoded ones at the beginning of each entry.

The term *tribe* itself is not accepted by all Native groups. The people living in North America before the Europeans arrived had many different ways of organizing themselves politically and relating to other groups around them—from complex confederacies and powerful unified nations to isolated villages with little need for political structure. Groups divided, absorbed each other, intermarried, allied, and dissolved. The epidemics and wars that came with non-Native expansion into North America created a demographic catastrophe to many Native groups and greatly affected tribal affiliations. Although in modern times there are actual rules about what comprises a tribe (federal requirements for recognition of tribes are specific, complicated, and often difficult to fulfill), the hundreds of groups living in the Americas in early times did not have any one way of categorizing themselves. Some Native American peoples today find the word *tribe* misleading. In a study of Indian peoples, it can also be an elusive defining term. But in facing the challenges of maintaining traditions and heritage in modern times, tribal or community identity is acutely important to many Native Americans. Tremendous efforts have been undertaken to preserve native languages, oral traditions, religions, ceremonies, and traditional arts and economies— the things that, put together, make a tribe a cultural and political unit.

Advisors and contributors

For the invaluable contributions, suggestions, and advice on the *U•X•L Encyclopedia of Native American Tribes,* special thanks are due to: Edward D. Castillo, (Cahuilla-Luiseño), Director, Native American Studies Program, Sonoma State University, California; Ned Blackhawk; Elizabeth Hanson, Ph.D., Research Associate to the Dean, The College of Charleston, South Carolina; Daniel Boxberger, Department of Anthropology, Western Washington University; John H. Moore, Ph.D., Anthropology Department, University of Florida, Gainesville; Amanda Beresford McCarthy; George Cornell, Ph.D., Associate Professor, History and American Studies, Michigan State University; Brian Wescott, Athabascan/Yup'ik; Gordon L. Pullar, Director, Department of Alaska Native and Rural Development, College of Rural Alaska,UAF; and Barbara Bigelow.

Comments and suggestions

In this first edition of the *U•X•L Encyclopedia of Native American Tribes* we have presented in-depth information on eighty of the hundreds of tribes of North America. While every attempt was made to include a wide representation of groups, many historically important and interesting tribes are not covered in these volumes. We welcome your suggestions for tribes to be featured in future editions, as well as any other comments you may have on this set. Please write: Editors, *U•X•L Encyclopedia of Native American Tribes,* U•X•L, 27500 Drake Road, Farmington Hills, Michigan 48331–3535; call toll-free 1-800-347-4253; or fax: 313-699-8066; or send e-mail via http://www.galegroup.com.

Words to Know

A

Aboriginal: native, or relating to the first or earliest group living in a particular area.

Activism: taking action for or against a controversial issue; political and social activists may organize or take part in protest demonstrations, rallies, petitioning the government, sit-ins, civil disobedience, and many other forms of activities that draw attention to an issue and/or challenge the authorities to make a change.

Adobe: (pronounced *uh-DOE-bee*) a brick or other building material made from sun-dried mud, a mixture of clay, sand, and sometimes ashes, rocks, or straw.

Alaska Native Claims Settlement Act (ANCSA): an act of Congress passed in 1971 that gave Alaska Natives 44 million acres of land and $962.5 million. In exchange, Alaska Natives gave up all claim to other lands in Alaska. The ANCSA also resulted in the formation of 12 regional corporations in Alaska in charge of Native communities' economic development and land use.

Allotment: the practice of dividing and distributing something into individual lots. In 1887 the U.S. Congress passed the Dawes Act, or the General Allotment Act, which divided Indian reservations into privately owned parcels (pieces) of land. Under allotment, tribes could no longer own their lands in common (as a group) in the traditional way. Instead, the head of a family received a lot, generally 160 acres. Land not allotted was sold to non-Natives.

American Indian Movement (AIM): an activist movement founded in 1966 to aggressively press for Indian rights. The movement was formed to improve federal, state, and local social services to Native Americans in urban neighborhoods. AIM sought the reorganization of the Bureau of Indian Affairs to make it more responsive to Native

American needs and fought for the return of Indian lands illegally taken from them.

Anthropology: the study of human beings in terms of their populations, cultures, social relations, ethnic characteristics, customs, and adaptation to their environment.

Archaeology: the study of the remains of past human life, such as fossil relics, artifacts, and monuments, in order to understand earlier human cultures.

Arctic: relating to the area surrounding the North Pole.

Assimilate: to absorb, or to be absorbed, into the dominant society (those in power, or in the majority). U.S. assimilation policies were directed at causing Native Americans to become like European-Americans in terms of jobs and economics, religion, customs, language, education, family life, and dress.

B

Band: a small, loosely organized social group composed of several families. In Canada, the word *band* originally referred to a social unit of nomadic (those who moved from place to place) hunting peoples, but now refers to a community of Indians registered with the government.

Boarding school: a live-in school.

Breechcloth: a garment with front and back flaps that hang from the waist. *Breechcloths* were one of the most common articles of clothing worn by many Native American men and sometimes women in pre-European/American settlement times.

Bureau of Indian Affairs (BIA): the U.S. government agency that oversees tribal lands, education, and other aspects of Indian life.

C

Census: a count of the population.

Ceremony: a special act or set of acts (such as a wedding or a funeral) performed by members of a group on important occasions, usually organized according to the group's traditions and beliefs.

Clan: a group of related house groups and families that trace back to a common ancestor or a common symbol or totem, usually an animal such as the bear or the turtle. The *clan* forms the basic social and political unit for many Indian societies.

Colonialism: a state or nation's control over a foreign territory.

Colonize: to establish a group of people from a mother country or state in a foreign territory; the colonists set up a community that remains tied to the mother country.

Confederacy: a group of people, states, or nations joined together for mutual support or for a special purpose.

Convert: (as verb) to cause a person or group to change their beliefs or practices. A *convert* (noun) is a person who has been *converted* to a new belief or practice.

Coup: (pronounced *COO*) a feat of bravery, especially the touching of an enemy's body during battle without causing or receiving injury. To *count coup* is to count the number of such feats of bravery.

Cradleboard: a board or frame on which an infant was bound or wrapped by some Native American peoples. It was used as a portable carrier or for carrying an infant on the back.

Creation stories: sacred myths or stories that explain how the Earth and its beings were created.

Culture: the set of beliefs, social habits, and ways of surviving in the environment that are held by a particular social group.

D

Dentalium: (pronounced *den-TAIL-ee-um*; from the Latin word for tooth). Dentalia (plural) are the tooth-like shells that some tribes used as money. The shells were rubbed smooth and strung like beads on strands of animal skin.

Depletion: decreasing the amount of something; *depletion* of resources such as animals or minerals through overuse reduces essential elements from the environment.

Dialect: (pronounced *DY-uh-lect*) a local variety of a particular language, with unique differences in words, grammar, and pronunciation.

E

Economy: the way a group obtains, produces, and distributes the goods it needs; the overall system by which it supports itself and accumulates its wealth.

Ecosystem: the overall way that a community and its surrounding environment function together in nature.

Epidemic: the rapid spread of a disease so that many people in an area have it at the same time.

Ethnic group: a group of people who are classed according to certain aspects of their common background, usually by tribal, racial, national, cultural, and language origins.

Extended family: a family group that includes close relatives such as mother, father, and children, plus grandparents, aunts and uncles, and cousins.

F

Federally recognized tribes: tribes with which the U.S. government maintains official relations as established by treaty, executive order, or act of Congress.

First Nations: one of Canada's terms for its Indian nations.

Five Civilized Tribes: a name given to the Cherokee, Choctaw, Chickasaw, Creek, and Seminole during the mid-1800s. The tribes were given this name by non-Natives because they had democratic constitutional governments, a high literacy rate (many people who could read and write), and ran effective schools.

Formal education: structured learning that takes place in a school or college under the supervision of trained teachers.

G

Ghost Dance: a revitalization (renewal or rebirth) movement that arose in the 1870s after many tribes moved to reservations and were being encouraged to give up their traditional beliefs. Many Native Americans hoped that, if they performed it earnestly, the Ghost Dance would bring back traditional Native lifestyles and values, and that the buffalo and Indian ancestors would return to the Earth as in the days before the white settlers.

Great Basin: an elevated region in the western United States in which all water drains toward the center. The *Great Basin* covers part of Nevada, California, Colorado, Utah, Oregon, and Wyoming.

Guardian spirit: a sacred power, usually embodied in an animal such as a hawk, deer, or turtle, that reveals itself to an individual, offering help throughout the person's lifetime in important matters such as hunting or healing the sick.

H

Haudenosaunee: (pronounced *hoo-dee-noh-SHAW-nee*) the name of the people often called Iroquois or Five Nations. It means "People of the Longhouse."

Head flattening: a practice in which a baby was placed in a cradle, and a padded board was tied to its forehead to mold the head into a desired shape. Sometimes the effect of flattening the back of the head was achieved by binding the infant tightly to a cradleboard.

I

Immunity: resistance to disease; the ability to be exposed to a disease with less chance of getting it, and less severe effects if infected.

Indian Territory: an area in present-day Kansas and Oklahoma where the U.S. government once planned to move all Indians, and, eventually, to allow them to run their own province or state. In 1880 nearly one-third of all U.S. Indians lived there, but with the formation of the state of Oklahoma in 1906, the promise of an Indian state dissolved.

Indigenous: (pronounced *in-DIJ-uh-nus*) native, or first, in a specific area. Native Americans are often referred to as *indigenous* peoples of North America.

Intermarriage: marriage between people of different groups, as between a Native American and a non-Native, or between people from two different tribes.

K

Kachina: (pronounced *kuh-CHEE-nuh*) a group of spirits celebrated by the Pueblo Indians; the word also refers to dolls made in the image of *kachina* spirits.

Kiva: (pronounced *KEE-va*) among the Pueblo, a circular (sometimes rectangular) underground room used for religious ceremonies.

L

Lacrosse: a game of Native American origin in which players use a long stick with a webbed pouch at the end for catching and throwing a ball.

Language family: a group of languages that are different from one another but are related. These languages share similar words, sounds, or word structures. The languages are alike either because they have borrowed words from each other or because they originally came from the same parent language.

Legend: a story or folktale that tells about people or events in the past.

Life expectancy: the average number of years a person may expect to live.

Linguistics: the study of human speech and language.

Literacy: the state of being able to read and write.

Longhouse: a large, long building in which several families live together; usually found among Northwest Coast and Iroquois peoples.

Long Walk of the Navajo: the enforced 300-mile walk of the Navajo people in 1864, when they were being removed from their homelands to the Bosque Redondo Reservation in New Mexico.

M

Matrilineal: tracing family relations through the mother; in a *matrilineal* society, names and inheritances are passed down through the mother's side of the family.

Medicine bundle: a pouch in which were kept sacred objects believed to have powers that would protect and aid an individual, a clan or family, or a community.

Midewiwin Society: the Medicine Lodge Religion, whose main purpose was to prolong life. The society taught morality, proper conduct, and a knowledge of plants and herbs for healing.

Migration: movement from one place to another. The *migrations* of Native peoples were often done by the group, with whole nations moving from one area to another.

Mission: an organized effort by a religious group to spread its beliefs to other parts of the world; *mission* refers either to the project of spreading a belief system or to the building(s)—such as a church—in which this takes place.

Mission school: a school established by missionaries to teach people religious beliefs, as well as other subjects.

Myth: a story passed down through generations, often involving supernatural beings. *Myths* often express religious beliefs or the values of a people. They may attempt to explain how the Earth and its beings were created, or why things are as they are. They are not always meant to be taken as factual.

N

Natural resources: the sources of supplies provided by the environment for survival and enrichment, such as animals to be hunted, land for farming, minerals, and timber.

Neophyte: (pronounced *NEE-oh-fite*) beginner; often used to mean a new convert to a religion.

Nomadic: traveling and relocating often, usually in search of food and other resources or a better climate.

Nunavut: a new territory in Canada as of April 1, 1999, with the status of a province and an Inuit majority. It is a huge area, covering most of Canada north of the treeline. *Nunavut* means "Our Land" in Inukitut (the Inuit language).

O

Oral literature: oral traditions that are written down after enjoying a long life in spoken form among a people.

Oral traditions: history, mythology, folklore, and other foundations of a culture that have been passed by spoken word, often in the form of stories, from generation to generation within a culture group.

P

Parent language: a language that is the common source of two or more languages that came into being at a later time.

Per capita income: *per capita* is a Latin phrase that means "for each person." Per capita income is the average personal income per person.

Petroglyph: a carving or engraving on rock; a common form of ancient art.

Peyote: (pronounced *pay-OH-tee*) a substance obtained from cactus that some Indian groups use as part of their religious practice. After eating the substance, which stimulates the nervous system, a person may go into a trance state and see visions. The Peyote Religion features the use of this substance.

Pictograph: a simple picture representing a historical event.

Policy: the overall plan or course of action issued by the government, establishing how it will handle certain situations or people and what its goals are.

Post-European contact: relating to the time and state of Native Americans and their lands after the Europeans arrived. Depending on the part of the country in which they lived, Native groups experienced contact at differing times in the history of white expansion into the West.

Potlatch: a feast or ceremony, commonly held among Northwest Coast groups; also called a "giveaway." During a *potlatch,* goods are given to guests to show the host's generosity and wealth. Potlatches are used to celebrate major life events such as birth, death, or marriage.

Powwow: a celebration at which the main activity is traditional singing and dancing. In modern times, the singers and dancers at powwows come from many different tribes.

Province: a district or division of a country (like a state in the United States).

R

Raiding: entering into another tribe or community's territory, usually by stealth or force, and stealing their livestock and supplies.

Rancheria: a small Indian reservation, usually in California.

Ratify: to approve or confirm. In the United States, the U.S. Senate *ratified* treaties with the Indians.

Red Power: a term used to describe the Native American activism movement of the 1960s, in which people from many tribes came together to protest the injustices of American policies toward Native Americans.

Removal Act: an act passed by the U.S. Congress in 1830 that directed all Indians to be moved to Indian Territory, west of the Mississippi River.

Removal Period: the time, mostly between 1830 and 1860, when most Indians of the eastern United States were forced to leave their homelands and relocate west of the Mississippi River.

Reservation: land set aside by the U.S. government for the use of a group or groups of Indians.

Reserve: in Canada, lands set aside for specific Indian bands. *Reserve* means in Canada approximately what *reservation* means in the United States.

Revitalization: the feeling or movement in which something seems to come back to life after having been quiet or inactive for a period of time.

Ritual: a formal act that is performed in basically the same way each time; rituals are often performed as part of a ceremony.

Rural: having to do with the country; opposite of urban.

S

Sachem: the chief of a confederation of tribes.

Shaman: (can be pronounced either *SHAY-mun* or *SHAH-mun*) a priest or medicine person in many Native American groups who understands and works with supernatural matters. *Shamans* traditionally performed in rituals and were expected to cure the sick, see the future, and obtain supernatural help with hunting and other economic activities.

Smallpox: a very contagious disease that spread across North America and killed many thousands of Indians. Survivors had skin that was badly scarred.

Subsistence economy: an economic system in which people provide themselves with the things they need for survival and their way of life rather than working for money or making a surplus of goods for trade.

Sun Dance: a renewal and purification (cleansing) ceremony performed by many Plains Indians such as the Sioux and Cheyenne. A striking aspect of the ceremony was the personal sacrifice made by some men. They undertook self-torture in order to gain a vision that might provide spiritual insight and knowledge beneficial to the community.

Sweat lodge: an airtight hut containing hot stones that were sprinkled with water to make them steam. A person remained inside until he or she was perspiring. The person then usually rushed out and plunged into a cold stream. This treatment was used before a ceremony or for the healing of physical or spiritual ailments. *Sweat lodge* is also the name of a sacred Native American ceremony involving the building of the lodge and the pouring of water on the stones, usually by a medicine person, accompanied by praying and singing. The ceremony has many purposes, including spiritual cleansing and healing.

T

Taboo: a forbidden thing or action. Many Indians believe that the sacred order of the world must be maintained if one is to avoid illness or other misfortunes. This is accomplished, in part, by observing a large assortment of taboos.

Termination: the policy of the U.S. government during the 1950s and 1960s to end the relationships set up by treaties with Indian nations.

Toloache: a substance obtained from a plant called jimsonweed. When consumed, the drug causes a person to go into a trance and see visions. It is used in some religious ceremonies.

Totem: an object that serves as an emblem or represents a family or clan, usually in the form of an animal, bird, fish, plant, or other natural object. A *totem pole* is a pillar built in front of the homes of Natives in the Northwest. It is painted and carved with a series of totems that show the family background and either mythical or historical events.

Trail of Tears: a series of forced marches of Native Americans of the Southeast in the 1830s, causing the deaths of thousands. The marches were the result of the U.S. government's removal policy, which ordered Native Americans to be moved to Indian Territory (now Oklahoma).

Treaty: an agreement between two parties or two nations, signed by both, usually defining the benefits to both parties that will result from one side giving up title to a territory of land.

Tribe: a group of Natives who share a name, language, culture, and ancestors; in Canada, called a band.

Tribelet: a community within an organization of communities in which one main settlement was surrounded by a few minor outlying settlements.

Trickster: a common culture hero in Indian myth and legend. *Tricksters* generally have supernatural powers that can be used to do good or harm, and stories about them take into account the different forces of the universe, such as good and evil or night and day. The Trickster takes different forms among various groups; for example, Coyote in the Southwest; Ikhtomi Spider in the High Plains, and Jay or Wolverine in Canada.

Trust: a relationship between two parties (or groups) in which one is responsible for acting in the other's best interests. The U.S. government has a *trust* relationship with tribal nations. Many tribes do not own their lands outright; according to treaty, the government owns the land "in trust" and tribes are given the use of it.

U

Unemployment rate: the percentage of the population that is looking for work but unable to find any. (People who have quit looking for work are not included in *unemployment* rates.)

Urban: having to do with cities and towns; the opposite of rural.

V

Values: the ideals that a community of people shares.

Vision quest: a sacred ceremony in which a person (often a teenage boy) goes off alone and fasts, living without food or water for a period of days. During that time, he hopes to learn about his spiritual side and to have a vision of a guardian spirit who will give him help and strength throughout his life.

W

Wampum: small cylinder-shaped beads cut from shells. Long strings of *wampum* were used for many different purposes. Indians believed that the exchange of wampum and other goods established a friendship, not just a profit-making relationship.

Wampum belt: a broad woven belt of wampum used to record history, treaties among the tribes, or treaties with colonists or governments.

Weir: a barricade used to funnel fish toward people who wait to catch them.

Timeline

25,000–11,000 B.C.E. Groups of hunters cross from Asia to Alaska on the Bering Sea Land Bridge, which was formed when lands now under the waters of the Bering Strait were exposed for periods of time, according to scientists.

1400 B.C.E. People who live along the lower Mississippi River are building large burial mounds and living in planned communities.

1 C.E. Small, permanent villages of the Hohokam tradition emerge in the Southwest.

400 Anasazi communities emerge in the Four Corners region of the Southwest. Anasazi eventually design communities in large multiroomed apartment buildings, some with more than 1,200 rooms. The Anasazi are farmers and skilled potters.

900 The Mississippian mound-building groups form complex political and social systems, and participate in long-distance trade and an elaborate and widespread religion.

1000–1350 The Iroquois Confederacy is formed among the Mohawk, Oneida, Onondaga, Cayuga, and Seneca nations. The Five Nations of the Haudenosaunee are from this time governed by chiefs from the 49 families who were present at the origin of the confederation.

Anasazi ruins at Pueblo del Arroyo, Chaco Canyon, New Mexico.

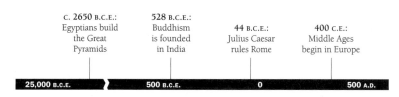

c. 2650 B.C.E.:
Egyptians build
the Great
Pyramids

528 B.C.E.:
Buddhism
is founded
in India

44 B.C.E.:
Julius Caesar
rules Rome

400 C.E.:
Middle Ages
begin in Europe

25,000 B.C.E.   500 B.C.E.   0   500 A.D.

1040: Pueblos (towns) are flourishing in New Mexico's Chaco Canyon. The pueblos are connected by an extensive road system that stretches many miles across the desert.

1350 Moundville, in present-day Alabama, one of the largest ceremonial centers of the Mound Builders, thrives. With 20 great mounds and a village, it is probably the center of a chiefdom that includes several other related communities.

1494: Christopher Columbus begins the enslavement of American Indians, capturing over 500 Taino of San Salvador and sending them to Spain to be sold.

1503 French explorer Jacques Cartier begins trading with Native Americans along the East Coast.

1539–43 Spanish explorers Hernando de Soto and Francisco Coronado traverse the Southeast and Southwest, bringing with them disease epidemics that kill thousands of Native Americans.

1609 The fur trade begins when British explorer Henry Hudson, sailing for the Netherlands, opens trade in New Netherland (present-day New York) with several Northeast tribes.

1634–37 An army of Puritans, Pilgrims, Mohican, and Narragansett attacks and sets fire to the Pequot fort, killing as many as 700 Pequot men, women, and children.

1648–51 The Iroquois, having exhausted the fur supply in their area, attack other tribes in order to get a new supply. The Beaver Wars begin, and many Northeast tribes are forced to move west toward the Great Lakes area.

1660 The Ojibway, pushed west by settlers and Iroquois expansion, invade Sioux territory in Minnesota. After fighting the Ojibway, many Sioux groups move to the Great Plains.

1760–63 The Delaware Prophet tells Native Americans in the Northeast that they must drive Europeans out of North America and return to the customs of their ancestors. His message influences the Ottawa leader Pontiac, who uses it to unite many tribes against the British.

The attack on the Pequot fort in 1637.

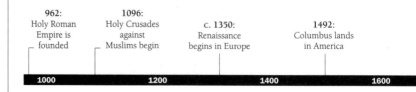

962:
Holy Roman
Empire is
founded

1096:
Holy Crusades
against
Muslims begin

c. 1350:
Renaissance
begins in Europe

1492:
Columbus lands
in America

| 1000 | 1200 | 1400 | 1600 |

1763 England issues the Proclamation of 1763, which assigns all lands west of the Appalachian Mountains to Native Americans, while colonists are allowed to settle all land to the east. The document respects the aboriginal land rights of Native Americans. It is not popular with colonists who want to move onto Indian lands and becomes one of the conflicts between England and the colonies leading to the American Revolution.

1769 The Spanish build their first mission in California. There will be 23 Spanish missions in California, which are used to convert Native Californians to Christianity, but also reduces them to slave labor.

c. 1770 Horses, brought to the continent by the Spanish in the sixteenth century, spread onto the Great Plains and lead to the development of a new High Plains Culture.

1778 The treaty-making period begins, when the first of 370 treaties between Indian nations and the U.S. government is signed. The treaty-making period ends in 1871.

1786 The first federal Indian reservations are established.

1789 The Spanish establish a post at Nootka Sound on Vancouver Island, the first permanent European establishment in the territory of the Pacific Northwest Coast tribes.

1805–06 Explorers Meriwether Lewis and William Clark, led by Sacajawea, travel through the Plateau area, encountering the Cayuse, Nez Perce, Walla Walla, Wishram, and Yakima.

1830 The removal period begins when the U.S. Congress passes the Indian Removal Act. Over the course of the next 30 years many tribes from the Northeast and Southeast are removed to Indian Territory in present-day Oklahoma and Kansas, often forcibly and at great expense in human lives.

Franciscan priest with an Indian child at a Spanish mission, California.

Sacajawea points out the way to Lewis and Clark.

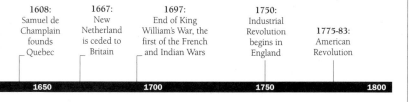

1608: Samuel de Champlain founds Quebec	1667: New Netherland is ceded to Britain	1697: End of King William's War, the first of the French and Indian Wars	1750: Industrial Revolution begins in England	1775-83: American Revolution

1650	1700	1750	1800

1851 Early reservations are created in California to protect the Native population from the violence of U.S. citizens. These reservations are inadequate and serve only a small portion of the Native Californians, while others endure continued violence and hardship.

1870 The First Ghost Dance Movement begins when Wodzibwob, a Paiute, learns in a vision that a great earthquake will swallow the Earth, and that all Indians will be spared or resurrected within three days of the disaster. Thus, their world will return to its state before the Europeans had arrived.

1870–90 The Peyote Religion spreads through the Great Plains. Peyote (obtained from a cactus plant) brings on a dreamlike feeling that followers believe moves them closer to the spirit world. Tribes develop their own ceremonies, songs, and symbolism, and vow to be trustworthy, honorable, and community-oriented and to follow the Peyote Road.

1876 The Indian Act in Canada establishes an Indian reserve system, in which reserves were governed by voluntary elected band councils. The Act does not recognize Canadian Indians' right to self-government. With the passage of the act, Canadian peoples in Canada are divided into three groups: status Indian, treaty Indian, and non-status Indian. The categories affect the benefits and rights Indians are given by the government.

1880s The buffalo on the Great Plains are slaughtered until there are almost none left. Without adequate supplies of buffalo for food, the Plains Indians cannot survive. Many move to reservations.

1884 Potlatches are banned by the Canadian government. The elaborate gift-giving ceremonies have long been a vital part of Pacific Northwest Indian culture.

1887 The Dawes Act, or the General Allotment Act, is passed by Congress. The act calls for the allotment (or parceling out) of tribal lands. Tribes are no longer to own their lands in common in the traditional way. Instead, the land is to be assigned to

Preparing for a potlatch ceremony in the Pacific Northwest.

1812:
The War
of 1812

1861-65:
American
Civil War

1867:
Russia sells
Alaska to the
United States

1870:
The Fifteenth
Amendment guarantees
male citizens the vote

| 1850 | 1860 | 1870 | 1880 |

individuals. The head of a family receives 160 acres, and other family members get smaller pieces of land. Many Native Americans, unable to make a living from their land, end up having to sell their parcels. All Indian lands that are not allotted are sold to settlers. Millions of acres of Indian lands are lost.

1889 The Oklahoma Land Runs open Indian Territory to non-Natives. (Indian Territory had been set aside solely for Indian use.) At noon on April 22, an estimated 50,000 people line up at the boundaries of Indian Territory. They claim two million acres of land. By nightfall, tent cities, banks, and stores are doing business there.

1890 The second Ghost Dance movement is initiated by Wovoka, a Paiute. It includes many Paiute traditions. In some versions, the dance is performed in order to help bring back to Earth many dead ancestors and exterminated game. Ghost Dance practitioners hope the rituals in the movement will restore Indians to their former state, before the arrival of the non-Native settlers.

1912 The Alaska Native Brotherhood is formed to promote civil rights issues, such as the right to vote, access to public education, and civil rights in public places. The organization also fights court battles to win land rights.

1920 The Canadian government amends the Indian Act to allow for compulsory, or forced, enfranchisement, the process by which Indians have to give up their tribal loyalties to become Canadian citizens. Only 250 Indians had voluntarily become enfranchised between 1857 and 1920.

1924 All Indians are granted U.S. citizenship. This act does not take away rights that Native Americans had by treaty or the Constitution.

1928 Lewis Meriam is hired to investigate the status of Indian economies, health, and education, and the federal adminis-

The day school at the Sac and Fox Agency in Indian Territory, between 1876 and 1896.

1893:
Henry Ford tests his first car

1898:
Spanish-American War

1902:
Wright brothers' first airplane flight

1914:
World War I begins

1917:
Russian Revolution

1890   1900   1910   1920

tration of Indian affairs. His report describes the terrible conditions under which Indians are forced to live, listing problems with health care, education, poverty, malnutrition, and land ownership.

1934 U.S. Congress passes the Indian Reorganization Act (IRA), which ends allotment policies and restores some land to Native Americans. The IRA encourages tribes to govern themselves and set up tribal economic corporations, but with the government overseeing their decisions. The IRA also provides more funding to the reservations.

1946 The Indian Lands Commission (ICC) is created to decide land claims filed by Indian nations. Many tribes expect the ICC to return lost lands, but the ICC chooses to award money instead, and at the value of the land at the time it was lost.

1951 A new Indian Act in Canada reduces the power of the Indian Affairs Office, makes it easier for Indians to gain the right to vote, and helps Indian children enter public schools. It also removes the ban on potlatch and Sun Dance ceremonies.

1952 In an all out effort to make Native Americans "blend in" or assimilate with the rest of society, the U.S. government begins a policy of moving Indians from reservations to cities. The government hopes that Native Americans will find jobs in the city and adopt an "American" lifestyle. Then the government will be able to "terminate" the tribes and eliminate the reservations.

1954–62 The U.S. Congress carries out its policy of "termination." At the same time laws are passed giving states and local governments control over tribal members, taking away the tribes' authority to govern themselves. Under the policy of termination, Indians lose their special privileges and are treated as any other U.S. citizens. The tribes that are terminated face extreme poverty and the threat of loss of their

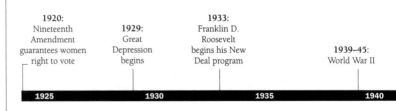

1920:
Nineteenth
Amendment
guarantees women
right to vote

1929:
Great
Depression
begins

1933:
Franklin D.
Roosevelt
begins his New
Deal program

1939–45:
World War II

1925   1930   1935   1940

community and traditions. By 1961 the government begins rethinking this policy because of the damage it is causing.

1955 The Indian Health Service (IHS) assumes responsibility for Native American health care. The IHS operates hospitals, health centers, health stations, clinics, and community service centers.

1960 The queen of England approves a law giving status Indians the right to vote in Canada.

1965 Under the new U. S. government policy, the Self-Determination policy, federal aid to reservations is given directly to Indian tribes and not funneled through the Bureau of Indian Affairs.

1968 The American Indian Movement (AIM) is founded in Minneapolis, Minnesota, by Dennis Banks (Ojibway) and Russell Means (Lakota). AIM is formed to improve federal, state, and local social services to urban neighborhoods and to prevent harassment of Indians by the local police.

1969 Eighty-nine Native Americans land on Alcatraz Island, a former penitentiary in San Francisco Bay in California. The group, calling itself "Indians of All Tribes," claims possession of the island under an 1868 treaty that gave Indians the right to unused federal property on Indian land. Indians of All Tribes occupies the island for 19 months while negotiating with federal officials. They do not win their claim to the island but draw public attention to their cause.

1971 The Alaska Native Claims Settlement Act (ANCSA) is signed into law. With the act, Alaska Natives give up any claim to nine-tenths of Alaska. In return, they are given $962 million and clear title to 44 million acres of land.

1972 Five hundred Indians arrive in Washington, D.C., on a march called the Trail of Broken Treaties to protest the government's policies toward Native Americans. The protestors occupy the Bureau of Indian Affairs building for a week,

The Menominee tribe was terminated by the U.S. government but after much protest, won back federal recognition.

1946:
Cold War between the United States and the Soviet Union begins

1950–53:
Korean War

1955:
Martin Luther King, Jr., leads bus boycott

1959:
Alaska and Hawaii are admitted to the union

| 1945 | 1950 | 1955 | 1960 |

*The armed takeover of
Wounded Knee in 1973.*

causing considerable damage. They present the government with a list of reforms, but the administration rejects their demands.

1973 After a dispute over Oglala Sioux (Lakota) tribal chair Robert Wilson and his strong-arm tactics at Pine Ridge Reservation, AIM leaders are called in. Wilson's supporters and local authorities arm themselves against protestors, who are also armed, and a ten-week siege begins in which hundreds of federal marshals and Federal Bureau of Investigation (FBI) agents surround the Indian protestors. Two Native American men are shot and killed.

1974 After strong protests and "fish-ins" bring attention to the restrictions on Native American fishing rights in the Pacific Northwest, the U.S. Supreme Court restores Native fishing rights in the case *Department of Game of Washington v. Puyallup Tribe et al.*

1978 U.S. Congress passes legislation providing support for additional tribal colleges, schools of higher education designed to help Native American students achieve academic success and eventually transfer to four-year colleges and universities. Tribal colleges also work with tribal elders and cultural leaders to record languages, oral traditions, and arts in an effort to preserve cultural traditions.

1978 The American Religious Freedom Act is signed. Its stated purpose is to "protect and preserve for American Indians their inherent right of freedom to believe, express, and exercise their traditional religions."

1978 The Bureau of Indian Affairs publishes regulations for the new Federal Acknowledgment Program. This program is responsible for producing a set of "procedures for establishing that an American Indian group exists as an Indian tribe." Many tribes will later discover that these requirements are complicated and difficult to establish.

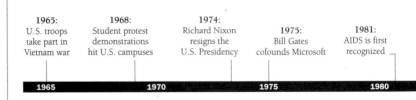

1965: U.S. troops take part in Vietnam war	1968: Student protest demonstrations hit U.S. campuses	1974: Richard Nixon resigns the U.S. Presidency	1975: Bill Gates cofounds Microsoft	1981: AIDS is first recognized
1965	**1970**	**1975**	**1980**	

1982 Canada constitutionally recognizes aboriginal peoples in its new Constitution and Charter of Rights and Freedoms. The Constitution officially divides Canada's aboriginal nations into three designations: the Indian, the Inuit, and the Métis peoples. Native groups feel that the new Constitution does not adequately protect their rights, nor does it give them the right to govern themselves.

1988 The Federal Indian Gambling Regulatory Act of 1988 allows any tribe recognized by the U.S. government to engage in gambling activities. With proceeds from gaming casinos, some tribes pay for health care, support of the elderly and sick, housing, and other improvements, while other tribes buy back homelands, establish scholarship funds, and create new jobs.

1989 U.S. Congress approves a bill to establish a National Museum of the American Indian under the administration of the Smithsonian Institution in Washington, D.C. (As of 1999, the Museum has not been built.)

1990 Two important acts are passed by U.S. Congress. The Native American Languages Act is designed to preserve, protect, and promote the practice and development of Indian languages. The Graves Protection and Repatriation Act provides for the protection of American Indian grave sites and the repatriation (return) of Indian remains and cultural artifacts to tribes.

1992 Canadians vote against a new Constitution (the Charlottetown Accord) that contains provisions for aboriginal self-government.

1999 A new territory called Nunavut enters the federation of Canada. Nunavut is comprised of vast areas taken from the Northwest Territories and is populated by an Inuit majority. The largest Native land claim in Canadian history, Nunavut is one-fifth of the landmass of Canada, or the size of the combined states of Alaska and Texas. Meaning "Our Land" in the Inukitut (Inuit) language, Nunavut will be primarily governed by the Inuit.

Chinook Winds Casino, Oregon, 1997.

After many years of struggle, the Inuit celebrate the establishment of a new Canadian territory, Nunavut, or "Our Land," in 1999.

1983: The Internet is born

1989: The Berlin Wall is destroyed

1993: Apartheid is outlawed in South Africa

1999: NATO forces bomb Serbian military sites

1985   1990   1995   2000

Historic Locations of
U.S. Native Groups

Menominee

Sauk

Fox

Dakota

Kickapoo

Winnebago

Potawatomi

Abenaki

Penobscot
Pennacook

Mohawk

Tuscarora
Oneida
Cayuga

Onondaga
Manhattan
Iroquois

Mohegan

Seneca

Nipmuk
Stockbridge

Massachuset

Munsee
Mahican
Wappinger

Unami

Narraganset

Delaware
Nanticoke

Schaghticoke
Susquehanna
Brothertown

Pequot
Podunk

Wampanoag

Montauk
Shinnecock

Paugussett

Peoria

Illinois

Erie

omaha

Iowa

Cahokia

Adena

Miami

Hopewell

Oto

Kaskaskia

Piscataway

aw (Kansa)

Missouri

Shawnee

Mattaponi
Pamunkey

Monacan

Mississippian

Powhatan
Chickahominy

Osage

Tutelo

Rappahannock
Nansemond

onkawa

Saponi

Meherrin

Waco

Koasati

Lumbee

Pamlico

wakoni

Quapaw

Cherokee

Waccamaw

chita

Chickasaw

Catawba

Caddo

Etowah

Cheraw

Coharie

Yuchi

Pedee

Hasinai

Santee

Kichai

Choctaw

Creek

Edisto

Tunica

Hitchiti

Cusabo

Natchez

Alabama

Yamasee

Guale

Houma

Mobile

Yazoo

Biloxi

Coushatta

Apalachicola

Chitimacha

Apalachee

Seminole

Timucua

Atlantic
Ocean

Gulf
of
Mexico

Miccosukee

Calusa

Pacific
Ocean

Historic Locations of
Canadian Native Groups

Inuit

Inuit

Inuit

Inuit

Inuit

Inuit

Inuit

Inuit

Inuit

Inuit

Inuit

Inuit

Inuit

Inuit

Intuit

Beothuk

Inuit

Naskapi

Innu

Cree

Montagnais

Maliseet

Micmac

Passamaquoddy

Ojibwa

Algonkin

Nippissing

Ottawa

Huron

Tobacco

Wenrohronon

Nuetral

Wyandotte

The Great Basin

The Great Basin

The vast, expansive region of the American West, between the Rocky Mountains in the east and the Sierra Nevada Mountains in the west, is commonly referred to as the Great Basin. The region is roughly comprised of what are now known as the states of Nevada, western Colorado, eastern Oregon, southern Idaho, and parts of eastern California. With no river outlets to the sea or easily traveled trails, this region was the last area of the continental United States to be explored and settled by Europeans and Euro-Americans. When it was finally mapped and crisscrossed in 1844, this dry, sparsely populated area was called one "Great Basin." Although the term has gained popular usage, the area is in fact not simply one immense basin but a series of mountain ranges and river valleys.

For thousands of years the Great Basin region has been home to hundreds of Indian groups that spoke similar languages but were distinct from each other politically. These groups have undergone profound cultural and political changes in the past few centuries of European and Euro-American contact and colonization and have skillfully adapted to the many changes brought by the foreigners.

Archaeologists and geologists (scientists who study the remains of past civilizations and the earth itself for clues about peoples and the environment of earlier times) have determined that great lakes and glaciers covered this region during the ice ages and began to evaporate around roughly 11,000–8,000 B.C.E. One of the oldest mummified skeletons in the world has been found in the Lahontan Cave, outside Fallon, Nevada, and is estimated to be over nine thousand years old. There is great debate over how much meaning can be attributed to the Lahontan Mummy and other archaeological findings from this area, which provide only faint glimpses into the material conditions of these precontact societies. What meanings, beliefs, and rituals these peoples attributed to their practices and lives over countless centuries cannot be adequately assessed. It is, therefore, difficult to make extensive, meaningful determinations about the lives of the Indian peoples throughout these many centuries.

An illustration of Ute on horseback by Frederic Remington. The use of the horse for travel, hunting, and war brought tremendous changes to some of the Great Basin groups.

The Spanish bring horses

Beginning in the early 1600s, European presence greatly changed the lives of the Great Basin peoples living in what are now eastern Utah and Colorado. Located directly north of the Spanish colony of New Mexico, the Utes were the first Great Basin group to experience the pressures introduced by Europeans in the American West. In the seventeenth century Spanish-introduced trade items, particularly the horse, began to make their way out of New Mexico and into the eastern Great Basin. The Ute at this time were not one unified tribal group but many different political units, organized under different leaders and living in different parts of Utah and Colorado. The Eastern Ute quickly adopted the horse and began hunting buffalo and trading in the Southern Plains and New Mexico. Many of the Western Ute, however, were slower to adopt the equestrian (horse-riding) culture and economy of their eastern brethren.

With the adoption of the horse, the Ute changed many aspects of their economies and cultures. Previously, like most of the other Numic-speaking (see "Language") peoples of the Great Basin, they had hunted on foot and gathered useful foods from their local environments. The Ute now vigorously competed for precious Spanish resources in and around New Mexico with the many other tribes around them, such as the Comanche to the east, Navajo to the Southwest, and Apache to the Southeast. In order to gain firearms, horses, and other goods to meet the demands of the New Mexican market, these tribes often raided each other and other neighboring groups (meaning they stole the goods from them). Their economies and political relations now revolved around the horse while many other Great Basin peoples still lived in societies without horses.

Europeans settle in the Great Basin

In addition to introducing the horse trade, beginning in the mid-1700s the Spanish began solidifying their control on the American Southwest and established settlements in California in 1769. In order to link up the New Mexican and California colonies, Spanish traders and explorers forged the Spanish Trail between Santa Fe and Los Angeles, which led directly through parts of the southern Great Basin, home to Southern Paiute groups in southern Nevada, western Utah, and northern Arizona as well as Chemehuevi, Kawaiisu, Owens Valley Paiute, and Western Shoshone groups. These Indian peoples now experienced the many pressures of European trading, particularly the newcomers' need for Indian slaves, food resources, and water supplies.

The 1800s brought revolutionary changes to all the Great Basin groups. The Western Shoshone of Nevada and eastern California, the Gosiute Shoshone of eastern Utah, the Northern Paiute of northern Nevada and eastern Oregon, and the Southern Paiute, Chemehuevi, Kawaiisu, and Washoe of California all found their previous economies, political organization, and cultural practices fundamentally disrupted by first British and American traders and settlers. Previously organized in hundreds of small bands that moved seasonally throughout local environments hunting and gathering needed resources, some smaller groups were forced to band together under powerful leaders while others migrated out of areas infested with European disease into more remote mountain locations.

In the early 1800s, both Britain and the United States vied for control of the western half of North America. Quickly displacing the Spanish, British and then American traders moved rapidly into the northern Great Basin along the Snake and Humboldt rivers and with the aid of local Bannock, Shoshone, and Paiute guides trapped any animals they could. With the American conquest of northern Mexico in the Mexican-American War (1846–48), the United States acquired control of the Southwest and California in 1848. In the late 1840s and 1850s the California Gold Rush attracted over 100,000 miners and settlers. Tens of thousands of these pioneers on their way to California and Oregon passed directly through the Great Basin along both the Overland Trail and Oregon Trail, destroying the fragile ecology with their many horses and cattle as well as sometimes attacking whatever small bands of Northern Paiute and Western Shoshone they encountered.

Greed becomes abuse

Because of their limited technologies, non-equestrian cultures, and sparse material conditions, most Great Basin peoples have always

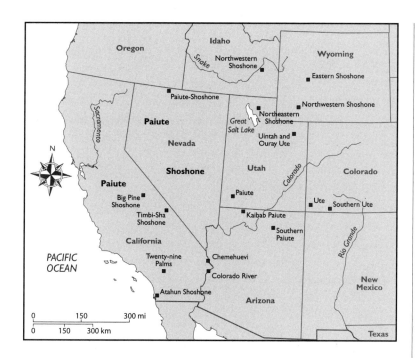

A map of some contemporary Native American communities in the Great Basin region.

been considered by Europeans to be inferior. Racism was a precondition for American expansion and development throughout California and the Great Basin, as Euro-American settlers firmly believed in their right to take and abuse Indian lands and Indian peoples, and they used both religious and intellectual justification for their violent and criminal acts. Thousands of Indian peoples, especially around the mining settlements in California and Nevada, did not survive these turbulent years of foreign intrusion, while others struggled desperately.

Eastern California and Nevada proved to be extremely abundant in timber, water, and minerals, resources that the growing American economy sought. The American public wanted Indian lands and there was little protection for the Great Basin groups. Although the United States negotiated treaties in the mid-1800s with nearly all the Great Basin Indian groups outside of California, the government played only a limited role in the supervision of the rights granted to Indian peoples by these agreements. Consequently, the reservation lands and annual annuities payments legislated by these treaties were not sufficiently enforced to meet the survival needs of many of these peoples. With the near-destruction of their subsistence economies (in which individuals work to provide the goods needed for their own survival and not for trade or money) and their lands occupied by foreigners, the Great Basin peoples experienced extreme hardships. Forced to work on white ranches, in mines, as domestic servants in white households, or in any capacity possible, many Indian people throughout the region found themselves dealing with wage labor for the first time.

U.S. policies

This period of difficult transitions was made even harder in the late 1800s and early 1900s when the U.S. government began policies that attempted to assimilate Indian peoples and Indian lands into the mainstream of American society. Boarding schools were established for Indian children that attempted to remove children from their traditions and native languages and, often painfully, separated them from their parents. New laws, such as the Dawes Act (1887), were passed that curbed tribal ownership of lands and gave reservation lands to Indians individually. The results of these policies were disastrous for Indian peoples. The Southern Ute Reservation in western Colorado lost over eight million acres, or 99 percent of the reservation. The Ute Mountain Reservation lost 94 percent.

Throughout the early 1900s, the Indians of the Great Basin continued to deal with harsh economic, political, and social impositions by state and federal institutions. Only in the 1930s did Indian policy move away from these assimilation efforts as Indian tribal governments received some limited autonomy (self-rule) over their own lives. This Indian New Deal (1930s) also led to the recognition of many new Indian governments as well as the creation of new Indian reservations, such as several for the Western Shoshone of Nevada. Unfortunately for Indian peoples, this era of limited autonomy was quickly followed in the 1950s by another attempt by the government to end the unique legal status of Indian tribes. This policy of termination directly affected several Southern Paiute reservations, such as the Shivwits Reservation in Southwestern Utah, which lost its status as a tribal government entitled to federal resources and exempt from state laws and taxation. In addition, the U.S. government attempted to integrate Indians into the larger U.S. economy through relocation programs, which moved Indian peoples away from their reservations to work in cities. Only in the 1970s did these assimilation efforts give way to an era of Indian self-determination, after which Indian peoples and tribal governments helped determine and enforce the laws under which they lived.

Great Basin Indian peoples have maintained their distinct political and cultural identities despite the tremendous changes brought by European and American contact and colonization. Although American pressures have irrevocably altered the quality of life for the Great

Basin Indian peoples, throughout this vast region Indian peoples continue to live according to their own beliefs and traditions. From Colorado to California they carry on cultures and traditions that are thousands of years old despite the loss of most of their ancestral lands, the economic difficulties of reservation life, as well as the often overwhelming presence of an intrusive American culture. Struggling to learn the many complexities of living in American society and dealing with a powerful, imposed American government, Indian peoples throughout Nevada, California, Utah, Eastern Oregon, Southern Idaho, and Western Colorado have become politically and economically active and productive members of their societies. The Indian peoples of the Great Basin have survived and creatively adapted to their changing world by learning the ways of the larger society and blending their own unique traditions with those of American society.

Religion

The dramatic disruptions accompanying American contact and colonization have irrevocably altered the ways in which Great Basin peoples understand and give meaning to their lives. Through Indian oral histories and the work of anthropologists (people who study human societies and cultures), it is relatively clear that many Great Basin peoples at the time of contact lived in a highly spiritual world where humans were simply one part of a greater cosmos (universe). Animals, the deceased, mountains, and the land itself all had spiritual significance in Great Basin cosmology.

Although it is difficult to measure the amount of religious change brought by American contact, a great deal of religious blending and mixture has occurred throughout the region. Different religious missionaries and denominations, such as the Mormon religion in Utah, have achieved small to large followings among contemporary reservation peoples. Following a new religion, however, does not necessarily mean that these individuals and groups no longer follow ancestral teachings and practices. The adoption of certain religious teachings from American society in many ways parallels the many other adoptions and adaptations Great Basin peoples have undergone. Gaining spiritual strength from outside religions and using it for everyday guidance are integral aspects of communities and cultures that have changed and continue to change according to their own needs.

Language

Related to linguistic groups found outside of the Great Basin, such as the Hopi of Arizona and the Comanche of the Southern

Plains, Numic, the primary Great Basin language, has been divided by linguists into three subgroups, Western, Central, and Southern, depending on the location in the Great Basin. Numic is a branch of a larger language family known as Uto-Aztecan, one of the largest North American language families, which stretches south of the Great Basin all the way into central Mexico. The different Paiute, Shoshone, Ute, Chemehuevi, and Kawaiisu peoples of the Great Basin all speak similar yet regionally unique versions of Numic. The Washoe people of western Nevada and eastern California are the only Great Basin groups that do not speak the Numic language. Washoe is a very unique language that is only distantly related to another North American language family, known as the Hokan. Linguists guess that this uniqueness comes from the long-standing presence of Washoe peoples in their Sierra Nevadan homeland near Lake Tahoe, California.

The Great Basin languages have in recent years fallen into disuse. Children at boarding schools in the region were punished for speaking their language, and discrimination in surrounding English-speaking communities forced many Great Basin peoples to learn English in order to survive. Elders and more traditional Indians have fought to keep the language alive, and many tribal leaders have instituted language retention programs in their tribal schools. Only in recent decades have some Great Basin languages been written down and translated. Recording the languages either electronically on tapes or textually on paper is another example of Great Basin Indians adapting their cultures to a technologically changing world.

Subsistence

For centuries the economies of the Great Basin peoples revolved around the gathering of local plants and seeds and the hunting of deer, antelope, rabbits, and various small game. Fishing was common for many groups, such as the Pyramid Lake Paiute, who had access to fish in this generally water-scarce region. For the Northern and Eastern Shoshone, the Bannock, and the Ute, the adoption of the horse brought a fundamental change to their economy. Mounted and mobile, these equestrian hunters roamed the northern plains in search of buffalo. The groups also hunted larger game, such as bear and elk, in the mountain regions of the Rockies. For most Great Basin groups, however, the gathering of local foods remained the main form of subsistence for centuries. The pine nut, or piñon, is a very delicious and nutritious nut found in the mountains throughout the Great Basin. Shoshone, Paiute, and other groups have gathered this food for centuries and use it in many different ways. Ground up, pine nuts form a paste that can either be rolled into dough for bread or boiled with other vegetables to form soup. Roasted, they can keep for many months. Nearly all Great Basin groups harvested piñons in the fall, and then saved much of their supply for the cold winter months in underground storage areas. The pine nut plays a significant cultural as well as an economic role, appearing in many Great Basin stories and legends.

American contact fundamentally altered the subsistence economies of all Great Basin tribes. For the Great Basin peoples who hunted on the Northern Plains, the virtual extermination (the killing of nearly all) of the buffalo forever changed their lives. For the non-equestrian Great Basin tribes, the settlement of American miners and ranchers disrupted their extremely fragile ecologies. Since small bands so heavily depended on the seasonal harvest of pine nuts and other grasses as well as the hunting of small game, the loss of access to mountain ranges and water valleys plunged many groups into terrible poverty. The mining industries of Nevada and eastern California, for instance, sometimes used up all local timber and water resources, destroying entire stands of piñon trees. Ranching and pioneer travel through the region destroyed fertile marshes and grasslands along the major rivers. Cattle, horses, and sheep ate many of the grasses and seeds that some groups depended on in order to live. Following these ecological disasters, Great Basin peoples came to depend heavily on local white communities and the government for their survival. The government has administered food and other payments to these groups, but poverty and economic problems continue to plague many of these communities.

Customs

All Great Basin groups have maintained social practices and customs that reflect as well as reinforce many of the broader cultural values of their communities. Although it is difficult to make generalizations that apply to all of these different groups, the various artistic, marital, child-rearing, puberty, and burial traditions of these groups offer interesting comparisons and contrasts.

In general, artistic expression and traditions have served both functional and creative purposes. Many of the equestrian Great Basin groups developed artistic styles combining their pre-equestrian traditions with those of their Plains neighbors. The Ute, for instance, embellished their child-carrying cradleboards with many beading and decorative techniques utilized by Plains groups but also used a willow cover for the child's head as practiced among other Great Basin groups. (Such woven, willow covers, both among the Ute and other groups, serve to protect the child from the sun as well as to designate the gender of the child.) The equestrian groups likewise adopted some of the Plains buffalo dances and ceremonies not found throughout the Great Basin. They also took up the hide-painting traditions of their Plains neighbors, often depicting important events and ceremonies on the hides of large elk and buffalo.

Most Great Basin groups did not have access to the same animal, leather, and wood resources as the equestrian tribes. Yet these groups did develop highly sophisticated forms of functional art, such as baskets. Intricate Washoe, Paiute, Shoshone, and other Great Basin baskets provide clear examples of the creativity and intellectual traditions of these different peoples. Made of woven and coiled branches and other grasses, Great Basin baskets are considered among the highest quality in the world. Washoe baskets became so highly coveted by art collectors in the early 1900s that weavers could not fulfill the demand.

Current tribal issues

Currently, the Great Basin tribes are mainly located on reservations and colonies in Idaho, Utah, Nevada, Oregon, and eastern California. These different lands are legally recognized by the federal government as home to the many specific tribes and are subject to the particular laws of these tribes. Many smaller political groups make up the larger Paiute, Ute, and Shoshone tribes. The Ute live on the largest Great Basin reservation, the Uintah-Ouray Reservation, in eastern Utah and on two other reservations in southwestern Colorado. There are three main Shoshone groups, the Western, Northern, and Eastern, each with numerous different tribes and reservations, especially the Western Shoshone. The many Shoshone reservations are quite spread out and stretch from eastern California to Wyoming. The Southern and Northern Paiute, like the Western Shoshone, consist of numerous smaller tribes living on many different reservations throughout southern Nevada and Utah for the Southern Paiute and northwestern Nevada and eastern Oregon for the Northern Paiute. The Washoe live close to the Nevada-California border, near their ancestral homes around Lake Tahoe.

Numerous interrelated concerns and challenges confront these different tribes and reservation communities. In their efforts to combat the many social problems that stem from economic poverty and joblessness, tribes throughout the region have attempted various economic development plans. Some tribes have used the federal court system to sue the government for failed treaty payments and lands. Others have received federal resources for education and other anti-poverty programs and channeled them into job training and job placement programs. Many of the Great Basin tribes, however, are located in remote locations, far from economic centers. Several tribes have adopted ranching on their open ranges as well as various other timber and water resource development projects.

In addition to economic concerns, numerous cultural and political issues are of critical importance. Culturally, most of the Great Basin groups are attempting to develop strong education programs for their youth and to teach their children some of the older traditions and teachings. Many pan-Indian (including Indians from all tribes) cultural and recreational activities, such as powwows and athletic tournaments, have become increasingly popular in recent years. Politically, tribes throughout the region continue to resist state and federal incursion onto their lands and jurisdictions (places where they have the authority to make and enforce their own law). Many Western Shoshone groups, such as the Te-Moak Tribe of Nevada, are still in court trying to recover some of the millions of acres of land lost to the U.S. government in the nineteenth century. The U.S. Bureau of Land Management (BLM) and Department of Defense, for example, have illegal ownership of nearly 90 percent of Nevada's land. Meanwhile, the BLM and military use the lands in ways that are offensive to Indian peoples. The military, for instance, tests nuclear and other weapons in Nevada, and the BLM prohibits Indian cattle ranching and pine nut harvesting on traditional Indian lands. Throughout the Great Basin, contemporary political, economic, and social issues continue to concern these many different neighboring tribes.

Ned Blackhawk

FURTHER READING

Bergon, Frank. *Shoshone Mike.* New York: Viking Penguin, 1987.

Crum, Steven J. *The Road On Which We Came: A History of the Western Shoshone.* Salt Lake City: University of Utah Press, 1994.

Harney, Corbin. *The Way It Is.* Nevada City: Blue Dolphin Publishing, 1995.

Hebard, Grace Raymond. *Washakie: Chief of the Shoshones.* Reprint. Lincoln: University of Nebraska Press, 1995.

Hyde, Dayton O. *The Last Free Man: The True Story Behind the Massacre of Shoshone Mike and His Band of Indians in 1911.* New York: Dial Press, 1973.

Martineau, LaVan. *Southern Paiutes: Legends, Lore, Language, and Lineage.* Las Vegas: KC Publications, 1992.

Pettit, Jan. *Utes: The Mountain People.* Revised edition. Boulder: Johnson Books, 1994.

Smith, P. David. *Ouray: Chief of the Utes.* Rideway, CO: Wayfinder Press, 1990.

Vander, Judith. *Shoshone Ghost Dance Religion: Poetry, Songs, and Great Basin Context.* Urbana: University of Illinois Press, 1997.

Paiute

Name

Paiute (pronounced *PIE-yoot*). The name means "true Ute." (The group was related to the Ute tribe; see entry.) The Spanish called both the Paiute and the Ute "Yutas," and this served as the origin of the name of the state of Utah.

Location

The Paiute occupied the Great Basin desert areas of Nevada, California, Oregon, Idaho, Arizona, and Utah. Modern-day members of the tribe live on more than two dozen reservations located throughout Nevada, California, Oregon, Utah, and Arizona. The largest numbers of Paiute live in California, Nevada, and Utah.

Population

In 1845, there were an estimated 7,500 Paiute. In a census (count of the population) taken in 1990 by the U.S. Bureau of the Census, 11,369 people identified themselves as Paiute. California was home to 4,605 Paiute; Nevada was home to 3,887; and Utah was home to 753.

Language family

Numic (Uto-Aztecan).

Origins and group affiliations

Native peoples have lived in the land of the Paiute for many hundreds of years. The Paiute are closely related to the Shoshone peoples of the Great Basin (see entry). The tribe is divided into three groups: Northern, Southern, and Owens Valley Paiute. The Northern Paiute were relatives of the Bannock. (See box titled "Bannock Break Away from Northern Paiute.") The Owens Valley Paiute were very similar to the Northern Paiute but did not speak the same language or live in the same area. (They shared their territory with the Washoe tribe.) The Southern Paiute, who moved into the Southwest around the year 1000 C.E., lived near some Pueblo people and learned farming from them. A group called the Chemehuevi broke away from the Southern Paiute sometime in the mid-eighteenth century.

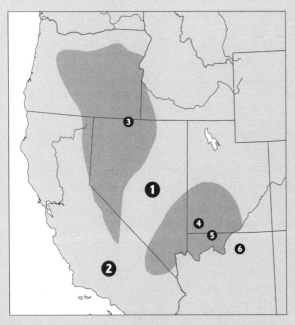

PAIUTE

Shaded area: Traditional lands of the Paiute in present-day Nevada, California, Oregon, Idaho, Arizona, and Utah.

Most Paiute were peaceful wanderers who roamed through the forested highlands of the Rocky Mountains, the Sierra Nevada mountain range, and the desert lowlands between the two ranges. Some led comfortable, settled lives with abundant resources; others struggled to survive in an extremely harsh environment. Although they tried to resist the hordes of American settlers and gold seekers who swarmed into their territory beginning in the mid-1800s, Paiute lands were taken over and the people were moved to many small reservations.

HISTORY

Before their first contact with non-Natives in the 1820s, the lifestyle of the various bands of Paiute depended largely on the types of foods that were available to them. Groups were often referred to by the names of the foods they ate. For example, some Northern Paiute were called "Fish Eaters," but most of the other bands survived on small game, roots, seeds, and berries.

Northern and Southern Paiute

There are three Paiute groups: Northern, Southern, and Owens Valley Paiute. The Northern Paiute lived in parts of Nevada, California, Oregon, and Idaho. The Southern Paiute lived in parts of California, Nevada, Arizona, and Utah. The tribe had little contact with the early European explorers, trappers, and settlers who arrived in the New World in the sixteenth, seventeenth, and eighteenth centuries. Their troubles began in the 1840s with the discovery of gold in the West. American settlers and gold seekers flooded Paiute territory, demanding more and more land and destroying the environment at an alarming rate. The discovery of silver in western Nevada brought another stream of non-Natives in the 1850s and 1860s.

White settlers showed little, if any, respect for the Indians of the American West. They overran the Natives' ancestral land, brought livestock with them, and set up fencing to contain their animals. The livestock destroyed edible plants and spread diseases among local wildlife. The fences cut the Paiute off from their hunting and gathering grounds. In addition, settlers cut down the prized piñon trees (see box titled "The Prized Pine Nut") to use for fuel, displacing local wildlife.

Whites generally looked down on the Paiute because most of them traveled on foot rather than on horseback. When they saw the Paiute digging for edible roots, they expressed their scorn for them by calling the Natives "Diggers." The Indians responded by raiding livestock at ranches, farms, mining camps, and wagon trains. Sometimes these raids were carried out on foot by Paiute who did not own horses. A major clash occurred at Pyramid Lake, Nevada, in 1860, after a group of white men kidnaped two Paiute girls. Warriors responded by attacking and killing five whites in a rescue attempt. After several minor battles, the whites formed an 800-man volunteer army and defeated the Paiute. Thereafter, the move to reservations, which had begun the year before, was stepped up.

Reservations for Northern Paiute

Several large reservations were established for the Northern Paiute in Nevada and Oregon between 1859 and 1891. By the turn of

IMPORTANT DATES

1860: Paiute War between the Southern Paiute and a volunteer army begins and ends. The move to reservations quickens.

1889: Wovoka, a Southern Paiute, founds the Ghost Dance religion, which soon spreads to other Native peoples throughout the West.

1965: Southern Paiute in Utah are awarded $8.2 million for land wrongfully taken from them.

1970: Southern Paiute win $7.25 million for land wrongfully taken from them.

1980: The Paiute Indian Tribe of Utah receives federal recognition.

the twentieth century their traditional land had been reduced to a mere 5 percent of its original size. Many Paiute bands refused to move to reservations that were already occupied by other bands. Instead, these bands established settlements called colonies on the outskirts of American cities. There they worked as wage laborers. Between 1910 and 1930 the U.S. government established official relations with most of these Indian colonies, treating them as reservations.

Southern Paiute and Mormons in Utah

Meanwhile, the Southern Paiute of Utah met up with Mormons—members of the Church of Jesus Christ of Latter Day Saints—who began settling in the Salt Lake Valley in 1847. Mormons stress the importance of hard work, devotion to family life, and refraining from the use of alcohol and tobacco. They moved to Utah to escape religious persecution from Americans in the East.

The Mormons' firsthand experience with religious intolerance helped them forge a bond with the Paiute—a Native group that was just beginning to get a taste of the whites' capacity for discrimination and prejudice. Mormons protected the Paiute from bloodthirsty white settlers, gold seekers, and Ute slave raiders. In return the Paiute shared their food and their knowledge of the environment with the displaced whites. The Mormons were determined to settle in the area, though, so they in turn gave the Paiute food, clothing, and jobs to foster a relationship of trust and productivity between the two groups.

But Mormon encroachment (advancement) on Paiute land strained relations with the Indians. Too many settlers crowded onto Native lands, making it impossible for the Paiute to hunt and gather in the old ways. Hostilities grew as starving Indians began to raid Mormon settlements. U.S. Army troops were called in, and government agents began to handle all Indian matters in the West, including those in Utah. The first Southern Paiute Reservation in Utah was established in the 1880s. Several more were set up there and in Nevada, but most of these lacked sufficient farmland to support the population. Many people had to move away to find work elsewhere.

By the 1950s the U.S. government was making drastic changes in its Native American policies. In 1954, under the terms of a program known as Termination, the government declared that the Southern Paiute tribe in Utah no longer existed. Several groups filed a lawsuit, and in 1965 the Utah Paiute were awarded $8.2 million to compensate for 30 million acres of land wrongfully taken from them. Fifteen years later the government granted federal recognition to the Paiute Indian Tribe of Utah. (Federally recognized tribes are those with which the U.S. government maintains official relations. Without federal recognition, the tribe does not exist as far as the government is concerned and therefore is not entitled to financial assistance and other aid.)

Owens Valley Paiute

The Owens Valley Paiute lived near the Owens River in southern California. They were fortunate to have a reliable water supply, which allowed them to settle down, build irrigation canals, and practice a primitive kind of farming. By the early 1860s American settlers in the Los Angeles area were trespassing on the fertile lands of the Owens Valley and casting their eyes on the bountiful waters of Owens River. The Paiute held them off for a time, defeating a volunteer army in 1862, but they were no match for the increasing number of whites in the area.

Around the turn of the twentieth century many Owens Valley Paiute were moved to reservations located on or near the lands where they had long lived. Most of these reservations, however, were far too small to support their former way of life. In 1937 the rapidly growing city of Los Angeles convinced U.S. Congress to pass laws allowing the city to take over water rights and most of the Owens Valley Paiute land. In exchange the Owens Valley band was given 1,391 acres in nearby Big Pine, where their largest settlement had stood prior to the arrival of whites. Five Owens Valley Paiute reservations now are home to about 2,200 Native people.

On the reservations

In the early 1900s the Paiute were settled on more than two dozen reservations, most of them small. Their land and lives were controlled by federal or state governments that were often slow in delivering on promises of schools, health care, and adequate housing and sanitation.

The Paiute faced ongoing struggles over land and water rights as whites diverted rivers to fulfill their own needs. White ranchers continued to allow their cattle to graze on Paiute land, and Native populations declined from diseases and high rates of infant death.

For decades the Paiute's tribal development was seriously hampered by a lack of funding. This trend did not show signs of reversing itself until the 1960s, when tribal land claims suits began succeeding in the courts.

RELIGION

The Paiute believed in many supernatural beings that were present in elements of the natural world, such as water, thunder, and animals. For some groups the most powerful spirit was the Sun, called *Thuwipu Unipugant* or "The One Who Made the Earth." Other groups gave credit to Coyote and his wife for populating the Earth. The Paiute prayed to the spirits in order to influence them and show their respect. For example, they might pray for rain or a successful hunt.

The Mormon influence

Mormon missionaries worked among the Southern Paiute in Utah in the nineteenth century, and some Paiute converted to Mormonism. Other Paiute were influenced by other Christian missionaries who began to arrive in the late 1800s. In the late 1990s most Paiute attended religious services in some Christian denomination. Some also participated in Indian religious movements such as the Native American church. (See box in Makah entry.)

The Ghost Dance religion

The Paiute played a key role in one of the major Native American religious movements of the modern era. In 1889, when most of the tribe had been pushed off their ancestral lands and forced to live on reservations, a Southern Paiute named Wovoka founded the Ghost Dance religion. Wovoka's underlying message was steeped in Christian sentiment. An advocate of nonviolence, he urged the Indians to express themselves through song and dance while they awaited the great event—the day when the whites would disappear. Some Natives were so anxious for the event and danced so energetically, they fainted. A few tribes, like the Dakota and Lakota (see entry), believed the Ghost Dance could protect them in armed conflicts with whites, but Paiute followers embraced the religion as a source of strength and a form of passive resistance to white culture.

LANGUAGE

Members of the three Paiute groups spoke versions of the language that could not be understood by the other groups. Paiute groups have maintained their language to varying degrees. The San Juan Paiute, a Southern Paiute band whose reservation is completely within the boundaries of the Navajo Reservation in Arizona, is the only group that continues to teach Paiute to children as a first language. However, other Paiute groups have taken steps to preserve their Native languages.

GOVERNMENT

Paiute groups tended to be small, consisting mostly of an extended family (a mother, a father, their children, and close relatives) led by a headman. Although the opinion of the headman was greatly respected, he could not make major decisions without first consulting every adult in the community—both male and female. Each morning he gave a rousing speech, urging his people to live in peace and harmony. The headman held his position only as long as he carried out the wishes of the community.

In the early times the Paiute were peaceful and had no need for war chiefs. So much energy was required to gather food that there was no time for war. After their land was overrun by whites, however, some groups appointed war chiefs. The modern-day Paiute on reservations are governed by elected tribal councils.

ECONOMY

The early Paiute economy was based on hunting, gathering, and some farming. After the tribespeople were relocated to reservations, they were encouraged to farm but were given neither the instruction nor the modern equipment to do so. Many were forced to leave the reservation and earn a living by working for wages in nearby towns or on ranches. Some also raised cattle.

In 1970 the Southern Paiute received $7.25 million from the U.S. government in a lawsuit over tribal lands that had been wrongfully taken from them. Many bands used this money to improve living conditions and develop educational and employment opportunities. Some of the more common business ventures have included the ownership and management of minimarts (small convenience stores), smoke shops, and campgrounds.

Paiute acorn storehouses in the Yosemite Valley, c. 1870.

In the past, the Northern Paiute raised cattle and hay or worked for wages in a variety of professions. In more recent times they have looked for ways to benefit from tourism. The Las Vegas Paiute, for example, opened a golf course in 1995. The Owens Valley Paiute work primarily in mining and businesses that cater to tourists.

Since the 1960s, when federal funds became available, many Paiute bands have successfully used government development grants to improve conditions on the reservations. Houses, roads, community buildings, and sewer and water systems have been built. Because many reservation economies were long hampered by a lack of skilled workers, vocational training among the tribal members is now of primary importance.

DAILY LIFE

Buildings

The wandering Paiute bands built small, temporary huts called wickiups (pronounced *WIK-ee-ups*), made of willow poles covered with brush and reeds. Wickiups were often constructed near streams, where the people could fish or draw water for irrigation.

Clothing and adornment

Paiute men and women often wore a bark or antelope-skin breechcloth, which was something like an apron with both front and back flaps. Animal-skin moccasins or woven yucca sandals (the yucca is an evergreen plant) were worn on the feet. In the winter, the Paiute wrapped themselves in blankets made of strips of rabbit fur. The members of some Paiute bands wore hats decorated with bird feathers, and some very important men wore elaborately feathered crowns. Face and body paints were common for protection from the sun. Ear piercing was associated with long life and a sign to the god Coyote to allow the souls of the dead to cross to the other world. Some men may have pierced their noses as well.

Food

The Paiute wandered the Great Basin in search of food. They knew and understood their environment—what was ripening when and

where. Their diet depended largely on their location; plant foods gathered by the women made up the bulk of the food supply. Many of these wild foods, such as pine nuts and agave (pronounced *uh-GAH-vee*; a plant with tough, spiny, sword-shaped leaves that grows in hot, dry regions), were baked or roasted in earth ovens. The Paiute ate other vegetable foods, including cattails, roots, berries, and rice grass. They often used stones to grind seeds and nuts into flour to make bread.

The Paiute also hunted ducks, rabbits, and mountain sheep using bows and arrows or long nets. Some bands in mountainous regions fished, while others in arid desert regions dug for lizards, grubs, and insects.

The Southern Paiute learned to grow corn from the Pueblo (see entry). The Owens Valley Paiute developed irrigation techniques and engaged in a kind of farming that did not involve planting seeds. Instead, their canals brought water to small plots where plants were already growing, thereby allowing the plants to produce better yields.

Education

Paiute children learned by observing, imitating, and listening to adults. Sarah Winnemucca, the first Indian woman to publish a book,

Writer Sarah Winnemucca and her father Chief Winnemucca pose with Natchez and Captain Jim, Paiutes from Nevada, and a European American boy.

described Paiute teachings passed on to children: "My people teach their children never to make fun of anyone, no matter how they look. If you see your brother or sister doing something wrong, look away, or go away from them. If you make fun of bad persons, you make yourself beneath them."

By 1910 all Paiute reservations had at least one government-run school. A number of children from the tribe were sent to boarding schools far from home. Some never returned, either because they died from infectious diseases or because they chose to stay away from the poverty-stricken reservations. In the late 1990s Paiute children attended public schools, but many did not graduate. Small, rural communities are currently struggling with the problem of developing bicultural programs in their public schools.

Healing practices

Many Paiute believed illness was the work of evil spirits, ghosts, or other supernatural causes. Tribal healers were called shamans (pronounced *SHAY-menz*)—men or women believed to possess supernatural powers. Shamans formed magical relationships with one or more animal spirits, using the fur or feathers of the animal to call upon the spirits for assistance in their work. A shaman used little else in the way of tools but often accomplished remarkable feats such as curing poisonous rattlesnake bites, healing wounds, controlling the weather, and assisting in childbirth.

The Paiute sought the help of shamans well into the 1960s. The two most famous modern Paiute healers were Jimmy George (died 1969) and Joe Green (died c. 1950s). By the 1990s the people of the Paiute reservations were making many different arrangements for health care. Some operated their own health centers to care for minor problems and sent patients with serious health threats to large cities for treatment. Most of the dozen Paiute reservations have access to community health representatives, who provide specific types of health care, including care for diabetic adults. The Paiute are at higher risk of contracting adult-onset diabetes than the rest of the American population.

ARTS

Basketry, rock art, and duck decoys

For centuries the Paiute were known in international trading circles for their outstanding basketry. Paiute creations were often sought out by other tribes and later by European traders. The tradition continues today on some reservations. Weavers at the San Juan Southern Paiute have been recognized for excellence by the National Endowment for the Arts.

Much of Owens Valley contains remnants of Paiute rock art, most of which depict animals such as mountain sheep. These drawings may have served as a decoration, as the mark of a family's territory, or as a symbol that would help bring "hunting magic" to the tribe.

The Northern Paiute were expert makers of duck decoys (artificial ducks used to lure live ducks within gunshot range when hunting). The decoys were made from plants gathered from the deserts and marshes and the skin of one recently killed duck.

Oral literature

Aunts, uncles, and grandparents passed on tribal legends to Paiute children through bedtime stories. The child repeated each line just as the teller told it. One popular creation story described how Coyote carried two boys in a water jug from Canada to the Great Basin, where he released them. One of the boys became the father of the Shoshone tribe, and the other became the father of the Paiute tribe. Because the two tribes were related, they never fought.

CUSTOMS

Festivals and ceremonies

Certain Paiute groups celebrate the desert coming into bloom with a spring Flower Festival. At this festival Paiute girls, who are often named for flowers, compose songs about their names. Young people from the Paiute bands often engage in the Round Dance. Formerly an all-night social affair, the dance features an ever-widening circle of men and women holding hands, singing, and moving to the beat.

Puberty and childbirth observed

The Paiute observed two related rituals to celebrate major life events: one for a young woman entering puberty and one for a woman expecting her first child. In the puberty ritual the young woman was isolated for four days. During this time she could not touch her face or hair with her hands, eat animal foods, or drink cold liquids. After the four days had passed she was bathed in cold water, her face was painted, and the ends of her hair were burned or cut. Then she ate a special meal of animal foods mixed with bitter herbs and spat into a fire.

The ritual for a woman expecting her first child was very similar but traditionally lasted for thirty days instead of four. The pregnant woman also received advice on childbearing from older women.

Courtship and marriage

Potential mates were judged on their performance of gender-based roles. The chief qualification for a good husband was his skill at hunting. A young girl—even one who was not yet physically mature—was considered a good candidate for marriage if she possessed outstanding homemaking skills.

Babies

Fathers buried the umbilical cord of a newborn boy in a hole made by a squirrel or the track of a mountain sheep to insure his hunting ability. A girl's cord was buried in an anthill or small rodent lair to insure that she would be a hard worker.

Death and burial

Author Sarah Winnemucca shed some light on ancient Paiute burial rituals when she described the last hours in the life of her beloved grandfather, who was called Chief Truckee by white settlers. While the chief lay on his deathbed, fires were lit on mountaintops so people would know it was time to pay him their last respects. After his death Chief Truckee's body was wrapped in blankets and buried in the ground. The burial service ended with the killing of six horses, which were intended to provide him with a swift journey to the next world.

According to Paiute traditions the dead were generally either buried or cremated. Paiute mourners abstained from eating meat for four days. Some cut gashes on their arms and legs or cut their hair off. The deceased person's property was destroyed, and his or her name was never spoken again. Often the tribe moved away from the site where the death had taken place, at least for a time.

A ceremonial funeral rite known as the Cry was introduced to the Paiute in the 1870s. The Cry took place over one or two nights after a person's death, before the funeral. It was repeated a year or two later as a memorial. During the Cry ceremony, which is still held by some groups, two groups of singers perform song cycles known as Salt Songs and Bird Songs. Between the singing, people close to the deceased give emotional speeches and the person's valuables are distributed among the guests.

CURRENT TRIBAL ISSUES

Conditions on Paiute reservations have improved since the 1960s. The quality of housing has gotten better, and most people of the tribe have access to utilities (electricity, plumbing, heat) and schooling for their children. But the situation for the Paiute is far from ideal. The tribe is still plagued by problems such as substance abuse, low educational attainment, higher than average unemployment, and the loss of Native language and customs.

Their inability to make a decent living in traditional ways has led the Paiute to seek out new sources of income for tribal members. Economic difficulties prompted two Paiute bands to consider controversial projects in the early 1990s. The Northern Paiute of the Fort McDermitt Reservation in Nevada discussed the possibility of building a storage facility for nuclear waste on their lands, while the Southern Paiute of the Kaibab Reservation in Arizona debated about whether to construct a hazardous waste incinerator. The financial rewards of these projects made them appealing, but both projects were ultimately turned down due to environmental concerns.

Wovoka (c. 1856–1932), known by American settlers as Jack Wilson, was a Southern Paiute who founded the Ghost Dance religion in 1889. He is believed to have been the son of Tavibo (c. 1835–c. 1915), another Paiute who had magnificent visions—visions of unfenced plains full of buffalo, freedom from whites, and peaceful communities of Indians living in harmony with the Earth. Sometime in the late 1880s Wovoka became seriously ill with a high fever. At the height of his illness he experienced a vision much like that of his father. Wovoka preached that the Native peoples could inherit a virtual paradise by purging themselves of white influences (such as alcohol) and by praying, meditating, and dancing. Wovoka's vision formed the foundation of the Ghost Dance religion, which was based upon the belief in a time in the future when all Indian people—the living and those who had died—would be reunited on an Earth forever free from death, disease, and all other miseries. Word of the new religion spread quickly among Indian peoples of the Great Basin and Plains regions, even though Wovoka himself never traveled far from his birthplace. Wovoka was revered by Indians, but local settlers denounced him as an impostor and a lunatic.

Another prominent Paiute was Thocmetony (name means "Shell Flower"), better known as Sarah Winnemucca (1844–1891). Her grandfather had befriended some whites and grew to trust them. At his urging, Winnemucca was educated at a Roman Catholic mission school in California. She later served as an interpreter and scout for the U.S. Army. Electrifying audiences with her lectures on Indian rights, Winnemucca became the first Indian woman to publish a book. Titled *Life among the Paiutes: Their Wrongs and Claims,* it describes the history and culture of the Paiute people.

FURTHER READING

Morrison, Dorothy Nafus. *Chief Sarah: Sarah Winnemucca's Fight for Indian Rights.* New York: Atheneum, 1980.

Scordato, Ellen. *Sarah Winnemucca: Northern Paiute Writer and Diplomat.* Broomall, PA: Chelsea House, 1992.

Winnemucca, Sarah. *Life among the Paiutes: Their Wrongs and Claims.* Privately printed, 1883; Reno: University of Nevada Press, 1994.

Shoshone

Name

Shoshone (pronounced *shuh-SHOW-nee*) or Shoshoni. The name may mean "high growing grass." The Shoshone refer to themselves using several similar words that mean "people." Other tribes and whites often referred to them as "Snake" people for two reasons: (1) their location near the Snake River, which runs through Wyoming, Idaho, and Oregon, and (2) the tribal warriors' wartime practice of carrying rattles that looked like snakes and using them to frighten the enemies' horses.

Location

Formerly in parts of California, Oregon, Nevada, Idaho, Utah, and Wyoming. Modern-day Shoshone live on or near reservations in their former territory.

Population

In 1845, there were an estimated 4,500 Northern and Western Shoshone. (Early estimates are not reliable because they often included members of other tribes.) In a census (count of the population) taken in 1990 by the U.S. Bureau of the Census, 9,506 people identified themselves as Shoshone (see box entitled "Shoshone Population: 1990"). The largest numbers lived in Wyoming (1,752), Idaho (676), Nevada (2,637), and California (1,595).

Language family

Uto-Aztecan.

Origins and group affiliations

Early Shoshone probably moved north from the Southwest between about 1 C.E. and 1000 C.E. Some of the many groups who make up the Shoshone tribe are related to the Paiute, Comanche, and Ute tribes (see entries).

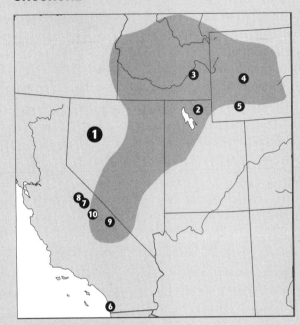

SHOSHONE

Contemporary Communities

1. **Nevada** 12 Shoshone communities

Utah

2. Northeastern Band of Shoshone Indians

3. Northwestern Band of Shoshone Nation, Utah and Idaho

Wyoming

4. Eastern Shoshone Tribe

5. Northwestern Band of Shoshone Nation, Wyoming

California

6. Atahun Shoshone of San Juan Capistrano

7. Big Pine Band of Paiute Shoshone Indians

8. Bishop Reservation

9. Death Valley Timbi-Sha Shoshone Band

10. Lone Pine Reservation

Shaded areas: Traditional lands of the Shoshone in present-day Idaho, Nevada, Utah, Wyoming, California, Oregon, and Montana.

Many different Shoshone groups (called bands) lived throughout the Great Basin—an area sandwiched between the Rocky Mountains and the Sierra Nevada mountain range. Theirs was a sparsely populated region where life was hard; some groups even tried to eke out a living in Death Valley, the lowest point in the Americas with little rain and very high temperatures. The Shoshone are perhaps best known for being the tribe of Sacajawea (pronounced *sak-uh-juh-WEE-uh*; also spelled "Sacagawea"), who helped guide the historic expedition in which American explorers Meriwether Lewis and William Clark mapped out the West for the first time. The Shoshone at first had friendly relations with white settlers, but this changed as they found themselves forced onto reservations. They face modern struggles over rights to their ancestral lands.

HISTORY

Before the whites arrived

Many bands make up the Shoshone tribe. Members of the bands speak the same language, but they developed different lifestyles based on the areas where they lived and how they supported themselves. Historians call the groups Northern, Western, and Eastern Shoshone, but the Shoshone do not refer to themselves that way.

Around the time of their move from the Southwest into the Great Basin, the Shoshone tribes separated and settled in different areas. They dominated the Great Basin until the arrival of other tribes such as the Blackfoot and Sioux from the East (see entries).

The Shoshone adapted well to their new surroundings. The Northern and Eastern groups, for example, adopted a wandering lifestyle, hunting and gathering where resources were plentiful. Soon they began to hunt the buffalo, a task made easier after they acquired horses late in the seventeenth century. The tribe eventually expanded its hunting territory and ran into conflict with other buffalo-hunting tribes like the Blackfoot and Arapaho (see entries). This constant friction, coupled with a 1782 smallpox epidemic, caused the Eastern Shoshone to move into Wyoming.

Shoshone help American explorers and settlers

The Shoshone saw Spanish settlers who arrived in the New World in the 1500s, and later they met up with other explorers, but contact with the foreigners was minimal. Their relations with whites really began with the 1804–1806 Lewis and Clark expedition into the American West. The pair first encountered a Shoshone Indian when they hired French-Canadian fur trapper Toussaint Charbonneau to serve as their interpreter. Charbonneau agreed to help the explorers, but it was his Shoshone wife, Sacajawea, who proved to be the important presence on the expedition. (See "Notable People.") With her help, Lewis and Clark and crew made their way from the Missouri River through to the Pacific Ocean, encountering many Shoshone bands along the way.

An illustration of Sacajawea with Meriwether Lewis and William Clark. Sacajawea had been kidnaped from the Shoshone by the Hidatsa at the age of twelve and was later bought from the Hidatsa by her husband, Toussaint Charbonneau. The expedition helped her to reunite with her people.

American settlers began arriving soon after Lewis and Clark charted the West. When the explorers returned to St. Louis, Missouri, in 1806, pioneers, trappers, and traders started pressing onto Shoshone lands. They were followed by a religious group called the Mormons, who founded Salt Lake City, Utah, in 1847. The lure of gold in California sent more whites west in 1849, as did the discovery of silver in Nevada in 1857. The American westward movement forever changed the lives of the Shoshone.

Shoshone resistance

Most Shoshone military resistance to white expansion took place in the early 1860s. Indian war parties attacked wagon trains, pony express riders (mail carriers on horseback), and telegraph line crews. They were reacting to the disappearance of buffalo herds from overhunting and to the influx of huge numbers of whites. To protect American settlers from Indian raids, California sent an army to establish Fort Douglas near Salt Lake City. In January 1863, 300 army troops went on a punishing raid against Chief Bear Hunter of the Northern Shoshone at Bear Hunter's village, 140 miles away from Fort Douglas.

The Indians prepared their village for the soldiers' arrival by building barricades. But the Shoshone had never experienced the full force of the U.S. Army. The soldiers flooded the village with gunfire on the morning of January 29th. In four hours they killed 250 Shoshone, ruined 70 homes, and captured 175 horses while suffering only 14 deaths and 49 injuries. The Bear River Massacre (1863), as it came to be called, was the turning point in Shoshone-American relations. According to Virginia Cole Trenholm and Maurine Carley in *The Shoshonis: Sentinels of the Rockies,* Mormons sent to view the battle site reported "the dead eight feet deep in one place. . . . The relentless slaughter of the Indians, for the first time, served as [a] . . . lesson. The natives now realized that the [U.S.] army had the power to deal them a crushing defeat"

Northern and Eastern Shoshone make peace

The Northern and Eastern Shoshone were ready to make peace with the whites after the Bear River Massacre. Later in 1863 Shoshone chiefs signed the first of several treaties in which they agreed to sell much of their land to the U.S. government for payments that were usually never made. The federal government began to assign all Native Americans to reservations. Many of the branches of the Shoshone tribe resisted the idea of moving from their homelands, but as time went on they were left with no choice but to agree to U.S. terms. Finally, all the Northern Shoshone, together with the Bannock (see Paiute entry), were moved to the Fort Hall Reservation in eastern Idaho.

By the beginning of the twentieth century most Northern Shoshone were living at Fort Hall, which was located in an area of dry, poor soil. The Shoshone saw reservation acreage reduced from 1.8 million acres to 544,000 acres, as white timber lords, railroad companies, and miners grabbed Shoshone lands. The hostility that whites continued to express toward the Shoshone prevented the Natives from exercising their treaty rights—the rights to hunt, fish, and gather on their own land.

The Wind River Reservation was established for the Eastern Shoshone later in 1863. It consisted of 44 million acres of land in Wyoming. After about five years a new treaty reduced the band's acreage to less than 2.8 million acres. But the Eastern Shoshone did not break their peace with the white Americans. In fact, under the leadership of Chief Washakie (see "Notable People"), they aided the Americans in their wars against the Sioux throughout the 1870s. After all their help, though, the Wind River band felt betrayed when the

federal government moved their old enemies, the Arapaho, to the Wyoming reservation in 1878.

After the death of Washakie in 1900, the Eastern Shoshone suffered one tragedy after another. Their population plummeted due to starvation, epidemics of measles and tuberculosis, and other problems. (Tuberculosis, often called TB, is an extremely contagious bacterial disease that usually attacks the lungs.)

Western Shoshone

The Western Shoshone signed the Treaty of Ruby Valley in 1863. In it they agreed to keep the peace, allow settlers to set up some businesses on their land, abandon "the roaming life," and at some future date live on reservations. It is important to note that in this treaty they did not give up their lands.

For the first three decades of the twentieth century many of the Western Shoshone avoided or tried to avoid moving to the reservations being established by the federal government. For many of them the U.S. government agreed to the creation of colonies (small Indian settlements near larger white settlements) in Nevada as alternatives to reservation life. By 1927 only about half of the Western Shoshone lived on reservations. This pattern continued into the twenty-first century.

Shoshone in the twentieth century

In the 1930s new government policies brought reforms to the Shoshone in the form of self-government, and the quality of their lives began to improve. The Shoshone began sharing their culture with white Americans and worked diligently to retain many of their traditional cultural practices. They taught and used the Shoshone language, built schools and cultural centers, and began holding pow-wows (traditional song-and-dance celebrations).

The Shoshone people live on or near eighteen reservations and colonies in Utah, Idaho, Nevada, Wyoming, and California. Many of the reservations also serve as homes to Arapaho, Bannock, Paiute, and Goshute peoples.

RELIGION

The many Shoshone peoples have a wide range of religious beliefs and practices. Some believe the Sun created the Heavens and the Earth, while others believe that either Coyote or Wolf or a kindly spirit called "Our Father" was the Creator. The aid of these and other spirits is often sought, but first the seeker has to undergo purification in a sweat lodge (a building where steam is produced by pouring water over heated rocks). Many groups do not have priests or other religious leaders. Instead, individuals seek out supernatural powers on their own, through visions and dreams.

A fairly recent addition to Shoshone spiritualism is the Peyote (pronounced *pay-OH-tee*) religion, which originated in Mexico and the southwestern United States and spread throughout North America in the late nineteenth and early twentieth centuries. Many Shoshone welcomed the Peyote religion as a source of comfort and strength in the face of hardship. Peyote is a type of cactus; when parts of it are chewed, the user sees visions. For a people like the Shoshone, who always believed in strong links to the supernatural and the powers of spirits, peyote is a tool to communicate better with spirits and to discover supernatural powers.

The Shoshone also welcomed the messages of the Ghost Dance religions of 1870 and 1889. Ghost Dancers believed that the performance of their special dance would hasten the day when the traditional Indian way of life would be restored and Native peoples would be freed from the burden of white intervention.

LANGUAGE

All Shoshone groups speak dialects (versions) of the same language. Though the dialects differ slightly among the divisions, they are, for the most part, understandable by all Shoshone.

GOVERNMENT

The Western Shoshone were the most loosely organized of the three groups. Their small, wandering bands sometimes had headmen, leaders who had little real authority. Shoshone groups who hunted buffalo were more likely to have chiefs with a greater degree of authority. This type of organization was necessary for the group to be effective against enemies coming into buffalo-hunting territory at the same time the Shoshone wanted to hunt. Such chiefs made decisions after consulting with a council, and they came and went as their popularity rose or fell.

Among the Eastern Shoshone, chiefs played a more important role. Men like Washakie—older men who had proved their worth in past battles—were chosen to lead.

In the 1930s new government policies brought reforms to the Shoshone in the form of self-government. In modern times the many Shoshone reservations and colonies are governed by elected tribal councils and business councils.

ECONOMY

The Shoshone were hunter-gatherers, but the things hunted and gathered differed according to where they lived. For example, those who lived near water could fish. No groups owned land; it was shared by all, as were the fruits of hunting and gathering. The Shoshone also engaged in extensive trade. They received metal arrow points from the Crow Indians in exchange for horses. Later they traded furs with whites for horses and weapons.

In the late 1800s and early 1900s many Shoshone who refused to move to reservations became dependent on wages paid by white employers. Those who lived on reservations were encouraged to farm, even where the land was not at all suitable for farming. They suffered hardships when government agents failed to deliver promised supplies, seeds, and instructions on how to farm. At the dawn of the twenty-first century many Shoshone still lived in poverty.

The Eastern Shoshone at Wind River have been hit the hardest by economic suffering. The reservation is located in a rugged, remote, mountainous area, with limited opportunities for agricultural activity. Income is generated by leasing land for grazing and by raising horses and cattle. Some income is earned from tourists, who are drawn by the excellent fishing, tours of Fort Washakie Historic District, and the reservation's location near the Rocky Mountains, the Continental Divide, and Yellowstone and Grand Teton national parks. A large percentage of tribal members are employed in government programs such as social services.

The Northern Shoshone have fared better, in part by opening a variety of shops and gambling establishments and by farming. Their reservation covers some prime farming land. The tribe grows potatoes, grain, and alfalfa, raises cattle, and leases land to other farmers. The Northern Shoshone have won many contracts and grants from the federal government for various projects, and tribal members are employed on those projects. Still, the tribe suffered when a phosphate mine on the reservation was closed in 1993 after nearly fifty years in operation.

The Western Shoshone support themselves by cattle ranching, and they continue their struggles with the U.S. government over land rights. (See "Current tribal issues.")

DAILY LIFE

Buildings

Some Northern Shoshone lived in tepees made from buffalo hides or interwoven rushes (marsh plants with hollow stems used for weaving) and willows. Others built conical dwellings of brush and grass. All Northern groups built and maintained sweat lodges and huts where women retreated during their menstrual period. (Menstrual blood was considered evil, even dangerous.)

The Western Shoshone lived in camps that were somewhat more permanent than other Shoshone divisions because they did not have to chase buffalo. They usually did not use animal hides in their homes and buildings. For the winter months they constructed cone-shaped huts with bark walls. Rings of stone supported the walls and kept the structure erect. Some built sun-shades and circular cottages out of brush and light timber. Many of the mountain-dwelling Western Shoshone lived in wickiups (pronounced *WIK-ee-ups*), frame huts covered with brush or bark matting. Others did not build homes at all but sought shelter in caves when the weather turned bad. All Western Shoshone built sweat lodges and most built menstrual huts.

The Eastern Shoshone built substantial tepees. Each of these structures required the hides of at least 10 buffalo. The chief's tepee might be painted with a yellow band to set it apart from the others.

Clothing and adornment

Most Shoshone wore few clothes, especially during the summer months. Women and girls usually wore only skirts and hats, while young boys went naked. During times of extreme cold they sewed small animal furs and hides into dresses, shirts, and robes, and the best hunters and their kin wore larger pieces of clothing made from deer and antelope skins. The clothing of the Eastern Shoshone tended to be more decorative than the Northern and Western divisions.

Buffalo-hunting groups wore buffalo robes in winter and elk skins in summer. Also common were leggings and breechcloths (garments with front and back flaps that hang from the waist). Many went barefoot; those who did not wore moccasins of buffalo hide.

Both sexes pierced their ears and wore many necklaces. Western Shoshone also practiced face and body painting and some facial tattooing.

Food

Shoshone bands were often named for the main foods they consumed, so names like "Salmon Eaters" and "Squirrel Eaters" were typical. Like many of the tribes of the region, some Northern and Eastern Shoshone bands depended on buffalo hunts for their main food. Men also chased down sheep and antelope to add to their wild game menu. In September they often combined forces with the Bannock and Flathead for a massive buffalo hunt. Some caught fish—primarily salmon, sturgeon (pronounced *STIR-juhn*), and trout—and gathered other wild foods. They are said to have used torches to attract fish at night, then netted or trapped them.

Shoshone women were skilled at making cakes from dried berries, nuts, and seeds of all sorts. They cooked turnips and other tubers in pits beneath hot rocks until the vegetables were soft and brown.

The Western Shoshone used sticks to dig up a variety of nuts, berries, and roots. They wandered more than other Shoshone bands, looking for places where edible plants and wild growth were most plentiful. The Western Shoshone did not hunt buffalo; their hunting was confined to smaller game—such as antelope, rabbits, and rodents—and to fishing. They also collected grasshoppers in large numbers by sweeping through open fields to send the hoppers scattering.

Education

Children were taught by the elderly and the handicapped, who sang songs and told stories while parents were busy gathering food. At the beginning of the twentieth century, when the U.S. government was handling Indian affairs on the reservations, Christian missionaries were invited to establish schools. Some Shoshone children were sent to boarding schools located far from home and family. At these schools children were encouraged to speak English and to give up their Native tongue, but among the Shoshone these efforts to eliminate Native traditions were largely unsuccessful.

In the 1950s Shoshone children were integrated (merged or blended) into America's public school system. Educational attainment improved, but test results from the 1990s showed that some Shoshone children still lag behind other students. One reason for the low test scores may be related to language and cultural differences. Frequently the public schools are the Shoshone child's first encounter with mainstream American society. Native students are often hampered by the language barrier and the lack of Native American history and culture in the curriculum. Students at the Wind River Reservation are fortunate to have their own Wyoming Indian High School, which teaches the Native culture and language. Other communities operate their own Head Start programs for preschoolers.

Healing practices

The Shoshone had healers, men or women called shamans (pronounced *SHAY-menz*), who knew how to use roots, herbs, charms, and chants to cure ailments. More serious cases were cured by spirit power. The shaman obtained spirit powers through visions, usually seen during a fast in a secluded place like a mountain peak. The shaman applied spirit power while laying hands on the patient or sucking out the disease-causing object.

Old rituals and ways declined after the move to reservations. People starved when the government did not provide adequate food, and tuberculosis was common. Government reforms that began in the 1930s brought better health care. The last half of the twentieth century saw many improvements in health care, and as a result the Shoshone population increased.

ARTS

Painting and basketry

All Shoshone groups have long and complicated artistic traditions. The Eastern Shoshone at Wind River Reservation preserve hundreds of ancient pictographs depicting Water Ghost Beings, Rock Ghost Beings, and other fearful creatures. Once they began using horses and traveling greater distances, many groups started learning some of the artistic practices and teachings of their new Plains neighbors. Elk- and buffalo-hide paintings, for instance, were used to record tribal histories.

The Western Shoshone artistic traditions are very different from the Northern and Eastern groups. Lacking water and wood supplies, Western Shoshone societies made extremely complex baskets and tools for carrying water, foods, and other objects. Not having leather like other groups, the Western Shoshone perfected the weaving of various willows, grasses, and other materials into a beautiful yet functional art.

Literature

The Shoshone have a longstanding commitment to the written word. Sacajawea's brother is credited with producing the first written Shoshone story. Shoshone authors have written tribal histories, and newspapers are produced at the Wind River and Fort Hall reservations.

CUSTOMS

Festivals and ceremonies

All three Shoshone divisions practiced a variety of dances and ceremonies. Major dances with religious themes included the Round Dance, the Father Dance, and the Sun Dance. The Round Dance (also performed by the Paiute; see entry) was performed when food was plentiful or as part of an annual mourning ceremony. The Father Dance, possibly a form of the Round Dance, paid tribute to the Cre-

COYOTE WANTS TO BE CHIEF

The Shoshone have many tales of Coyote, the trickster and alleged creator of people. Coyote is a prominent figure in many tales by tribes from the western parts of North America.

People from all over the country—all kinds of animals, even Stink Bug—gathered together in a valley for a council. Rumors were going around that a lot of them wanted to make Coyote the head man. Meadowlark told Coyote that Coyote was going to be a great chief. As he was going along, Coyote met Skunk, who told him the same thing, that Coyote was going to be the biggest chief there ever was. Then Coyote met Badger and he said the same thing. Every time Coyote heard this he got so swelled and he wished he would meet some more people who would tell him the same things.

Coyote wanted to find [Wolf] his brother. Wolf had been away for a long time. Coyote ran around that valley so fast, looking for Wolf, that he got all tired out.

The council was to start before the sun came up. Coyote didn't sleep the night before, [so] he was so weary. In the middle of the night Coyote got sleepy. He still had a long way to go to get to the council. Coyote sat down to rest a little while in some timber. He didn't want to go to sleep but he was very weary. His eyes began to close. He picked up some little yellow flowers and propped his eyelids open with them. He fought sleep but he was so tired. Finally he fell asleep and didn't wake up till noon the next day. He got up and ran toward the valley. To his surprise he began meeting people. They were coming back from the council. He started asking, "What did you talk about? Who became a chief?" And they all told him, "Your brother did. He is the biggest man in the country now. He is the chief."

Coyote wanted to find his brother. Then Coyote found his brother and asked him if he were the biggest chief. Wolf said, "Yes." The people all wanted him to be the biggest chief.

SOURCE: Tom Steward. *Shoshone Tales*. Edited by Anne M. Smith. Salt Lake City: University of Utah Press, 1993.

ator and asked him to keep the people healthy. In the old times the Sun Dance was performed after a buffalo hunt. The head of the buffalo was prepared so that it seemed to be alive. In modern times a mounted buffalo head is used. It is then kept at the home of the sponsor of the following year's Sun Dance. Sponsoring a Sun Dance is an expensive proposition and is considered a great honor. The Sun Dance has become a focal point for all Shoshone people. It expresses Indian unity and renews the people's connections to their spiritual side.

Modern-day Shoshone host celebrations called fandangos (festivities include prayers and games) and powwows. The powwow—a traditional song-and-dance celebration— is a very recent introduction, having come to the Shoshone in 1957. Shoshone powwows include dancers from many Plains tribes.

War rituals

Some Shoshone warriors took the scalps of their enemies as a symbol of victory. Upon returning to his village, a triumphant warrior would place each scalp atop a pole and dance around it. Military societies called the Yellow Brows and the Logs existed among the Eastern Shoshone. Yellow Brows were young men who underwent an interesting initiation ritual in which all speech was backwards, so that "yes" meant "no," for example. They painted their hair yellow and took a vow to remain fearless in battle, not giving up even when certain death was upon them. When preparing for battle a Yellow Brow and his horse performed a frenzied dance called Big Horse Dance. Behind the Yellow Brows in battle were older soldiers called Logs, who painted their faces black.

Courtship and marriage

Courting couples looked forward to socializing at Round Dances, although some men got their brides by kidnaping them—not caring if the women were single or already married. Good hunters were considered especially desirable husbands, and they often had more than one wife. Divorce was common and frequent remarriage was normal. The choice of residence for the newlyweds—with the bride's family or the groom's family—varied from group to group.

The role of women

In early times Shoshone women were considered inferior to men, especially when they were young. This is partly because they menstruated, and menstrual blood was considered evil. (Women were isolated in special huts during their periods.) A woman's status in the society was based upon that of her husband. As they grew older, women could attain a higher status by curing, assisting at births, and demonstrating skill at gambling. The coming of Europeans elevated the status of Shoshone women, who often acted as go-betweens with trappers and traders (as Sacajawea did).

By the late 1990s Shoshone women had expanded their roles in many ways, especially in tribal ceremonies. Thanks to their efforts, many traditional dances and music (formerly performed only by men) that might have been forgotten have been kept alive.

Death and burial

Sometimes when food was extremely scarce, the old and the feeble were abandoned by their group and soon died. Some Shoshone wrapped their dead in blankets and placed them in rock crevices. They believed the souls of the departed journeyed on to the lands of Coyote or Wolf. Mourners cut their hair and destroyed the deceased's property, horse, and tepee. The Western Shoshone practiced cremation and often burned the dead in their dwellings. The ghosts of the dead were feared, and even dreaming about someone who had passed on was considered a bad omen.

CURRENT TRIBAL ISSUES

The Western Shoshone have had longstanding land claims disagreements with the federal government. They continue to reject government offers of money and instead hope to regain some of the 22 million acres lost since the nineteenth century, when nearly all of their homeland was seized illegally. The treaty they signed in 1863 permitted railroad, mining, and timber activities on their territory, but the Shoshone could not have imagined how many people would come and live on—and mistreat—the land.

The federal government continues to give permission to various white business groups—mining companies, for example—to carry out activities on Shoshone land. Shoshone outrage at the misuse of their land has led to radical action. In 1972 the tribe joined with an organization called the American Indian Movement (AIM) in a demonstration called the Trail of Broken Treaties, in which 500 Indians, who arrived in Washington D.C. to protest the government's policies toward Native Americans, occupied the Bureau of Indian Affairs building for nearly a week.

NOTABLE PEOPLE

Washakie (c. 1804–1900) was a chief of the Eastern Shoshone and became the most powerful leader of his tribe. His name may mean "Gourd Rattle," "Rawhide Rattle," or "Gambler's Gourd" because during battle he would ride toward his enemies and shake his rattle to frighten their horses. In the 1820s and 1830s Washakie and the Shoshone were on good terms with white frontierspeople, trappers, and traders. They participated in Rocky Mountain get-togethers with fur trappers and joined them in battles against the Sioux, Blackfoot, and Crow Indians—traditional enemies of the Shoshone. Washakie signed the Treaty of Fort Bridger in 1863, guaranteeing U.S. travelers safe passage through his band's territory. His good relations with the U.S. government made it possible for him to secure the Wind River Reservation in Wyoming for the Eastern Shoshone. Washakie died in 1900 at Flathead Village in Montana's Bitterroot Valley and was buried with full military honors at Fort Washakie, Wyoming. His tombstone reads: "Always loyal to the Government and his white brothers."

Sacajawea (c. 1784–c. 1812) played an important role as a guide to American explorers Lewis and Clark during their westward trek (1804–6) across the country. She was born sometime between 1784 and 1790 among the Lemhi Shoshone of Idaho-Montana. Around the age of 10, Sacajawea was kidnaped by the Hidatsa tribe in a raid. In 1804 a French-Canadian trader, Toussaint Charbonneau, purchased her and married her. Charbonneau joined Lewis and Clark as an interpreter shortly before Sacajawea gave birth to their child, Jean Baptiste Charbonneau. The only woman on the expedition, Sacajawea proved invaluable in leading the explorers through the wilderness. She was a symbol to all people they encountered that theirs was a peaceful mission. Sacajawea's date of death is even less certain than her date of birth. One account reported her dying of a disease in 1812—six years after the return of the expedition—aboard a trader ship on the Missouri River. Another account suggested that she returned to her homeland, lived with the Wind River Shoshone led by Washakie, and died at about 100 years of age. (This would put her death date around the year 1884, not 1812.)

Other notable Shoshone include: Pocatello (c. 1815–1884), who put up the fiercest Shoshone resistance to white settlement; Bear Hunter (d. 1863), killed resisting a U.S. Army raid; and Shoshone-Goshute-Paiute author Laine Thom (1952–), who has edited two critically acclaimed books about the Native American experience: *Becoming Brave: The Path to Native American Manhood* and *Dancing Colors: Paths of Native American Women*.

FURTHER READING

Dramer, Kim. *The Shoshone*. Broomall, PA: Chelsea House, 1997.

Trenholm, Virginia Cole, and Maurine Carley. *The Shoshonis: Sentinels of the Rockies*. Norman: University of Oklahoma Press, 1964.

Ute

Name

Ute (pronounced *yoot*). The Ute call themselves *Noochew,* which means "Ute People." The name of the state of Utah comes from the Spanish word for the Ute (*Yutah*), which means "high land" or "land of the sun."

Location

Ute territory once included most of Colorado and Utah and parts of New Mexico, Arizona, and Wyoming. Today, the Northern Ute live on the Uintah and Ouray Ute Reservation, the second-largest Indian reservation in the United States, with headquarters in Fort Duchesne, Utah. The Southern Ute live on their own reservation in the southwestern corner of Colorado near Ignacio. The Ute Mountain Ute moved to the western end of the Southern Ute Reservation in 1897; their reservation is located near Towaoc, Colorado, and includes small sections of Utah and New Mexico.

Population

In the 1600s, there were about 4,000 Ute. In a census (count of the population) done in 1990 by the U.S. Bureau of the Census, 7,658 people identified themselves as Ute (572 Uintah Ute, 5,626 Ute, and 1,460 Ute Mountain Ute).

Language family

Uto-Aztecan.

Origins and group affiliations

The seven to twelve bands (groups) who made up the Ute people probably left western Canada and Alaska and moved into their current homeland during the thirteenth century. They may have contributed to forcing the ancient Anasazi (see entry) to move from the mesa tops to sandstone caves for defense purposes. The Ute bands looking for food fought with numerous other tribes, including the Arapaho, Cheyenne, Comanche, Sioux, Kiowa, Pueblo, Apache, Hopi, Navajo, Shoshone, and Paiute (see entries).

Today the Ute bands form three main groups: the Northern Ute (the largest), the Southern Ute, and the Ute Mountain Ute.

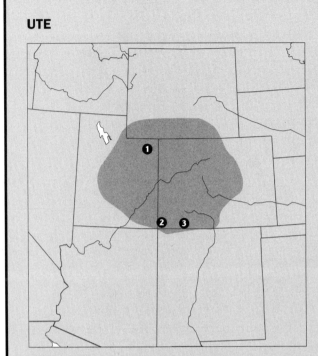

UTE

Contemporary Communities

Utah
1. Uintah and Ouray Ute Tribe

Colorado
2. Ute Mountain Ute Reservation
3. Southern Ute Tribe

Shaded area: Traditional lands of the Ute in present-day Colorado and Utah and parts of northern New Mexico and southern Wyoming.

The Ute were a fearless people; some historians say they were equal in skill and cunning to the Apaches. They once roamed over 79 million acres of the Great Basin area. Through many centuries their feet carved out trails in the beautiful mountainous landscape of the West, and the signs they left to guide themselves proved invaluable to the white settlers who took their lands from them. Although they struggle with poverty and other problems today, they retain an unconquerable spirit, a sense of humor, and many of their ancient customs.

HISTORY

Early relations with Spanish

Before they first met white men, the Ute were a varied and widespread tribe. They ranged over 79 million acres, from the forested slopes of the Rocky Mountains to the barren deserts of Utah. They never really formed a "tribe," as we usually think of one. Instead, individual members gave their loyalty to their extended family group or to a small, independent band led by a chief. They did this because food was scarce, and small groups had to cover a lot of territory to find enough to feed themselves.

At first the Ute wandered their territory on foot, hunting and gathering food. In the 1600s they acquired horses from the Spanish, and their lives underwent a tremendous change. Because their land was well-suited to grazing livestock, over time the lifestyle changed. Where they had once gathered and hunted small game, they began to hunt buffalo and raise horses, cattle, and sheep.

Riding on horseback increased their ability to travel long distances—as far away as the territory claimed by other tribes. The Ute began raiding neighboring tribes and also the Spanish settlements springing up in New Mexico. These raids were for the purpose of taking hostages, horses, and other goods. Their raiding skills earned the Ute a reputation as a warlike people.

The Spanish sent expeditions into Ute country in the 1600s looking for gold, and there are many written accounts of meetings with the Ute. One account noted: "They were said to be very skillful with the bow and arrow and were able to kill a buffalo with the first shot." In 1670, the Spanish signed a peace treaty with the Ute, but this did not stop the Utes from raiding the Spanish and others—their desire for horses was too great. The Spanish penetrated further into previously unknown Ute territory, and set up an extensive trading network.

Loss of land to Mexicans

When Mexico took control of the territory (lands that would later be parts of Colorado, Utah, Arizona, and New Mexico) in 1821, the pattern of trading and exploration of Ute land continued. The Mexicans wanted to own Ute land, because it was both beautiful and excellent for grazing livestock. The Mexican government began granting to its citizens farm and ranch land in Ute territory, and naturally the Indians were angry. As the years went by, Ute raids on Mexican settlements continued.

IMPORTANT DATES

1637: First known contact between Utes and Spanish. Utes soon acquire horses from the Spanish and their lifestyle begins to change.

1670: Utes sign a peace treaty with Spanish.

1861: Uintah Reservation (later the Uintah and Ouray Reservation) is established in Utah.

1868: A reservation is established for the Colorado Utes.

1879: Utes kill 13 U.S. soldiers and 10 Indian agency officials, including Nathan Meeker, in a conflict that becomes known as the "Meeker Massacre."

1895: The Weminuche band moves to the western end of the Southern Ute Reservation and becomes the Ute Mountain Ute.

1896: Colorado and Utah (Northern) Utes form the Confederated Bands of Ute Indians and file claims for lands illegally taken.

1950: Confederated Ute Tribes receive $31 million from the U.S. government for lands wrongfully taken in the 1800s.

When the United States won its war with Mexico in 1848 and took over the land of the Ute, it agreed to respect the land grants given to settlers by the Mexican government. While the Ute were unhappy about this, they overcame their feelings because they believed the Americans were going to make better trading partners than the Mexicans had been. In fact, the Ute did have good relations with the trappers and "mountain men" who came into their territory. Those men had no interest in settling on Ute land. The Ute shared their knowledge of the vast area of their homelands with these early visitors.

In 1849 the first treaty between Ute and the United States was signed. Ute bands acknowledged that the United States was now in charge, and agreed to peace and friendship. They promised not to leave their usual territory without permission and to allow U.S. citizens to build military posts and Indian agencies on Ute lands.

Losing land to Americans in Utah and Colorado

Utah was at the time being settled by Mormons, members of the Church of Jesus Christ of Latter Day Saints, who began moving there in the 1840s. In no time, they were trying to convert the Ute and were calling Ute land their own. The fighting that resulted led President Abraham Lincoln to establish the Uintah Valley Reservation for the Utes in Utah in 1861. In 1886 the reservation became the Uintah and Ouray Ute Reservation.

Back in Colorado, gold was discovered in 1859, and white miners and settlers began to pour in. In 1863, a treaty was signed in which some Utes agreed to give up mineral rights (gold) in exchange for an 18-million-acre reservation (it later became the Southern Ute Reservation). The bands who signed the treaty kept their own hunting grounds and signed over the lands of other Utes who were not present at the treaty meetings.

In 1868, most Colorado Utes signed a treaty in which their land was reduced to 15 million acres. Two Indian agencies were established, at White River and Los Pinos. Five years later, when more gold was discovered, the Ute were forced to give up 3.4 million acres from their Colorado reservation.

Continued conflict erupts in "massacre"

Conflict continued between white settlers and Ute bands in Colorado. White missionaries and Indian agency officials tried to convert the Ute to Christianity and to convince them to adopt a farming

lifestyle, but the Ute resisted. They could not understand why they should sit still and farm on reservations, where the hunting was poor and there was not enough room to roam. After Colorado became a state in 1876, the non-Native inhabitants decided "the Utes must go."

The conflict came to a head in 1879 when an Indian agent at White River named Nathan Meeker grew frustrated by the Utes' refusal to become farmers. He called in government troops to help him plow the Indians' horse-racing track, so they would stop amusing themselves there and start farming. The Ute considered Meeker's actions a declaration of war and warned that the army would not be allowed to enter their territory. When a force of 150 U.S. soldiers arrived, the White River Ute ambushed them at Milk Creek. After nearly a week of fighting, the Ute had killed thirteen soldiers and wounded forty-eight others. With the support of two late-arriving backup regiments, the troops finally managed to push forward to the Indian agency, where they found Meeker and nine of his white employees dead. The Ute had also taken several women and children hostage.

An illustration of a group of Ute encountering a gold prospector on reservation land during the gold rush.

Chief Ouray, a respected Ute leader (see "Notable People"), helped negotiate an end to the hostilities and arranged for the release of the women and children. White settlers, however, used the "Meeker massacre" as a rallying cry in their battle to remove the Ute from Colorado. The Meeker tragedy was one of the last major Indian uprisings in the United States. After Ouray died in 1880, the White River Ute were forced to move to the Uintah Reservation in Utah. Members of other Colorado Ute bands were forced at gunpoint to move to the Ouray reservation adjacent to Uintah in 1882.

The allotment period

The Ute (and many other Native Americans) would not settle down to farming fast enough to suit white Americans. Also, Americans were land-hungry, and many believed that too much land had been set aside for Indians. To respond to their complaints, the U.S. Congress passed the General Allotment Act in 1887.

The Allotment Act was supposed to speed up the process of assimilation, whereby Indians became more like white Americans. Reservation land was divided into parcels (allotments) that would be owned by individual Indians rather than by the tribe as a whole. The land "left over" was opened to white settlement.

To the Ute, who did not like farming and did not believe in individual ownership of land, the allotment policy was unwelcome. Some successfully resisted, perhaps because their land was not considered desirable. They occupied the western end of the Southern Ute Reservation, and their land eventually became the Ute Mountain Ute Reservation. Land at the Southern Ute Reservation and the Uintah and Ouray Reservation were allotted to Indians and the remainder was sold, so that both reservations today are checkerboards of Indian-owned and non-Indian-owned land.

The Ute in modern times

In 1896, the Colorado and Utah (Northern) Ute formed the Confederated Bands of Ute Indians. They pressed the U.S. government to pay them back for land they said was wrongfully taken from them, by treaties and by the allotment policy. Finally, in 1950, the Ute were awarded $31.7 million. Since then, they have engaged in many complex talks with local governments, trying to clarify issues such as hunting and water rights, taxes, and territorial boundaries. They have met with successes (being allowed to hunt outside the state-ordered hunting season, for example) and frustrating delays (trying to clarify their water rights; see "Current Tribal Issues").

RELIGION

The Ute believe in a Supreme Being and a number of lesser gods, such as the gods of war, peace, thunder and lightning, and floods. The Ute also have a strong faith in life after death and believe that a good spirit will lead them to the Happy Hunting Ground when they die. They believe in an evil spirit called the skinwalker. Long ago, skinwalkers were esteemed Navajo warriors who could change themselves into coyotes or foxes and sneak into enemy camps. Once the Indian wars were over, skinwalkers used their powers for evil. The Ute believe that skinwalkers can steal a person's soul.

Some Utah Ute converted to the Mormon religion in the 1800s. A Catholic Church was established in Ignacio, Colorado, in 1898, and found some converts among the Southern Utes. Many Utes today participate in the Native American Church, which was formed in Oklahoma in 1918 (see box in Makah entry). The church brought together several groups of Native North Americans who had been practicing the peyote (pronounced *pay-OH-tee*) religion since the 1880s. Peyote is a substance obtained from cactus; when eaten, it causes a person to see visions. The religion involves an all-night service held in a tepee.

LANGUAGE

The language spoken by the Ute people is called Shoshonean; it is a variation of the Uto-Aztecan language that was spoken by the Hopi, Paiute, Shoshone (see entries), and others. According to the 1990 U.S. Census, more than 1,100 people spoke Ute at home. The tribe also uses their language during cultural events and public meetings. According to a 1990 study, about half of the residents of the Ute Mountain Ute Reservation and about one third of the residents of the Northern and Southern Ute Reservations knew at least some of their Native languages as well as English. Growing numbers of young people on all three reservations speak only English, however, causing some concern about how long the Native language can last.

GOVERNMENT

Utes were organized into extended family groups or small independent bands led by a chief, who was chosen for his wisdom or skills. Families were held together by their respect for their chief. Those who lost their respect left and moved in with relatives.

After they began to hunt the buffalo, the Ute organized into larger groups with more powerful leaders. These leaders were in charge of moving camp and directing hunts, raids, and war parties.

After many years under the supervision of U.S. government agents on the reservations, in the 1930s the three major Ute groups adopted elective forms of government. The Uintah and Ouray Reservation is overseen by a tribal business committee, while the Ute Mountain Utes and the Southern Utes are governed by tribal councils.

ECONOMY

The Ute's early economy was based on hunting and gathering and some trade with neighboring tribes. After they acquired horses, they could trade more extensively, raise cattle, and raid to provide for themselves. The Ute traded their dried buffalo meat and hides for Pueblo farm products, cotton blankets, pottery, salt, and turquoise. From the Hopis they got the red ocher paint (obtained from minerals) they sometimes used to decorate their faces and bodies. From the tribes on the Pacific Coast they got sea shells. The Ute often acquired women and children in raids, and either adopted them into the tribe or traded them for products; for example, the Spanish traded horses for children they used as slaves.

After the arrival of white settlers in the 1800s, the Ute saw their territory disappear at an alarming rate. Eventually, they were confined to reservations and attempts were made to force them to become farmers. Most Ute strongly resisted the agricultural lifestyle and instead raised livestock while continuing to hunt and gather their food.

Between the 1890s and the 1930s, the Ute had a terrible time supporting themselves. They lived on government food handouts (mostly salt and beans) and raised small herds of livestock (cattle and sheep). Many took jobs as day laborers; many still lived in tents. The Ute also received some income from land leases.

In 1950, the Confederated Ute Tribes received $31 million from the U.S. government after winning a lawsuit over territory that had been wrongfully taken in the 1800s. The three major Ute groups divided the money among themselves. Around the same time, oil and natural gas deposits were discovered on the reservations, giving the Utes another source of income. This allowed the Ute to make a number of improvements on their reservations, including the construction of modern homes for most of the tribe. The Northern Ute and the Southern Ute also used some of the money to start businesses related to tourism, such as motels, restaurants, convention facilities, craft shops, a pottery factory, casinos, rodeos, and horse-racing tracks. Tourism is now the leading industry.

Statistics paint a grim picture of Ute life today. By 1990, half of all Ute households had an annual income of less than $15,000, making the Ute nearly three times more likely than their white neighbors to live in poverty. The Ute Mountain Ute Reservation ranks among the poorest in the United States, with unemployment rates near 57 percent (5.7 people out of 10 who want to work cannot find work).

DAILY LIFE

Families

The extended family was the basic unit of Ute society (parents, children, grandparents, close relatives). Everyone shared responsibility for caring for children, but the primary caretakers were often young girls, who took over the job when they were about ten years old. The girls carried infant siblings around on wooden boards called cradle boards. Both boys and girls assisted with food gathering as soon as they were old enough.

Education

For centuries, everyone in a camp shared in the education of young children. Once they were confined to reservations, Ute parents were encouraged to send their children to government-run boarding schools, where they were not allowed to speak their own language and were punished for observing their old ways. Some held on to their old customs anyway.

In the twentieth century, Utes demanded non-segregated public schooling for their children (Indian children were educated separately from white children). Since the 1960s, Ute children on the reservations have been attending public schools in nearby communities. Often there are difficulties because the children do not speak English well enough to understand what is going on in the classroom. Children suffer from poverty and poor self-esteem, and schools can be insensitive to the Indian culture. To illustrate this, newspaper reporter and author Jim Carrier described the experience of an eight-year-old Ute girl who was given this writing assignment: "The year is 1800. You and your family are traveling by covered wagon over the mountains to your new home in the West. You keep a diary and write down your exciting experiences. You have bad weather, Indian trouble and many other problems. Write down what you see, feel and hear."

Buildings

Ute homes varied depending on where they lived. Most common were domed (round) houses; they were round because the Ute believed the circle was a sacred shape. These houses were about eight feet high and fifteen feet around, and consisted of a pole frame covered with willow branches or bark. Some groups built cone-shaped houses with pole frames covered with brush, bark, or reeds. Groups who hunted on the Great Plains used small tepees covered with elk or buffalo skin. They often painted the tepees with brightly colored decorative scenes and symbols. Sweathouses (or sweat lodges, buildings where steam is produced for ritual cleansing) were common then, and they are still used today.

The Ute lived in their traditional types of homes until the 1950s, when settlements and housing funds allowed them to build modern homes.

Food

In the very early days before the Ute had horses, the seven bands divided into small family groups for a large part of the year to gather what they could find in the large territory they occupied. Food was scarce, and groups had to cover great distances to find it.

From spring until fall, family units hunted for deer, elk, and antelope. They gathered roots, seeds, and wild fruits and berries. They caught insects, lizards, rodents, and other small game. Crickets and grasshoppers were dried and mixed with berries to form a fruitcake. Some groups planted corn, beans, and squash in meadows and returned to harvest them in the fall.

In late fall, the small groups rejoined the larger band and left the mountains to find sheltered areas for the winter. After they acquired horses in the 1630s, they could hunt farther afield and capture more animals. Buffalo became a major source of food, clothing, and other items. The Ute were especially fond of jerky (meat—either buffalo or deer—that is cut into strips and dried). This meat specialty is still prepared on the reservations; today they use deer and elk meat they get from hunting. The jerky is mixed with corn to make a stew, ground up and fried in lard, or eaten as a snack. Another modern specialty is frybread, plate-sized disks of bread that are fried in hot fat.

Clothing and adornment

Ute women were described by early observers as being extremely skilled at tanning hides, which were used in trade and for making clothing. They used the hides of buffalo, deer, elk, and mountain sheep. Ute women wore long, belted dresses, leggings, and moccasins. Men wore shirts, leggings, and moccasins for everyday activities, and they added elaborate, feathered head-dresses on special occasions. Many men decorated their bodies and faces with paint, using yellow and black during times of war. Women sometimes painted their faces and the part in their hair. Some Utes pierced their noses and inserted small polished animal bones in the hole; some tattooed their faces using cactus thorns dipped in ashes. Necklaces of animal claws, bones, fish skeletons, and juniper seeds were sometimes worn by both sexes.

Paint, fringes of hair, rows of elk teeth, or porcupine quills dyed in bright colors decorated the clothing worn in early Ute ceremonies. Later, when the Ute acquired beads from European traders, their costumes included intricate beadwork.

An illustration of two Ute men in southern Colorado.

Healing practices

Among the Ute, shamans (pronounced *SHAY-muns*)—medicine men and women—were healers as well as religious leaders. They acquired supernatural powers through their communication with the spirits of animals and dead people. Most shamans knelt down next to a sick person and sang a special curing song, often accompanied by the patient's family. Some shamans also carried small bags containing special materials to aid in healing, including deer tails, small drums and rattles, and herbs. Sometimes medical treatment included placing sick people in a sweathouse and then plunging them into cold water to make their body unappealing to evil spirits.

Today, all the old-time Ute healers are dead. People use modern health-care facilities in urban areas, but those who still wish to consult medicine men can call on Navajo medicine men in Arizona (see Navajo entry).

ARTS

The traditional Ute crafts had nearly died out by the 1930s but have been revived. Some Utes maintain tribal customs by weaving baskets, creating pottery (the Ute Mountain Ute have their own pottery manufacturing plant), or working with beads or leather. They use these traditional works of art in ceremonies or sell them in gift shops.

Oral literature

Many Ute stories explained features of their natural surroundings. For example, they tell the legend of Sleeping Ute Mountain, which resembles a sleeping Indian with his headdress pointing to the north. The sleeping Indian was once a Great Warrior God who was wounded and fell into a deep sleep. Blood from his wound became water, and rain clouds fell from his pockets. The blanket that covers him changes colors with the seasons.

CUSTOMS

Hunting rituals

A Ute boy was considered a man when he proved he could provide meat. He was forbidden to eat his first kill, and a woman was forbidden to eat deer meat during her menstrual period, because to do so would spoil her man's hunt.

Utes used deerskins as disguises when hunting that animal. They hunted elk on snowshoes, driving the animals into deep snow before killing them.

Sun Dances

The two ceremonies that were most important to the Utes were the Sun Dance and the Bear Dance; both are still performed annually.

The Sun Dance is a personal quest by the dancer for power given by the Great Spirit. But each dancer also represents his family and community, so the dance is a way of sharing. The Sun Dance originated from a legend in which a man and a woman left the tribe during a time of terrible famine. While on their journey, the couple met a god who taught them the Sun Dance ceremony. After they returned and performed the ritual with the tribe, a herd of buffalo appeared and the famine ended.

The Sun Dance ceremony includes several days of secret rites followed by a public dance performance around a Sun Dance pole, which is the channel to the Creator. The rites involve fasting, praying, smoking, and preparing ceremonial objects.

Newspaper reporter Jim Carrier described a modern Sun Dance on top of Sleeping Ute Mountain: "Night and day, for four days, the dancers charged the pole and retreated, back and forth in a personal gait. There were shuffles, hops, a prancing kick. While they blew whistles made from eagle bones, their bare feet marked a twenty-five-foot path in the dirt."

Bear Dances

The Bear Dance takes place every spring and honors the grizzly bear, who taught the Utes strength, wisdom, and survival. In the early days, the Bear Dance was held at the time when bears emerged from hibernation, and was intended to waken the bear so he could lead the people to the places where nuts and berries were plentiful. It was a grand social occasion after a long hard winter. The dance is "lady's choice"; it allows a Ute woman to show her preference for a certain man.

The Bear Dance ceremony traditionally lasted for four days and four nights. It involves building a large, circular enclosure of sticks to represent a bear's den. Music played inside the enclosure symbolizes the thunder that awakens the sleeping bears.

CURRENT TRIBAL ISSUES

One of the major issues facing the Ute in the 1990s involves water rights. Treaties dating back as far as 1868 guarantee water rights on reservation lands. The Ute Mountain Ute in Colorado never had safe drinking water on the reservations until the mid-1990s, when one part of a proposed $73 million water project was completed. It is unclear whether the rest of the project will be funded; some people object to spending that much money to provide water to a reservation. Some of the Ute Mountain Utes' land is parched because white farmers dammed the rivers that used to irrigate it.

The Ute Mountain Ute became involved in another controversy in 1986 when they took part in a business venture to transport tourists from Ute lands by helicopter to view ancient Anasazi ruins at the adjacent Mesa Verde National Park. The National Park Service argued that vibrations from the frequent helicopter flights damaged the ruins. They asked the Bureau of Indian Affairs to determine their impact on the environment. The Ute, meanwhile, hoped to use the income from this and other tourist enterprises to improve the tribe's education levels and employment opportunities. They are exploring ways to divert Mesa Verde visitors to attractions on their reservation.

Today the Ute struggle with health issues such as obesity, diabetes, strokes, and alcoholism. On the Ute Mountain Ute Reservation,

Thunderheads over the Rocky Mountains, a view from the Ute Mountain Ute Reservation, Colorado.

life expectancy for men is only thirty-eight years, because of the high number of deaths from alcohol-related accidents and violence.

NOTABLE PEOPLE

Chief Ouray (c.1833–1880) became a prominent spokesman and negotiator on behalf of the Ute people, thanks to his ability to speak several languages and other skills. He was born in Taos, New Mexico, and spent his youth working as a shepherd on Mexican-owned ranches, where he learned to speak Spanish. He moved to Colorado at the age of eighteen and soon became a leader in the Ute tribe. At first he was revered as a cunning and dangerous warrior, but his career shifted as he came to realize that white settlement in his tribe's territory could not be halted.

Ouray helped to arrange treaties between the Utes and the U.S. government in 1863 and 1868. In 1867, he assisted Kit Carson, a U.S. Army officer, in suppressing a Ute uprising. In 1868, he accompanied Carson to Washington, D.C., and acted as spokesman for the seven Ute bands. In the negotiations that followed, the Ute retained 16 million acres of land. More miners trespassed on Ute lands, and in 1872, Ouray and eight other Ute again visited Washington, D.C., in an attempt to stress peace over warfare. In these talks, the Ute were pressured into giving up four million acres for an annual payment of $25,000. For his services, Ouray received an additional payment of $1,000. After the Nathan Meeker massacre (see "History"), both the Indians and the U.S. government chose Ouray to represent them in peace talks. In 1880 Ouray again traveled to Washington, D.C., where he signed the treaty by which the White River Ute were relocated to the Uintah-Ouray Reservation in Utah. Soon after his return from Washington, Ouray died in 1880 while on a trip to Ignacio, Colorado, where the Southern Ute Agency had been relocated. Lacking a strong voice for their interests, the Ute were removed from Colorado the following year.

Another notable Ute is tribal leader Walkara (1801–1855), who was probably the most powerful and renowned Native American leader in the Great Basin area from 1830 until the time of his death.

FURTHER READING

Carrier, Jim. *West of the Divide: Voices from a Ranch and a Reservation.* Golden, Colorado: Fulcrum, 1992.

Dutton, Bertha P. *The Rancheria, Ute, and Southern Paiute Peoples.* Englewood Cliffs, NJ: Prentice-Hall, 1975.

Dutton, Bertha P. "The Ute Indians." *American Indians of the Southwest.* Albuquerque: University of New Mexico Press, 1983.

Pettit, Jan. *Utes: The Mountain People.* Colorado Springs, CO: Century One Press, 1982.

Southern Ute Homepage. [Online] http://www.southern-ute.nsn.us/index.html

Uintah and Ouray Reservation Homepage. [Online] http://www.uwin.com/ute/

Ute Mountain Ute Homepage. [Online] http://www.aclin.org/other/society_ culture/native_american/ute/index.html

Southwest

Southwest

The origins of the Southwest Indians are far-reaching, spanning two continents and many centuries. The term "Southwest Indians" refers to North American Indian groups living in the American Southwest (all or part of the present-day states of Arizona, New Mexico, Utah, Colorado, Nevada, and Texas) and in the region that is now northern Mexico. These groups include, among others, the Hopi and Zuni—Pueblo Indians of Arizona whose roots and language can be traced to Mexico and Central America—and the Navajo and Apache peoples—Athabaskan speakers from the Northeast who began migrating to the Southwest around 1000 C.E. The Southwest Indians are well known for their farming techniques (these are said to have originated in Mexico), their permanent, multistoried settlements, and their crafts, including distinctive painted pottery, basketry, and woven items.

Early history

Evidence of early Southwest Indian settlement may date back as far as 10,000 years. The Cochise (pronounced *koh-CHEES*) cultures most likely developed in present-day Arizona and New Mexico around 5000 B.C.E. In this mostly arid (dry) environment, these prehistoric societies constantly adapted their economic practices, social patterns, and living arrangements to meet the prevailing conditions. Moving with the change in seasons, they built homes among cliffs, in caves, and along desert valleys. By gathering many different types of plants, the Cochise peoples are believed to have paved the way for extensive agricultural (farming) development in the region by later peoples.

Ancient Indian cultures and traditions of the American Southwest

Four agricultural Indian cultures—the Hohokam, the Mogollon, the Patayan, and the Anasazi—dominated the prehistoric Southwest.

THE HOHOKAM Small, permanent villages appeared in the Southwest around 1 C.E., marking a shift in the region's nomadic hunting and gathering lifestyle. In the Sonoran Desert of present-day south-central Arizona, the Hohokam cultural tradition emerged. Originally from Mexico, the Hohokam were hunters and gatherers who turned to agriculture around 300 C.E. Over the next 200 years they developed massive irrigation systems to water the rugged terrain surrounding the Gila and Salt rivers in present-day central Arizona. The Hohokam are said to be ancestors of the Pima and Tohono O'odham (Papago) peoples.

THE MOGOLLON Around the year 200 C.E. in present-day southern New Mexico, eastern Arizona, and parts of Mexico, the Mogollon people developed small villages of semi-underground, earth-covered pithouses. The Anasazi (see below for a description of this later culture) would subsequently modify the Mogollon concept of the villages, creating what are now called pueblos (pronounced *PWEB-lowz*)—small towns made up of multistoried stone or adobe (earthen brick) buildings that often housed many families. The Mogollon people developed systems for farming in a dry climate and established themselves as the foremost potters of their time. Some people of the modern Western Pueblos are believed to be descended from the Mogollon.

THE PATAYAN The Patayan—contemporaries of the Mogollon (they lived at about the same time) and inhabitants of a vast stretch of land in what is now the state of Arizona—were among the first pottery producers in the Southwest. Their homes were small and made of wood or stone. The Patayan people hunted and farmed, growing squash and corn with the help of irrigation. Their culture is thought to have dominated the lower Colorado River region for some 1,500 years.

THE ANASAZI An agricultural group called the Anasazi (pronounced *on-uh-SAH-zee*; sometimes referred to as "Ancient Ones," although this is not a direct translation of the name) emerged around 400 C.E. in the Four Corners region of present-day Arizona, New Mexico, Utah, and Colorado. They eventually designed their communities in large multiroomed apartment-type buildings—some with more than 1,200 rooms. Though well known for their expertise in farming, the Anasazi were also skilled potters, credited with refining the potterymaking techniques first developed by the Mogollon. (The works of both cultures were distinguished by their black-on-white geometric designs.) Modern Pueblos of Arizona and New Mexico are descended from the Anasazi.

THE PUEBLO PEOPLE: ORIGINS OF THEIR NAME

Pueblo Indians—North American Indians of the southwestern United States —are so-named because they lived in villages of compact, flat-roofed, multistoried adobe or clay dwellings called *pueblos* (towns) by the Spanish. The word *pueblo* refers both to Indian villages of the American Southwest *and* to the people who lived in these villages.

*Kiva ruins at Pueblo del Arroyo,
Chaco Canyon, New Mexico.*

By about 900 C.E. the Anasazi inhabited multistoried cliff dwellings on the Colorado Plateau. Over the next 300 years large trading towns—possibly as many as 200 of them—flourished in the Southwest, especially in a region of present-day northern New Mexico known as Chaco Canyon. Some pueblos had hundreds of rooms. Among the largest were Pueblo Bonito and Chetro Ketl. The pueblos of Chaco Canyon were connected by an extensive road system that stretched many miles across the desert. Archaeological finds (remains of the past civilization) from the area indicate that the Indians of Central America, the U.S. Southwest, and the Pacific Coast region engaged in trade.

Aztlán

Back around the year 900 C.E., long before European colonization, the area that is now the southwestern United States and northern Mexico was called Aztlán. Aztlán was named by the Aztecs, builders of a powerful empire that stretched throughout the central highlands of Mexico. In spite of the desertlike conditions that exist in the Southwest, many agricultural communities grew throughout Aztlán. Southwestern farmers developed a variety of innovative irrigation and drainage systems to conserve the scarce rainfall in the region. Agriculture served as an advanced and effective food source for this dry territory.

Aztlán communities consisted of multistory villages (later named *pueblos*) and large ceremonial centers. The ceremonial centers resembled *kivas*, the round underground chambers found among the present-day Hopi in Arizona and the Pueblo in eastern New Mexico.

The Aztec empire expanded and prospered for several centuries, until the Spanish arrived in the New World around the turn of the sixteenth century. Aztlán continued to exist under Spanish control until 1821, when Mexico won its independence from Spain. The region was then subject to Mexican rule until the end of the Mexican-American War (1846-48; a two-year conflict between Mexico and the United States over territory that is now part of the American Southwest). The U.S. government annexed (incorporated into the United States) the northern part of Aztlán in 1848, following the victory of American military forces at war's end.

The tides turn

By the thirteenth century Athabaskan-speaking Navajo and Apache groups had migrated south (most likely from territory that is now part of Canada) and had begun trading with the Pueblo Indians. Their cultures and worldviews blended.

A severe drought then struck the region that is now the southwestern United States (probably between 1275 and 1300). As a result, Southwestern peoples left their once-thriving towns in search of water. Many settled in villages along the Colorado and Rio Grande rivers. Hunting and gathering became increasingly important throughout the Southwest during this time.

European contact

Indian societies in the United States were transformed radically by the arrival of Europeans between 1500 and 1700. Age-old Native cultures, customs, traditions, and political systems were disrupted and suppressed, but not entirely lost, under white dominance.

SPANISH REACH THE NEW WORLD Southwest Indian contact with whites probably began with the arrival of Spanish explorer Cabeza de Vaca in 1535. He entered present-day New Mexico and

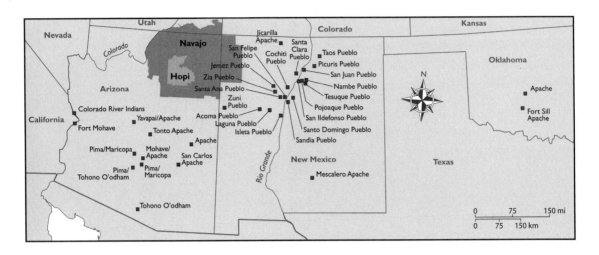

A map of some of the contemporary Native American communities in the Southwest region of the United States.

reported back to Spain on the land, the food resources, and, above all, the people he encountered. Five years later another Spanish explorer, Francisco Coronado, traveled into territory that is now part of Arizona and New Mexico, possibly going as far east as present-day Oklahoma. Coronado was searching for the legendary Seven Cities of Cíbola, which were believed to contain great wealth.

There were 98 pueblo villages in present-day New Mexico when the Spanish arrived. The Pueblo people had similar cultures, but they spoke four distinct languages: Zuni, Keres, Tiwa, and Tewa. Coronado came into contact with several Pueblo peoples, including the Hopi.

COLONIZERS AND MISSIONARIES Spanish colonization began in the Southwest in the late 1500s when Spanish expeditions began to enter what is now eastern New Mexico. Although they were driven back at first by Pueblo and Apache Indians, by 1598 a Spanish colony was established at San Juan Pueblo in northern New Mexico.

Spain already had a huge colonial empire in North America, meaning it had established control over lands in the New World. Spanish arrival in the Southwest had a major and lasting impact on the lives of the region's Native populations. Showing no respect for Indian rights or customs, the Europeans simply took over, snatching ancestral lands away, forbidding the Native people to practice their traditional ceremonies and rituals, and making them slaves on the ranches and farms of the Spanish upper class. And by 1628 Spanish missionaries had established a solid presence in the region. (Missionaries are organized members of a religious group who work to spread their beliefs in other parts of the world. In this case, Spanish missionaries sought to promote Christianity among the Native popula-

tions.) Their efforts to convert the Indians to Christianity further fractured the Indians' ties to the past.

THE EFFECTS OF INTRODUCED DISEASES The populations of the Hopi villages along the Colorado River dropped dramatically because many people died of the diseases brought by Spanish explorers. An estimated 10 pueblos were abandoned between 1519 and 1650. Evidence indicates that illness decimated (reduced severely) the population at various intervals between the late 1530s and 1598. Spiraling death rates seemed to correspond to uncontrolled outbreaks, or epidemics, of smallpox, measles, and the plague that hit the region during these decades. (Experts speculate that between 1500 and 1700 European diseases reduced Native American populations in the Northeast, Southeast, and Southwest to less than one-tenth of their original numbers.) By the early 1600s most Hopi had retreated to their present villages in northern Arizona. There the Spanish tried to rule them and spread Christianity, but the Hopi resisted.

AN UPRISING STAGED BY THE PUEBLO In 1680 Pope, a Pueblo spiritual leader, led his people in a successful rebellion against the Spanish. The Spanish and their Indian allies fled, moving on to present-day El Paso, Texas. Pope claimed that the spirits told him to drive away the Spanish and help the Pueblo return to their traditional life. But Spanish military forces eventually regained control, and by 1696 many Pueblo people had left their villages to join the Navajo bands that had moved farther north. The Pueblo who remained under Spanish rule were forced to convert to Catholicism, the dominant Christian religion in Spain.

THE COMANCHE MOVE SOUTH During the early 1700s the Comanche moved south to New Mexico from present-day Wyoming. They soon acquired horses from the Spanish. By the mid-1700s the Comanche had gained control of the horse and gun trade on the southern Plains and had established themselves as the most powerful bison-hunting tribe in the area.

The Spanish wrangled trade deals with the Comanche, using bribes and threats of war to achieve their goals. Conflicts arose pitting Indian against Indian as a large number of Comanche and Pueblo allied themselves with the Spanish against the horse- and sheep-raiding Apache and Navajo bands. Pueblo villagers ended up migrating to El Paso, following the Spanish retreat down the Rio Grande. Tensions continued throughout the early 1800s, during the period of rule by the Mexican Republic.

Pressures increase in the 1800s

The U.S. settlers who streamed into the Southwest after the United States won the territory from Mexico in 1848, met strong opposition from the Indians. The American military tried to subdue Indian uprisings throughout the Southwest, destroying Native land, livestock—even whole communities—in the process. Outbreaks of violence crossed tribal lines as various Native peoples rebelled against U.S. policies.

PUEBLO REVOLT The Taos Pueblo Indians, angered by the conduct of the United States during the Mexican-American War, attacked and killed the U.S. governor of New Mexico in 1847. American troops retaliated, attacking the Taos Pueblo and killing approximately 165 people.

NAVAJO RESISTANCE TO U.S. INFLUENCE For more than 200 years the *Diné* (Navajo for "the people," the name the Navajo people called themselves) spent considerable time and effort dealing with the *Nakai,* or Spanish. At the end of the Mexican-American War in 1848, white Americans poured into California and New Mexico. The Navajo—the largest Native American nation in the United States—were one of the first Indian nations in the American Southwest to confront the U.S. government in a prolonged struggle for their rights.

CATTLE RAIDS LEAD TO TROUBLE Cattle, sheep, and horses had been introduced to the Native peoples of the Southwest during the period of European domination. By the 1800s the Navajo had built up large herds of these animals by raiding the Spanish and other tribes. Even after the American victory in the war with Mexico, the Navajo people continued their raids, storming U.S. settlements in present-day New Mexico. These actions led to conflict between the Navajo and the U.S. Army. Fighting ensued. Many Navajo cornfields were burned, fruit trees were destroyed, sheep were slaughtered, and communities were ruined. The Navajo managed to resist for 17 years, but, facing starvation in 1863 and 1864, they finally surrendered.

LONG WALK OF THE NAVAJO The Navajo people's unsuccessful attack on Fort Defiance (an American base located in the middle of their territory) sealed their fate, resulting in their final defeat in 1864. The tribe was subsequently forced to march 800 miles to a 40-square-mile reserve at Fort Sumner, New Mexico. Two thousand died along the way from starvation and exposure (lack of shelter). The 9,000 survivors found themselves on land that lacked water and had poor soil. The nearest available wood was 5 to 18 miles away. Hordes of grasshoppers swept the area. The Navajo called the reservation *Hweeldi* (prison).

The Navajo were expected to farm this drought-ravaged land. The U.S. government did little to help the tribe until a Santa Fe newspaper wrote about the terrible conditions on the reserve. As a result, federal officials allowed the Navajo to return to a small portion (10 percent) of their original homeland. In later years more land was added as the Navajo population grew.

AFTER THE MEXICAN-AMERICAN WAR

As a result of the Treaty of Guadalupe Hidalgo (pronounced *Gwah-duh-LOOP-ay ee-DAHL-go*), which ended the Mexican-American War, the United States took control of the territory that now makes up the states of Arizona, California, Nevada, New Mexico, Utah, and parts of present-day Colorado and Wyoming. Indian nations such as the Kiowa, Modoc, Navajo, and Sioux nations fought against the U.S. Army in an attempt to prevent a land-hungry new government from seizing their land. Others tribes, including the Blackfeet, Caddo, Crow, Hopi, and Nespelem, did not fight. In what became the Southwest region of the United States, Native groups fared differently under the new government. The Apache and the Navajo, whose raids against Mexican and other Native villages were well known, were ruthlessly rounded up. The Pueblo peoples, who had been citizens of Mexico, automatically became citizens of the United States in 1848. (Other Native Americans were not granted citizenship until 1924.) But as citizens, the Pueblo did not receive the rights and protection granted to Indians as independent nations. For all Native groups, coming under the authority of the U.S. government meant loss of lands and rights to the expanding country.

COCHISE AND THE APACHE WARS Around the time of the ill-fated Navajo uprising, Cochise, an Apache warrior, led his people in a series of conflicts known as the Apache Wars (1863-72). From his stronghold in the Dragoon Mountains (located in southern Arizona), Cochise led an effective campaign against U.S. and Mexican forces. In 1871 he opposed efforts to relocate his people to a reservation in New Mexico. A year later the Apache leader finally agreed to end the tribe's attacks on the U.S. Army. This peace agreement hinged on the federal government's promise of reservation land for the Apache in eastern Arizona.

The twentieth century

The 1920s was a key decade in Native American history. In response to pressure applied by reformers who wished to see conditions improved for Native Americans throughout the country, U.S. Secretary of the Interior (the nation's internal affairs officer) Hubert Work appointed the Committee of One Hundred to investigate American Indian policies. The committee, which met in 1923, recommended increasing funding for Native American health care, public education, scholarships, and legal action to rule on Indian land claims.

Pueblo Lands Act

When the United States took over the American Southwest from Mexico in 1848, the Pueblo were the only Southwest tribe who had citizenship in Mexico. As Mexican citizens, they were automatically granted U.S. citizenship. As citizens, however, the Pueblo peoples did not receive the same rights and protections granted to federally recognized Indian nations. As a result, much Pueblo land—the finest farmland in the Southwest—was lost.

The Pueblo asked for—and then sued for—Indian status, which they gained in 1916. By that time, though, they had already been forced to surrender some of their best lands, including important religious sites. The All Indian Pueblo Council, a loose federation of Pueblo representatives, organized delegates from all the pueblos to rally for rights to their old lands. The resulting Pueblo Lands Act of 1924 restored Pueblo lands, but the battle was not over. At the end of the twentieth century the Pueblo continued the fight to obtain and keep their water rights. Their lands are secure, but useless, without water.

HOPI-NAVAJO JOINT USE AREA When the Navajo began settling on Hopi lands in the nineteenth century, dissension (frequent disputes or arguments) arose between the two tribes. It soon became clear that the conflict would not be settled without outside intervention, so U.S. courts created a Joint Use Area—1.8 million acres to be shared between the Hopi and the Navajo. Under the terms of the joint use agreement, only a portion of the Hopi reservation was held for the exclusive use of the Hopi, and by 1973 clashes were again erupting between the Hopi and the Navajo over rights to the area. The next year U.S. Congress passed the Hopi and Navajo Relocation Act, which divided the Joint Use Area between the two nations and provided $16 million to compensate (repay) 800 Navajo families who were required to relocate. Even after the settlement, though, tensions between the Hopi and the Navajo continued to exist.

The dawn of the twenty-first century

In spite of the disruptive effects of European colonization, white advancement, and U.S. law on Native populations, the spirit of the Southwest Indians has not been broken. Their Native identities, though influenced by the ideas and practices of invading forces, remain whole and intact. Southwest Native efforts in the late twentieth and early twenty-first centuries have focused mainly on countering the negative impact of white influence and preserving traditional Indian language and culture.

FURTHER READING

Champagne, Duane, ed. *Native Americans: Portrait of the People.* Detroit: Visible Ink, 1994.

Ortiz, Alfonso, ed. *Handbook of American Indians.* Vols. 9-10. *The Southwest.* Washington, DC: Smithsonian Institution, 1978-83.

Taylor, Colin F., ed. *The Native Americans.* New York: Smithmark, 1991.

Waldman, Carl, ed. *Encyclopedia of Native American Tribes.* New York: Facts on File, 1988.

Anasazi

Name

Anasazi (pronounced *on-uh-SAH-zee*), a Navajo word meaning "ancient enemies." This phrase is offensive to many Pueblo peoples; they prefer to translate the name as "ancient ones."

Location

Formerly in the Four Corners area of the United States, where Utah, Colorado, Arizona, and New Mexico meet. These are hot, dry areas of steep canyons and the high, flat hilltops the Spanish called *mesas* (meaning "tables"). Large numbers of Anasazi were located in three major areas: Mesa Verde (pronounced *MAY-sah VUR-dee* or *VAIR-day*, meaning "green table"), Colorado; Chaco Canyon, New Mexico; and Kayenta, Arizona. The most well-known Anasazi settlement is the one at Mesa Verde, stretching more than 150 miles from the Colorado River in Utah east to the Animas River in Colorado.

Population

Between the years 1000 and 1200 C.E., there may have been as many as 100,000 ancient peoples, including the Anasazi, the Mogollon, the Hohokam (see the box entitled "Hohokam, Mogollon, and Patayan Cultures"), and other trading partners who have since disappeared.

Language family

Uto-Aztecan.

Origins and group affiliations

The main theory on Anasazi origin is that the group's ancestors were part of the migration from Asia during the last Ice Age, which occurred about 20,000 years ago. These ancient peoples may have reached Mesa Verde, Colorado, some 10,000 years ago. Along with the Mogollon, the Hohokam, and the Patayan, the Anasazi became one of four major civilizations of farming peoples who lived in the Four Corners area of what is now the American Southwest (see the box entitled "Hohokam, Mogollon, and Patayan Cultures").

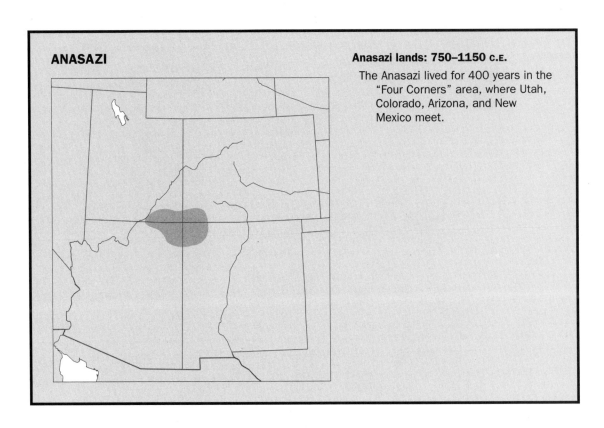

ANASAZI

Anasazi lands: 750–1150 c.e.

The Anasazi lived for 400 years in the "Four Corners" area, where Utah, Colorado, Arizona, and New Mexico meet.

For centuries the Anasazi have been a great American mystery. Many unanswered questions remain about the people and their culture. Why did they move suddenly from the fertile valleys and mesa tops of their Southwestern homeland to dangerous cliff alcoves? Why, less than 100 years later, did they abandon those cliffs altogether, mix with other cultures, and disappear as a separate people? How could they have become master builders without the aid of horses, other pack animals, or wheels? How did they manage to construct the wide boulevards that connect their villages and their huge, reddish-gold sandstone homes? The knowledge we have about these ancient peoples is actually a compilation of theories put together by archaeologists, people who collect and study the remains of past civilizations.

HISTORY

Basketmakers were their ancestors

The earliest Anasazi people were referred to as "Basketmakers." They wandered the Southwest for thousands of years. Theirs was an extremely hard life, one marked by a constant search for water and food—without the benefit of bows and arrows for hunting. The people apparently lived in shallow caves for a few days at a time, then moved on. The development of watertight baskets made a big difference in their way of life. Baskets could be used to hold, carry, and even cook food (when filled with water and hot rocks).

By about the year 1 C.E. the Basketmakers had learned how to grow corn and squash and had settled down to farm. They lived in more permanent homes—usually in pits that were partially underground.

About five and a half centuries later the Basketmakers were living in or near three major areas: Mesa Verde, Chaco Canyon, and Kayenta. The Anasazi learned from their neighbors, the Mogollon, how to make a primitive type of undecorated pottery, which allowed them to cook over a fire. This enabled them to prepare beans—beans need to be boiled for a long time to make them tender—and as a result beans became a staple crop.

Great building phase begins

Around the year 700 the Anasazi began to build the huge homes for which they will always be remembered. Over the next 400 years their civilization flourished. Chaco Canyon in northern New Mexico became the heart and soul of the Anasazi culture. It was the center of a vast trading network that may have extended all the way to the Pacific Coast. By 1050 more than 5,000 inhabitants had settled the Chaco Canyon area.

An extensive network of wide roads (more than 400 miles) connected other communities to Chaco Canyon. At points along the roads, signal stations were erected and fires were maintained as a way of communicating with and guiding travelers. Traders from faraway places traveled the roads, exchanging a variety of exotic goods— macaw feathers from Mexico, seashells from the Sea of Cortez, and turquoise from eastern New Mexico.

Twelve large pueblos were built in the valley of Chaco Canyon, but the greatest of all was Pueblo Bonito. (*Pueblo* is the Spanish word for city or village.) It is a D-shaped, four-story complex of 600 to 800 rooms and is considered the jewel in the crown of Anasazi architecture. Pueblo Bonita was large enough to hold 1,000 people; some of its rooms appear to have been used for storage of surplus crops, luxury items, and art treasures. Until 1882 Pueblo Bonito (though no longer inhabited) held the title "the world's largest apartment house"; that year a larger one was built in New York City.

Restoration of Anasazi ruins at Pueblo Bonito.

During the Developmental Pueblo period (700–1050) Anasazi people also moved from remote areas and small villages into apartment-style buildings in Mesa Verde, Colorado, and Kayenta, Arizona.

Cliff dwellings

Between 1050 and 1300 the Anasazi were at the height of their architectural genius. Then, for reasons that remain unclear, they began to move down from the tops of mesas and build dwellings under the edges of cliffs. These huge dwellings were very difficult to climb; ladders were often required to get from one level to another. Perhaps the people built them this way for protection against invaders. The fact that lookout towers were built around the same time lends support to this theory. Another possibility is that the population was growing so large that the Anasazi needed to free up land for farming. Either way, archaeological evidence indicates that the civilization began an irreversible decline around this time.

Many reasons have been given for the decline of the Anasazi. Tree ring studies seem to show that a 100-year drought began during the Classic Pueblo period of 1050-1300, causing crop failures and food shortages. Other studies indicate that trees may have been cut down to build houses, leaving no wood for fires and ruining the top soil in the process. Perhaps the Anasazi fled from enemy raids or left because they could not agree among themselves how to distribute dwindling food supplies. Whatever the reason, less than 100 years after their settlement the cliff dwellings were abandoned, and by 1300 all the Anasazi had left the region forever.

HOHOKAM, MOGOLLON, AND PATAYAN CULTURES

In addition to the Anasazi, three other early farming cultures dominated the Southwest: the Mogollon, the Hohokam, and the Patayan. A major difference among the groups was the irrigation technique they employed to farm in regions where water tended to be scarce. The Anasazi used several different methods, depending on where they lived. Some sought out ditches that collected rainwater, then built dams along the ditches in order to divert the water to nearby crops. Others conserved water by planting their gardens on hillside terraces (ridges), thereby taking advantage of the natural flow of water from upper to lower levels.

Mogollon culture

The Mogollon were mountain people who farmed the valleys of east-central Arizona and west-central New Mexico. Their small villages of earth-covered houses began to appear in the Southwest around the year 200 C.E. The earliest of the agricultural groups in the region, the Mogollon were fortunate enough to have a relatively abundant water supply. They planted their crops along the many streams in their homeland. This group is best known for its pottery, which depicted humans, animals, and insects outlined and painted in black over white clay.

The Mogollon culture survived until about 1300 C.E. and may be the ancestors of the present-day western Pueblo. The Hohokam and Anasazi cultures adopted or refined some of their practices, including the construction of semi-underground earth-covered pit houses.

Hohokam culture

The name Hohokam comes from a Pima word for "those who have gone before." The Hohokam migrated from Mexico around 300 B.C.E. and established their villages along the Gila and Salt rivers in central Arizona. Their greatest accomplishment was the development of an ingenious irrigation system that improved farm yields: a series of canals that channeled the rivers' flood waters directly to their dry fields. The Hohokam culture is believed to have faded around 1450 C.E. Its people may have been the ancestors of the Present-day Tohono O'odham and the Pima (see entries).

Patayan culture

The Patayan people lived in present-day Arizona along the lower Colorado River and in the desert nearby, beginning around 200 C.E. Like the Hohokam, this group took advantage of the annual flooding of nearby rivers to irrigate their fields. That same flooding swept away most of the remains of their culture, so not much is known about the Patayan people or their traditions. The Hualapai people who came after them gave them the name "Patayan," which means "the old people."

The Anasazi moved in a roundabout way and joined the Hohokam, the Mogollon, and other peoples on the Colorado and upper Rio Grande rivers. The Anasazi intermarried with those peoples, mixed their customs with those of their hosts, and ceased to exist as a separate people. The Hopi, Zuni, Rio Grande Pueblo, and Acoma (see entries) are thought to be the descendants of the Anasazi.

Cowboys find Anasazi ruins

One winter day in 1888 two cowboys named Richard Wetherill and Charlie Mason were out retrieving stray cattle in Colorado when in the distance they spied an amazing sight: a row of huge sandstone

Spruce Tree House, First Courtyard, the third largest cliff dwelling at Mesa Verde.

houses in an area where they had never seen any people. Wetherill later named the discovery "Cliff Palace." Cliff Palace was once a village housing more than 200 people.

Later that same day the explorers discovered "Spruce Tree House." The next morning they found a third village with a tall four-story tower; they named the village "Square Tower House." Over the next few years Wetherill and Mason discovered more than 182 sites in all.

Wetherill and Mason were not expert archaeologists. At first they hoped to make money from their find, selling the remains of the ancient culture to curiosity seekers. Later on, Wetherill decided that it would be in the best interest of scientific discovery if complete collections of artifacts were sold to museums. Over the next several years Wetherill made many more interesting discoveries. (See "Burial.")

Archaeologists who came after Wetherill have proposed different theories about the "ancient ones." Research continues to shed new light on the many mysteries of the ancient Anasazi. Their influence and history permeate the modern Southwest.

RELIGION

Old beliefs reflected in modern Pueblo practices

Although Anasazi religious beliefs are generally unknown, archaeologists have discovered rooms called *kivas* that were apparently constructed around 750 C.E. These chambers were actually the former pit houses of the early Anasazi. When the people began moving above ground, they retained the pit houses for use as spiritual centers, usually for the male members. The kivas were utilized for ceremonial and religious purposes in much the same way they are used today among Pueblo tribes (see entries).

Anasazi kivas were deeper than those of the Mogollon people. Each one was supported by about six columns, contained a hole in the roof for entry, and featured benches along the inside wall. In the floor of the kiva was a small, cup-shaped hole called a *sipapu*, which was believed to be a gateway to and from the spiritual world.

The *Kachina* religion practiced by the modern-day Pueblo people may have begun with the Anasazi. Kachina were said to be reincarnated ancestors (reborn after death) who served as messengers between the people and their gods. The term kachina also refers to (1) the dolls that represent Pueblo Indians' ancestral spirits and (2) the masked dancers who perform at agricultural ceremonies. Kachina masks dating back many hundreds of years have been unearthed from various Anasazi sites.

Influences from distant civilizations

There is strong evidence that the Anasazi had contact with distant civilizations, including the Aztec and Mayan peoples of Mexico, and

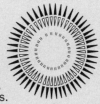

IMPORTANT DATES

100 B.C.E.–400 C.E.: Early Basketmaker period; the Anasazi use baskets as containers and cooking pots; they live in caves.

400–700: Modified Basketmaker period; the Anasazi learn to make pottery in which they can boil beans; they live in underground pits and begin to use bows and arrows.

700–1050: Developmental Pueblo period; the Anasazi move into pueblo-type homes above the ground and develop irrigation methods. A great cultural center is established at Chaco Canyon. Anasazi influence spreads to other areas of the Southwest.

1050–1300: Classic Pueblo period; Pueblo architecture reaches its height with the building of fabulous cliff dwellings.

1300–1700: Regressive Pueblo period; Anasazi influence declines; the people leave their northern homelands, heading south to mix with other cultures.

1700–present: Historic Pueblo period; Anasazi lands are taken over by Spanish, Mexicans, and Americans. Some Anasazi traditions are carried on by modern Pueblo tribes.

1888: Rancher and amateur archaeologists Richard Wetherill and Charlie Mason discover ancient cliff dwellings.

may, have shared some religious beliefs with them. Petroglyphs (paintings or carvings on rock) at Chaco Canyon are similar to those found in Mexico and parts of South America. For example, a spiral symbol that appears on Anasazi petroglyphs may represent a serpent in a coiled position, like the Mayan *Quetzalcoatl* (pronounced *KWET-sahl-koh-WAH-tuhl*) or plumed (feathered) serpent, a nature god.

The Mayan and Aztec cultures also sacrificed humans to the Sun god. Although it has not been proven that the Anasazi sacrificed humans for religious reasons, there is evidence they ate humans, a practice called cannibalism. (See "Current Tribal Issues.")

LANGUAGE

The Anasazi were a Nahuatl-speaking people. Nahuatl (pronounced *nah-WAH-tuhl*) is a branch of the Uto-Aztecan language spoken today by some of the Pueblo peoples in central Mexico. Diverse languages among the present Pueblo peoples indicate that their ancestors may long ago have had a complex and far-reaching interaction with outsiders. Pueblo languages show the influence of Numic peoples in the West (such as the Paiute; see entry) and Plains Indians in the East.

GOVERNMENT

It was long believed that all people in Anasazi society were considered equal. This assumption was based in part on archaeological evidence, which showed that no palaces or special buildings were set aside for wealthy and powerful people. However, opinions changed after Richard Wetherill's 1897 discovery of a mummified body (it was dried out and preserved) of a woman he nicknamed "Princess." Pictographs (paintings done on stone) had been painted above her grave. The lavish and careful burial of the Princess, along with the pictographs, was viewed as proof that she was a member of Anasazi royalty.

Belief in the existence of an Anasazi royal line was further supported by Peruvian scientist Guido Lombardi in 1998. Dr. Lombardi's theory was also based on mummies. It had long been assumed that the bodies of the Anasazi dead were mummified naturally over time—a direct result of the area's climate. But Lombardi contended that the mummification was done on purpose. It was not performed on all Anasazi dead—only on certain special persons.

ECONOMY

The Anasazi were farmers, hunter-gatherers, and traders. Shells and other items found in Anasazi ruins show that they traded with people who lived far from the Anasazi homelands. During the Developmental period the Anasazi began trading with their southern neighbors, who were cotton growers.

DAILY LIFE

Buildings

The Anasazi are often associated with unusual and startling cliff dwellings such as Cliff Palace and Spruce Tree House at Mesa Verde. But cliff dwellings existed for only a brief period of Anasazi history. More typical were blocks of rooms on mesa tops or underground pit houses clustered together to form communities.

In the eighth century descendants of the early Basketmakers began to build houses above ground. Setting poles upright in the ground to form the outline of a house, they wove sticks among the poles. Roofs were constructed the same way, with a thick coating of mud added to weatherproof the top and sides of the house.

Sometime before 1000 C.E. the Anasazi began using sandstone for masonry, replacing the traditional pole and mud construction of homes. These beautiful sandstone buildings were strong enough to support rafters and adobe roofs (pronounced *uh-DOE-bee*; a sun-dried mud made of a mixture of clay, sand, and sometimes ashes, rocks, or straw). They were expertly made, some standing as high as three stories and containing more than 50 rooms. The apartmentlike rooms were often built around a central courtyard or plaza that contained several kivas.

THE CLASSIC PUEBLO PERIOD Near the end of the twelfth century the Anasazi began to abandon the mesa tops, relocating to crevices in cliffs, where they built fabulous structures like Cliff Palace, the largest dwelling at Mesa Verde. It contained 217 rooms and 23 kivas. The rooms were low and narrow, stacked as high as four stories. The average size of a living room measured 6 feet by 8 feet and was only about 5 feet 6 inches high.

Life in the cliff dwellings must have been demanding. Farmers had to climb up or down from the crevices in the cliffs to work their fields on the mesas, a task that required some agility. Accidents were apparently common—crutches have been found among Anasazi ruins.

Food

Domestic routine was a central and time-consuming part of Anasazi life—from fetching and boiling water to grinding corn to powder with a mano (a hard smooth stone), to gathering and storing beans and piñon nuts. The kinds of crops grown were limited to what could thrive in the dry climate. The Anasazi grew beans, corn, and squash, but they also continued to hunt and gather, collecting timber and nuts from the surrounding forests and fish, fowl, and berries from the valley floors. By the late 600s the Anasazi were using the bow and arrow for hunting. Before that time they had used the *atlatl* (pronounced *AHT-lah-tuhl*; dart thrower). The group also domesticated (tamed) several animals, including dogs and turkeys.

Clothing and adornment

In the summer months the Anasazi wore little more than apron-like coverings tied around the waist. In winter robes and blankets of turkey feathers or rabbit skin were worn. Cotton was obtained in trade (some southern Anasazi also grew it) and used to make clothing and blankets, which were then painted or dyed with juices from plants and berries. Sandals made from plant fibers were an absolute necessity: they protected feet from the rugged terrain during farming and made it more comfortable to travel by foot in pursuit of wild game and wood for building and burning.

Both sexes wore jewelry, most of it studded with shells and turquoise from faraway places. The Classic Pueblo period was a time of tremendous artistic growth among the Anasazi. Archaeologists have discovered various decorative items, feather robes, girdles, belts, and wooden necklaces and earrings.

ARTS

Baskets and pottery

Anasazi artistic traditions are recognized far and wide. In addition to their architectural prowess, these Indians are known for their distinctive basketry and pottery. Some scholars believe that in Anasazi culture the men were the weavers and the women were the potters. Baskets were made by twisting plant materials into coils. These coils were wound one layer on top of another. Splints—often dyed red or black with juices from plants and berries—were used to hold the layers of the basket together. Pitch (a black, sticky substance) from piñon pine was used for waterproofing.

Anasazi ceramics fall into several different categories. The earliest pottery, which was first made around 600 C.E., was known as the White Ware style. It was actually gray in color because the Anasazi did not have kilns (heated enclosures that dry or "fire" the freshly shaped clayware). Pottery fired over open fires will not "take" colors, so it turns gray.

During the Classic period, Anasazi pottery reached its artistic height. The style for which the group is most famous is the Black-on-White style, common in Chaco Canyon and the Mesa Verde region. It consisted of black geometric designs on a white background. Black paint was produced from plant juices and ground-up minerals. The people in Kayenta, Arizona, produced the Red Ware style, also known as "polychrome ware" for its many colors. Designs were very distinctive, with broad lines and solid triangles.

Oral literature

Although the Anasazi left behind no written literature, they did produce thousands of petroglyphs and pictographs, and their oral histories no doubt helped to shape today's Hopi, Zuñi, and Rio Grande Pueblo cultures.

CUSTOMS

Moving on

Although agriculture changed the Anasazi way of life, the people were not content to stay in one area for long periods of time. Anasazi tradition is marked by a repeating pattern of settling and then abandoning their communities. It seems that no matter how successful their harvests might have been, the Anasazi never stayed in one place for long. They continued to rely on the old ways of hunting and gathering.

Warlike or peaceful?

It was long thought that the Anasazi were a peaceful people, until Richard Wetherill's "Cave 7" was rediscovered in 1990. This site had apparently been the scene of a bloody massacre more than 1,500 years ago, a battle that involved stabbing, poison darts, beatings with blunt instruments, scalping, and possibly even torture.

Head flattening

Like their Mexican trading partners, the early Anasazi adopted the practice of flattening the heads of infants. They strapped babies' heads to hard boards that over time flattened their naturally soft skulls. A flat head was considered an attractive feature among some Indian groups.

Burial

What is known about Anasazi burial practices has been learned by digging up burial sites. In 1893 Wetherill discovered a number of basketry containers filled with skeletons. The people he discovered (1) had no pottery, (2) used the *atlatl* (dart thrower) rather than bow and arrow, (3) made baskets of yucca, willow, and squawbrush, (4) were apparently taller than the cliff-dwelling Anasazi, and (5) had flattened skulls. Although Wetherill thought they were a different people, it is now known that these were the early Anasazi.

When Cliff Palace was excavated, archaeologists found that the entire area in front of the settlement had been used as a trash or refuse area. In addition to discovering food fragments, broken tools, and worn-out clothing, archaeologists determined that this section was used as a burial place for the dead, who were wrapped in yucca fiber mats, rabbit fur robes, or turkey feather blankets.

Other sites have revealed bodies buried with items to take to the next world, including new sandals, jewelry, and food. At some sites the bodies of children have been found buried beneath the floors of homes, whereas the bodies of older people were found buried at some distance away.

CURRENT TRIBAL ISSUES

Preservation of archaeological sites is an ongoing concern. At Grand Gulch Primitive Area in Utah, the collection of Anasazi specimens is disappearing as visitors help themselves to souvenirs. Conservation groups hope to have Grand Gulch and other areas designated as protected wilderness areas. Meanwhile, many of the cliff dwellings of the Anasazi are preserved at Mesa Verde National Park in southwest Colorado and at Chaco Culture National Historic Park in New Mexico, home of Pueblo Bonito, the largest Anasazi pueblo.

Archaeologists have been examining Anasazi relics for more than 100 years and are still coming up with theories to resolve unanswered questions about the culture. In 1998 *Discover* magazine reported on a controversial theory that some Anasazi may have been cannibals. While excavating at Cowboy Wash in Colorado, archaeologists discovered piles of human bones—bones which they maintain show clear evidence of the Anasazi people's cannibalistic activity. It is possible that drought caused starvation, which led a desperate people to survive by consuming human flesh. Another theory hinges on the notion of "prehistoric terrorism"—that is, when several groups were competing for scarce resources, the Anasazi tried to frighten the others away by openly engaging in the unaccepted practice of cannibalism.

FURTHER READING

Arnold, Caroline. *The Ancient Cliff Dwellers of Mesa Verde*. Clarion Books, 1992.

Ayer, Eleanor H. *The Anasazi*. New York: Walker Publishing, 1993.

Dold, Catherine. "American Cannibal." *Discover,* February 1998, vol. 19, no. 2, p. 64.

Fisher, Leonard Everett. *Anasazi.* New York: Simon & Schuster, 1997.

Phillips, Jeff. "Grand Gulch: On the Trail of Utah's Secret Kivas." *Sunset,* May 1998, vol. 200, no. 5, p. 131.

Siegel, Lee. "Mummies Might Have Been Made by Anasazi." *Salt Lake Tribune,* April 2, 1998.

Warren, Scott. *Cities in the Sand: The Ancient Civilizations of the Southwest.* San Francisco: Chronicle Books, 1992.

Apache

For more information on Apache groups, please see entries on Chiricahua Apache, San Carlos Apache, and White Mountain Apache that follow.

Name

Apache (pronounced *uh-PATCH-ee*). It may come from the Zuñi word *apachu,* meaning "enemy." The Apache most likely called themselves *Diné,* or "people."

Location

The Apache once lived in a vast region stretching from what is now central Arizona to central Texas, and from northern Mexico to the high plains of southeastern Colorado. Today, about 30,000 Apaches reside on nine reservations in Arizona, New Mexico, and Oklahoma. The remaining Apaches are scattered throughout the United States.

Population

At the end of the 1600s, there were an estimated 5,000 Apache. In a census (count of the population) done in 1990 by the U.S. Bureau of the Census, 53,330 people identified themselves as Apache, making the tribe the seventh largest in the United States (see box on page 415).

Language family

Athabaskan.

Origins and group affiliations

The Apache people made a gradual move from western Canada to the American Southwest between the thirteenth and sixteenth centuries. They were never one unified group but rather a number of bands who spoke similar languages and shared similar customs. Today they are divided into two groups: Western Apache and Eastern Apache (also known as Plains Apache).

Eastern Apache include the Chiricahua (pronounced *CHEER-uh-KAH-wuh*), Jicarilla (pronounced *hi-kah-REE-yah*), Lipan, Mescalero (pronounced *mes-KAH-lair-ro*), and Kiowa (pronounced *KYE-o-wah*) Apache peoples. Their descendants now live in New Mexico and Oklahoma. Western Apache include the Cibecue, Coyotero, Northern Tonto, Southern Tonto, San Carlos, and White Mountain Apache. Their descendants now live in Arizona.

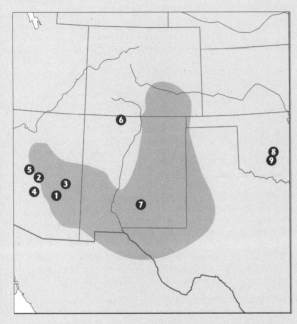

APACHE

Contemporary Communities

Arizona

1. San Carlos Apache Tribe
2. Tonto Apache Reservation
3. Fort Apache Reservation
4. Fort McDowell Mohave-Apache Indian Community
5. Yavapai-Apache Tribe

New Mexico

6. Jicarilla Apache Tribe
7. Mescalero Apache Tribe

Oklahoma

8. Apache Tribe of Oklahoma
9. Fort Sill Apache Tribe of Oklahoma

Shaded area: Traditional lands of the Apache in present-day Arizona, New Mexico, Texas, northern Mexico, and southeastern Colorado.

The Apache believe they once lived beneath the earth's surface. Long ago they came up from there and found themselves in the American Southwest, their sacred homeland. Apaches feel a powerful spiritual tie to their land, a place of majestic mountains, grassy hills, vast deserts, steep canyons, hot springs, and dense forests of pine, sycamore, cottonwood, juniper, and oak. They are a fierce, proud, religious people who, for centuries before Europeans came, wandered the Southwest, hunting game and gathering the abundant fruits and nuts there.

HISTORY

Trading and raiding

The Apache were wanderers in a harsh, dry land, where temperatures could abruptly change from extremely hot to extremely cold. They often quarreled among themselves and they had uneasy relations with their neighbors, especially the Pueblo and Pima tribes (see entries). They sometimes traded with those tribes, but because they were quick to anger, they could as easily take up their weapons and raid Pueblo and Pima villages.

When the Spanish arrived in 1540, bringing guns and horses, the Apache at first happily traded with them. For more than 300 years the Spanish had been listening to stories about seven lost cities of gold, and they believed Apache land was its hiding place. Relations between the Apache and the Spanish soon turned sour after the Spanish tried to take control of Apache land. The Apache began to carry out sneak attacks on Spanish settlements, stealing their guns, horses, cattle, and even their children (the Spanish, in return, took Apache women and children into slavery).

By 1700 the Comanche tribe (see entry) acquired horses, which allowed them to leave the Great Plains and travel greater distances than ever before. They entered Apache territory and forced the people out of their hunting grounds. Unable to hunt for buffalo, Apache carried out even more raids against Spanish settlements.

When the Spanish signed a peace treaty with the Comanche in 1786, they employed Comanche and Navajo (see entry) warriors to hunt down Apache. The Spanish then offered bribes if the Apache people would agree to settle near Spanish missions, stop raiding Spanish livestock, and live peacefully. One by one, Apache groups accepted the terms. Some fled to the mountains, however, and continued to carry out raids against Spanish settlements in what is now Mexico (see Chiricahua Apache entry). The Mexican government responded by offering to pay a price for every Apache scalp that was taken.

Apache come under U.S. control

In 1821 the Spanish gave to Mexico land in the Southwest that included Apache territory. In 1848 the United States took over part of the region under the terms of the Treaty of Guadalupe-Hidalgo, which settled the Mexican-American War. In the treaty, U.S. government officials promised Mexico that if any Indians on the new American lands carried out raids in Mexico, America would punish them. Now, instead of the Mexican government, the Apache had a new enemy—the U.S. army.

> **IMPORTANT DATES**
>
> **1540:** Spanish gold seekers encounter the Apache for the first time.
>
> **1847:** The Apache come under American control.
>
> **1886:** The final surrender of Geronimo's band marks the end of Apache military resistance to white settlement.
>
> **1934:** The Indian Reorganization Act results in self-government for Apache tribes.

American settlers and gold seekers streamed through Apache territory, and relations were very bad. The Americans did not try to get along with the Apache, as the Spanish had done. Instead, they called out the U.S. army to subdue them. The Apache put up such a fierce resistance, however, that they were not subdued until the final surrender of the feared and respected Apache leader Geronimo (c. 1827–1909) and his band in 1886 (see Chiricahua Apache entry). Newspaper headlines across the nation announced: "Apache War Ended!" The "roving Apache," as one army general called them, were now under the control of the U.S. government.

Some became prisoners of war, shipped first to Florida, then to Alabama, and finally to Fort Sill Military Reservation in Oklahoma. Others were placed on reservations in the Southwest. Different Apache groups found different destinies; more details on this can be found in the profiles of the Chiricahua, White Mountain, and San Carlos Apache tribes.

RELIGION

The Apache are very religious, and all of their actions are guided by their beliefs. They seek the help and guidance of the gods before hunting, farming, or going to war. The Apache believe in a creator called Ussen or Life Giver, who is the most important of their several gods. Other supernatural spirits include White Painted Woman, the symbol of life, and her children, Child of the Water and Killer of Enemies. The friendly Mountain Spirits are worshiped in special ceremonies led by spiritual leaders called shamans (pronounced *SHAY-mans*), who could also heal the sick.

Many Apache people converted to the Catholic faith under the influence of Spanish missionaries, but they never abandoned their ancient religion because it is such an important element of their way of life. In the late 1800s the U.S. government and Christian missionaries tried to suppress the old religion, but Apache still practice it today. It is common for Apache people to participate in both Christian and traditional religious ceremonies.

LANGUAGE

The Southwestern Athabaskan language, which is sometimes called Apachean, has seven dialects (varieties): Navajo, Western Apache, Chiricahua, Mescalero, Jicarilla, Lipan, and Kiowa Apache. All Apache dialects differ from one another in some ways, but members of the different groups can still understand one another. Most dialects, especially Western Apache, continue to be spoken today.

When the Spanish came to the New World in the mid-1500s, the Apache easily communicated with them using sign language.

GOVERNMENT

In the old times

For the Apache, the family is the most important unit. Until the twentieth century, they never had a government body that ruled over everyone. Instead, family groups usually acted independently. Apache groups moved about constantly from place to place, and government officials found it hard to find them and reach any agreements with them.

From time to time, a number of these family groups might come together to make important decisions, such as whether to form a war party. In those instances, the male heads of each family group formed a council, discussed the problem, and made a decision. Even if they decided to act together, though, the groups were never very large. When faced with threats from the Comanche tribe, the Spanish, the Mexicans, and the Americans, the Apache might have a war or raiding party consisting of a maximum of 100 men (and sometimes women).

Although Apache men made decisions about war and whether to move to a new location, women had influence too. The oldest woman in a household ruled the roost and was greatly respected.

On the reservations

Once on the reservations, the Apache came under the control of government agents, who did not always treat them well. The government established a U.S. Indian Police force to oversee law enforcement, health, and the use of land. Government agents—mostly white men—were mainly interested in making the Indians more like whites, and they devoted their efforts to getting the Indians to turn over decision-making power to them.

APACHE POPULATION: 1990

According to the U.S. Bureau of the Census, in 1990 53,330 people identified themselves as Apache, making the tribe the country's seventh largest. The breakdown of population figures looked like this:

Apache	32,912
Chiricahua	739
Fort Sill Apache	103
Jicarilla Apache	2,750
Lipan Apache	30
Mescalero Apache	4,144
Oklahoma Apache	563
Payson Apache	89
San Carlos Apache	2,300
White Mountain Apache	9,700

SOURCE: "1990 census of population and housing. Subject summary tape file (SSTF) 13 (computer file): characteristics of American Indians by tribe and language." Washington, DC: U.S. Department of Commerce, Bureau of the Census, Data User Services Division, 1995)

An Apache rancheria.

In 1934 the U.S. Congress passed the Indian Reorganization Act. American Indian tribes were given the opportunity to form their own elective tribal councils, a type of government the Apache still use today.

ECONOMY

Before the twentieth century

In the early days, the Apache carried on a lively trade, especially with the Pueblo and Pima tribes. The Apache were very clever at hunting and manufacturing items from buffalo, especially robes and jerky (meat that is cut into long strips and dried in the sun or cured by exposing it to smoke). In return for these in trade, the Apache received corn and beans, gourds, cotton cloth, and minerals.

Later, they traded with the Spanish, exchanging buffalo hides for grain and cattle as well as the horses and guns that allowed them to expand their hunting and trading opportunities. Raiding was as natural to them as trading, though, and they often took what they wanted from other tribes and from the Mexicans. Some Apache

THE RECREATION BUSINESS

Several Apache tribes have been successful at taking advantage of Americans' interest in outdoor recreation. For example, many members of the Mescalero Apache find employment at their ski resort, Ski Apache. Others work at the tribal museum and visitor center in Mescalero, Arizona. A large Mescalero enterprise, the Inn of the Mountain Gods in New Mexico, has a gift shop, several restaurants, and an 18-hole golf course. It also offers horseback riding, skeet and trap shooting, and tennis.

For the Yavapai Apache, whose small reservation has fewer than 300 acres of land suitable for agriculture, the tourist complex at the Montezuma Castle National Monument—where the tribe owns the 75 acres of land surrounding the monument—is an important source of employment and revenue. The Jicarilla Apache operate a ski enterprise, offering equipment rentals and trails for a cross-country ski program during the winter months. The gift shop at the Jicarilla museum provides an outlet for the sale of locally crafted Jicarilla traditional items, including basketry, beadwork, feather work, and finely tanned buckskin leather.

Tourism, especially for events such as tribal fairs and for hunting and fishing, provides jobs and brings money into the local economies at a number of reservations. Deer and elk hunting are especially popular on the Jicarilla reservation. The Jicarilla also maintain five campgrounds where camping is available for a fee. Other campgrounds are maintained by the Mescalero Apache, the San Carlos Apache, and the White Mountain Apache.

groups had relied on a limited amount of farming for food, but once they had horses, they depended even less on farming.

The U.S. government began moving the Apache onto reservations in the late 1800s. Life on the reservations was a great shock to a people who were accustomed to wandering. Men who were once warriors were expected to turn to farming, and they struggled to do so for a time. Some succeeded but others did not, because the land was poor and there was little water. Some left the reservations to work for wages paid by whites.

Twentieth-century economy

After World War I ended in 1918, the U.S. government encouraged the Apache to begin raising cattle, and some tribes have done so very successfully. Others engaged in processing lumber. When large numbers of Americans began to own cars and travel in the 1950s, many Apache turned to the outdoor recreation business (see box above).

Today Apache can be found pursuing careers in all the professions, though most of them must leave their communities to do so. Farming and ranching continue to provide employment for many Apache. The Apache are also known as some of the finest professional rodeo performers.

Those who live on the reservations face a persistently high level of unemployment. More than 50 percent of tribal members who want to work cannot find work.

An Apache dwelling in the 1880s.

DAILY LIFE

Families

Daily life revolved around the extended family, which included mother, father, children, grandparents, cousins, uncles, and aunts, who lived in single-family homes placed close together. Apache women bore few children. There was no word in the Apache language for "cousins," and children considered their cousins to be their brothers and sisters.

Buildings

The Apache usually built single-family homes called wickiups (pronounced *WIK-ee-ups*). These are cone- or dome-shaped structures with a framework of poles covered with brush, grass, reed mats, or sometimes skins. A fire pit in the center vented smoke through a hole directly above it. The Kiowa Apache and Jicarilla usually lived in Plains-style tepees covered with hides, although some Jicarilla are believed to have lived in Pueblo-style homes (see Pueblo entry).

Wickiups were easy to put up, take down, and carry to the several camps Apache bands lived in throughout the year. In very early times, before they acquired horses, they would strap their housing materials to the backs of dogs to carry to the new location.

Education

In early times, Apache children learned by listening to, observing, and imitating their parents. Both boys and girls learned survival skills like how to run swiftly, how to ride horses (the Apache were outstanding riders), and how to sneak up on enemy villages, because these skills might one day save their lives. Games and contests were held that were fun and also made contestants stronger.

Once they were on reservations and under the control of U.S. government agents, Apache children were expected to become "civilized," or more like whites. Not long after the 1879 founding of the Carlisle Indian School in Pennsylvania, many Apache children were sent there, to live unhappily far from their homeland and families. Government and mission schools were established among the Apache in the 1890s. All of these schools offered instruction only in English.

Today, the majority of the Apache population is under the age of eighteen. Education is highly regarded, and the Apache take an active role in making decisions about their children's education. This has resulted in some Apache public schools being singled out by the U.S. government as model schools for their bilingual and bicultural programs, especially in the elementary grades.

Food

The Apache were hunter-gatherers. They hunted bison, antelope, deer, elk, cougars, mountain sheep, and such birds as quail and wild turkey. Apache religion would not allow the eating of fish or bears. After they acquired horses in the late 1600s, some Apache groups hunted buffalo like their Plains neighbors, but buffalo were not plentiful. They had to travel great distances to find buffalo, and sometimes approached the animals by crawling a long way through the underbrush to disguise their scent.

Gathered foods included agave (pronounced *ah-gah-VEE*; a plant with tough, spiny, sword-shaped leaves that grows in hot, dry regions), cactus fruits, pecans, acorns, black walnuts, pine nuts, chokecherries, juniper berries, and raspberries. The climate of the Southwest was not good for farming and water was scarce. However, some Western tribes who were willing to carry water produced limited amounts of corn, beans, pumpkins, and squash.

Clothing and adornment

Apache men wore buckskin breechcloths (garments with front and back flaps that hung from the waist), ponchos (blanket-like cloaks with a hole for the head), and moccasins with attached leggings. Women wore buckskin skirts and similar ponchos and moccasins. Men usually cut their hair shoulder-length and tied a cloth headband across their forehead. Women wore their hair long.

SAN JUAN, HEAD CHIEF.

GORGONIO, MEDICINE-MAN.

NANTZILI, HEAD WAR CHIEF.

Three Mescalero Apache.

The Apache acquired cloth and wool through trade with other tribes. At the turn of the twentieth century, the Apache began to wear more American-style clothing, such as white cotton shirts and black vests for men and long-sleeved cotton blouses and full skirts for women. Even so, traditional clothing is worn on important occasions. A girl's puberty ceremony costume generally consists of a two-piece buckskin dress of the highest quality, which might be adorned with fringe, shells, beads, and metal pieces. A shaman's buckskin garment might have feathers, beads, and paint.

Healing practices

The Apache believed that sicknesses were often (but not always) sent by evil spirits to people who had offended them. Such ailments were cured by healers called shamans, who could be either male or female and who cured with herbs and by dancing and chanting. A suffering person requested the aid of a healer, then sprinkled the healer's head with pollen and offered a gift. The shaman would accept the gift only if he or she decided to take the case.

During the healing ceremony, the shaman sprinkled the patient with pollen and performed a ritual involving four dancers. The ceremony would be repeated over four nights.

Sometimes sweat baths were used as a remedy for colds and fever. The Apache also knew practical skills such as how to set broken bones with splints fashioned from cedar bark. Bleeding—the draining of blood from a sick person—was also a medical treatment, used for headaches and other ailments.

Twentieth-century health problems

Well into the twentieth century, ailing Apache continued to seek the services of shamans, but the kinds of ailments they suffer have changed. The Apache have suffered tremendous health problems associated with malnutrition (poor diet), poverty, and despair. They have suffered from incredibly high rates of contagious diseases such as tuberculosis. Once tuberculosis was introduced among the Jicarilla, it spread at an alarming rate. The establishment of schools in the early 1900s gave the tuberculosis bacteria a means of spreading rapidly throughout the entire tribe. By 1914, 90 percent of the Jicarilla suffered from tuberculosis. Between 1900 and 1920, one quarter of the people died. One of the reservation schools had to be converted into a tuberculosis sanatorium (a type of treatment facility) in an attempt to address the crisis. The sanatorium was not closed until 1940.

Like other tribes, the Apache have struggled with the ill effects of alcohol abuse. Alcohol, though long known to the Apache, has not always been a destructive force. In times past, the custom of sharing the drink *telapi,* made from fermented corn sprouts, "made people feel good about each other and what they were doing," said an Apache elder. Tribal leaders have attempted to address these health problems through education and by creating jobs that keep people from feeling despair.

ARTS

Crafts revival

Many Apache are demonstrating a new pride in traditional crafts as they attempt to survive in the larger American culture while still remaining Apache. Basketry and pottery making, which had nearly died out during the 1950s, are now valued skills once again, taught and learned with renewed vigor.

THE EMERGENCE: HOW THE APACHE CAME TO EARTH

Long ago they say. Long ago they made the earth and the sky. There were no people living on the earth then. There were four places under the earth where Red Ants were living. These Red Ants were talking about this country up here on the surface of the earth, and they wanted to come up here. Among them was the Red Ant chief and he talked about coming here. "All right, let's go to this new place above!" all the Ants decided. There was a big cane growing in that place. This grew upwards toward the sky. Then all the Red Ant People started off from the bottom of this cane and traveled up it. When they reached the first joint of the cane they made camp there all night. The next day they traveled on from there, still upwards.

They spent many nights on their way, always making their camp at the joints of the cane. They kept on traveling that way, upwards, and then finally the chief told them to look around this place where they were. So all the people went out and looked around this new country and all of them said that this was a nice place. There were lots of foods growing all around. The chief said, "Bring in all those foods that are good to eat, to our camp." So the people brought in the different kinds of foods and fruits that were good. They went all over the country for these wild foods. This way they found lots to eat and they found good places to live all over the new land.

After that the chief told the people to look around, and then he sang a song. At every song that he sang all the people were to come together again. Then the chief was singing and in his song he said, "You can go off any place you want to, and when you find a place that is good, then stop there and settle." So this was the first place that people were living, and these were the first people, the Red Ants.

Badger and Porcupine were the first ones on this earth also. Then all kinds of birds started to live on this earth; Eagle and Hawk and all the other kinds. Then God had made man on this earth and everyone was living well. This is the story about how man first became.

My yucca fruits lie piled up.

SOURCE: Bane Tithla, storyteller. *"Hatc'onondai* (the emergence, or the emerging place)." *Myths and Tales of the White Mountain Apache.* Glenville Goodwin. New York: American Folk-lore Society, 1939.

Oral literature

The Apache tell stories about the creation of the universe and the supernatural, but these stories are considered sacred and are kept secret. Other tales about the adventures of Coyote and Big Owl are told to instruct young people and to entertain, and some of these stories have been written down.

Coyote is sometimes portrayed as a hero because he taught the Apache how to care for themselves. At other times Coyote plays the role of a fool, for he frequently makes bad moral decisions and then suffers from the consequences. The Apache believe Coyote was responsible for bringing death and darkness into the world.

CUSTOMS

Festivals and ceremonies

The Apache did not have rituals celebrating the harvest, as many other tribes do. Apache ceremonies focused on celebrating important life events such as the naming of an infant, a child receiving his or her first pair of moccasins, a first haircut, puberty, healing by shamans, and asking supernatural beings for power. There might be hundreds of ceremonies celebrating life events each year.

Most rituals involved the use of pollen and the number four. Pollen is a symbol of life, fertility, and beauty. It is still thought to bring good luck and is still used in some ceremonies.

The number four represents the four directions (north, south, east, west), and rituals are often performed four times.

Puberty

Unlike many other tribes, Apache boys and girls did not go on vision quests to receive the spiritual guidance some call Power. Instead, Power came to them suddenly and unexpectedly, and this could happen several times throughout a person's life. Without Power, a man could not be a leader, and a woman had no influence.

A girl's coming-of-age was the occasion for a major ceremony, which lasted four days and was hosted by her parents. Part of the ceremony is called the Dance of the Mountain Spirits, in which masked participants pretend to be gods of the mountains. The young girl being honored impersonated White Painted Woman, who is like Mother Earth. Performance of the dance was supposed to bring good fortune to the entire tribe. During the ceremony, the young girl was attended by an older woman who would be her guide throughout life. After four days of constant singing and dancing, a girl took four days to recover. This puberty ceremony is still observed today.

The boy's version of a puberty ceremony was his first four raids on enemy settlements. After he completed them, he was considered an adult.

Courtship and marriage

Young Apache women were supervised to limit their contact with young men, and dances provided rare and welcome opportunities for socializing. The choice of a bride was a matter to be decided by a young man's entire family. Once all his relatives had voiced their approval of his choice, the young man's parents or their representative offered presents to the girl's parents.

If the bride's parents accepted the gift, the couple was often considered married with little or no further ceremony. Author Michael Melody described one simple Apache wedding that he observed: "A

basin made of buffalo hide was carried to a secluded place and filled
with fresh water. The bride and groom stepped into it, held hands, and
awaited the appearance of both sets of parents, who had to acknowl-
edge the matrimony." Afterward, the couple joined a public dance.

Married life

The Apache trace their ancestry through the mother, and married
couples set up housekeeping near the wife's parents in a separate
wickiup. The Apache believed a marriage would be happier if the
wife's mother never spoke to, or even appeared in the presence of, her
son-in-law. No such rule applied to the wife's grandmother, who
today remains a powerful presence in family life.

A man had to take care of his wife's family, and if she died, he had to marry her sister or unwed cousin. Several wives might be taken by those who could afford it, such as successful hunters or warriors. In the case of divorce, children remained with the wife's extended family. Modern-day Apache have adopted American marriage customs.

War rituals

Warfare was a major part of the Apache existence until almost 1900. Michael Melody wrote that most Apache battles "were undertaken to avenge deaths of group members, usually killed during raids. The slain warrior's family led the way during battle." It was the custom to request the help of the gods prior to battle in a ceremony that included warriors in costume. The dancers acted out the brave deeds they intended to perform. If the warriors were successful, another dance was held in which they acted out their achievements.

War parties might consist of a maximum of 100 warriors, who bravely faced much larger forces. During the late 1800s they took on the U.S. Army. When a cause seemed hopeless, warriors would scatter rather than fight to the bitter end.

Death and burial

Death of loved ones was a source of great dread for Apache, who feared they would be haunted by the ghost of the deceased. The face of a corpse was painted red, and the body was wrapped in skins and disposed of as soon as possible to hasten the spirit's journey to the underworld. The body was loaded onto a horse and taken to a cave or some other secluded area, where it was entombed and the tomb opening was sealed. Then the horse was killed and the deceased's house and belongings were destroyed. Survivors did not go near the burial ground, nor did they ever again speak the name of the dead person.

Today the Apache seek the services of funeral homes, in part because of state laws but also because it is a custom that allows for a quick disposal of a body.

CURRENT TRIBAL ISSUES

Poverty—and what to do about it—is a constant concern. The Apache have proved very modern in their efforts to resolve this issue.

Another issue is the illegal seizure of Apache lands. The Jicarilla Apache were awarded nearly $10 million in a lawsuit for land unjustly taken from them, but the United States will not return any of the land. In the lawsuit, the U.S. Supreme Court ruled that the Jicarilla have the right to impose tribal taxes on minerals extracted from their lands by others.

NOTABLE PEOPLE

In addition to the notable Apache discussed in the entries on the Chiricahua, San Carlos, and White Mountain Apache, others include Jicarilla Apache scholar Veronica E. Velarde Tiller, author of *Discover Indian Reservations USA, Tiller's Guide to Indian Country: Economic Profiles of American Indian Reservations, The Jicarilla Apache Tribe: A History,* and other works. Apache-Hopi-Pueblo author Michael Lacapa, who was raised as an Apache, has written award-winning children's books both alone and with his wife, Kathleen, a Mohawk. They co-authored *Less than Half, More than Whole* (Flagstaff, AZ: Northland, 1994), about a part-Native American child troubled by his mixed heritage. The works of poet and educator Jose Garza (Coahuiltec-Apache) and poet and short-story-writer Lorenzo Baca (Mescalero Apache), appear in *Returning the Gift: Poetry and Prose from the First North American Native Writers' Festival* (Joseph Bruchac, ed., University of Arizona Press, 1994) and elsewhere.

FURTHER READING

McKissack, Patricia. *The Apache*. A New True Book. Chicago: Children's Press, 1984.

Melody, Michael E. *The Apache*. New York: Chelsea House, 1989.

Chiricahua Apache

See Apache entry for more information on the Chiricahua Apache.

Name

The name Chiricahua (pronounced *CHEER-uh-KAH-wuh*) Apache may mean "chatterer," referring to their warriors' way of speaking to one another in code during battle. It may mean "grinder," because of their custom of breaking the bones of captured Mexican soldiers. They call themselves *de Apache,* meaning "man" or "person." The Chiricahua have also been called Mimbreños, Coppermine, Warm Springs, Mogollon, Pinery, and Cochise Apache.

Location

The Chiricahua Apache once lived in rugged, mountainous areas of what are now southeastern Arizona, southwestern New Mexico, and northern Mexico. Today, a little more than 100 Chiricahua live on individual plots of land in southwestern Oklahoma and are organized as the Fort Sill Apache Tribe with headquarters in Apache, Oklahoma. Other Chiricahua have intermarried with the Mescalero and Lipan Apache at Mescalero Reservation in New Mexico and are no longer considered a separate tribe.

Population

In the early to mid-1800s, there were an estimated 2,500 to 3,000 Chiricahua Apache. In 1886, there were just over 500. By 1959, there were about 91 full-blooded Chiricahua at the Mescalero Reservation in New Mexico, but in 1990 only 17 Chiricahua were living in New Mexico. In a census (count of the population) done in 1990 by the U.S. Bureau of the Census, 739 people identified themselves as Chiricahua (see box on page 435), and 103 people identified themselves as Fort Sill Apache.

Language family

Athabaskan.

Origins and group affiliations

The Chiricahua probably journeyed from western Canada to the Southwest between the thirteenth and sixteenth centuries. They are divided into three groups: Eastern Chiricahua (who call themselves "red paint people"); Central Chiricahua (the meaning of their name for themselves is unknown); and Southern Chiricahua ("enemy people").

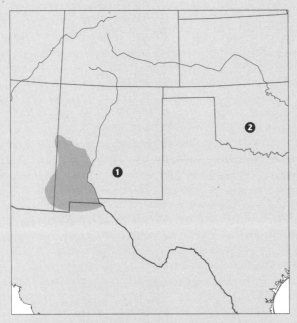

CHIRICAHUA APACHE

Contemporary Communities

1. Mescalero Apache Reservation, New Mexico
2. Fort Sill Apache Reservation, Oklahoma

Shaded area: Traditional lands of the Chiricahua Apache in present-day Arizona, New Mexico, and northern Mexico.

A pache groups put up perhaps the fiercest and most long lasting of Native American resistance to the invasion of their homelands by Spanish and white settlers. The names of certain Chiricahua men and women became known across America for their leadership of resistance groups. Legendary figures Cochise, Chato, Geronimo, and Victorio and his sister Lozen were all Chiricahua Apache, and many a U.S. Army commander tried and repeatedly failed to capture them. It was not until the surrender of Geronimo's band in 1886 that Apache armed resistance to white settlement finally ended.

HISTORY

Chiricahua have many enemies

The Chiricahua homeland was west of the Rio Grande and centered around Warm Springs (Ojo Caliente in Spanish) in present-day New Mexico. Spanish explorers passed by in the 1500s, but because they did not write about meeting the Chiricahua, some historians believed the Chiricahua were not yet living in the Southwest. Other historians believe the Spanish simply did not see the remote mountain homes of the Chiricahua, where they may have concealed themselves to avoid attack. They did not stay hidden from the Spanish invaders for long, however.

By the late 1500s the Spanish were building settlements and missions throughout the Southwest. At first the Chiricahua were willing to trade with them, but they soon grew unhappy with the newcomers' ways. Spanish soldiers considered Indians to be "savages," and took many to be their slaves. Spanish missionaries tried to turn them away from their religion. All Apache objected to the Spanish attitude, but in the Chiricahua people the Spanish soon found their bitterest enemies.

There followed centuries of battles between the Chiricahuas and the Spanish, and later the Mexicans, who became independent of Spain in 1821 but inherited Spain's enemies. There were frequent raids and murders carried out by all sides. During the conflict, the Chiricahua may have learned from the Mexicans the custom of scalping and then replacing their victim's hat. Despite the efforts of many military expeditions that were sent to subdue them, the Chiricahua stubbornly held on to their sacred homeland.

Under American control

In 1848 Mexico was defeated in its war with the United States and turned over vast tracts of the Southwest to its former enemy. The land included much of the Apache's territory in Arizona and New Mexico. The Apache now had a new and larger enemy than Mexico: the government of the United States. The United States soon made it clear that it would not put up with Apache raids and would not allow them to hunt on land that American settlers wanted. All the Apache put up resistance to the new white settlers, but none fought as long or hard as the Chiricahua.

Between the 1850s and 1875, Apache groups were settled on several reservations in Arizona and New Mexico. Then the American government decided that it was too expensive to maintain so many reservations and tried to move all the Apache to two reservations: Mescalero

---

IMPORTANT DATES

1540: Spanish expeditions begin crossing Apache territory.

1861: Cochise is arrested on a false charge, and the Apache Wars begin.

1874: Cochise dies.

1886: Geronimo and his band surrender.

1913: Majority of surviving Chiricahua resettle on Mescalero Reservation in New Mexico.

1977: Fort Sill (Oklahoma) Apache Tribe receives federal recognition.

Reservation in New Mexico and the barren San Carlos Reservation in Arizona. The Apache were outraged. Fights broke out, and many fled the reservations. The leaders of the groups that fled became legends.

Cochise and the Apache Wars

Cochise (pronounced *coh-CHEES;* c. 1812–1874), whose name means "hardwood" is one of the best known Chiricahua leaders and was an early opponent of white settlement in Apache territory. He was not a well known person when he was talked into moving with his people onto a reservation in 1853. But his unjust arrest in 1861 and his escape, which may have ignited the Apache Wars, brought his name to the attention of Americans all over the southwestern United States and as far east as the nation's capital. What happened was that a young army officer named Bascom arrested Cochise on a false kidnaping charge. Cochise was taken prisoner with some companions; he escaped but his people were murdered. The Apache Wars that followed lasted for more than three decades.

Cochise and his father–in–law, Mangas Coloradas, fought many battles with the U.S. military. Mangas Coloradas was captured in 1863, tortured, and killed. Cochise and his small group of followers held on for another ten years, until Cochise's white friend, Thomas Jeffords, convinced Cochise to end the wars by settling on a reservation in his homeland. After the death of Cochise in 1874, this agreement fell apart and the Chiricahua lost their reservation. They were moved to the San Carlos Reservation in Arizona. Unhappy with the area, with the Apache already living there, and with their treatment by U.S. government agents, some Chiricahua escaped, led by people such as Victorio (see page 432). Another decade of fighting began.

Geronimo

Geronimo (pronounced *juh-RON-uh-moe;* c. 1827–1909) was born in present-day Arizona, and his people often hunted and camped with Cochise's band. He was not a chief but was a medicine man and warrior. Geronimo believed, as many Apache do, that to be removed from one's homeland was to die. His battle against the Mexicans and U.S. settlers was for the preservation of the Apache people.

Geronimo was called Goyathlay, "One Who Yawns," by his people. When Mexican raiders killed his mother, wife, and three children in 1858, Geronimo vowed vengeance. He carried out deadly raids in Mexican territory and was given the name Geronimo by awed Mexican soldiers. (One story says that the Mexicans may have been crying

out in fear to St. Jerome when they saw Geronimo, or they may simply have been mispronouncing his Apache name.) He was caught more than once and returned to the reservation, only to escape again. His raiding and fighting in Mexico lasted until U.S. General George H. Crook's soldiers captured him in 1886.

It took an army of thousands of soldiers to finally capture Geronimo and his band; with him at the time of his surrender were thirty-six warriors, women, and children. They were forced to resettle in Florida and then in Alabama. Finally, in 1894 they were moved to a reservation at Fort Sill, Oklahoma. Geronimo lived out his years there, raising watermelons and selling his autograph to soldiers and at fairs. He died in 1909 after he fell off his horse into a creek and became ill.

Chato

With Geronimo at the time of an 1881 escape from the San Carlos Reservation was Alfred Chato (c. 1860–1934), known simply as Chato for most of his life. Chato rode with Geronimo and also led his own raiding parties throughout Arizona and New Mexico, stealing ammunition, killing white settlers, and spreading terror. He was convinced to return to San Carlos along with Geronimo in 1884, and thereafter his life took a different path from Geronimo's.

Chato adapted to reservation life and learned to farm. He was frequently employed by the U.S. army as a scout and consultant on Indian ways (he later received a medal for his service). In 1886, when the army commander in charge decided it was time to move the Chiricahua off the San Carlos Reservation and back to the home of their ancestors, Chato went to Washington, D.C., to discuss the move. Washington officials asked Chato to help convince the Chiricahua to move to Florida instead, but he refused. On Chato's return trip from Washington, he was arrested and sent to Florida, where Geronimo and his people had already been sent.

Conditions in Florida were very bad. In 1894 Chato and the other Chiricahua moved with Geronimo to Fort Sill, Oklahoma. Although it was not their homeland, at least it was closer to it than Florida had been. Chato was appointed leader of a small village near the reservation and was given a small plot of land for farming. At some point during his stay at Fort Sill, he converted to Christianity. He resumed work for the U.S. Army.

In 1913, Chato again traveled to Washington, this time to ask that his people be allowed to return to their homeland. After long discussions, and after white settlers in New Mexico voiced their fears that the Chiricahua would begin raiding again, the Apache were offered the opportunity to return to New Mexico.

Chato was respected by both the Indians and the white community in New Mexico, where he lived the remainder of his life. He died in an automobile accident in March 1934.

Victorio

Tribal leader Victorio (c. 1820–1880) is not as well known as Geronimo, but he too was a major obstacle to the U.S. Army. In 1879 he was told that his reservation at Warm Springs, New Mexico, would be opened to whites for settlement. Victorio responded: "If you force me and my people to leave [Warm Springs], there will be trouble. Leave us alone, so that we may remain at peace." Fearing he would be taken prisoner, as Geronimo had been, Victorio left the reservation, never to return.

African American soldiers (called Buffalo Soldiers) were sent to capture him, but Victorio eluded them. He was finally trapped by Mexican soldiers, who blasted Victorio's people out of their hiding place with dynamite. Sixty-one warriors and eighteen women and children were killed. Sixty other women and children, including two of his sons, were captured and taken into slavery. Victorio killed himself rather than be taken.

Chiricahua reservations

In 1913, Geronimo's followers at Fort Sill were given the choice of remaining in Oklahoma and receiving eighty acres of land apiece, or returning to New Mexico—their homeland—to live on the Mescalero Reservation. Eighty-seven chose to remain in Oklahoma, while the remaining 171 returned to New Mexico with Victorio.

The Mescalero Reservation was already home to Mescalero and Lipan Apache. For a time the Chiricahua kept an isolated area to themselves and held on to their tribal identity. Eventually they intermarried with the other Apache, though, and their culture was absorbed into the larger group.

The Fort Sill Chiricahua who received land instead of a reservation lived apart from each other on scattered plots. They have likewise intermarried with members of other tribes and with whites. Over time their tribal identity has been diluted.

RELIGION

In 1881 an Apache medicine man named Nochedelklinne began to preach about a vision he had, in which white men vanished from the earth and dead Apache came back to life. His vision included a dance, which he began to teach to increasing numbers of Apache. The dance was so lively, and dancers became so enthusiastic performing it, that white officials feared they might start an Indian revolution. Geronimo was an observer of some of these performances and his anger against white people was inflamed when Nochedelklinne was murdered by white soldiers together with his wife and son late in 1881.

Christian missionaries from the Reformed Church in America arrived at Fort Sill in 1899 and began the Apache Mission of the Reformed Church. They set up schools, tended the sick, and conducted religious services. Their success was assured when Geronimo agreed to convert, although he was soon expelled for gambling. The Church is still a strong presence at Fort Sill.

LANGUAGE

Because the Chiricahua had no reservation of their own, their language and culture were largely absorbed into other tribes or into white culture. Today, their language has almost disappeared. Robert W. Young in *Handbook of North American Indians* estimated that in 1981 there were only five Chiricahua speakers at Fort Sill, Oklahoma, "all over fifty years of age."

GOVERNMENT

Because the names of many Chiricahua leaders and warriors have become well known, some people think they were chiefs in charge of large groups of followers. This is not so. The Chiricahua did not have a "big chief" telling them what to do. Each small group had a leader, who was listened to because he had qualities his followers admired, such as wisdom, bravery, or a convincing way of speaking. While the leader may have had a great deal of influence, he did not make major decisions on his own; he had to consult the heads of other families in his group.

After the defeat of Geronimo, his survivors, who were the last of the Chiricahua, took different paths. Those who went to the Mescalero Reservation at first joined with the Mescalero and Lipan Apache in meetings with U.S. government agents who ran the reservations. Later, the government offered tribes on reservations the opportunity to organize and handle their own affairs.

At Mescalero, the three Apache groups accepted the opportunity offered by the federal government and organized as the Mescalero Apache. This entitled them to receive federal recognition. Federally recognized tribes are those with which the U.S. government maintains official relations. The Mescalero Apache formed a tribal council, which is made up of a president, vice-president, and eight elected members. The reservation has been blessed with strong leaders who have overseen advances in health care, education, and economic independence.

The Fort Sill Apache for a long time had only an informal business council. The U.S. government threatened to terminate (dissolve) the tribe in the 1950s. Termination would have brought an end to any relationship with the U.S. government. Members of the tribe rallied to fight termination by forming a tribal committee. In the 1970s the Fort Sill Apache formed a new government with elected members, and were granted federal recognition. They are recognized as a separate Chiricahua tribe, even though there are Chiricahua at the Mescalero Reservation.

ECONOMY

On the Mescalero Reservation in New Mexico, the people are fortunate to have land on which to develop businesses. Extremely successful timber and tourist operations have grown up, including the well known Inn of the Mountain Gods, a luxurious resort, and its sports center.

Things have not gone as well for the Fort Sill people, who do not have a reservation. When they moved onto their individual plots of land in 1913, the people raised cattle and farmed. When large farms blossomed in Oklahoma in the 1940s and 1950s, requiring large, expensive machinery, many Chiricahua could not afford to compete, and some left to find work wherever they could. In the 1970s the federal government began to give aid to Indian tribes, and the economy improved somewhat. Today, some people lease their land to whites for farming and cattle grazing, and other business opportunities are being explored. Still, while other Apache reservations are trying to deal with poverty and large numbers of unemployed people, the problem remains especially acute at the Fort Sill reservation.

DAILY LIFE

Buildings

The Chiricahua were wandering mountain dwellers who changed camps often. In the summer they lived in the highlands where it was cooler, and in the winter they moved down to the lowlands. Often their winter encampments included a sweat lodge for the men.

DISTRIBUTION OF CHIRICAHUA APACHE PEOPLE: 1990

In the 1990 census, 739 people identified themselves as Chiricahua, and 103 people identified themselves as Fort Sill Apache (descendants of the Chiricahua who chose in 1913 to move to Fort Sill Reservation in Oklahoma). The 739 people who said they were Chiricahua are scattered throughout the United States. Below are the states with the largest Chiricahua populations.

State	Chiricahua population
California	279
Washington	61
New York	40
Florida	35
Iowa	27
Arizona	26
Michigan	18
Nevada	18

SOURCE: Selected from "American Indian Population by Selected Tribes: 1990," U.S. Bureau of the Census, 1990 Census of Population, *Characteristics of American Indians by Tribe and Language*, 1990, CP-3-7, Table 1.

A portrait of a young Chiricahua Apache girl.

Food

Like other Apache, Chiricahuas were basically hunter-gatherers. The men hunted for deer and antelope using deer-head disguises and employing bows and arrows. They also hunted elk, mountain goats, and mountain sheep, but these were scarce. Small boys helped out by hunting cottontail rabbits, squirrels, birds, and opossums. Some animals, such as the badger and wildcat, were hunted only for their skins, and others, such as fish, bear, and turkey were not eaten by the Chiricahua. The bear was not hunted by most Apache tribes because it stood upright and was believed to be too much like a man. However, it was hunted by the Chiricahua, probably only for bear grease and fur.

Clothing and adornment

Like the other Apache, before the coming of Europeans, Chiricahua men and women wore clothing made of tanned animal skins. Because they lived near the Mexican border, they began early to adapt some of the Mexican-style clothing. Most common were white cotton shirts for the men, long white cotton breechcloths (garments with front and back flaps that hung from the waist), and tall leggings that were part of boot-like moccasins. At the waist they wore cartridge belts (belts with loops or pockets for carrying ammunition). In the later nineteenth century, they began wearing American-style black vests or jackets.

The women also began to adapt American clothing in the late nineteenth century by wearing long-sleeved blouses and full skirts with the addition of a decorative border at the bottom.

Men often wore a scarf around the neck, and women had necklaces made of shells or beads. Both sexes wore unpainted wood charms for personal protection and men carried leather cases with ornate beadwork.

Healing practices

The Chiricahua were skilled in the use of herbs for healing. Well into the twentieth century they prepared a potion for the elderly to help keep their blood thin. It was made from a weed called zagosti, which has been used by modern medical experts to prepare blood thinner for heart patients. The Chiricahua used roots such as the osha, either chewed or ground up in tobacco, for the common cold. Apache plume was used for diarrhea and constipation. Mud baths were also prescribed for many ailments. A hot cloth spread with grease and ashes was sometimes used for such maladies as mumps.

Education

By the time he was confined on the Fort Sill Reservation in 1894, Geronimo realized that the old ways of educating Apache children would no longer work in American society. He encouraged children on the reservation to learn the ways of the "White Eyes." Some Fort Sill children were sent away to the Carlisle Indian School in Pennsylvania. Others were taught white ways by Christian missionaries, who set up schools at Fort Sill. At many schools, children were forbidden to speak their native language. Today, Fort Sill children attend local public schools in the five counties where Chiricahua own plots of land.

Children at the Mescalero Reservation attend elementary school on the reservation and public middle and high schools nearby. Plans were under way in the 1990s to open a middle school, a high school, and a community college on the reservation.

CUSTOMS

Festivals and ceremonies

The Apache Dance for the Mountain Spirits, originally held for every young girl's puberty ceremony, is now an annual event. The Fort Sill Apache host the dance in September, while the Mescalero hold it as part of their Fourth of July celebration. That July Ceremonial is a four-day gala event (four is their lucky number); it pays tribute to young girls who have reached puberty and includes feasting and a rodeo.

Fort Sill Apache keep in touch with other Native nations by hosting both rodeos and powwows. A powwow is a celebration at which the main activity is traditional singing and dancing. In modern times, the singers and dancers at powwows come from many different tribes. While at Fort Sill, visitors can view the works of famed Chiricahua sculptor Allan Houser at the tribal headquarters.

CURRENT TRIBAL ISSUES

Poverty—and what to do about it—is a constant concern. Some Apache solutions have raised controversy. For example, in 1996 the

Mescalero Apache accepted a $2 billion contract to house nuclear waste in a remote part of their reservation in New Mexico. They say the money will provide jobs and business opportunities. Critics say the decision is an environmental disaster waiting to happen.

At Fort Sill, tribal members are involved in tracing Apache genealogy (ancestry) and in reviving aspects of the culture that seemed to be vanishing as tribal members moved away in the 1940s and 1950s.

NOTABLE PEOPLE

Allan Houser (1914–1994) was a Chiricahua Apache sculptor who has been acclaimed throughout the world for his six decades of work in wood, marble, stone, and bronze. In April 1994, he presented an 11-foot bronze sculpture entitled "May We Have Peace" to first lady Hillary Rodham Clinton in Washington, D.C., as a gift from the American Indians to all people. Houser's work is on view in museums all over the world, and he has won many awards, including the Prix de West Award in 1993 for a bronze sculpture titled "Smoke Signals," now a part of the permanent collection of the National Cowboy Hall of Fame.

Lozen (c. 1840s–1886) was the sister of Chiricahua war leader Victorio and is the most famous of the Apache War Women. Though they were few in number, their accomplishments were significant, especially at a time when women everywhere enjoyed little freedom. She is said to have been a medicine woman and an accomplished horsewoman whose advice and guidance was sought by both men and women of her band. She rode to battle with Victorio and later with Geronimo, with whom she was photographed several times, although one cannot tell from these photographs that she is a woman. She was taken with Geronimo as a prisoner to Florida. She died, most probably of tuberculosis, in 1886.

FURTHER READING

Buchanan, Kimberly Moore. *Apache Women Warriors.* Southwestern Studies No. 79.

Debo, Angie. *Geronimo: The Man, His Time, His Place.* Norman: University of Oklahoma Press, 1976.

Geronimo. *Geronimo: His Own Story*, edited by Frederick W. Turner III, New York: Dutton, 1970.

Roberts, David. *Once They Moved Like the Wind: Cochise, Geronimo, and the Apache Wars.* New York: Simon & Schuster, 1993.

Sweeney, Edwin R. *Cochise: Chiricahua Apache Chief.* Norman: University of Oklahoma Press, 1991.

White, Julia. "Lozen—Chiricahua Apache." [Online] http://www.twelvestring.com/innerspace/lozen.htm

San Carlos Apache

See Apache entry for more information on the San Carlos Apache.

Name

The name San Carlos Apache (pronounced *sahn CARR-los uh-PATCH-ee*) refers to the area where the tribe lives, along the San Carlos River in Arizona.

Location

The Apache who make up the San Carlos Apache tribe are descended from members of many Apache groups. The traditional Apache homeland included a vast region stretching from what is now central Arizona to central Texas, and from northern Mexico to the high plains of southeastern Colorado. The modern-day San Carlos Apache live on the San Carlos Indian Reservation, which covers 1.8 million acres in Gila, Graham, and Pinal counties in central Arizona. The reservation is located 20 miles southeast of Globe and 100 miles east of Phoenix, Arizona.

Population

In 1930, there were 3,000 San Carlos Apache. In a census (count of the population) taken in 1990 by the U.S. Bureau of the Census, 32,912 people identified themselves as Apache; of that number, 2,300 said they were San Carlos Apache. The San Carlos Indian Reservation claims an enrollment of 10,500.

Language family

Athabaskan.

Origins and group affiliations

All Apache peoples made a gradual move from western Canada to the American Southwest between the thirteenth and sixteenth centuries. They were never one unified group but rather a number of bands who spoke similar languages and shared similar customs. The people who now make up the San Carlos Apache tribe are descended from the Aravaipa, Chiricahua (see entry), Coyotero, Mimbreño, Mogollon, Pinaleno, San Carlos, and Tonto Apache peoples.

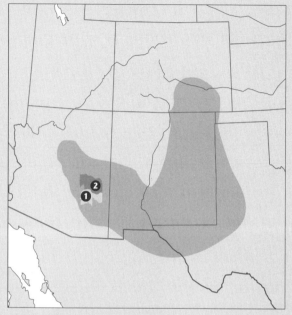

SAN CARLOS APACHE

Two Reservations

1. San Carlos Reservation
2. White Mountain Reservation

Shaded area: Traditional lands of the Apache, in present-day Arizona, New Mexico, Texas, northern Mexico, and southeastern Colorado.

The San Carlos Indian Reservation was established in 1871 to hold members of many Apache groups and stop their raiding of American and Mexican settlements. The confining nature of reservation life caused considerable unrest among the Apache, who were used to living in small family groups. The trouble was compounded by persistent, grinding poverty, pressure to give up their Indian ways, and mismanagement of the fragile Arizona landscape where they lived. The San Carlos Apache have yet to overcome these problems, but some advancements have been made in recent years.

HISTORY

San Carlos Indian Reservation established

In 1848 the United States took over Apache lands from Mexico. The American government soon made it clear that it would not tolerate Apache raids or allow Natives to hunt on land claimed by settlers. (See Apache and Chiricahua Apache entries.) Following years of resis-

tance by Apache groups, some were moved in 1871 to a new site, Arizona's White Mountain-San Carlos Indian Reservation, located at the place where the Gila River joined the San Carlos River. By 1890 all Apache groups had submitted to the government's reservation policy.

In 1897 the White Mountain-San Carlos Indian Reservation was divided into the San Carlos Indian Reservation and the Fort Apache Reservation (where the White Mountain Apache now live; see entry). The adjustment to reservation life was very hard for these wandering peoples, who were not used to living in large communities. Historians indicate that many still have not adapted to white ways.

Early days on the reservation

From the beginning, government officials were put in charge of running the San Carlos Reservation. They expected the Apache to become farmers—to take up a way of life that was totally alien to them. While the land was beautiful, much of it was desert—dry and not at all suited for agricultural use.

Slowly the Apache tried to adapt to their new lives, but it was not long before their land was found to be rich in mineral resources. Between 1872 and 1902 the U.S. government took away reservation land five times at the urging of white business owners. Copper and silver mines were opened, and the San Carlos Apache found their reservation reduced to about one-third of its original size.

Coolidge Dam brings lake to reservation

Construction of the Coolidge Dam across the Gila River changed the lives of the San Carlos Apache. The Coolidge Dam stretches across

the portion of the Gila that runs through southeast-central Arizona, forming San Carlos Lake (now a popular fishing and water sports center). Completed in 1928, the dam was intended to help both Indian and white farmers in the region by sending much-needed water their way. But when backed-up waters flooded San Carlos in 1929, headquarters were then moved upstream on the San Carlos River to the village of Rice (later renamed San Carlos).

RELIGION

Although many modern-day San Carlos Apache are Christians, some tribespeople still retain certain old Apache beliefs. They have also adopted features of other Southwestern religions.

Like many Native Americans, the San Carlos Apache have long considered their religious beliefs to be a private matter—one not to be discussed among outsiders. It is not widely known, then, that members of the tribe still travel to Mt. Graham in the Coronado National Forest in Arizona to conduct spirit dances in honor of the mountain spirits. Mt. Graham, one of the Pinaleno Mountains, was taken away from the Natives by government order in 1873, but it is still considered sacred. San Carlos Apache priests were forced to openly discuss their belief that the mountain range is sacred after the University of Arizona announced in the early 1980s that it would build multiple telescopes there.

The building of telescopes in the mountains has generated considerable controversy both as an issue of religious freedom and as an environmental issue. It has pitted nonreligious Apache people against the traditional Apache, and Natives and environmentalists against astronomers, politicians, and the Roman Catholic church. In 1990 the Apache Survival Coalition was formed to save the sacred mountain. Although the group failed in this effort—a telescope was erected and dedicated there in 1994—it remains active in the struggle for the religious freedom and rights of the San Carlos Apache.

LANGUAGE

Government schools built around the turn of the twentieth century routinely punished children for speaking their Native languages on the reservation, but the Apache have managed to retain their language. Many fear that it may soon be lost as the American culture takes over and Apache people intermarry with non-Natives.

GOVERNMENT

The San Carlos Apache tribe is run democratically (by the people) according to a constitution. An elected tribal council has a chairperson, vice-chairperson, and nine representatives from four districts. A secretary and treasurer are appointed.

ECONOMY

Land-based economy

After enduring years of poverty as the Apache tried to adjust to life on the reservation, the economy at San Carlos improved somewhat when cattle were introduced around 1930. Overgrazing occurred, however, and cattle monies declined. At the turn of the twenty-first century San Carlos cattle operations were the tribe's third-largest source of money, generating about $1 million in sales annually.

One-third of the tribe's land is forest or woodland, and timber operations are another source of income. Arizona is one of only three places in the world where the rare peridot (a transparent yellowish-green mineral) gemstones can be found, and the San Carlos tribe earns money from mining it.

The San Carlos Apache have been slow to adjust to a rapidly changing world. They have been haunted by poverty and lack of opportunity, and their standard of living remains well below the national level. In recent years, though, the San Carlos tribe has placed a high priority on the development of agriculture. Irrigation facilities are being modernized, and an Agricultural Development Committee has been formed to guide the process. Alfalfa (a haylike plant) and jojoba beans (pronounced *huh-HOBE-uh*; edible seeds that are also prized for their thick moisturizing liquid center) are promising crops.

Government and recreation as employers

Recreation yields a significant amount of money for the tribe. San Carlos Lake, the state's largest body of water, offers fishing opportunities, but from time to time the lake dries up completely. Hunters pay fees to track big and small game like elk, bighorn sheep, antelope, and migratory birds. Campgrounds, boat ramps, stores, tackle shops, and a warm-water fishery are available to tourists, and visitors are also permitted to observe Apache ceremonies while in the area. The

Apache Gold Casino, which includes a hotel, restaurant, and RV (recreational vehicle) park, opened in 1994 and is expected to be a big moneymaker for the tribe.

The federal government is a major employer of San Carlos Apache. It operates health, education, and other services on the reservation and employs members of the tribe. Despite these enterprises, reservation members still contend with unrelenting poverty and high unemployment.

DAILY LIFE

Education

In 1900 a boarding school was opened by the U.S. government on the San Carlos reservation. Children were taken from their families and forced to attend the school, where they were not allowed to speak their Native language or practice their age-old religion. The experiment proved to be a failure, and it left many Apache with a long-standing feeling of resentment toward white schools and the white style of education. This has contributed to very low levels of educational attainment on the reservation.

Apache leaders are trying to address these critical educational issues. The reservation houses a library, and the tribe was proud to announce the opening of its first cultural center in 1995. Located in Peridot, Arizona, the center tells the story of the Apache people in their own words and offers educational programs in cooperation with Arizona schools and other groups.

Healing practices

In modern times some San Carlos Apache place their trust in medicine men, who journey to Mt. Graham to look for healing herbs—special plants and plant parts that can only be found there—and to learn healing techniques from the mountain spirits.

The U.S. Public Health Service operates a hospital on the reservation. The San Carlos Apache tribe faces serious health problems, including alcoholism (and the illnesses that result from it) and high rates of infant death and teenage suicide.

ARTS

Basketry

The Apache tribe is known for its outstanding basketmakers and artists. Efforts were under way in the 1990s to develop an arts and crafts guild at the new San Carlos Apache Cultural Center. There artists will work, teach their skills, and display and sell their creations. In addition, the guild intends to make sure that local artists obtain fair prices for their work.

CUSTOMS

Festivals and ceremonies

The San Carlos Indian Reservation hosts an annual Holy Ground Summer Blessing Ceremony. Recent controversies over the building of telescopes on Apache sacred land have sparked a renewed interest in this traditional religious practice.

The tribe also celebrates the coming-of-age of its young women in a Sunrise Ceremony, formerly called the Changing Woman Ceremony. (The puberty ceremony is described in the Apache entry.)

CURRENT TRIBAL ISSUES

The San Carlos Apache are currently engaged in efforts to reverse the trends of alcoholism, suicide, crime, and violence that plague their people. According to experts, serious problems like these often result from decades of poverty and high unemployment. Many homes lack electricity and indoor plumbing. Disputes between the tribe and mining companies over rights to Arizona's scarce water supplies are also a nagging issue.

NOTABLE PEOPLE

Evalena Henry (1939–) is a San Carlos Apache known for her award-winning baskets. Her works are on display at the Heard Museum in Phoenix and are held by art collectors all over the world. Her goal is to pass on her basketmaking methods to future generations.

FURTHER READING

Martin, Evelyn. "The Last Mountain (Mount Graham in Arizona)." *American Forests,* March-April 1993, vol. 99, no. 3-4, p. 44.

Melody, Michael E. *The Apache.* New York: Chelsea House Publishers, 1989.

Warshall, Peter. "The Heart of Genuine Sadness: Astronomers, Politicians, and Federal Employees Desecrate the Holiest Mountain of the San Carlos Apache." *Whole Earth,* Winter 1997, no. 91, p. 30.

White Mountain Apache

See Apache entry for more information on the White Mountain Apache.

Name

The name White Mountain Apache refers to the White Mountain region of Arizona where the tribe resides.

Location

Formerly in east-central Arizona, between the Pinaleno Mountains to the south and the White Mountains to the north. Presently the tribe lives on the Fort Apache Reservation, which covers 1.7 million acres in Arizona's Navajo, Apache, and Gila counties.

Population

In 1850, there were an estimated 1,400 to 1,500 White Mountain Apache. In a census (count of the population) taken in 1990 by the U.S. Bureau of the Census, 9,700 people identified themselves as White Mountain Apache.

Language family

Athabaskan.

Origins and group affiliations

The Apache people made a gradual move from western Canada to the American Southwest between the thirteenth and sixteenth centuries. They were never one unified group but rather a number of bands who spoke similar languages and shared similar customs. Whites referred to the Apache people as Western Apache or Eastern Apache. Those called White Mountain Apache are descendants of the easternmost group of Western Apache. The White Mountain people most likely learned agricultural techniques from the Navajo or Pueblo (see entries).

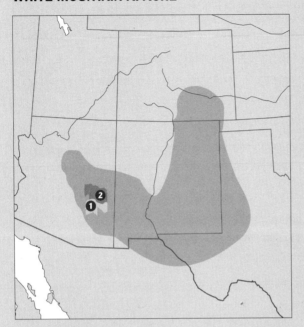

WHITE MOUNTAIN APACHE

Two Reservations

1. San Carlos Reservation
2. White Mountain Reservation

Shaded area: Traditional lands of the Apache, in present-day Arizona, New Mexico, Texas, northern Mexico, and southeastern Colorado.

The White Mountain Apache differed from other Apache groups for two main reasons: (1) they farmed, and (2) they interacted more with other tribes, which led to significant changes in their culture. The White Mountain people served as scouts for the U.S. Army to help round up other Apache groups—including the group led by Chiricahua Apache warrior Geronimo—who refused to move to reservations. In August 1998 *Newsweek* called the White Mountain Apache one of five Native North American "tribes to watch" because of their astonishing economic successes.

HISTORY

Cooperative relations with United States

The land belonging to the White Mountain Apache ended up in U.S. hands in 1853, when the Gadsden Purchase—a land deal with Mexico—was sealed. Although the tribe continued the longstanding Apache custom of raiding Mexican settlements for food, they avoided confronting the U.S. Army. In fact, they aided the army by providing scouts and fighters. And when American forces established Camp Ord on White Mountain Apache land to protect white settlers in Arizona, the tribespeople did not object. Camp Ord later became Fort Apache Reservation.

In 1874 the U.S. government adopted a peace policy and began to place all Indians on reservations. General George Crook and his White Mountain Apache scouts tracked down every hostile band. Without the Indian scouts, this feat might have proved impossible. The White Mountain people believed that their traditional Native way of life was over. They cooperated with the government's reservation policy and were moved to the White Mountain-San Carlos Indian Reservation, established in 1871.

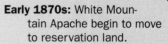

IMPORTANT DATES

1853: The United States acquires White Mountain Apache land in the Gadsden Purchase.

Early 1870s: White Mountain Apache begin to move to reservation land.

1897: The White Mountain-San Carlos Indian Reservation is divided into two reservations. The White Mountain Apache are given their own reservation (now called Fort Apache Reservation).

1938: White Mountain Apache constitution is ratified and a tribal council is elected.

In 1897 the White Mountain-San Carlos Indian Reservation was divided into the San Carlos Indian Reservation and the Fort Apache Reservation. The White Mountain Apache were a more unified group than the Natives confined to San Carlos, but they did have to abandon most of their old ways in order to survive. While under military supervision at Fort Apache, they learned to farm, build irrigation dams, and tend livestock. Armed with this knowledge, they were able to create a strong economy over the course of the twentieth century. The population has grown tremendously, thanks to better health care and improvements in sanitation and housing. More than 10,000 people are enrolled in the Fort Apache tribe; about 2,500 are from other tribes, mainly Navajo.

LANGUAGE

In the late 1990s approximately 75 percent of the White Mountain people spoke Apache in their homes.

GOVERNMENT

The Apache were divided into small local groups that governed themselves. White Mountain groups were often named after the location of their farmland. They had chiefs who organized food-gathering, farming projects, and interactions with other local groups.

In 1934 the U.S. government passed the Indian Reorganization Act, which encouraged Native American communities to govern themselves and set up tribal economic corporations. The White Mountain Apache adopted a constitution in 1938 and formed a tribal council, consisting of a chairperson, a vice-chairperson, and nine members elected from four voting districts. Tribal headquarters is in Whiteriver, Arizona. Although this type of government had never been tried by Apache communities before, it worked well throughout the rest of the century.

ECONOMY

Before 1918

The White Mountain Apache lived in a region made up of dry deserts and watered valleys. About 75 percent of the food economy was based on hunting and gathering; the rest was based on gardening. When families left their fields and moved back to winter quarters, the men of the tribe took to raiding (stealing from other groups) livestock, including horses, which they used mostly for food.

On the reservation in the early 1900s, the people of Fort Apache began to earn wages by working for whites. They cut hay for U.S. Cavalry horses stabled at Fort Apache. They also leased land to white cattle ranchers and then went to work for them.

Cattle and timber boost economy

After World War I ended in 1918, the U.S. government began supplying cattle to Indians. Four hundred head of cattle were given to residents of Fort Apache, and the cattle-raising business took off. As of 1998 the tribe boasted a herd of 15,000 purebred whiteface cattle. They also owned and managed a fish hatchery.

Since 1934 the White Mountain Apache Tribal Council has overseen the building of a strong economy on the Fort Apache Reservation. The council is responsible for an 800,000-acre forest, which supports a substantial lumber business. The Fort Apache Timber Company in Whiteriver, Arizona, is owned and operated by the White Mountain Apache and employs about 400 Apache workers. It has an annual income of approximately $30 million.

Tourism thrives in late twentieth century

Tourists in White Mountain Apache country are entertained at a large complex of operations that includes hunting, fishing, winter sports, and water sports. Big-game hunting draws wealthy people and celebrities, and the new Hon-Dah Casino is also a big attraction. The tribe owns the White Mountain Apache Motel and Restaurant, the Sunrise Ski Resort, and the Sunrise Park Hotel. The complex is open year-round and contributes both jobs and tourist dollars to the local economy. The ski area has seven lifts and generates $9 million per year.

Over the years, various members of the tribe have made a name for themselves in the field of firefighting. White Mountain Apache people are in demand all over the western United States as forest fire-fighting specialists.

DAILY LIFE

Food

About one-quarter of the White Mountain tribe's food was supplied by farming. Summer camps were set up along streams, where dams and channels were constructed to irrigate their small fields. They grew limited amounts of corn, beans, pumpkins, and squash. Once the seeds were planted, the women moved out across the land in gathering groups, collecting such foods as acorns, mescal (pronounced *MESS-kal*; a type of small cactus), and berries. The men left to hunt for deer, elk, mountain sheep and goats, and pronghorn sheep. Birds were not eaten but were hunted for their feathers. (Eagle feathers were especially prized.) Fish were not eaten either because they were considered unclean.

Education

The children of the White Mountain Apache tribe are educated at public schools in Whiteriver or can attend one of two government-run schools or a Lutheran school on the reservation. A branch of the Northland Pioneer College also operates in Whiteriver.

OLD FORT APACHE PRESERVES CULTURE Old Fort Apache, now owned and preserved by the tribe, is on the National Register of Historic Places. Visitors to the fort can learn about Apache culture and history at the Heritage Museum and at various archaeological sites (places where experts remove the remains of past cultures for study).

Healing practices

The ancient Apache people believed in the power of supernatural spirits. Some spirits were said to be benevolent (to be kind or do good), but evil witches were thought to cause sickness, insanity, and even death. Suspected witches were still feared by some tribes at the end of the twentieth century. According to Native tradition, witches could make people sick by poisoning them, by thinking evil thoughts, or by "shooting" victims with a piece of wood or charcoal, a pebble, a bead, or an arrowhead. A victim of witchcraft could either seek treatment through a ceremony conducted by a medicine man or shaman (pronounced *SHAH-mun*) or do nothing and allow the condition to get worse.

Traditional White Mountain healing ceremonies were performed at night. Before beginning, the shaman was given a piece of shell with an eagle feather attached to it; white shells were used for female patients, and turquoise shells were used for males. If the ceremonies worked, the witch would die and the victim would begin to recover. Modern-day White Mountain Apache seek the assistance of shamans and health care professionals at an Indian Health Service hospital in Whiteriver. If more specialized care is needed, a helicopter can airlift patients to Phoenix, Arizona.

CUSTOMS

Festivals and ceremonies

The White Mountain Apache held a ceremony after returning from a raid. If a woman chose to join in the ceremonial dancing, the successful raider had to give her one of the livestock captured in the raid.

Some of the rich culture of the Apache people faded away during the twentieth century, but the White Mountain people are working to restore some key traditions, including the Girls' Puberty Ceremony. During this major annual event, young girls perform the Sunrise Dance to receive special blessings.

CURRENT TRIBAL ISSUES

Problems still exist for the White Mountain Apache on the reservation. Too many people are out of work. Too much of the available housing is poor. School attendance is low, while alcoholism, drug use, and teen suicide rates are high. But the White Mountain Apache are taking renewed pride in their language and tradition. Experts feel that the outlook for the tribe is improving.

FURTHER READING

Mails, Thomas E. *The People Called Apache.* New York: BDD Illustrated Books, 1993.

Perry, Richard J. *Western Apache Heritage.* Austin: University of Texas Press, 1991.

Hopi

Name

Hopi is the shortened form of the tribe's original name *Hopituh- Shi-nu-mu*. Its most commonly given meaning is "peaceful people." The Hopi are sometimes referred to as the Moqui, the named given to them by the Spanish.

Location

The 2.5 million-acre Hopi federal reservation is located in northeast Arizona, just east of the Grand Canyon, in the Four Corners area (where Arizona, Utah, Colorado, and New Mexico meet). The Hopi inhabit fourteen villages, most of them situated atop three rocky mesas (called First Mesa, Second Mesa, and Third Mesa) that rise 600 feet up from the desert floor. A mesa (the Spanish word for table) is a large hill with steep sides and a flat top.

Population

In 1680, there were an estimated 2,800 Hopi. In a census (count of the population) done in 1990 by the U.S. Bureau of the Census, 11,791 people identified themselves as Hopi.

Language family

Uto-Aztecan.

Origins and group affiliations

Scientists say the Hopi tribe has lived in its present location for at least a thousand years. Hopi tales tell how their ancestors developed from small creatures in another world (see box entitled "Hopi Origin Tale"). The Hopi are the westernmost of the Pueblo Indian tribes. The Hopi, however, are the only Pueblo people that speak a Shoshonean language of the Uto-Aztecan language family.

HOPI

Two Reservations Today

Hopi Nation Reservation (lighter shading), surrounded by the Navajo Nation Reservation (darker shading).

Lighter shaded area: Hopi Nation, in present-day Arizona at the Four Corners area, where Arizona, Utah, Colorado, and New Mexico meet.

The Hopi people regard themselves as the first inhabitants of America. They excel at the painstaking challenge of farming and gardening in their extremely dry climate. According to this deeply religious tribe, their way of life focuses on humility, cooperation, respect, and taking care of the earth. Their isolated location, customary secrecy, and the fact that their community remains largely closed to outsiders has helped them to preserve their culture.

HISTORY

The Hopi before contact with the Spanish

Most scholars believe that the region where the Hopi live has probably been occupied for at least 10,000 years. Evidence suggests that as long as 1,500 years ago ancestors of the Hopi made use of ceremonies, technology, and architecture very much like that seen on the Hopi reservation today.

During the years 1350 to 1540 C.E., Hopi villages began to grow larger and require greater social organization. At that time chieftains, or heads of the villages, began to experience an expansion of power. The period also saw the first use of *kivas*, the underground ceremonial chambers found in every village. In addition, coal was mined on Hopi land and the Hopi people were among the world's first to use coal for firing pottery to strengthen it.

Other Native Americans call the Hopi, whose complex culture was firmly in place by the 1550s, "the oldest of the people." The Hopi culture included an annual series of ceremonies and a social system based around clans (groups of related families that traced themselves back to a common ancestor). Their village of *Oraibi* dates back to at least 1550 and is without a doubt the oldest continuously occupied settlement in the United States.

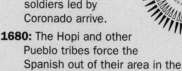

IMPORTANT DATES

1540: The Hopi first meet Europeans when Spanish soldiers led by Coronado arrive.

1680: The Hopi and other Pueblo tribes force the Spanish out of their area in the Pueblo Revolt.

1882: President Chester A. Arthur establishes the Hopi Indian Reservation.

1934: The Hopi Tribal Council starts to deal with Hopi-U.S. government relations.

1974: The Navajo-Hopi Settlement Act returns 900,000 acres to the Hopi that had been taken over by the Navajo.

Spanish try to impose Christianity

The Hopi had their first contact with Europeans in 1540, when a group of Spanish soldiers, led by the explorer Francisco Vásquez de Coronado, arrived in Hopi territory. They were looking for the legendary "Seven Cities of Gold"—places that were supposed to be full of riches. When the Spaniards searched and found no gold in Hopi villages, they destroyed part of a village and left. The Hopi did not face further interference from the Spanish until 1629, when the first Spanish missionaries arrived. These Roman Catholics built missions in Oraibi, and at two other villages. Most tribal members pretended to adopt the new religion while practicing their own in secret.

The people finally cast off Spanish rule and religious oppression when they joined the rest of the Pueblo people in a unified revolt known as the Pueblo Revolt of 1680 (see Pueblo entry). During this uprising, the Indians took the lives of Catholic priests and Spanish soldiers and kept up a several-day attack on Santa Fe, New Mexico. After the battle, the Hopi returned to their villages and killed all the missionaries.

Spanish interference ends

To protect themselves from retaliation, the Hopi moved three of their villages to the mesa tops. The Spanish returned in 1692 and

reconquered the nearby Rio Grande area (the Rio Grande is the river that separates Mexico from Texas). Many Rio Grande Natives fled west to the Hopi lands, where they were welcomed. Over the next few years, a number of the people who lived at the Hopi village of Awatovi invited the Spanish priests back. This situation caused a serious break between those who wanted to preserve the old ways and those who embraced Christianity. Finally, in 1700, Hopi supporters of the old ways killed all the Christian men in Awatovi and then destroyed the village.

The destruction of Awatovi marked the end of Spanish interference in Hopi life. For the most part, there was no further contact between the Hopi and white people until about 1850. At that time the U.S. government appointed an Indian agent to oversee the Hopi and other Indian inhabitants of their region. Visits to Hopi lands by U.S. officials resulted in a terrible smallpox epidemic that killed hundreds of people in 1853 and 1854. A drought that took place soon after reduced the population of Oraibi from 800 people to 200. When the American Civil War (1861–65) broke out, the American military withdrew from the Southwest to go and fight in the war. Without the soldiers there to stop them, the Navajo (see entry), ever on the lookout to take over Hopi land, stepped up their attacks on Hopi villages.

Navajo intrusion on Hopi land

In 1882, aware that the Navajo were attacking the Hopi and taking over their land, U.S. President Chester A. Arthur (1830–1886) ordered the establishment of the Hopi Reservation. He granted the tribe 2.6 million acres of land. But because of the way his order was worded, the Navajo takeover of Hopi land was allowed to continue for nearly a century, until the passage of the Navajo-Hopi Indian Land Settlement Act of 1974. The act returned approximately half of the disputed land to the Hopi. However, some land disputes between the Hopi and Navajo still remain unresolved (see "Current Tribal Issues").

In 1950 the U.S. Congress passed the Navajo-Hopi Act and spent $90 million to improve the facilities on the reservation, such as roads, schools, hospitals, water, electricity, and sewers. In 1961 the Hopi tribal council was granted permission to lease tribal lands to outsiders. As a result, the council allowed the Peabody Coal Company to begin leasing 25,000 acres of land for mining, a process that began at Black Mesa in 1970, and has brought some money to the Hopi. Since the 1960s, farming has greatly decreased on Hopi lands, and by 1980 the major source of income had become wage labor (see "Economy"). Today, most Hopi work at jobs in area coal mines, in the service industry, or as part of the tourist trade.

RELIGION

Religious Hopi depend on the gods

The Hopi religion is a highly developed belief system. It has many gods and spirits, such as Earth Mother, Sky Father, the Sun, the Moon, and the many *kachinas,* or invisible spirits that inhabit living and non-living things. The religion features a yearlong schedule of rituals, songs, recitations, and prayers that are as unusual and complex as any in the world.

The Hopi have long believed that the non-religious elements of their lives must be based upon their religious patterns, the patterns of Creation. As of 1992, it was reported that more than 95 percent of the people remained faithful to their Hopi religious beliefs.

The Hopi believe that they are deeply connected to the Earth. They also believe that if they perform their cycle of ceremonies successfully, the world will remain in harmony, the gods will be pleased, and there will be sufficient rainfall.

Kivas and prayer feathers

Central to the religious ceremonies of the Hopi are the kiva, the *paho,* and the Corn Mother. The kiva (the underground ceremonial chamber) is usually rectangular in shape (although the ancient ones were circular) and sunk into the village square. It symbolizes the

"Mong Kachinas," a painting by Hopi artist Waldo Mootzka.

place of emergence of the original Hopi people into this world. The kiva has a small hole in the floor that represents the entrance to the underworld and a ladder extending above the roof opening that represents the way to the upper world.

At the end of secret ceremonies held inside the kiva, ceremonial dances are performed in the square. The paho, a prayer feather, usually that of an eagle, is used to send prayers to the Creator. Pahos are used at all kiva ceremonies.

The Corn Mother and kachinas

Corn, which has sustained the Hopi for centuries, plays a large role in Hopi ceremonies. For example, cornmeal is sprinkled to welcome the kachinas to the Corn Mother. The Corn Mother, who has been described as "a perfect ear of corn whose tip ends in four full kernels," is saved for rituals.

Hopi kachinas are said to inhabit the sacred San Francisco Peaks and come to live in Hopi villages for six months of the year to perform certain necessary ceremonies and dances. They are mostly good spirits who have the power to pass on prayers for rain to the gods. Masked people dressed as these spirits perform the kachina dances, which are tied to the growing season, beginning in March and lasting into July.

LANGUAGE

The Hopi speak a single language, Hopi, a Shoshonean form of the Uto-Aztecan language family. Different Hopi groups vary in their dialects (varieties) and the Hopi people of the village of Hano speak *Tewa,* a Pueblo language derived from the *Azteco-Tanoan* language family.

The Hopi language is difficult to translate, and only recently has it been placed into written form. But the strong Hopi oral tradition has preserved it and passed it down from generation to generation, so that today most Hopi, including the young people, still speak Hopi as well as English.

GOVERNMENT

Each independent Hopi village is governed by a *Kikmongwi,* or village chief. The Hopi villages are only loosely connected politically as a confederation, although they have strong cultural connections in their shared history and religion, and the similarity in their ceremonies.

The Hopi tribe has always been organized according to a system of clans based on the mother's ancestry. Today, there are some thirty clans. Clan membership helps to provide a singular Hopi identity. Although an elected Hopi Tribal Council has existed since 1934 to deal with matters between the Hopi and the federal government, it does not govern the tribe. The council is made up of a chairperson and vice-president, who serve four-year terms, and by council members who serve two-year terms.

THE POWAMU CEREMONY AND BEAN DANCE

The Hopi Powamu Ceremony is performed to request plentiful crops from the gods and to initiate children into a Kachina society. It is a sixteen-day collection of rites that begins on the new moon in February and prepares the Hopi and their dry lands for the upcoming planting season. Beans are blessed, planted in moist sand in boxes, then grown in the hothouse environment of underground kivas. Ceremonies that center on planting are considered very important since they help make sure seeds sprout and thrive when warm weather comes.

The Bean Dance celebrates the germination of the seeds. Kachinas dance into the village square along a path of cornmeal that has been sprinkled before them by priests. The dancers call on the mysterious forces of nature and stay in the village for six months, dancing for rain, fertility, and other blessings.

The Crow Mother kachina walks through the village on the last day of the Powamu Ceremony, carrying a basket of fresh bean sprouts that germinated in the kiva and signify the abundance of crops to come. The Crow Mother is accompanied by her two sons, called the Whipper Twins. With eyes bulging and hair flying, they bare their teeth as they pretend to whip the children of the village with yucca fronds.

ECONOMY

For many centuries the Hopi stayed in one place and farmed. The men handled the work of planting and harvesting the crops, while the women gathered other needed food. When a great drought occurred from 1279 to 1299, the Hopi adopted inventive farming methods that took advantage of every possible source of moisture and are still in use today.

One Hopi irrigation method made use of the wind to blow sand up against the sides of the mesas, forming dunes that trapped moisture. Crops were then planted in these dunes. Hopi farmers also planted in the dry washes (low ground that is flooded part of the time) as well as in the mouths of the streams. They sometimes irrigated crops by hand. The Hopi raised cotton in addition to the edible crops, and men spun and wove cotton cloth into clothing and textiles for their own use and for trade.

Today, small farms and cattle and sheep ranches are a major part of the tribal economy. A number of tribesmen work on the reservation in the construction industry, either for private developers or for the tribal government. Several ongoing activities on the reservation include building houses; developing the Hopi Industrial Park; establishing the Hopi Water Utility authority, which the tribe can operate as a business; renovating the Hopi Cultural Center Museum and crafts shops; building a small shopping mall and a motel-restaurant complex; and developing a 30-acre tract of land for businesses. Tourism is also important, as visitors come to see Hopi historical sites such as Oraibi Village.

DAILY LIFE

Buildings

For centuries, Hopi villages were made up of houses built of local native stone and arranged around a center containing one or more kivas. Hopi villages are set up in much the same way today.

From 1100 to 1300 C.E. the climate became drier, and people were forced to move into villages. It became difficult for farmers to grow enough food for all of them. To house the growing population, buildings in the villages grew larger, with some containing hundreds of rooms. Houses built from 1350 to 1540 C.E. were made of stone cemented with adobe (pronounced *uh-DOE-bee*; a sun-dried mud

Terraced houses in the ancient Hopi village of Oraibi with the entrance to a kiva in the foreground. The illustration was made from a description of Oraibi by an observer in the 1870s.

made of a mixture of clay, sand, and sometimes ashes, rocks, or straw) and then plastered inside. They were very similar to the older houses of present-day Hopi, except that they often had many stories. The houses of that time were heated with coal.

Today the Hopi live in both the older houses and modern ones. The kiva remains largely the same as in ancient times: a rectangular room built of native stone, mostly below ground. Sometimes kivas are widened at one end, to form the same T-shape as the doorways found in all ancient Hopi ruins. Kivas contain an altar and a central firepit below the roof opening, with a ladder extending above the edge of the roof. They also serve as meeting rooms.

Clothing and adornment

In earlier times Hopi men wore fur or buckskin loincloths (flaps of material that covered the front and back and were suspended from the waist). Some loincloths were painted and decorated with tassels, which symbolized falling rain. The men also wove robes and blankets out of the cotton they grew. Observers who were in the region in about 1861 reported that women were wearing loose black gowns with a gold stripe around the waist and at the hem, while men wore shirts and loose cotton pants, covered with a blanket wrap.

Married women wore their long hair straight or in braids. Unmarried girls wore their hair in large twists on either side of the head in a

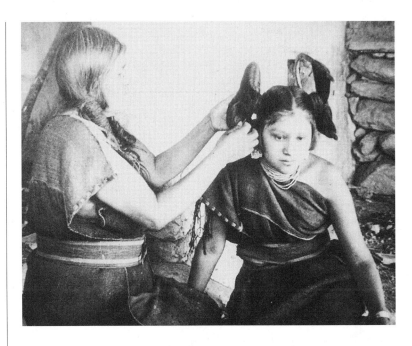

shape that resembled the squash blossom, a symbol of fertility. Unmarried women still wear this time-consuming hairstyle today, but only for ceremonies. Some Hopi men still wear the traditional male hairstyle with straight bangs over the forehead and a knot of hair in the back with the sides hanging straight and covering the ears.

In modern times, some Hopi women and girls still wear the traditional Hopi dress, which is black and embroidered with bright red and green trim. Hopi men wear elaborate costumes that feature special headdresses, masks, and body paints for ceremonies and dances. The costumes vary according to clan and ceremony.

Food

In earlier days, the staple crops of the Hopi were corn, squash, beans, and some wild and semi-cultivated plants such as Indian millet and wild potato. Salt was obtained during long, difficult excursions to the Grand Canyon area. It was the job of the Hopi women to gather pine nuts, prickly pear, yucca, berries, currants, nuts, and various seeds. In the sixteenth century, the Spanish introduced wheat, onions, peaches and other fruits, chilies, and mutton (sheep meat) into the Hopi diet.

Many modern Hopi farmers still use the old methods. They primarily raise corn, melons, gourds, and many varieties of beans. The

six traditional Hopi varieties of corn include yellow, blue, red, white, purple, and sweet. Corn is ground for use in ceremonies, such as the annual corn roast, as well as to make *piki,* a traditional bread baked in layers on hot stones.

Hundreds of years ago, wild game was more plentiful than it is today, and Hopi men hunted deer, antelope, and elk. They also hunted rabbit using boomerangs (flat, curved sticks that can be thrown so that they will return near the thrower). By 1950, wild game had dwindled, leaving only rabbit and a few quail and deer.

Education

The Hopi made use of the original "interactive method" of learning—speaking and listening. This was their main method for teaching their children about the Hopi ways. Today, Hopi children are educated at six elementary schools, a junior high school and a high school on the reservation, and at a community college nearby.

Healing practices

Many Hopi healing methods rely on the power of suggestion—the fact that often people begin to feel better if something is said or done that makes them believe they are going to feel better. The Hopi are also knowledgeable about the healing properties of certain plants and herbs.

There are several healing societies that perform curing rituals; some concentrate on only one type of illness. For example, snakebite is treated by the Snake Society on First Mesa, while rheumatism (muscle or joint discomfort) is treated by the *Powamu* Society.

Hopi myths teach that the Hopi originated in the first of Four Worlds, not as people but as insect-like creatures who fought among themselves. Displeased that the creatures did not seem to grasp the true meaning of life, the Creator, the Sun spirit *Tawa*, sent Spider Woman, another spirit, to guide them on a journey. By the time they had reached the Third World, they were human beings, and they reached the Fourth, or Upper World, by climbing up from the underworld through a hollow reed.

When the Hopi reached the Fourth World, they were given four stone tablets by *Masaw*, the spirit that protected the world and taught the people the proper way to live. Masaw described the travels they were to take—to the ends of the land in each of the four directions—and how in time they would find the place where they were meant to settle.

As the migrations began, various clans started out in each direction. Their routes eventually formed a cross, the center of which was the Center of the Universe, their intended permanent home. According to this Hopi story of creation, their journeys finally led them to the plateau that lies between the Colorado River and the Rio Grande, in the Four Corners region (where four of the United States join). The Hopi believe they were led there so that they would have to depend upon the scanty rainfall. The need for rain has caused them to pray and remain close to the Creator they rely on to fulfill their needs for rain and other things.

Because the number four holds great significance in the Hopi religion, many ritual customs often call for repetitions of four.

Sometimes people become members of curing societies after suffering an accident or illness. For example, lightning-shocked people and those whose fields have been lightning-struck join the Flute Society, whose members can cure earache in babies. Other healers can suck out diseases from infants and children by holding cornmeal in the mouth and then symbolically "spitting away" the disease. Certain kachina dances (including the Horned Water Serpent and the Buffalo Dance) are held specifically to help afflicted persons.

In addition to these age-old healing techniques, modern-day Hopi use modern medical science, including doctors and hospitals. There are health clinics on the reservation and hospitals nearby. The U.S. Indian Health Service provides mental health services and substance-abuse programs.

ARTS

Hopi women are known to make fine multicolored pottery. They also produce traditional textiles for trade or sale, Hopi kachina dolls, hand-woven baskets, and ornate jewelry.

Oral literature

Hopi stories present Hopi knowledge in such a way that both children and adults can learn something new from them at each hearing. Each clan has its own stories that contain information valuable to its members, and people learn only the stories of their own clan. The stories contain more than enough truth to ponder for a lifetime. The Hopi consider their stories sacred and private.

CUSTOMS

Naming ceremonies

Newborn babies are kept from direct view of the Sun for their first nineteen days, and then a naming ceremony is held. A baby belongs to its mother's clan, but it is named for the father's. Since one cannot be Hopi without a clan of birth, if the mother is not Hopi, neither will her children be.

For the ceremony, a traditional Hopi stew is prepared at the home of a baby's maternal grandmother—its mother's mother. During the naming ritual, the grandmother kneels and washes the mother's hair, then bathes the new baby, who is wrapped snugly in a blanket with only its head visible. Using the baby's special ear of corn called the Corn Mother, the grandmother rubs a mixture of water and cornmeal into the baby's hair, applying it four times. Then each of the baby's paternal aunts (from the father's side) does the same, and each gives a gift and suggests a name. The grandmother chooses one of the names. Then she introduces the baby to the Sun god just as the Sun comes up. A feast follows the naming ceremony.

Adolescence

Both boys and girls are initiated into a kachina cult between the ages of eight and ten. The initiation ceremony includes fasting, praying, and a light whipping with yucca leaves. Each child is assigned a ceremonial mother (for the girls) or father (for the boys), who sees them through the ordeal. Boys usually join the society of their ceremonial fathers. There are four such societies—*Kwan, Ahl, Tao,* or *Wuwutcimi.* Joining one of these groups usually is part of the *Powamu* ceremony, a four-day tribal initiation rite for young men that traditionally takes place at planting time (see box on page 461).

Ten-year-old girls once took part in a ceremony that involved grinding corn for an entire day at the girl's paternal grandmother's house. Some girls ground corn for four days to mark their first menstrual period, received a new name, and adopted the squash blossom hairstyle (see "Clothing and adornment").

The Hopi Snake Dance.

Festivals

The cycles of Hopi rituals are conducted in secrecy within the kivas. The dances that follow in the village square are rhythmic, mystical, and colorful. Outsiders are sometimes allowed to watch them.

One of the most important Hopi ceremonies is held at the Winter Solstice (the time when the Sun is farthest south of the equator and appears to stand still). This ceremony, called the *Soyal,* is the first ceremony of the year and the first kachina dance. The people believe this ceremony will make the Sun return sooner. The Niman Ceremony or Home Dance, the last kachina dance of the year, is held in thanksgiving at the Summer Solstice in late July (when the Sun is closest to the equator). By this time, the last of the crops have been planted and the first corn has been harvested.

Other dances of less religious importance are the Buffalo Dance, held in January to commemorate the days when buffalo were plentiful; the Bean Dance (see box on page 461), held in February to ask the kachinas to bless the next planting; and the Navajo Dance, which celebrates the neighboring Navajo tribe.

The relatively short (one hour) Snake Dance is preceded by eight days of secret preparations. During this rite, priests handle and even put in their mouths snakes that have been gathered from the desert. The secret of how they do this without being bitten has never been revealed to outsiders. At the end of the dance, the snakes are released back into the desert to ensure that the rains will come. Alternating every other year with the Snake Dance is the Flute Dance, which honors the spirits of people who have died during the preceding two years. Women's dances, like the Basket Dance, are held near the end of the year.

Courtship and marriage

Some of the ancient Hopi marriage customs still survive, but many have fallen into disuse. For example, around 1950 courtship was still an elaborate procedure that involved a rabbit hunt and corn grinding, and marriages could only take place with family approval. A bride wore a traditional white tasseled robe that was woven for the occasion by her uncles. A similar, smaller white robe was carried rolled up in a type of suitcase. This gown would later serve as the woman's burial clothes. The young couple lived with the mother of the bride during their first year together.

Today, courtship is much less formal. A couple is often married in a church or by a town official and then returns to the reservation. Since many men no longer know how to weave, most uncles no longer produce the traditional robes.

There are several Hopi marriage customs still in practice today. These include a four-day stay by the bride-to-be with her future in-laws. During this period she grinds corn all day and prepares all the family's meals to show that she knows how to cook. Prior to the wedding, the aunts of both the bride and groom engage in a sort of good-natured free-for-all, throwing mud and trading insults, each side suggesting that the other's is no good. Then a ceremonial washing of the couple's hair with yucca by the groom's parents takes place. A huge feast follows at the house of the bride's mother.

Clan membership continues to play a role in partner selection. There are still rules that discourage marrying into one's own clan, but such marriages are no longer forbidden. The fact that marriage to non-tribal members is extremely rare has helped to preserve Hopi culture.

Funerals

Among the Hopi it is desirable to grow old because it indicates that the journey of life is almost complete and the soul will go on to a better place. Because their religion holds that the soul's journey to the land of the dead begins on the fourth day after death, bodies are customarily buried as quickly as possible. Any delay in burial could interfere with the soul's ability to reach the underworld.

One ritual calls for the hair of the deceased to be washed with yucca shampoo by a paternal aunt, who then decorates the hair with prayer feathers and covers the face with a mask of raw cotton that symbolizes clouds. The body is wrapped—a man in a deerskin robe and a woman in her wedding robe. The oldest son buries the corpse in a sitting position along with food, water, and cornmeal. Finally, a stick is inserted into the soil of the grave, creating a place for the soul to exit. If rain follows, it signifies that the soul has experienced a successful journey.

CURRENT TRIBAL ISSUES

Land claims

The Hopi today are very concerned about the Navajo tribe taking over their land bit by bit, and they also want to regain the land already taken by the Navajo. When the Hopi Reservation was originally established in 1882, nearly 2.5 million acres were set aside in northeastern Arizona for the Hopi and whatever other Indians the government might decide to settle there. The Hopi Reservation was centered within a larger area that the Hopi considered to be their ancestral land, but it was designated the Navajo Reservation.

As their population increased, the Navajo expanded their settlements well beyond their own borders, and pushed onto the Hopi Reservation. The situation went on for many decades. Although the Hopi complained, the U.S. government failed to act. In time the Navajo took over 1.8 million acres of the land originally designated for the Hopi, leaving the tribe with only about 600,000 acres. Recognizing the problem, Congress finally passed the Navajo-Hopi Settlement Act in 1974. The act returned 900,000 acres to the Hopi. But as late as the 1990s, the dispute over resettlement and the remaining 900,000 original acres continued.

Preserving the Hopi Way

The Hopi are also concerned about the preservation of the Hopi Way. Their concerns have divided the tribe into two factions: Traditionalists and Progressives. Traditionalists, who want to keep the old ways, fear that white influence will further break down the Hopi culture. On the other hand, Progressives feel that adoption of some aspects of modern American life is necessary if the tribe is to survive and grow.

Hopi people are disturbed that the privacy surrounding their rites and practices has been violated for the benefit of non-Hopi people. For example, stories told to visitors and photographs of rites have been published in books without permission, observers have taped Hopi ceremonies and sold the tapes to the public, clothing items and ceremonial dance steps have been copied and sold in non-sacred settings, and designs from Hopi potters and kachina doll makers have been reproduced without their permission.

NOTABLE PEOPLE

Louis Tewanima (1879–1969) was a world-class Hopi athlete. He won a record-setting silver medal in the 1912 Olympic Games in Stockholm, Sweden, in the 10,000-meter race. Tewanima returned to his home on the reservation to tend sheep and raise crops but still kept active well into his nineties. In 1954 he was named to the All-Time United States Olympic Track and Field Team. In 1957 he was the first person to be inducted into the then-new Arizona Sports Hall of Fame.

Hopi Charles Loloma (1921–1991) designed jewelry that is among the most distinctive in the world. His unique designs combined non-traditional materials like gold and diamonds with typical Indian materials like turquoise. He also received great recognition as a potter, silversmith, designer, and painter of murals.

Other notable Hopi include: geneticist and the first Hopi to receive a doctorate in sciences Frank C. Dukepoo (1943–); traditional artist Fred Kabotie (born c. 1900); the "single most influential Indian woman creator in clay," Otellie Loloma (1922–1992); award-winning artist and teacher, Linda Lomahaftewa (1947–); a ceramicist who helped revive Indian arts, Nampeyo, (c.1860–1942); influential periodical publisher and editor, Rose Robinson (1932–); anthologized poet, Wendy Rose (1948–); and weaver, Ramona Sakiestewa (1949–).

FURTHER READING

Benedek, Emily. *The Wind Won't Know Me: A History of the Navajo-Hopi Land Dispute.* New York: Knopf, 1992.

Indian Reservations: A State and Federal Handbook. Compiled by the Federation of American Indians. Jefferson, NC: McFarland and Company, 1986.

Kavasch, E. Barrie. *Enduring Harvests: Native American Foods and Festivals for Every Season.* Old Saybrook, CT: The Globe Pequot Press, 1995.

Leitch, Barbara A. *A Concise Dictionary of Indian Tribes of North America.* Algonac, MI: Reference Publications, Inc., 1979.

Page, Susanne, and Jake Page. *Hopi.* New York: Harry Abrams, 1982.

Parsons, Elsie Clews. *Hopi and Zuñi Ceremonialism.* New York: Harper and Bros., 1950. Reprint. Millwood, NY: Kraus Reprint, 1976.

Thompson, Laura, *Culture in Crisis: A Study of the Hopi Indians.* Ann Arbor, MI: University Microfilms, 1969.

Waters, Frank. *Book of the Hopi.* New York: Viking Press, 1963.

Mohave

Name

Several meanings for the name Mohave (pronounced *moe-HAH-vee*) have been suggested. It may come from the Native word *hamakhava,* which means "mountain peaks," referring to the Needles Mountain peaks (California). Or it may come from the word *ahamakav,* which means "people who live along the river."

Location

The Mohave lived in sprawling settlements on both sides of the Colorado River, which separates California and Arizona and extends into lower Nevada. Their homeland was once about 200 miles long and 25 miles wide. Modern-day members of the tribe live with descendants of three other tribes (Chemehuevi, Hopi, and Navajo) on or near the 270,000-acre Colorado River Indian Tribes Reservation (located mostly in Arizona, with about 43,000 acres on the California side). Some Mohave also live on or near Fort Mohave Reservation, which has acreage in California, Arizona, and Nevada, and tribal offices in Needles, California.

Population

In 1800, there were about 3,000 Mohave. In 1900, there were about 2,000, with 500 on the Colorado River Reservation, about 1,000 near Fort Mohave, Arizona, and about 200 in Needles, California. In a census (count of the population) taken in 1990 by the U.S. Bureau of the Census, 1,645 people identified themselves as "Colorado River." No one identified themselves as "Mohave."

Language family

Yuman (rhymes with "human").

Origins and group affiliations

The Mohave were the largest of the Yuman-speaking tribes (the other Yuman-speaking tribes were the Yavapai, Maricopa, Quechan, Hualapai, and Havasupai). The Mohave were a desert people descended from the Patayan (see box in Anasazi entry) of late prehistoric times. Most Mohave migrated to the Mohave Valley (where Fort Mohave Reservation now stands) from the Mohave Desert to the east, settling along the Colorado River around 1150 C.E. The tribe later divided into two factions or groups: one favoring peace with whites and neighboring tribes, the other favoring war.

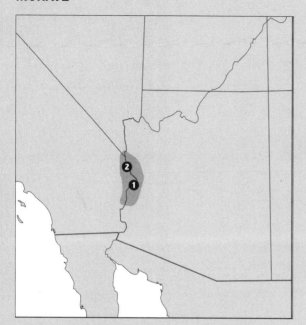

MOHAVE

Contemporary Communities

1. Colorado River Indians, Arizona
2. Fort Mohave Indian Tribe, California

Shaded area: Traditional lands of the Mohave, along both sides of the lower Colorado River separating present-day California and Arizona.

The Mohave have lived, they say, longer than anyone—living or dead—could ever remember, in a hot, dry area made fertile by the yearly flooding of the Colorado River. An active and adventurous people, they made a name for themselves as expert runners. The Mohave traveled far and wide to trade and created a trail to the Pacific Coast that white settlers later found very useful. But the tribe was also feared because of its warring ways. Although the Mohave say they were always cooperative until provoked, white trappers and settlers characterized them as being calculating and dangerous. Reports of their attacks on California-bound wagon trains brought them to the attention of the U.S. military, and by 1865 they were being settled on reservations. There the tribespeople lived unhappily and impoverished for many years. By the late 1990s, though, with modern irrigation methods in place for more than 35 years, the Mohave were enjoying considerable prosperity.

HISTORY

Uneventful contacts with Spanish

Long before the Spanish first saw them, the Mohave were a large, unified tribe, even though families lived on sprawling, individually-owned farms rather than in villages. Their lives were simple and marked by few ceremonies or festivals. The Mohave people came together to defend their territory or to attack other tribes. The first overwhelming threat to their way of life came hundreds of years after their first contact with whites.

The tribe first met a Spaniard in 1604, when Juan de Oñate of Mexico explored the region where the Colorado and Bill Williams rivers come together. It was another 172 years before the Spanish actually reached the Mohave Valley. When a Spanish priest, Father Francisco Garcés, arrived in 1776, he estimated the Mohave population to be three thousand. But as far as the Spanish were concerned, the Mohave Valley was too dry, barren, and remote to bother with. Contact between the two groups remained minimal, except for the occasional Mohave raid for horses at Spanish missions in California.

War with whites and neighboring tribes

During the 1820s American fur trappers began traveling through Mohave country, prompting considerable bloodshed. One of the best known battles occurred in August 1827, when the Mohave nearly wiped out a trapping expedition led by American fur trader and explorer Jedediah Smith (1799–1831). And a group led by Lorenzo Sitgreaves, who was looking for a route for a transcontinental railroad, was attacked by the Mohave in 1851. The tribe claimed to have cooperated with the whites to a great extent. They did, for example, guide an expedition of white travelers through the desert to the Pacific Coast in 1853–54. But when faced with the destruction of their natural resources by thoughtless whites, they attacked.

Throughout the early period of American trapping and westward expansion, the Mohave were also busy warring with neighboring tribes. Between 1827 and 1829 they fought against the Halchidhoma,

IMPORTANT DATES

1827: A battle breaks out between the Mohave and Jedediah Smith's expedition.

1858: Fort Mohave is established to protect American settlers from Mohave attacks.

1859: The Mohave are defeated, ending resistance against white settlement.

1865: The Colorado River Reservation is established, with acreage in Arizona and California.

1870: Fort Mohave Reservation is established, with acreage in California, Arizona, and Nevada.

c. 1945: Members of the Hopi and Navajo tribes join the Mohave and Chemehuevi on the Colorado River Indian Tribes Reservation.

1963: The Colorado River Indian Tribes win an important water rights case, and the reservation economy begins to improve.

1983: State of California passes legislation calling for the development of a radioactive waste depository. Ward Valley, 22 miles from Fort Mohave Indian Reservation, is chosen as the site. Indian opposition to the proposal begins.

An illustration of three Mohave people.

a hostile tribe that invaded their land. The Mohave successfully expelled the tribe from their valley. Later the Mohave permitted the poverty-stricken Chemehuevi to occupy their lands until war broke out between the tribes in 1865. The Chemehuevi were driven back into the desert, but they reached a peace with the Mohave in 1867.

The Mohave suffered a disastrous military defeat at the hands of the Pima and Maricopa tribes in 1857, but they still persisted with attacks on white settlers. Their 1858 attack on a wagon train bound for California was a call to arms for the U.S. military. It resulted in the establishment of a U.S. military post in the Mohave Valley for the protection of white settlers. (The post was later named Fort Mohave.) The post's commander was ordered to bring the Mohave "to submission" (to bring them under U.S. authority). Mohave resistance did not end until after an 1859 battle in which many Mohave warriors were slain by American soldiers.

Reservations established—lands lost

The Colorado River Indian Reservation was established in 1865 for all the Indians along the Colorado River and its tributaries. The Mohave and the Chemehuevi were confined to nearly 270,000 acres on both sides of the river. The government promised to build modern irrigation works on the reservation, and Mohave Chief Irretaba settled there with a fairly large group of people. But another Mohave chief named Hamoseh Quahote, along with a great majority of the tribe, refused to leave the Mohave Valley. Later, after a railroad was built through Mohave lands, some of the Native people changed their minds and moved south to the Colorado River Indian Reservation. Those who remained behind were settled at Fort Mohave Reservation, established in 1870, where they endured prejudice and humiliation by white settlers.

The Mohave had been settled on their reservations for only a short time before their lands were reduced. By 1887 the Santa Fe Railroad company owned a large portion of Fort Mohave Reservation land.

In 1941, when the Japanese bombed Pearl Harbor, Hawaii, and the United States was brought into World War II (1939-45), the federal government adopted a policy of internment of Japanese-Americans, confining them to camps purely because of their race. (The government feared that Americans of Japanese descent might try to help Japan invade the United States, although no evidence of this ever existed.) Many Japanese-Americans were confined at the Colorado River Indian Tribes Reservation. In return for accommodating these prisoners, the U.S. War Department promised the Indians it would not keep the land permanently and would make land and irrigation improvements on the reservation.

After World War II the United States developed a new policy of moving "surplus" Indians from one reservation to another. The government offered farming land on the Colorado River Indian Tribes Reservation to some people from Hopi and Navajo reservations, and members of those tribes are now considered Colorado River Indians.

Government tries to "civilize" Mohave

As the Mohave mourned the loss of their ancient homeland, the government set about "civilizing" and educating them in white ways. Schools and churches were built, and the Native people were instructed in modern farming techniques. Between 1870 and 1890 the Mohave were plagued by disease and poverty. Improved irrigation methods brought some prosperity in the twentieth century, but much of the traditional culture has been lost over the years.

An elderly Mohave man.

RELIGION

The Mohave believe they were sent forth from Spirit Mountain (Mt. Newberry in Nevada) by their spiritual guides, Mutavilya and Mastamho, to be Earth's caretakers. Mutavilya is said to have built a Great Dark House, the place where the first Mohave dreamers received knowledge from their spirit guides.

The Mohave have always relied upon dreams for spiritual guidance and knowledge. All the talents, skills, and successes they enjoy in life are thought to be received in ordinary dreams. Great dreams would come only to a few chiefs, braves, healers, and singers, who had to perform great deeds to show their dreams were real. According to Mohave beliefs, these great dreams occurred first in the womb, were forgotten, and then reoccurred in adolescence. There were few religious ceremonies among the Mohave; religious expression was demonstrated mainly through the singing of songs. (See "Oral literature.")

The Mohave did not believe in heaven. They believed that four days after a body was cremated (burned), the spirit went to the land of the dead, where the ghost was met by deceased relatives. A pleasant, pain-free period followed, with plenty of good things to eat. The soul then died again and was cremated by other ghosts, repeating the cycle until, eventually, the soul turned to charcoal in the desert. The Mohave who had not been tattooed in life were thought to pass down a rat hole at death.

Religious leaders, called the "one who is good," gave feasts and hosted victory celebrations. Their importance declined after European contact, when public religious ceremonies began to vanish in Mohave life.

Christian missionaries came to the reservations to convert the Mohave at the beginning of the twentieth century. The first Presbyterian church was built in 1914, and many other groups have had an influence on the tribe since then. Religious denominations with followers on the reservations include the Catholics, Pentecostals, Mormons, and Jehovah's Witnesses. A small number of Mohave still practice the Native religion.

LANGUAGE

The Mohave are regarded as the first speakers of the Yuman language. In 1997 about 5 percent of Fort Mohave tribal members still spoke the language; the figure at the Colorado River Indian Reservation was 15 percent. In addition to English, many tribal members speak Spanish. Efforts to revive the Native language have been undertaken by Fort Mohave's Aha Makav Cultural Society.

GOVERNMENT

The Mohave did not have a formal government, but they felt themselves to be a unified tribe and came together to form a cooperative defense against enemies. Very long ago the position of head chief was claimed by a man who had special power bestowed on him in a dream, but at some point in the tribe's history the chief position became hered-

Two Mohave men.

itary, that is, passed down from father to son. Even though there was a chief, no single person or group held a great deal of power over any other. The tribal chief served mainly as an overseer, looking after tribal welfare and providing an example of proper behavior to his people. During wartime he was in charge of the war chiefs chosen by him.

The last Mohave chief died in 1947. Present-day Mohave reservations are governed by elected tribal councils in accordance with the Indian Reorganization Act of 1934. At the Colorado River Indian Reservation, the tribal council is advised by the Mohave Elders Standing Committee. The task of the tribal councils is complicated by the fact that, when governing, they must take into account tribal laws and the laws of the states of California, Arizona, and Nevada.

ECONOMY

Farming was the main economic activity among the Mohave. The men cleared the land and planted and tended the fields, which were then harvested by women. Unlike many other Native groups, among

the Mohave private ownership of property was recognized. A piece of land that was not already in use was simply taken over, cleared, and planted; it was then considered private property. In years when the Colorado River did not rise high enough to flood their fields, the Mohave became dependent on hunting, fishing, and gathering food.

On the reservations the Mohave endured poverty and hardship when the federal government was slow to deliver on promises of improved irrigation techniques. When a reliable system was introduced in the early twentieth century, the economy began to improve.

Farming remains the major source of income for the Mohave, with cotton, alfalfa, wheat, feed grains for livestock, lettuce, and melons being their major crops. The Mohave attained a higher standard of living beginning in the 1960s when they started leasing reservation lands to development corporations and farming operations. Unemployment on the reservations remained extremely high at the end of the twentieth century, with 41 percent of job seekers at Fort Mohave and 25 percent of job seekers at the Colorado River reservation unable to find work. The opening of casinos in the 1990s was expected ease the unemployment situation by providing jobs and income.

DAILY LIFE

Families

Families usually consisted of seven or eight persons, including parents, children, and other relatives. Families that were related to each other through the male line might settle for a time near one another, but the Mohave tended to move about frequently.

Buildings

During most of the year the Mohave lived in single-family, open-sided, flat-roofed structures that provided shade more than shelter. Winter homes were low, sloping, rectangular structures made of arrowweed attached to poles and covered with mud. A low door on the eastern side of the dwelling served as both an entrance and an escape hole for smoke from indoor fires. Although they lived along the Colorado River, the Mohave did not build boats or canoes.

Clothing and adornment

The Mohave were big-boned, exceptionally tall, and physically stronger than any other tribe in the United States. The desert region where they lived was subject to extremes of heat and cold, and when it was hot the Mohave wore little or no clothing. Men sometimes wore narrow breechcloths, garments with front and back flaps that hung from the waist. Women might wear front and back aprons or short skirts woven from the fibrous inner layer of willow bark.

Blankets of rabbit skin or badger skin provided warmth in the evenings and the cold weather, and badger skin sandals were used to protect the feet during travel. Both men and women wore their hair in bangs over the forehead. Women let their hair hang long in back, while the men twisted theirs into many thin strands. Both sexes took pride in their long, glossy black hair, frequently cleaning it by plastering it with a mixture of mud and boiled mesquite bark. Both sexes painted their faces, and body tattooing was common.

Modern-day Mohave men often wear a pair of overalls, a painted tight-fitting undershirt and a bright handkerchief around the neck. Creative glass bead adornments are common among Mohave women.

Food

PLANT LIFE The Mohave lived in small farming communities scattered in clusters along the bottomlands of the lower Colorado River. The region's vegetation consisted of piñon (pine nut) trees, desert shrubs, cactus, mesquite shrubs, and screwbeans (the spiral-shaped pod of the screwbean tree). In the river bottoms grew arrowweed, cottonwoods, cane, and willows. The sandy earth sloping upward from the river supported cacti and creosote bushes (pronounced *KREE-uh-sote*; evergreen desert shrubs).

More than one-half of the food consumed by the Mohave people was grown by them. Their crops included corn, melons, pumpkins, gourds, beans, sunflowers, grasses, and herbs. They also grew tobacco and cotton. Men punched holes in the moist river soil using a planting stick with a wedge-shaped point. Women followed, dropping seeds in each hole and covering them with soil by hand. No fertilization was necessary because flooding enriched the soil. After harvesting, crops not used immediately were dried in the sun and stored in huge baskets.

ANIMAL LIFE Scarce food and water forced wildlife to roam widely, and the Mohave rarely saw big game. They hunted an occasional deer, a project that required a profound understanding of life in the desert and a keen eye. When a deer was caught, the hunter traded it to other Mohave for fish and farm products because it was considered bad luck for him to eat his own kill. Mostly, though, meat came from rabbits, rodents, and river fish. The Mohave broiled bland mullett or humpfish on hot coals or prepared them with corn as a stew.

Sometimes communal rabbit drives were held. The Mohave occasionally relied on insects, snakes, and lizards for food when game was scarce, or they burrowed for nourishing roots.

Education

There was little pressure placed on children to learn because it was believed that skills and talents came through dreaming. Children spent much time in play activities, often imitating adult behavior.

Once the Mohave were on reservations, the U.S. government took over the schooling of the children. Boarding schools were built for Native youth with the intention of doing away with their connections to their culture. Children were forbidden to speak their Native language and were even given new "American" names. By the end of the twentieth century a few Mohave reservation children were still attending government-run boarding schools, but most children were enrolled in area public schools.

Healing practices

A medicine man's power came from dreams, which were sent before birth or in early childhood by Tinyam, "The Night." Tinyam would stand beside the young child and provide instruction on how to perform certain cures. Mohave medicine men were specialists; that is, each could only cure one type of illness. Evil medicine men could cause illness.

The curing specialist might blow breath or spit on a patient with a fever, or suck a swollen part of the ill person's body to release the evil. The identity of an evil medicine man who had caused an illness usually came to the patient in a dream. In the early days relatives of sick people sometimes killed a medicine man who was thought to have caused an illness. Some medicine men welcomed such a death, because they believed a special fate would be theirs if they died violently.

Mohave medicine men had a great mistrust for white remedies. During the 1900s their influence all but disappeared, in part because the U.S. government discouraged their practices. Modern-day Mohave on the reservations have access to community hospitals and to hospitals operated by the Indian Health Service. The Colorado River Indian Tribes employ health experts and operate facilities on the reservation to deal with psychological problems and alcohol abuse.

Games

The Mohave apparently enjoyed gambling and games involving skill, strength, and endurance. Among these was a hoop and pole game that required a person to have both a sure aim and good judgment under pressure, since participants bet heavily on the outcome. A hoop was set rolling, then one player slid a pole along the ground, trying to calculate when the hoop would roll onto the pole and stop. Dice-like counting games were played by women, with counters made from shells.

ARTS

Petroglyphs

Petroglyphs (carvings or drawings on rock) left behind by ancient Mohave peoples can still be seen on the walls of Grapevine Canyon, the entrance to Spirit Mountain (Mt. Newberry in Nevada) where the Mohave people believe they originated. The petroglyphs tell how the Mohave came to be and record important information such as who passed through their territory and where water sources were located.

Later Mohave seem not to have been interested in creating works of art. This may be because people's possessions were burned when they died.

Oral literature

Mohave song cycles passed along tribal history, morals, and myths, which were extremely long and complicated and full of details about time and place. For example, Mohave Bird Songs describe a travel route through the desert to the Pacific Coast—and list every type of bird encountered on the way. One song cycle could be made

up of 50 to 200 songs, and 30 cycles were sung at one time. The words to the songs came to the singer in dreams. Some song cycles required several days and nights to perform; they were often accompanied by the music of a gourd rattle or by drumming on a basket. By the 1970s there were few Mohave people left who knew how to perform the song cycles, and only fragments of the tribe's oral literature were remembered.

CUSTOMS

Festivals and ceremonies

The Mohave culture did not make use of masks or ceremonial costumes. Rituals were not used to bring about rain or crop growth, except in the very early times, when members of the tribe sometimes drank a cactus wine to bring forth rain.

Mohave   **485**

War rituals

The Mohave were warlike because their spirit guide, Mastamho, predicted that each generation would have men with war powers. Therefore, when not hunting or gathering, Mohave warriors fulfilled that prophesy by going to war. Warfare was carried on by men who had experienced "great dreams" that gave them power in battle. However, if they were needed, most Mohave men were willing to fight, whether they had had a great dream or not.

When small raids were carried out, 10 to 12 men simply went out and performed the task without ceremony or ritual. For major battles, scouts were sent ahead to stake out a route to be traveled, noting the location of water holes and enemy camps. Surprise attacks on the enemy were then made at dawn.

Mohave warriors divided into two groups: the first group were archers, who used 5-foot-long bows and arrows for long-distance fighting; the second group were clubmen, who rushed in for close fighting, using heavy clubs and sticks. Each warrior carried round shields made of hide and feathered staves (narrow pieces of wood). A fighter would plant his stave firmly in the ground and defend it to the death.

A special scalper always accompanied war expeditions, and the return of warriors was celebrated with a victory dance around enemy scalps mounted on poles. Young female prisoners were given to old men of the tribe as a way of insulting the enemy.

Running

Much of Mohave traveling took place on foot, and men were especially adept, often covering up to 100 miles a day across the desert. Running was seen as an opportunity to meditate and to escape from evil spirits; it served a practical purpose as well. Teams of relay runners could communicate the location of enemies or water holes—important knowledge for a warlike desert tribe.

Puberty and pregnancy

Unlike many other tribes the Mohave did not regard puberty and pregnancy as occasions for complicated rituals. Menstruating girls simply sat in a secluded corner of their homes, resting quietly and avoiding meat and salt. At night they were laid in a warm pit. A pregnant woman was cared for tenderly, since the unborn child would be having its first—and possibly "great"—dream, and the dream might be adversely affected if the mother were unhappy or upset.

Courtship and marriage

A Mohave man courting his future bride brought her many gifts. If the young woman accepted the man's advances, the couple simply began to live together. No ceremony was necessary to validate the marriage. The couple could live wherever they chose. They might, for example, take up residence at the bride's home with her parents until they built a home of their own. If the partners' union failed, they separated. Such "divorces" were fairly common. Most men had only one wife, although it was permissible to have more than one. Divorces and remarriages remain common in modern Mohave society.

Funerals

The funeral involved more ritual than any other Mohave ceremony. Mourners typically gathered around the dying person to sing and wail. After death, the corpse was wrapped in a blanket and burned, while mourners continued to wail and watch as the body departed to the afterworld. The person's home and personal possessions were also burned. The Mohave never again spoke the name of the dead person.

A special mourning ceremony was held for certain warriors and chiefs after the cremation. This ceremony involved a 10-hour ritual in which men in war costumes ran back and forth carrying replicas of real weapons. The special house that was built to hold the spectators at this ritual was later burned together with the replica weapons. Runners then fled to the river and jumped in for purification.

The cremation and wailing ceremony continues to be the manner in which most Mohave mourn their dead. Some personal property also continues to be burned upon a person's death.

CURRENT TRIBAL ISSUES

In the nineteenth century the Mohave gave up a large part of their homeland to the American government. At the end of the twentieth century they were being pressured by the state of California to permit the building of a radioactive waste dump in Ward Valley, a site 22 miles west of Needles in traditional Mohave territory. The Mohave and the Chemehuevi, who are also affected by the proposal, claim such a dump would contaminate the sacred Colorado River, threaten the tribes' health and livelihood, and destroy the habitat of the desert tortoise, an important tribal symbol. Furthermore, the tribes assert that the project is a violation of their rights and yet another attack by the white culture on Indian culture, lands, and futures.

Little of traditional Mohave culture remains, thanks to long-standing efforts on the part of the federal government and other well-meaning agencies to force the people to assimilate (become part of the larger American culture). However, recent efforts have been made to revitalize aspects of the culture. The tradition of running, for example, is gaining renewed meaning and popularity at Fort Mohave. Runner clans—groups of men and women who receive in dreams the desire and the power to run—have been formed at the reservation. And Ward Valley, site of the proposed waste dump, became the site of "Spirit Runs," communal relay runs with both a political and spiritual purpose.

FURTHER READING

Curtis, Edward S. *The North American Indian*. New York: Johnson Reprint Corporation, 1908.

Josephy, Alvin M., Jr. *The Indian Heritage of America*. New York: Alfred A. Knopf, 1968.

Ortiz, Alfonso, ed. *Handbook of North American Indians*, Vol. 10: *Southwest*. Washington, DC: Smithsonian Institution, 1978.

Swanton, John R. *The Indian Tribes of North America*. Washington, DC: Smithsonian, 1979.

Navajo

Name

Navajo (pronounced *NAH-vah-ho*). The name comes from a Tewa (Pueblo) Indian word meaning "cultivated fields." The Navajo call themselves Diné ("the People").

Location

The Navajo make their homes on a federal reservation called the Navajo Nation. The largest reservation in the United States, it covers more than 26,000 square miles of their former homelands in the canyons, mountains, deserts, and forests of northeastern Arizona, northwestern New Mexico, and southeastern Utah.

Population

In 1868, there were about 10,000 Navajo. In a census (count of the population) done in 1990 by the U.S. Bureau of the Census, 225,298 people identified themselves as Navajo, making the tribe the second largest in the United States.

Language family

Athabaskan.

Origins and group affiliations

Navajo accounts of their own history correspond with what scientists and historians say about Navajo ancestors moving from the far North to the Southwest over long periods of time. The Navajo traditions tell of the First World (or Black World), which is similar to that of a frigid flatland area, possibly the far north in Alaska. The Navajo Second World (or Blue-Green World) features landmarks and animal life similar to those found in western and central Canada. The Navajo Third World (or Yellow World) contains mountains and plains that resemble those on the eastern slope of the Rocky Mountains and the Southwest. The Navajo Fourth World (or Glittering World) reflects the surroundings at the Navajo Nation today in northwestern New Mexico. The Navajo have probably inhabited the Southwest for nearly a thousand years. Their closest allies were the Apache and the Pueblo (see entries).

NAVAJO

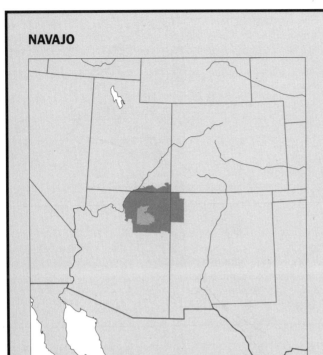

Navajo Nation today

Federal reservation—26,000 square miles of former homelands in northeastern Arizona, northwestern New Mexico, and southeastern Utah.

Darker shaded area: Navajo Nation.

Lighter shaded area: Hopi Nation, surrounded by Navajo Nation.

Once a group whose fierce warriors struck fear in the hearts of their enemies, the Navajo are a mysterious, complex people who have maintained more of their culture than most other tribes. Today, the majority of Navajo are under the age of thirty, and nine out of ten tribal members inhabit reservation lands. Although the people live a variety of lifestyles and work at many different sorts of jobs, they value their traditions and strive to keep alive the ancient Navajo ways.

HISTORY

Outside influences

The Navajo may have arrived in the American Southwest as early as the eleventh century. Until around 1650, the people were mainly hunters and gatherers who noted the practices of other societies and adopted those that they thought would be useful to them.

The Spaniards came to the land of the Navajo in the seventeenth century and tried to convert the Indians to the Spanish way of life. From around 1650 to 1775, the Navajo learned from both the Spanish and the Pueblo how to farm corn, herd sheep, weave wool, and work silver. The Spanish also taught them how to grow new fruits and vegetables, such as peaches, wheat, and potatoes, and introduced them to the cattle, sheep, and horses that over time would become so important to the Navajo way of life. By the 1600s the use of horses allowed the Navajo to travel far distances on horse raids and increase the scope of their trading. But very few Navajo were converted to the Catholic religion of the Spanish, perhaps because the Indians resented the fact that many of the Spanish showed disrespect for the Native culture.

Beginning in the late 1600s the Navajo moved westward into lands in what are now New Mexico and Arizona. This was done in response to hostilities with Comanche and Ute tribes (see entries) and Spaniards who lived on three sides of their territory. The Navajo did not like the customs of the Spanish, who fought with the Indians and sometimes took them as slaves. The tribe joined with the Pueblo and Apache to fight off the Spanish. Around 1750, the Navajo established a fortified town in Canyon de Chelly (pronounced *SHAY*). The next several decades were marked by the development of the arts and intricate ceremonies.

U.S. government deals with "Navajo problem"

Even though they were becoming mainly farmers and herders, the Navajo sometimes raided neighboring societies. This was usually because they could find no other way to feed themselves after a crop failure, they needed more horses and other livestock, or they sought the return of their children who had been captured for the slave trade.

In the early 1800s, the original Spanish colonists in the Southwest rebelled against Spain and founded the modern nation of Mexico. Although they claimed the northern territory where the Navajo lived as their own, most Mexicans lived further south. Then the United States took possession of most of the Southwest in 1848, as a result of the Treaty of Guadalupe-Hidalgo, which ended the Mexican-American

IMPORTANT DATES

1626: Spanish first encounter the Navajo people.

1864: The devastating Long Walk, a forced removal from their homelands, leads the Navajo to a harsh exile at Bosque Redondo.

1868: The Navajo reservation is established by treaty with the United States, and the people return from Bosque Redondo.

1923: The Navajo unify under a tribal council.

1941–45: Navajo Code Talkers send and receive secret messages in their Native language, making a major contribution to the U.S. war effort during World War II.

1974: The U.S. Congress passes the Navajo-Hopi Land Settlement Act, which establishes a Joint-Use Area and requires the relocation of individual tribe members to the their own tribal lands.

Navajo memorial to the Bosque Redondo, "Long Walk," beside the Pecos River, Ft. Sumner, New Mexico.

War (1846–48). At first the Americans made an effort to establish a treaty-based relationship with the Navajo. However, the Americans mistakenly assumed that the leaders of the Navajo bands (headmen) who signed various treaties represented all Navajo people. In fact, each headman actually represented only his own band.

When bands that had not signed treaties continued to raid, the Americans thought their agreements had been violated. Over time, the Navajo disputed with America over land, lies were told on both sides, and people, both white and Indian, were killed. In 1864, the U.S. government decided to settle the "Navajo problem" once and for all, and adopted an-all out policy of subduing the entire Navajo population. Kit Carson, an early frontiersman, guide, and Indian fighter, was brought in to lead American troops. Rather than engaging in military battles, Carson and his army proceeded through the Navajo lands, taking Navajo's livestock and burning their homes and crops. In the process, some women and children were molested, and some of the captured women were sold into slavery. Finally, Carson's troops attacked Canyon de Chelly, crushing most of the remaining Navajo resistance. Thousands of nearly starving Navajo surrendered.

The Long Walk

During 1864, 8,000 Navajo were resettled at a place called Bosque (pronounced *BOSK*) Redondo near Fort Sumner in east central New Mexico. They made the 300-mile journey on foot, a terrible event that has become known as the Long Walk. Those who could not keep up were either taken into slavery or were shot by military guards. People who complained of illness, including women soon to give birth, were also shot. More than 2,000 died during the forced march.

Once they arrived at the 40-square-acre reservation at Fort Sumner, the brokenhearted Navajo found the land unsuitable for growing adequate food. The water was bad, firewood was in short supply, and they suffered from plagues of insects. On this land where farming was impossible, the Navajo were expected to become farmers. They also fell victim to raids by their Indian enemies. More than 2,000 more Navajo died at Bosque Redondo from starvation and diseases.

During their period of exile at Bosque Redondo, survived by only about half of the Navajo, hundreds of people escaped and returned to their homelands to join the thousands of fellow tribesmen who had remained free. While hiding on their lands, the people grew crops, gathered wild foods, and raised livestock, confident that in time the others would come home from the Long Walk. They built homes and planted gardens, trying to reestablish their former way of life before their kinsmen returned.

The U.S. government did little to help the sick and dying Navajo until a Santa Fe newspaper wrote about the terrible conditions on the reservation and the American public protested. In time, the U.S. government admitted that the resettlement had been a terrible mistake. In 1868 Congress created a reservation within the original Navajo homelands, and invited Navajo people to return from Bosque Redondo. But they were only permitted to return to an area called "Treaty Reservation," a section of land that was only 10 percent of their former lands. This land was then surrounded by non-Indians who had moved in while the Navajo were gone and established towns and trading posts. Before long, the Santa Fe Railroad brought even more whites to the area.

The four Navajo reservations

The 3.5-million-acre Navajo Nation reservation established by the U.S. government was expanded over time by additional grants of land. The reservation is now the largest Indian reservation in the United States, includes more than 17 million acres and is about equal to the size of West Virginia.

After their departure from Bosque Redondo, three bands of Navajo chose to settle apart from the main tribe. These bands established three small, isolated offshoot reservations in western New Mexico. Today, more than 5,000 Navajo live on the Ramah Reservation, the Cañoncito Reservation, and the Alamo Reservation. The vast Navajo Nation boasts spectacular scenery, but not much of the land is useful for farming or grazing.

Life in the twentieth century

Coal and oil were first found on the Navajo Nation around 1920, and the Navajo have made some money from these resources.

Many Navajo volunteered for military service in World War I (1914–18). In 1924 all Indians were granted U.S. citizenship in large part due to the services Indian soldiers performed during the First World War. The Navajo made a very important contribution during World War II (1939–45). Men called Navajo Code Talkers (see box)

THE NAVAJO CODE TALKERS

After Japan bombed Pearl Harbor, Hawaii, on December 7, 1941, the U.S. government declared war on Japan and entered World War II (1939–45). It was discovered that the Japanese were eavesdropping on the U.S. Marines and decoding all their secret coded messages. In early 1942, a white man who had been brought up at the Navajo Nation suggested that the military could use Navajo men to devise unbreakable codes. This was because other than 50,000 Navajo, not more than 30 other people in the world knew the Navajo language—and none of them were Japanese.

Young Navajo men were recruited as Code Talkers. Because the Navajo language lacked words for modern military terms, Navajo Code Talker Carl Gorman and others worked out a two-tier code in which English military words were represented by different Navajo words. For example, various kinds of planes were represented by Navajo words for different kinds of birds. When the Japanese finally figured out the Marine radio operators were speaking Navajo, they tried to force a captured soldier who spoke the language to translate. But he could not do so. Although he could figure out that a term such as *chay-da-gahi* meant turtle, he didn't know that "turtle" meant "tank" to the code talkers.

The young Navajo soldiers proved to be adept at night scouting and were terrific undercover fighters. They lived off the land in Japan, and made stew from chickens, goats, and horses they killed with their sling shots. It is ironic that the Navajo, who at one time were forbidden to speak their own language by the Bureau of Indian Affairs, used that language to help the United States win the war. In 1982, President Ronald Reagan proclaimed August 14 as National Navajo Code Talkers Day. Most of the Code Talkers who are still alive do not partake in celebrations, however, as they do not believe in glorifying war.

used the Navajo language to send secret messages to branches of the American military. Their messages baffled the enemy Japanese codebreakers. Survivors of the 420 men who served in this way with the U.S. Marines remain among the most respected elders of the modern Navajo Nation.

The Navajo-Hopi land dispute

Ever since the founding of their reservations, the Navajo and Hopi have been engaged in a land dispute. The original Navajo Nation authorized by Congress included only ten percent of the tribe's original land. The Hopi reservation was created adjoining the Navajo Nation in 1882, and in 1934 Congress expanded the Navajo reservation so that it completely surrounded the Hopi reservation. Each tribe thought that land given to the other was rightfully their own.

In 1962, a federal court ruling established an area surrounding the Hopi land as a Joint Use Area (JUA) for both tribes. The discovery of oil and coal in the JUA made the tribes more interested in clearly defining ownership. When the U.S. Congress passed the Navajo-Hopi Settlement Act in 1974, it authorized the division of the JUA between the two tribes and required people living on the other tribe's land to relocate (this applied to nearly 10,000 Navajo). Thousands of people voluntarily moved, but many became separated from their extended families and relocated to suburban-area homes where they could not find work. In time, one-third of them lost their new homes.

After a long delay, the matter neared a resolution in 1997. The Navajo still living on Hopi land were permitted to stay in their homes if they signed a non-renewable, 75-year lease and agreed to live under Hopi regulations. The choice was a difficult one for the Navajo because of spiritual ties, the fact that they would be obliged to ask for Hopi permission to conduct many of their ceremonies, and because they would not be allowed to bury their dead on the leased land. Still, most Navajo signed the lease in March 1997. But the long dispute disrupted many lives and further strained relations between the two tribes.

At the end of the twentieth century, the Navajo educational system, economy, and government have grown strong despite some leaders who misused tribal money. Young Navajo continue to learn their language and participate in tribal ceremonies, and their ancient culture is being preserved.

RELIGION

The Navajo religion helps the people strive for harmony with nature and with other people. The Navajo see the universe as orderly. Everything in it, no matter how tiny or insignificant, has an important place.

Among the Navajo gods are many Holy People, including Changing Woman (who created the People from cornmeal and flakes of skin that had fallen away from her own body), Spider Woman (who taught the People to weave), Talking God (who showed the People how to build their houses), and Coyote (an occasionally helpful, clever prankster whose tricks provide many lessons). Ceremonies called "Blessing Ways" are given in thankfulness for a long and happy life, or to celebrate the occasion of a new house or a new marriage.

Mountain Earth bundles are the most important ceremonial objects. They are made of tanned, undamaged buckskin that is taken from a deer suffocated during a special ritual. The bundle contains small pouches of soil and other items that have been brought from the top of each of the four sacred mountains that surround the Navajo homeland.

Navajo Christians

The Roman Catholic missionaries in the 1600s were only the first of various Christian groups that tried to convert the Navajo to their faith. In the late 1860s and 1870s, Presbyterians and Mormon missionaries were a presence on the reservation. In the 1890s, Catholic priests began a mission, St. Michael's, and later opened a mission school that became a center for studying the Navajo religion, language, and way of life. In time, other Protestant denominations also began churches and schools and many Navajo became Christians.

Present-day Navajo often combine Christianity with their traditional religious beliefs and practices. About 25,000 Navajo are members of the Native American Church, which was formed in 1918 by followers of the Peyote (pronounced *pay-O-tee*) religion who had developed an intricate belief system embracing traditional Native American values and visions of the spiritual world attained through the use of dreams, prayers, and rituals and the peyote plant. Thousands more participate in its peyote ceremonies without claiming membership in the church. Peyote is a substance that comes from cactus; when it is consumed, it causes the taker to go into a trance-like state and see visions. The use of peyote was prohibited on the Navajo Nation for twenty-seven years, until its religious use was legalized by the tribal council in 1967.

LANGUAGE

Navajo, along with six Apache dialects (varieties), makes up the southwestern branch of the Athabaskan language family. The language includes sounds from the natural world and pronunciation requirements are very strict. Spoken Navajo has a mechanical flavor about it that almost sounds like the talk of a robot. Language experts say that the only people who can pronounce Navajo perfectly are the native-born.

The Navajo believe that some words have the power to ward off evil, while others are so dangerous that only special persons under specific conditions can speak them. Unlike many other tribes, the Navajo rarely add words from other languages into their vocabulary. Instead, they use combinations of traditional terms to describe new objects or events. For example, the Navajo word for "elephant" literally means "one that lassoes with his nose." They call an automobile a "chuggi," which sounds like a car's engine, and gasoline is described as "car's water."

GOVERNMENT

Until modern times, the tribe had no overall structure. It was made up of small, independent bands headed by chiefs or headmen. The discovery of coal and oil on the Navajo Nation in about 1920 made it necessary for the tribe to organize in a new, modern way. The Navajo Business Council was founded in 1922 by the U.S. government to grant oil and mineral leases in the name of the Navajo Nation, but many of the leases granted were not favorable to the Navajo.

In 1938 the Navajo rejected the Indian Reorganization Act (IRA), which would have given them a federally structured tribal government and constitution. Instead, they held their own constitutional convention, with the federal government's permission. The Navajo wrote a constitution that would give them independence from the federal Bureau of Indian Affairs (BIA). The U.S. government rejected this plan and instead formed a new Navajo Business Council. This council was composed of 74 elected Navajo members and became known as the "Rule of 1938." This was the basis for the present Navajo Tribal Council.

Navajo Tribal Government Center, Window Rock, Arizona.

ECONOMY

Farming and ranching

Traditionally, the Navajo were farmers who did not irrigate their fields. Their seeds could be sustained by underground water. But farming methods have changed. In the 1960s, Congress approved the Navajo Irrigation Implementation Project (NIIP). The system made use of canals, pipelines, pumping stations, and sprinklers to irrigate crops. The water needed was stored thirty miles away, behind a new dam on the San Juan River. As of the mid-1990s, a 70,000-acre tribal farm called Navajo Agricultural Products Incorporated (NAPI) was producing profitable harvests of alfalfa, pinto beans, potatoes, onions, and mushrooms. In addition to growing crops, NAPI processes and packages them.

Traditional ranching, too, has undergone changes. Since the seventeenth century, sheep herding has been a vital part of Navajo life. The sheep provided meat plus tendons that were used to make bows and wool for clothing and weaving. During the late 1930s an extreme

A Navajo family at the blanket loom.

drought made the central and southern United States so dry the affected area was called the "dust bowl." At this time, the U.S. government decided that the Navajo were raising too many sheep and that their grazing would cause soil erosion, by stripping plant cover off topsoil, which would then dry out and blow away. Agents of the Agricultural Department killed tens of thousands of Navajo sheep. For several decades after this, relations between the Navajo and the U.S. government were hostile. During the twentieth century, cattle raising has largely replaced sheep herding on the reservation.

Other sources of income

Today, the Navajo Nation gains income by leasing out its land for gas and oil drilling, and through coal mining, forestry, and the operation of seven industrial parks. In the mid-1990s, the Navajo Oil and Gas Company was planning its own oil refinery. Manufacturing businesses on reservation lands produce wood products, circuit boards, locomotive computers, modems, and other computer products. More than 250 trade operations, including shopping centers and banks, also operate on the reservation, and construction workers are employed building new homes and buildings there.

Navajo weavers command good prices for their handmade woolen rugs, belts, and blankets. Navajo trading posts sell crafts objects such as silver work, an art form they learned from the Mexicans. Navajo artisans make silver bracelets, rings, earrings, necklaces, and belts that are decorated with the handsome blue stone called turquoise.

Service businesses make substantial profits from the more than 800,000 annual visitors who come to the reservation. Several resort facilities operate there, including the Chinle Holiday Inn and the Navajo Nation Inn in Window Rock. In 1997 the tribe entered into a partnership with the U.S. National Park Service to develop a new resort and marina complex at Antelope Point on Lake Powell.

DAILY LIFE

Families

Navajo family units were made up of two or more families centered on a mother and her daughters. The unit was bound together

Navajo log hogan, Canyon de Chelly, Arizona.

by ties of marriage and close relationships. Women held an important social position.

Navajo society is based on clans (groups of people who claimed descent from a common ancestor). Some clans trace their origins to creation by the Holy People. The original clans were Towering House, Bitterwater, Big Water, and One-who-walks-around. Other clans arose when new groups chose to become Navajo. Each Navajo person is associated with four different, unrelated clans.

Among the Navajo, a person's ancestry is traced through the mother's side of the family and it determines the clan to which a person belongs. A child must marry outside his or her clan. Navajo relationships are often hard for outsiders to understand as the people have unfamiliar terms or groups of words for aunts, uncles, cousins, and other relatives.

Buildings

Traditional Navajo houses are called hogans. The older versions, built around a wooden post frame, were cone-shaped. Beginning in the mid-1800s, log cabins with beehive-shaped log roofs became more popular. Usually the roofs, and sometimes the walls, were covered with packed earth, and a smoke hole was left at the center of the roof. When wood was scarce, hogans could be built of stones held together with mud mortar.

In recent years, modern-style cinderblock houses have become more popular, and family homes usually include several additional structures. There are corrals made of brush, open-walled work spaces with flat roofs, and storage structures or dugouts. Usually a sweat lodge, built like a small version of the old, conical hogans, sits nearby in a secluded spot, since curing ceremonies can only be conducted in the traditional structure. Newly built hogans are sprinkled with corn pollen or meal, and prayers are offered to ensure they will be places of happiness. According to legend, the first hogans were built by the Holy People from such precious materials as turquoise, jet, or shell. Now, as then, hogan doors must face eastward, toward the rising sun. Navajo families often have two homes: one to live in during the cold winter months, and one to stay in while farming in the summer.

Clothing and adornment

Early Navajo clothed themselves in breechcloths (flaps of material that cover the front and back and are suspended from the waist), leggings, skirts, and blankets woven from the yucca plant or cedar bark, or made of fur. Animal skins were used to make moccasins with braided yucca soles.

By the early seventeenth century, the men were clothing themselves in tanned buckskin, while the women wore dresses made of newer fabrics, often wool. By the time of the Long Walk, their clothing had become quite colorful. Some men wore knee-length buckskin pants decorated with brass and silver buttons along the outer seams, and woolen leggings dyed blue and decorated with bright red garters. Women's ankle-length dresses, fashioned from two woven panels and sewn together along the sides and over both shoulders, were belted at the waist with a red woven sash. Women also wore leggings made by wrapping strips of dyed buckskin around the legs from ankle to knee; these were decorated with silver buttons.

During the late nineteenth century and early twentieth century, women usually wore long, full skirts of cotton with bright blouses, often made of velveteen fabric. Men usually wore blue jeans, colorful shirts (sometimes of velveteen), and boots; belts decorated with decorative silver disks, and headbands made of rolled kerchiefs. Both men and women have traditionally worn their hair long, wound into an hourglass shape at the base of the neck, and bound with wool string. Silver and turquoise necklaces, earrings, and bracelets have long been popular with both men and women.

Food

When they first moved to the Southwest between the ninth and twelfth centuries, the Navajo got their food by hunting and by gathering wild vegetation. Before long, they learned from the Pueblo Indians how to grow crops like corn, beans, and squash. The Spanish, who came in the 1600s, taught the Indians to grow wheat and oats, and herd sheep and goats. By the time of their exile to Bosque Redondo, the Navajo commonly ate mutton (sheep meat), corn, frybread (plate-sized disks of bread that are fried in hot fat), and coffee laced with sugar and goat's milk. Corn was usually picked early to avoid frost damage, husked, ripened, sun dried, removed from the cob, and stored in bags for later use. Fresh corn served as a special treat. The people often ate a cooked mush made from cornmeal or wild seed meal mixed with water or goat's milk. The substance was used in the preparation of many types of foods. The addition of garden vegetables and meat—prairie dog continues to be a favorite—made the mush into a well-balanced meal.

Education

For centuries, Navajo children learned the skills required to become adult members of the tribe by observing their parents and members of their extended families. During the nineteenth century, various efforts to start white-style schools for Navajo children met with great opposition from the Navajo people. They saw the schools as a threat to the Navajo way of life and the Navajo family. Some children were taken away from their parents on the reservation and sent to boarding schools where they were taught to speak and dress like whites. During World War II (1939-45) many families lived off the reservation to take advantage of work opportunities, and their children attended public schools.

Today, the Navajo Nation's educational facilities include state schools that serve grades K–12, as well as several Bureau of Indian Affairs boarding schools. Diné Community College (formerly Navajo Community College) at Tsaile, Arizona, along with its five branch campuses, offers students a choice of a variety of courses of study.

Healing practices

For the Navajo, sicknesses are an indication of disharmony. Curing ceremonies are designed to treat the cause of the ailment rather than the symptoms. When a person gets sick, he or she normally goes to a person called a stargazer or hand trembler, who tells the patient the cause of the illness. The stargazer then recommends that the person see a special medicine person and take part in a particular ceremony. Illnesses can be caused by the accidental or intentional breaking of one of the society's many taboos (see "Taboos" in "Customs"), by contact with a ghost, or by the spell of a witch.

The medicine person recommended by the stargazer is known as a *Hataali* ("singer"). The Hataali conducts a ceremony in which both the patient and his or her relatives participate. The ceremony may last as many as nine nights and include the performance of more than 500 separate songs. Sometimes the singer is assisted by dancers who wear masks representing appropriate spirits, called *Yeis*. A sand painting, created during the ritual, is destroyed at the completion of the ceremony. (Sand painting is a Navajo and Pueblo tradition in which sands of different colors are used to create a ceremonial design.) During a ceremony the healer may employ objects with special powers, medicines made from plants, and lengthy prayers. Ideally, curing rituals are followed by the singing of the Blessing Way, a prayer to restore harmony that has been called the backbone of the Navajo healing system.

In modern times, with the breakdown of some of the traditional, family- and clan-based educational systems, Diné Community College and other institutions have begun to teach Native healing arts. At the Medicine Man School in Rough Rock, Arizona, aspiring singer-healers are taught their trade from experienced healers. The students learn during actual ceremonies because it is thought to be wrong to address the spirits without a genuine need for healing or blessings.

Navajo medicine man at a dedication ceremony for a new hospital at Fort Defiance, Arizona, 1938.

Because the training period cannot be scheduled and the ceremonies are complex, it can take four to six years to learn one of the longer rituals. Each singer is trained in a specialty that includes being able to perform between one and six different ceremonies. Although women are permitted to become singers, they rarely do. This may be because they fear that some event or spirit the woman could encounter could affect a child she might later bear.

Today, Indian Health Service hospitals on the reservation have special rooms where medicine men can conduct traditional curing ceremonies. This new spirit of cooperation between modern and traditional medical people is bringing more Navajo people in for treatment. Medicine men display a knowledge of the use of native herbs for birth control, mild diabetes, and seizures.

ARTS

Craftwork

Navajo women in traditional times were known for their excellent pottery, including ladles, jars with pointed bottoms, and variously shaped decorated bowls. They also made coiled baskets, food containers, and water bottles. The women learned to weave from the Pueblo people and produced rugs and blankets with intricate, unique designs, colored with natural dyes.

CUSTOMS

Taboos

The Navajo believe that the sacred order of the world must be maintained if one is to avoid illness or other misfortunes. This is accomplished, in part, by observing a large assortment of taboos (forbidden things or acts). Here are a few of the thousands of actions or acts that are forbidden: lightning-struck trees are not to be touched; coyotes, bears, snakes, and some kinds of birds must never be killed; people are never to comb their hair at night; no one must ever step over the body of another person sleeping in a hogan, no matter how crowded it may be. Certain people, such as pregnant women and their husbands, or a person who has recently undergone a curing ritual, may have to observe even more taboos.

Puberty

Young girls undergo one of the oldest ceremonies of the Navajo culture, the "kinaaldá." The two-day ritual takes place after a girl's first menstrual period and is designed to teach her lessons she will need in adult life. The girl must perform several exhausting runs to assure her physical conditioning and endurance. In addition, she must grind by hand at least some of the cornmeal and wheat she will use to prepare a traditional cake; in the process, she is accompanied by the chanted prayers of a medicine man. Near the end of the ceremony, a female relative massages the girl's body to make it more beautiful. Then the girl prays over a group of young children that have been brought to her. Following the ritual, she is accepted into the community as an adult and is considered ready for marriage.

Ceremonies and festivals

Rituals were developed by the Navajo in ancient times to cope with the dangers and uncertainties of the universe. The Navajo have been able to preserve their traditional beliefs and practices in the face of long-time pressure from white culture.

Many Navajo ceremonies are healing rituals used for many types of physical and emotional imbalances and problems of social maladjustment. The most commonly held ceremony may be the War Dance, which has the official name of The Enemyway. It is a three-day ceremony held in summer that comes from the legend of Changing Woman's twin sons, who went to see their father, the Sun, to seek his help in slaying the monsters who inhabit the earth so they could make it safe for the Navajo people. The Enemyway sounds like a ceremony to get ready for war, but it actually is a way for a patient to be rid of the effects of some "enemy." For example, it is held for people who feel weak or faint from the sight of blood or who have scary dreams. The ceremony involves the use of a Rattle Stick, a piece of juniper about eighteen inches long that is carved with meaningful designs. Burnt herbs and melted wax are placed on the stick and on the face of the afflicted, and a complicated ceremony follows, ending with the "killing" of the enemy ghost and a scattering of his ashes, followed by a big feast and final dance.

Throughout the year, a number of fairs, festivals, and rodeos are held at various sites around the reservation. As part of their ceremonies, the people make use of sand painting, singing, dancing by masked impersonators of Holy People, and the use of cornmeal, corn pollen, feathered prayer sticks, and bundles containing sacred items.

Each year more than 100,000 people attend the Navajo Nation Fair, a five-day festival that takes place in Window Rock, Arizona, the capital of the Navajo Nation. The fair features a celebration of Navajo traditions centering on the sacredness of food. It also offers art, craftworks, and the performance of chants, dances, and stories.

Courtship and marriage

Relatives usually arrange Navajo marriages after the boy reaches the proper age. Often an expensive gift (sheep or horses) is given to the girl's family by the family of the boy. When a couple marries, the grandmother of the bride presents the new couple with a basket of cornmeal at the wedding site. Then the bride and groom exchange a pinch of cornmeal, from which they receive the strength and blessing of the spirit world.

Newly married couples usually build their houses near the wife's mother's home. This permits the wife and children to have close contact with the maternal grandmother. But a large space is left between the homes, because it is forbidden for a man to look at or speak to his mother-in-law.

Funerals

The Navajo feared dead persons and ghosts. Immediately upon the death of a family member, close relatives began mourning by weeping and wailing, cutting their hair, and putting on old clothing. Elderly relatives washed the hair and body and dressed the deceased in fine clothes. Burial took place in the daytime, and as soon as possible. The corpse was placed on a horse along with many personal possessions and was taken far away, possibly to the hill country. A crevice in the rocks that could be covered with brush served as a grave. The horse was killed at the grave site, because the dead person would need it in the afterworld.

Those who accompanied the body returned home and burned their own clothing. Then all the mourners burned sage, or some other strong-smelling plant, and bathed in the smoke. Ashes were scattered around the camp to discourage the return of the dead one. The remaining personal possessions were broken or burned, and nothing was kept that would remind the living of the dead person. The name of the deceased was never mentioned again. The building in which the death occurred was moved to another site. For a time, the mourning relatives did not participate in social events.

CURRENT TRIBAL ISSUES

A current Navajo land ownership issue revolves around a 7,000-square-mile area known as the Checkerboard. When railroads were being built in the late 1800s, alternating sections in this region were granted to the railroad companies. Federal programs in the early twentieth century further fragmented lands in the area. At present, nearly 30,000 Navajo live in the Checkerboard. The tribe is making efforts to trade or buy land so that larger, more useful parcels can be created.

NOTABLE PEOPLE

Navajo Peterson Zah (1937–), once a teacher on his reservation, served for ten years as executive director of an organization to help poor Native people. He has served as chief executive officer of the Navajo Nation government and chief fundraiser for the Navajo Education and Scholarship Foundation. In 1988, he founded a private firm that provided educational services to school districts on and off the reservation and worked to secure funds for new school construction on the Navajo and San Carlos Apache reservations.

Annie Dodge Wauneka (1910–1997), the first woman to be elected to the Navajo Tribal Council, was a strong advocate for the Navajo people in politics, economics, and health. In 1964 she became the first Native American to receive the Presidential Medal of Freedom.

Manuelito (1818–1894) was a powerful warrior in raids against the Mexicans, Hopi, and Zuñi, and rose to prominence within his band. Of all the resistant Navajo bands, Manuelito's held out the longest against Kit Carson's troops, who were trying to kill hostile

Navajo and relocate the rest to Bosque Redondo. Faced with army pursuit and starvation, Manuelito surrendered with his remaining warriors. He later traveled to Washington, D.C., to petition for the return of the Navajo homelands, then successfully served as principal Navajo chief and chief of tribal police.

Over a period of seventy years, Henry Chee Dodge (c. 1857–1947) played a major role in forming a modern identity for the Navajo nation. Following the death of Manuelito, Dodge was chosen to be Navajo head chief. Under his leadership, the tribe began to actively participate with the federal government in making and carrying out policies for mineral development, land rights issues, and federal programs like school development. In 1923 he was elected chairperson of the first Navajo tribal council.

Other notable Navajo include: war chief Barboncito (c. 1820–1871); nuclear physicist and professor Fred Begay (1932–); painter Harrison Begay (1917–); artist and Navajo Code Talker Carl Nelson Gorman (1907–1998); artist R. C. Gorman (1931–); educator and tribal councilman Ned Hatathli (1923–1972); tribal chairperson Peter MacDonald (1928–); tribal leader Raymond Nakai (1918–); and award–winning poet Luci Tapahonso (1953–).

FURTHER READING

Dutton, Bertha P. *Indians of the American Southwest*. Englewood Cliffs, NJ: Prentice-Hall, 1975.

Glipin, Laura. *The Enduring Navajo*. Austin, TX: University of Texas Press, 1968.

Iverson, Peter. *The Navajos*. New York: Chelsea House Publishers, 1990.

Osinski, Alice. *The Navajo*. Chicago, IL: Children's Press, 1987.

Trimble, Stephen. *The People: Indians of the American Southwest*. Santa Fe, NM: School of American Research Press, 1993.

Pima

Name

The Pima (pronounced *PEE-mah*) referred to themselves as *Akimel O'od-ham* or *Akimel Au-Authm* ("River People"). Legend has it that Spanish explorers asked several questions of the first Pima Indians they encountered. When the Natives answered their questions with the phrase "*Pi-nyi-match*" ("I do not know"), the Spanish misunderstood and thought they were saying *Pima.* Thereafter, the Spanish explorers referred to the tribespeople as Pima.

Location

The Pima were desert dwellers from various portions of the 100,000-square-mile Sonoran Desert. Those the Spanish called Upper Pimans came from southern Arizona and southeastern California; Lower Pimans inhabited western Sonora (a section of the desert that extends into Mexico). Modern-day descendants of the Upper Piman Indians live with members of the Maricopa tribe on the Gila River Reservation and the Salt River Reservation in southern Arizona. Some Pima also live on the Ak-Chin (Maricopa) Reservation in Maricopa, Arizona. (Lower Pimans are now called Tohono O'odham; see entry.)

Population

In 1694, there were an estimated 2,000 to 3,000 Pima. In a census (count of the population) conducted in 1990 by the U.S. Bureau of the Census, 15,074 people identified themselves as Pima, making the tribe the sixteenth-largest in the United States.

Language family

Uto-Aztecan.

Origins and group affiliations

The Pima believe they originated in the Salt River valley and later spread to the Gila River area. They are probably descended from the prehistoric Hohokam people (see box in Anasazi entry), whose culture had faded by about 1450. The Pima Nation shares a similar language and certain traits with tribes in Sonora, Mexico—especially with the neighboring Tohono O'odham (often called the Papago). The Pima were friends and allies of the Maricopa and enemies of the Apache and Quechan tribes, who often raided and stole from them.

PIMA

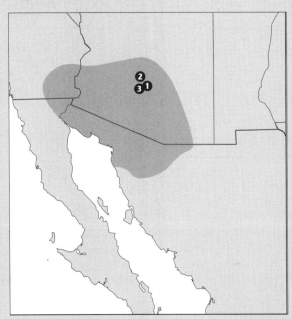

Shaded area: Traditional lands of the Pima in the Sonoran Desert in present-day southern Arizona, southeastern California, and northern Mexico.

Contemporary Communities

Arizona

1. Gila River Pima–Maricopa Indian Community
2. Salt River Pima–Maricopa Indian Community
3. Ak-Chin Indian Community

Once a primitive farming people, the Pima employed Spanish agricultural know-how and technology to become large-scale, prosperous farmers in their own right. Their newfound wealth was said to have changed them from a gentle people into warriors forced to protect their surplus crops from enemy raiders. The Pima frequently supplied produce to American settlers passing through their seemingly barren desert territory. Carrying on a tradition now hundreds of years old, the tribespeople continue to farm the arid (dry) lands of Arizona, but their difficult job has been eased somewhat by modern irrigation techniques.

HISTORY

Early encounters with the Spanish

No one knows for sure how long the Pima Indians have lived in Arizona and Mexico. By the time the Spanish encountered them in 1694, the tribespeople had adapted to the widely varying environments in their homeland, which ranged from extremely dry sections where food and water were in short supply to regions that supported crops quite well.

Historians believe that when the Spanish first encountered them, the Pima were weak, having suffered from plagues of diseases for the previous 170 years. The Pima lived in several farming communities, where people worked together to plant and harvest crops. For some time after their arrival in the New World, the Spanish were busy in other regions, trying to convert Indians to the Catholic faith and make them a useful part of the Spanish empire. Tribes such as the Pueblo rebelled against the Spanish (see Pueblo entries), but Pima participation in the revolts was minimal for three main reasons: (1) their location was remote, (2) they were busy with their farms, and (3) they had little contact with outsiders.

The Spanish government knew little about the Pima, but they approved of the tribe's industrious nature and its policy of noninvolvement in the numerous Native uprisings that occurred in the eighteenth century. Hoping to win the tribe's confidence and support, the Spanish decided to introduce some modern farming techniques to them.

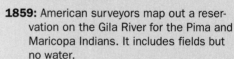

IMPORTANT DATES

1694: First contact with Spanish explorers.

1848: Pima lands become U.S. territory following the Mexican-American War.

1859: American surveyors map out a reservation on the Gila River for the Pima and Maricopa Indians. It includes fields but no water.

1871: New non-Indian settlements reduce the water supply to Pima lands, thus destroying the tribe's farms.

1879: Salt River Indian Reservation is established.

1895: Congress formally establishes the Gila River Indian Community, setting aside 375,000 acres of land for Native Americans.

Spanish innovations make prosperous farmers

The Pima reaped instant benefits from Spanish innovations. They gained a new food crop—winter wheat—and were thus able to farm year-round. After learning to grow more food by means of advanced irrigation methods, the tribe became an important economic force in the region. Years of prosperity followed.

A surplus of grain and cotton allowed the Pima to engage in trade. Their visibility in the trading community brought them to the attention of the Apache (see entry), who took note of Pima surpluses and began to raid their communities. This forced the Pima to cut down on their travel, to move into fewer, larger settlements for protection, and to sharpen their fighting skills.

In 1848, following the American victory in the Mexican-American War, the United States acquired Pima lands. The Pima hoped to learn more about farming from the Americans, but they were disap-

Pima home, 1907.

pointed when no such help was given. For their part the Pima proved to be good friends to the United States. They supplied food and live-stock to pioneers who traveled through Pima lands during the California gold rush, which began in 1848. They also helped the U.S. Army protect settlers against Apache raiders and supplied farm goods to U.S. troops. The Pima hoped to receive guns and shovels in return for their help, but they were deeply offended when U.S. government officials failed to deliver on their promises. The tribe's anger and confusion grew when the federal government—without explanation—supplied farming implements to the Pima people's traditional enemy, the Apache. (Apache Indians were not farmers and therefore were not even likely to use the implements.)

Around the same time the Apache were also raiding Maricopa Indian villages to the west, forcing the Maricopa toward Pima territory. In 1859 American surveyors plotted out the Salt River Pima-Maricopa Indian Community Reservation for both the Pima and Maricopa Indians. The reservation included only fields—no water—and the era of Pima farming wealth quickly began to fade.

"Years of famine"

The Pima economy collapsed in 1871, after the construction of a dam that diverted water from the Gila River to lands settled by whites. Some Pima moved south to a location on the Salt River; in 1879 their new settlement became the Salt River Indian Reservation.

The Pima way of life disappeared completely between 1871 and World War I (1914–18), a period the tribe remembers as the "years of famine." Those who wanted to work became dependent on wages earned performing labor for whites. Presbyterian missionaries arrived on the scene, discouraged the Pima from practicing their traditional religion, and assumed control of the education of their children. Many members of the tribe turned to alcohol for solace. Tensions within the tribe escalated. Isolated from the world and unwilling to learn English or adopt white ways, the people fell into poverty and despair.

Becoming a part of the outside world

Pima Indian contact with the outside world was almost nonexistent at the beginning of the twentieth century. Their isolation lessened somewhat after they acquired battery-powered radios and began to learn English. Some Pima men served in the U.S. military during World War II (1939–45) and returned to the reservations with a wider worldview and a determination to bring their fellow Pima into modern life. This process was further hastened by a tremendous postwar population explosion in the nearby city of Phoenix, which grew from about 107,000 people in 1945 to 790,000 people 30 years later.

Major technological advances took place in Arizona in the first half of the twentieth century. Among them were the expansion of the Southern Pacific Railroad, the building of the Roosevelt Dam on the Salt River, and other significant water projects that returned some water to the Pima. Since then the Pima have become involved in the expanding economy of the surrounding urban areas. Forward-looking Pima leaders are working hard to take on the challenges of the twenty-first century. They predict that the tribe will (1) embrace and adopt worthwhile aspects of the larger American culture, (2) modify its farming lifestyle to keep up with the competition, and (3) expand its economic base by developing nonagricultural means of support.

RELIGION

Not much is known about early Pima religious practices. According to the Pima origin story, the Earthmaker created a world that was populated by supernatural beings such as Coyote the trickster and a man-eating beast. A great flood later caused the supernatural beings to flee, but Elder Brother returned, created the Pima and their neighbors, and taught them the few arts and ceremonies they are known to have had. Like other Southwestern Indians, the Pima celebrated the corn harvest, fertility (the ability to conceive and bear children), and rainmaking.

Early Spanish Catholic missionaries had little influence on the Pima. The people accepted some Catholic rituals such as baptism but blended them in with their own traditional ceremonies. Presbyterian missionaries were much more successful. They arrived during the 1870s and had a profound effect on the Pima. By the 1890s they claimed about 1,800 Pima as members. Officials of the Catholic church returned and started the first missions among the Pima around 1900, but the tribe was not happy with this new attempt to convert them to another kind of Christianity.

LANGUAGE

The Pima speak a single dialect (variety) of the Piman language. By way of comparison, their relatives—the Tohono O'odham (see entry)—speak the same language but have maintained several distinct dialects. As longtime allies and neighbors the Pima and Maricopa traditionally have known each other's languages. In the twentieth century the Pima people began learning English.

GOVERNMENT

Long ago the Pima were a loosely organized society. Each independent farming community had a designated leader and one or more influential persons called shamans (pronounced *SHAH-menz*), who specialized in healing, controlling the weather, or ensuring success in battle. As the Pima began farming on a greater scale and interacting more with outsiders during trade and warfare, the position of leader (or governor) became increasingly important and was passed down from father to son.

The Pima people earned considerable distinction as farmers and then as soldiers. Their uncompromising work ethic and impressive organizational skills secured their title as a "nation" in the eyes of the Spanish, Mexican, and U.S. governments. The Pima Nation elected its own governor and tribal council.

The Pima of the late twentieth century lived on reservations held jointly with the Maricopa tribe, a traditional neighbor and ally. The Gila River Indian Community is governed by a 17-member elected tribal council with a governor and a lieutenant governor. The tribal council encourages and facilitates youth participation in government.

The official governing body of the Salt River tribe is the Salt River Pima-Maricopa Indian Community Council, whose seven elected members include a president and a vice-president.

ECONOMY

The Pima Indians have always been farmers. Tribal members became traders only after the Spanish arrived in the New World. Before the Pima developed their own "buying and selling" economy like that of white settlers, they had an interesting way of exchanging goods: they distributed most items as gifts. In this system of give and take, a person offered a possession to another person who had to accept it. The giver gained power or importance, and the recipient was obliged to return the gift in some way. Sometimes the presenter used lines to mark the value of a gift. For example, when presenting grains or beans in a basket, lines were drawn on the basket marking how high up the sides the grain or beans came. This ensured that when an item was returned in the basket, it matched or exceeded the original in worth. Merchandise also changed hands based on the outcome of games and foot races.

After contact with the Spanish, the Pima began growing winter wheat and used more elaborate irrigation methods to increase the productivity of their crops. Agricultural development supported more people and allowed the Pima to trade surplus grain with other tribes and with non-Natives. Eventually the Pima sold crops for gold and silver.

During the period of their greatest prosperity, the tribe's surplus goods made them an attractive target for Apache raiders. To get back at the Apache thieves, the Pima would sometimes kidnap and sell Apache children to the Spanish for use as slaves. They later traded wheat, baskets, and blankets to the Mexicans and to other tribes for items like hides and wild peppers—things not available in Pima homelands.

Where they had once grown only as much food as their own needs demanded, the Pima responded to increased outside demands for their grains and produce by growing more. The resulting wealth introduced the concepts of personal possessions and wealth to Pima culture. By the time they lost the water they needed to grow so many crops, the Pima had also lost the old ways of farming their land as a cooperative group and sharing the proceeds with others. Farming was not reestablished as a productive way of life for nearly a century.

The water crisis of the late 1800s and the period of famine that followed forced some Pima to turn to low-paying wage jobs and government welfare until farming became practical once again. The reservations looked to other ways of using their land, such as leasing it to outside industries—research and development companies, a brass foundry, telecommunications businesses, and manufacturing plants among them. These industries brought jobs to the reservations.

With modern irrigation techniques in place, agriculture is once again an important source of income for the Pima. In addition to their very fine Pima cotton (see box), the tribe grows wheat, millet (small-seeded cereal grasses), alfalfa, barley, melons, pistachios, olives, citrus fruits, and vegetables. The location of the reservations in prime Sunbelt territory attracts many tourists, who are drawn by artifacts offered at the Hoo-hoogam Ki Museum and the Gila Indian Center. Golf courses, a marina complex, an international racepark, and many tribal annual events are also open to the public.

DAILY LIFE

Families

Pima families included a husband and wife, their young children, the families of their married sons, and their unmarried adult daughters.

Buildings

The early Pima built a type of small, round, flat-roofed house called a *ki* (pronounced *kee*). The typical *ki* measured 10 to 25 feet in diameter. Materials such as arrowwood, cattail reeds, wheat straw, or corn stalks covered a cottonwood frame. Four posts and two main support beams propped up the roof. The support beams, in turn, braced several lighter cross poles. Light willow poles were bent in a circle around this square frame and tied to it. Dirt on top of brush or straw covered the light, domed frame. Although they often leaked, these homes could survive strong winds.

Other structures in the traditional Pima village included a rectangular council house, storehouses, a lodge for women who were menstruating, and cottonwood arbors that protected people from the heat of the sun.

Even after centuries of contact with people who lived in adobe (pronounced *uh-DOE-bee*) homes (see Pueblo entries), the tribe persisted in building the *ki* style single-family home until the late 1800s.

(Adobe is a sun-dried mud made of a mixture of clay, sand, and sometimes ashes, rocks, or straw.) The Pima began building pueblo-style adobe houses around the turn of the twentieth century, but cement-block construction later became a more popular method of construction.

Clothing and adornment

Before the Spanish arrived in Pima territory, the tribespeople wore little clothing. Men dressed in breechcloths, garments with front and back flaps that hung from the waist. Women wore skirts made of cotton or the inner part of cottonwood bark; padding under the skirts made them stand away from the body. Sandals and cotton blankets added protection and warmth when needed. Later on, Pima men began to wear Spanish clothing as a sign of their importance.

The Pima paid particular attention to hair styles, body painting, and tattooing. Men and women wore their hair long. While women wore it loose with bangs, men braided or twisted it into locks and added human or horse hair and sometimes woven headbands to produce a bulky mass they considered attractive. Frequent brushings and a dressing of river mud and mesquite gum kept the hair dark and shiny. The Pima sometimes painted their hair, faces, and bodies. Both sexes had their lower eyelids lined with tattoos, usually at the time of puberty or marriage. Men also tattooed lines across the forehead; women added lines along each side of the chin. Grease applied to the face protected against chapping.

Food

For many centuries Pima farmers used just two implements: a digging stick and a sharpened board that served as both hoe and harvester. They concentrated on farming the islands in the Gila River and the land on the surrounding floodplain. The tribe's most important crops were corn and tepary beans (pronounced *TEH-puh-ree*), supplemented with wild foods such as mesquite beans and saguaro (pronounced *suh-WAHR-uh*) cactus fruit.

Although their methods were primitive, the Pima usually met their primary food needs without having to hunt or gather. When drought or other catastrophes damaged their crops, they turned to hunting activities and searching for food to make up for the lost grains and vegetation.

Education

In early times Pima chiefs and parents were a child's primary source of knowledge. Their role was taken over by missionaries and government agents during the early reservation period, but the Pima were so impoverished at the time that they had little interest in education of any kind.

The present-day Pima recognize the importance of education and training to ensure that young people attain good, high-paying jobs. Education starts early with a Head Start program for preschoolers. There are elementary schools on the reservations, and children attend high school at public schools in nearby cities. Pima children are encouraged to attend college and return home to use the skills they acquire for the betterment of the tribe.

Healing practices

The early Pima believed that people could be made ill by behaving badly toward animals or by offending clouds or lightning. They called on shaman-healers for help. Shamans gained their powers through dream visions in which they met powerful supernatural beings. Later, they could call upon these beings to help heal the sick.

To find out what ailed a person, the shaman breathed tobacco smoke over the patient's body and sometimes used an eagle feather or crystal to connect with the spirit world. This ritual allowed the shaman to see what spirits had visited the body and harmed its health. If these steps did not work, the shaman sang to the spirits, asking them to communicate the nature of the illness. Then a curing ritual was performed.

The Pima thought of shamans as heroes, but white missionaries encouraged the people to look upon shamans with suspicion. Because of this, three shamans were blamed for causing a plague (an outbreak of disastrous illness) and were killed by the Pima. In the late twentieth century shamans had regained the respect once given them, but the number of shamans had decreased dramatically.

Modern-day Pima have become a subject of great interest to U.S. health officials. The tribespeople are apparently more likely than other Americans to contract diabetes, a disorder involving the breakdown of energy-releasing carbohydrates. In diabetic patients, a gland called the pancreas fails to produce insulin (a chemical messenger) in amounts needed to control the breakdown of sugars in the body. As a result, blood sugar levels rise above normal limits. The frequency of a certain type of diabetes at the Gila River Indian Reservation is the highest known in the world. Pima diabetics are treated for the disease at a sophisticated health center located on the reservation. Other health care is provided by the Community Health Center, the Phoenix Indian Medical Center, and HuHuKam Memorial Hospital.

ARTS

The Pima made beautiful and functional baskets and woven cotton blankets, but their pottery was said to be quite ordinary—evidently more practical (useful) than decorative in nature.

CUSTOMS

Festivals and ceremonies

In the old times few ceremonies were practiced among the Pima, although there may have been a simple puberty ritual for girls. Modern Pima celebrate many occasions, adding a Native flare to non-Native-style events. Annual happenings include a New Year's Chicken Scratch Dance; the "Mul-Chu-Tha," a tribal fair that raises money for youth activities and features a parade, Indian rodeo, arts and crafts, and dances; and the Red Mountain Eagle Powwow. A powwow is a traditional song-and-dance celebration. Modern-day powwows include singers and dancers from many different tribes.

War rituals

The Pima began as a society of gentle people who valued peace. The wealth they gained from growing surplus crops changed their lives. They were forced to station guards around their settlements and defend themselves from raids by tribes who wanted what they had. Warring became far more frequent as the tribe carried out counter-raids to punish the thieves. The Pima trained their men to be outstanding warriors—they fought with heavy clubs and shot arrows treated with rattlesnake poison. But the concept of war was still considered an evil among the tribespeople. When a Pima warrior killed someone, he tried to make up for the person's death by secluding himself for a 16-day purification, which involved fasting and special rites performed by a shaman to cleanse the warrior's weapons.

Marriage and divorce

Parents usually arranged marriages for their children, but children could freely express their wishes about their future mates. Marriages in Pima society were quite informal: the couple lived together and declared themselves married with no ceremony to mark the occasion. Divorce and remarriage were also relatively simple matters.

CURRENT TRIBAL ISSUES

Like other Southwestern tribes, the Pima are working to improve the quality of education and health care on their reservations. While other Southwest tribes have at least partially closed their communities to outsiders and seek to protect aspects of their culture through secrecy, the Pima have allowed outsiders to observe their culture. Modern Pima regard themselves as a people with their own history and traditions, which they have retained despite all outside attempts to change them.

NOTABLE PEOPLE

Ira Hamilton Hayes (1923–1955) was probably the most famous Native American soldier of World War II. In February 1945 his unit landed on Iwo Jima, a barren island in the Pacific Ocean. Iwo Jima served as a base for launching U.S. air strikes against Japan, America's greatest rival in the war. Hayes became one of six marines who raised the U.S. flag on the summit of the island's now-famous Mount Suribachi in the midst of heavy enemy fire. The Associated Press photograph that captured the moment on film became the basis for the renowned bronze monument in Washington, D.C., that commemorates the battle of Iwo Jima. After he finished his military service, Hayes returned to the Pima Reservation, but the taste of fame that came with his war exploits had a destructive effect on him in the postwar years. He became a drifter, an alcoholic, and a lawbreaker. Hayes died of exposure (unprotected from severe weather) in the Arizona desert on January 24, 1955. He was buried alongside many of his fallen comrades in Arlington National Cemetery, not far from the bronze statue that captures the pivotal moment in his life.

The 1961 film *The Outsider,* starring Tony Curtis, is loosely based on the life of Ira Hayes. Folksinger-songwriter Bob Dylan's single "The Ballad of Ira Hayes," released in 1965, provides a far more realistic account of this tragic hero's experiences. For a generation of young Native Americans who came of age during the late 1960s and early 1970s, Hayes took on new prominence, becoming a modern symbol of the wronged Indian warrior: he fought for the United States and gained celebrity, but he died in near-obscurity.

FURTHER READING

Ezell, Paul H. "History of the Pima." *Handbook of North American Indians,* Volume 10, *Southewest.* Ed. Alfonso Ortiz. Washington, D. C.: Smithsonian Institution, 1983.

Innis, Gilbert C. "Pima." *Native America in the Twentieth Century.* Ed. Mary B. Davis. New York: Garland Publishing, 1994.

Russell, Frank. *The Pima Indians.* Tucson: University of Arizona Press, 1975.

Pueblo

For more information on the Pueblo people, see entries on Acoma Pueblo, Jemez Pueblo, San Juan Pueblo, Taos Pueblo, and Zuñi Pueblo that follow.

Name

Pueblo (pronounced *PWEB-loh*). Early Spanish explorers gave this name to various Indian tribes living in territory that is now part of the American Southwest. A *pueblo* is a stone and adobe village inhabited by various tribes in the southwestern United States. The broad Spanish name for the tribes now refers to both the Pueblo people and the pueblos (cities) where they live.

Location

The Pueblo people have always lived in New Mexico and northeastern Arizona. The surviving New Mexico pueblos are located at Acoma, Cochiti, Isleta, Jemez, Laguna, Nambé, Picuris, Pojoaque, Sandia, San Felipe, San Ildefonso, San Juan, Santa Ana, Santa Clara, Santo Domingo, Taos, Tesuque, Zia, and Zuni. Most are located on the Rio Grande River and its branches. The Hopi people (see entry) live in Arizona, and Ysleta del Sur Pueblo, near El Paso, Texas, was begun by refugees from the New Mexican Isleta Pueblo.

Population

There were an estimated 250,000 Pueblo in the early 1600s. They lived in 134 or more villages in the early sixteenth century. Between 1540 and 1700 the number of villages dwindled to 19, which it remains today. In a census (count of the population) taken in 1990 by the U.S. Bureau of the Census, 55,330 people identified themselves as Pueblo (see box on page 531).

Language family

Pueblo languages belong to four different families: the Keresan, Tanoan, Zunian, and Uto-Aztecan.

Origins and group affiliations

Ancestors of the Pueblo people were called the Anasazi ("ancient ones"; see entry)—a group of wandering hunters who settled down between 400 C.E. and 700 C.E. They began growing corn and other crops, and built houses in caves and cliffs. At the end of the twentieth century the people called Pueblo were actually 19 independent tribes in New Mexico, one in Arizona, and one in Texas.

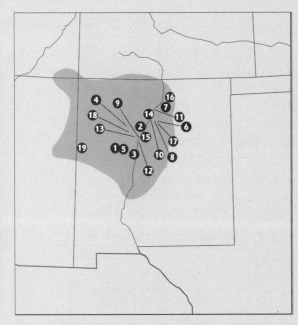

PUEBLO

Pueblo Communities in New Mexico

1. Acoma Pueblo
2. Cochiti Pueblo
3. Isleta Pueblo
4. Jemez Pueblo
5. Laguna Pueblo
6. Nambé Pueblo
7. Picuris Pueblo
8. Pojoaque Pueblo
9. San Felipe Pueblo
10. San Ildefonso Pueblo
11. San Juan Pueblo
12. Sandia Pueblo
13. Santa Ana Pueblo
14. Santa Clara Pueblo
15. Santo Domingo Pueblo
16. Taos Pueblo
17. Tesuque Pueblo
18. Zia Pueblo
19. Zuñi Pueblo

Shaded area: Traditional lands of the Pueblo in present-day New Mexico and northeastern Arizona.

The Pueblo believe that the first humans came out of the Earth through an opening called *sipapu.* Unlike Indian tribes who were moved onto reservations by the U. S. government, the Pueblo still inhabit their ancestral lands, and their culture has not undergone a great deal of change. Historically, the many Pueblo groups were alike in key ways: they built permanent homes, had similar religious customs, made pottery, and grew corn, beans, and other crops.

HISTORY

The "ancient ones"

Note: Please see entry on Anasazi for more information.

Although the ancestors of the Pueblo lived in the American Southwest for more than 12,000 years, not much is known about them—partly because the Pueblo will not allow archaeologists to dig extensively on Pueblo land. (Archaeologists are scientists who recover and study the evidence of past cultures.) It is known that thousands of years ago the ancestors of the Pueblo—known as the Anasazi—lived in the Four Corners area of the present-day United States, where the states of Arizona, Colorado, New Mexico, and Utah meet.

Until the 700s C.E. the Anasazi lived modestly, mainly by hunting and growing small crops of corn and beans. Over the next few centuries they began to cultivate cotton, create pottery, and build *kivas* (rooms where ceremonies and sacred meetings took place). They also built cities, later called "pueblos" by the Spanish, who arrived in the New World in the 1500s. In time, Spanish colonists gave each pueblo a Spanish name based on a geographic trait, a Catholic saint's name, or a Spanish pronunciation of the Indian name for the pueblo.

IMPORTANT DATES

1539: Pueblo encounter Spanish explorers.

1680: Pueblo Revolt drives out the Spanish.

1692: Spanish begin their reconquest of Pueblo land.

1850: New Mexico, land of the Pueblo people, is declared a U.S. territory.

1922: The All Indian Pueblo Council meets to fight for land and water rights.

Pueblos thrive, then decline

By the 1300s the pueblos were flourishing. Pueblo architecture grew more complex, pottery and weaving methods improved, and farming practices were refined. The ancient Anasazi people built spectacular cities, including the famed Pueblo Bonito, which was constructed between 920 C.E. and 1130 C.E. The city centered on a huge, D-shaped apartment building of 800 rooms that rose 5 stories high.

A severe drought struck the Southwest around 1276 and lasted into the early 1300s, forcing many of the Pueblo peoples to abandon their villages in search of water. At that time they joined other Puebloans farther north in central New Mexico and northeastern Arizona. A second series of migrations took place during the fifteenth century. When the Spanish arrived on the scene in the 1500s, they discovered many abandoned Pueblo towns.

Spanish drawn to Pueblo lands

In 1529 four Spanish shipwreck survivors spent eight years wandering the Southwest before finding their way back to their countrymen. With great excitement they returned to Spain telling tales of magnificent Indian cities of gold. It was not long before treasure-seeking Spanish explorers made their way to the new land. The Spanish began exploring Pueblo country in 1539, 81 years before the Pilgrims landed at Plymouth Rock. Some of the cities they visited were already

Chaco Canyon, New Mexico.

250 years old. Historians estimate that at the time some 250,000 Pueblo people were living in at least 134 villages.

The Spanish introduced horses and firearms to the Pueblo. Later batches of European settlers brought new crops, various inventions, and white diseases to which the Indians had no immunity. Some anthropologists (scientists who study ancient cultures) believe that during the period between 1540 and 1700, when the Spanish controlled what is now New Mexico, the Pueblo population decreased by half and the number of villages fell to nineteen.

Spanish settlers had little regard for the Native people's land, their culture, or their traditions. In 1540 a Spanish expedition led by Francisco Vásquez de Coronado (1510–1554) landed in the region. They camped in the Tiwa province of Tiguex, putting 12 villages of people out of their homes. Using the area as a base camp, the party searched in vain across the plains of Kansas for an incredibly wealthy mythical city, then returned to Mexico empty-handed.

Starting around the year 1580, new groups of Spaniards arrived in Pueblo territory. They sought to establish settlements and bring Christianity to the Indians. Juan de Oñate set up a government at

Santa Fe, New Mexico, and quickly began stripping the Natives of their freedoms. The Indians were required to give corn and woven cloth to the Spanish settlers; they were forced to perform backbreaking labor for the Spanish; and their traditional religious practices were banned as superstitious. Indians who refused to follow Spanish rule might pay for their disobedience with the amputation of a hand or foot, forced slavery, or even execution.

An illustration of a Pueblo village.

The "First American Revolution"

The Pueblo Revolt of 1680 was the first and only successful move by Native North Americans to throw colonists off their lands. By that time the Indians were thoroughly disgusted with Spanish rule and determined to put an end to it. They organized what some call the "First American Revolution." The Jemez (pronounced *HAY-mez*)—one of the Pueblo groups of New Mexico—took a major part in insuring the success of the revolt that was organized by Popé, a religious leader from the San Juan Pueblo (see "Notable People"). For the first time in their history, the many different Pueblo groups acted as a single force, and one day in August 1680 they killed 400 Spaniards, including 21 Catholic priests. The tribes succeeded in driving the Spanish out of New Mexico, but only for a short time.

Twenty percent of the Spaniards in the region are believed to have died in the Native rebellion, and those who survived fled to Mexico. But not all the Pueblo people agreed that the Spanish should be expelled. Some believed that it was important to keep the foreigners nearby for the protection they provided from the Apache and the Navajo (see entries), especially since those tribes had acquired horses and firearms. Some Pueblo even followed the Spanish to the South. Within a few years other groups had invited the Spanish to return.

The return of the Spanish

For 12 years the Jemez made efforts to reestablish their pueblos and their way of life. But in 1692 Don Diego de Vargas returned to the area to reclaim New Mexico for Spain. De Vargas forcibly took over San Diego Canyon in 1694, killing 84 warriors and taking 361 Jemez as prisoners. The Spanish once again established colonies in the Pueblo region. For many years the Pueblo who remained in the area under Spanish rule were forced to convert to Catholicism and to work on the ranches of Spanish officers and other wealthy people. Over time Spanish rule became less strict and officials permitted the Indians to resume some of their traditional religious practices.

After the Mexican Revolution of 1821, Mexico became independent of Spain and the new Mexican government took charge of the pueblos. Twenty-five years later Mexico went to war with the United States over land in what is now the American Southwest. America's victory in this conflict (known as the Mexican-American War) made New Mexico—the land of the Pueblo peoples—part of U.S. territory. The Pueblo, as Mexican citizens, were automatically granted U.S. citizenship (Indians as a whole were not granted U.S. citizenship until 1924). As U.S. citizens, the Pueblo did not receive the rights and protections granted through treaties to Indians as independent nations.

Pueblo lose, then regain land

Spanish laws passed in 1689 had given the Pueblo ownership of their ancestral lands. After New Mexico became part of the United States, the American government pledged that it would recognize this agreement. Under the terms of ownership, then, white settlement should not have been allowed on Pueblo land. Near the end of the nineteenth century, though, there was a great increase in illegal settlement on the lands by white Americans. The Pueblo asked for, and then sued for, Indian status, which they gained in 1916.

The All Indian Pueblo Council (see "Government") came together in the early 1920s to oppose U.S. government interference with Pueblo land ownership and water rights. Using tactics like an around-the-country lecture tour and appearances before Congress, the council succeeded in securing passage of the Pueblo Lands Act of 1924. This act returned to the Pueblo any land that had been owned by non-Indians for less than 20 years. It also provided money for lost lands. The Pueblo people used the money to purchase other land for irrigation projects.

In the early 1970s the All Indian Pueblo Council once again acted on behalf of the united Pueblo people to oppose federal action that would have interfered with their tribal water rights. In 1996 representatives from all the New Mexico pueblos, as well as two Apache tribes and the Navajo (see entry) Nation, began holding quarterly meetings with New Mexico state officials to improve communication and cooperation among the various groups.

RELIGION

Ancient beliefs and practices preserved

The Pueblo considered a person's spiritual beliefs central to his or her daily life. They saw themselves as Earth's caretakers and called upon supernatural beings to help ensure health, happiness, and abundant crops.

Many Pueblo were converted to Christianity by Catholic and Protestant missionaries, but these missionaries were not successful in their attempts to eliminate traditional beliefs and practices. Even at the end of the twentieth century many Pueblo Catholics adhered to the beliefs of their ancestors and practiced their ceremonies. Tribal members belong to religious societies devoted to weather, fertility, healing, hunting, even entertainment. Centuries ago the Pueblo people learned to keep their ceremonies secret during times of religious intolerance, and many of their religious ceremonies still remain shrouded in mystery.

Kachinas

The Pueblo believe in a Creator ("Great Spirit") who is always present. They honor the Earth as their Mother and respect everything in it, whether living or not. According to Pueblo belief, every visible object has a spirit (the *kachina*) that is as real as the thing itself. The Pueblo honor 300 major *kachinas* that represent the most important objects in their lives.

The Kachina religion practiced by the modern-day Pueblo people may have begun with the ancient Anasazi. Kachinas were said to be reincarnated ancestors (reborn after death) who served as messengers between the people and their gods. The term *kachina* also refers to the dolls that represent Pueblo Indians' ancestral spirits and the masked dancers who perform at agricultural and religious ceremonies (see box on page 530.)

Pueblo Indians of the late 1990s still stayed in touch with the spirit world. For example, hunters asked permission of the spirit of an animal before killing it for food, and persons seeking strength often prayed to be endowed with the spirit of an especially powerful or beloved kachina.

Many Pueblo tales featured Salt Woman or Salt Mother, an elderly woman who freely helped anyone who asked her. The Pueblo used salt for healing rituals, burial ceremonies, food preparation and preservation, and even love potions. It was also used for trade. People made pilgrimages to the place where Salt Woman lived in order to obtain the precious substance.

Religious freedom

During the 1920s various outside groups of whites tried to stop the Pueblo from practicing their traditional religious ceremonies. Laws passed in the 1930s were supposed to protect the tribe's freedom of religion, but they did not. Even as late as the 1960s U.S. government officials were attempting to "civilize" the Indians by forcing them to give up their old religious ways. The Pueblo were finally assured an important religious freedom in 1970, when legislation returned to the Taos Pueblo the sacred area of Blue Lake and 55,000 surrounding acres of land. The Pueblo had been struggling for 30 years for the return of this land, which they consider to be the place where the Creator first created people (see Taos Pueblo entry).

LANGUAGE

Most of the Pueblo tribes speak dialects (varieties) that derive from four separate language families: Tewa, Tiwa, Towa, and Keresan. Although the Pueblo share similar cultures, they are not typically fluent in each other's languages. Throughout their history, though, some Pueblo people have been able to speak several Pueblo languages. During the time of Spanish rule many also spoke Spanish. Even though the Pueblo languages are still unwritten, they continue to survive in most of the villages. In fact, most modern Pueblo speak both English and their Native tongue.

GOVERNMENT

In early times the Western Pueblo were ruled by religious leaders. Public opinion, expressed through gossip, was used to keep people in line. The Eastern Pueblo separated religious and political authorities and developed a stronger central government. A tribal council decided how land was to be divided and could revoke (or take back) a person's right to live in a given pueblo.

Beginning in 1620 a Spanish-style system of government—one featuring a tribal governor and his assistants—became widespread among the tribes. By the twentieth century each pueblo maintained its own separate elected government.

All of the pueblos are self-governed and fiercely independent, but they all participate in the All Indian Pueblo Council, a loose federation or grouping. The All Indian Pueblo Council began with the Pueblo Revolt against the Spanish in 1680. It became the important force in the 1920s in organizing delegates from all the pueblos in the effort to regain the land illegally seized from them by American settlers. Through their participation in the All Indian Pueblo Council, the governors of the New Mexico pueblos continue to meet and discuss issues such as water rights, education, health, and economic development.

ECONOMY

Prior to the arrival of the Europeans, the most important task at each pueblo was the construction of homes. Workers were paid with food, but because food was so costly only a minimal number of builders were used on each project. Members of the tribe used stone or bone to make their own personal tools, such as grinding stones, knives, hammers, arrows—even fireplaces and ovens. Men usually made the adobe (pronounced *uh-DOE-bee*) bricks, while women did the plastering and constructed the roofs of the houses. (Adobe is a sun-dried mud made of a mixture of clay, sand, and sometimes ashes, rocks, or straw.)

The Spanish introduced sheep and cattle ranching and new crops in the 1600s, and these economic activities were still important among the Pueblo at the end of the twentieth century.

PUEBLO POPULATION: 1990

According to the U.S. Bureau of the Census, 55,330 people identified themselves as Pueblo in 1990. The breakdown of population figures looked like this:

Pueblo group	Number identified
Acoma	3,938
Arizona Tewa	423
Cochiti	1,184
Hopi	11,791
Isleta	3,306
Jemez	2,238
Keres	36
Laguna	6,424
Nambé	300
Picuris	245
Piro	15
Pojoaque	39
Pueblo	2,664
Sandia	291
San Felipe	2,218
San Ildefonso	411
San Juan	1,081
Santa Ana	596
Santa Clara	1,180
Santo Domingo	2,865
Taos	1,875
Tesuque	225
Tewa	1,640
Tigua	1,271
Zia	793
Zuñi	8,281
Total	**55,330**

Many Pueblo fought during World War II (1939–45), and when they returned home they used their war benefits to obtain higher education or to open businesses. During the 1960s federal programs were set up to provide financial assistance to Native Americans, and tourism on Pueblo lands began to thrive. Tourists are drawn to New Mexico by their fascination with the ancient pueblos and the Pueblo lifestyle.

Some modern-day Pueblo people continue to work their own farms but make use of modern equipment. Others have taken nonagricultural jobs off the reservation and have moved to cities.

DAILY LIFE

Families

In Pueblo families, children belonged to their mother's clan (a group of related families). A household was made up of a husband and wife, their children, her brothers, and their wives and children.

Pueblo women and girls built houses and ovens, made baskets and pottery, and tended the small vegetable gardens. Men and boys took care of the corn fields, hunted, and did the weaving, knitting, and embroidering.

Buildings

ARCHITECTURE The unusual Pueblo style of construction dates back to the Anasazi culture of about 700 C.E. and remains popular with some of the modern Pueblo people. Structures were made either of sandstone slabs cemented into place with mud or, more commonly, of adobe. Because adobe was also used in countries on the Mediterranean Sea in Europe, the Spanish were already familiar with it when they discovered the Pueblo. In fact, the Spanish taught the Indians to make adobe bricks. Thereafter, bricklaying replaced the earlier practice of forming mud walls between wooden poles.

The Pueblo carried on the architectural traditions of their ancestors. They built multistoried apartment-style buildings, usually from three to six stories tall. First-floor rooms were used mostly for food storage, while the living quarters were located on upper levels. To provide safety from invaders, the first floor was left without doors. Lower rooms were entered through hatches (holes in the ceiling), and during rainstorms the hatches could be covered with large slabs of stone. Modern homes have doors on the first floor.

Upper stories were terraced (staggered) toward the rear of the building. As a result, each upper-story room had a patio area provided by the roof of the room below. People used ladders or, less often, adobe stairs, to go from one level to the next. The ladders could be pulled up in case of an enemy attack. Sometimes the ladders were wide enough for two people to pass at the same time.

HOUSE INTERIORS Because wind and rain wore away at the earthen walls of the pueblos, a coating of mud plaster had to be reapplied to the exterior every year. To make the dwelling clean and attractive, interior surfaces were whitewashed. This time-consuming

An illustration of the interior of a traditional Pueblo dwelling.

process involved combining a mineral substance called gypsum with cattle dung and baking the mixture like pottery. The substance was then pounded into a powder, mixed with water, and applied to the walls. The thick adobe walls kept the rooms cool in the summer and warm in the winter.

Families slept on rugs or animal skins that were rolled up in the morning and used for seating. Pegs and poles, somewhat like the towel racks we use today, served as clothes hangers. In one corner of the room sat the fireplace. Nearby were cooking pots and gourds (dried, hollowed-out vegetables) for carrying water. Before the nineteenth century smoke was vented through the pueblo's entrance. Later, a hood and flue (or pipe) sent smoke outside the house. Special storage containers for grain were built into the floor.

During planting season, whole families sometimes camped in the fields, living in the remains of ancient settlements or building temporary villages. Light shelters of brush and stone were constructed to give protection from the blazing sun.

At the end of the twentieth century the majority of Pueblo residents lived in modern, single-family homes, most made of cinder block. But at Acoma and Taos some people still inhabited their centuries-old, apartment-style adobe buildings, chopping wood for fuel and living for the most part without modern conveniences.

A mural from a Pueblo kiva, from sometime around 1500.

KIVAS Central to the spiritual life of each pueblo was a circular room called the kiva, which was often built below ground level. Some pueblos had one or two kivas, while others had many. Most kivas contained a fire pit, an adobe bench attached to the wall, possibly an altar, and a *sipapu*, a hole through which *kachinas* could emerge from the underworld for ceremonies. The men of a religious society used kivas to prepare for tribal ceremonies and to hold social gatherings. Traditionally, women were allowed into a kiva only to plaster the walls and to attend occasional ceremonies.

CHURCHES During the period of Spanish rule a Catholic church was constructed in each pueblo. These huge adobe structures had walls as much as 9 feet thick and were up to 40 feet tall. Their bell towers stretched even higher. The churches' roofs were made with strong wooden poles long enough to span the entire width of the structure. The poles were laid at intervals to make a base, with several layers of smaller wooden branches and brush in alternating directions arranged over them, then covered with packed earth. In the case of the larger mission churches, tree trunks 40 feet long and weighing hundreds of pounds were harvested from the nearest forest. They were then hand-carried 30 miles or more to the construction site.

Clothing and adornment

The Pueblo wore cotton clothing as early as 800 C.E. In climates where it was too cold to grow cotton, animal skins were used. Winter coats were made by forming fluffy ropes from small animal pelts and turkey feathers. Rows of these ropes were sewn together with yucca twine, much like a basket is woven. After the Spanish taught the Indians to spin and weave wool, woolen clothing became popular. In the early days weaving was considered a male occupation.

Men usually wore a type of knee-length skirt or loin cloths (flaps of material that covered the front and back and were suspended from the waist). A piece of cloth with a hole in the center was slipped over the head to serve as a shirt. The Pueblo either went barefoot or wore sandals made of yucca fiber. Around 1300 C.E. they learned from other Indian cultures to make animal skin moccasins and leggings. The tribespeople did not begin wearing long pants until around 1880. Even then, they sometimes slit the legs to accommodate tall moccasins or boots.

Women often wore simple, knee-length dresses called *mantas* (pronounced *MAHN-tuhs*), made from a straight piece of cloth wrapped around the body and tied with a sash at the waist. The fabric passed under the left arm and was fastened above the right shoulder. Black wool has been used to make mantas since the time of Spanish rule. In the nineteenth century women began wearing brightly colored silk blouses under their mantas. They later added colorful fringed shawls.

Clothing was usually left undyed, but sometimes fabrics were colored with a bright blue-green dye made from copper sulfate. Later, when European fabrics became available, bright red cloth was especially popular among the Pueblo people. The fibers from such fabrics were carefully unraveled so the threads could be rewoven as decorative elements in Pueblo cloth.

Most Pueblo people wore their shoulder-length hair either loose or tied back, with bangs cut straight across the forehead. Men often tied their hair back at the nape of the neck, folded it up in half, and wrapped it with a leather strip into a long bundle called a *chongo*. Influenced by Plains Indians, some men in the Northern Pueblos braided their hair. Men painted their bodies for ceremonies, and women often decorated their cheeks with red powder made from crushed flowers.

Food

Because they farmed and did not have to wander about looking for food, the Pueblo were able to settle in permanent cities. Their main crop—corn—made up about 80 percent of their diet. It was so important to Pueblo life that it was used in some form—as corn, cornmeal (see box), or corn pollen—in nearly every ceremony. Fresh corn was boiled or roasted or dried, ground, and stored in the form of cornmeal. The Pueblo groups cultivated many varieties, including a type called flint corn that could be stored for years because it was resistant to mold and rodents. Aside from the familiar white and yellow varieties, the tribes raised red, blue, dark purple, and speckled corn. The people often stored seed corn with an evergreen sprig or prayer feather in hopes of keeping the seeds fresh.

In addition to corn the Pueblo raised squash, sunflower seeds, and several types of beans. The Spanish colonists introduced new crops, including apples, apricots, pears, grapes, wheat, and a variety of vegetables. Individual Indian families grew their own onions, peppers, chilies, and tobacco. The Pueblo also made use of various wild plants, such as prickly pear cactus, berries, pine nuts, and yucca fruit. Other parts of the yucca plant were used to make soap, fiber for sandals, and material for brooms and hairbrushes.

The Pueblo lived in a desert climate and their crops were often harmed by drought. They planted in fields most likely to catch the summer rain and built dams to keep thunderstorm runoffs from washing away their crops. Corn was planted in holes up to 18 inches deep to allow the plant roots to make use of moisture well below the surface. A ridge of soil was formed around each plant to retain water. As a result, cornfields took on a wafflelike appearance.

Meat was used by the Pueblo only on occasion. Sometimes large animals like deer, antelope, and buffalo were hunted by using the "drive" method. A group of men and boys surrounded their prey and drove it into a canyon or corral where it could be killed easily. More commonly, rabbits, gophers, squirrels, and other small animals were caught in traps or killed with clubs.

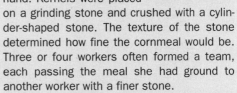

THE USES OF CORN-MEAL

Pueblo girls and women spent three to four hours a day grinding several quarts of cornmeal by hand. Kernels were placed on a grinding stone and crushed with a cylinder-shaped stone. The texture of the stone determined how fine the cornmeal would be. Three or four workers often formed a team, each passing the meal she had ground to another worker with a finer stone.

Cornmeal added to boiling water produced a favorite morning drink. For travelers, cornmeal that had been thoroughly toasted between successive grindings and crushed extra fine could be carried easily and mixed with cold water for a nourishing beverage. Lumps of cornmeal dough dropped into boiling water made dumplings. A favorite food now known by its Mexican Indian name, *tamale* (pronounced *tah-MAH-lay*), consisted of meat or other filling that was encased in cornmeal, wrapped with a corn husk, and then boiled.

Cornmeal was also used for various types of bread, including tortillas (pronounced *tor-TEE-yahz*). *Piki* (pronounced *PEE-kee*) bread was prepared by quickly spreading thin batter made from blue cornmeal on a hot stone and almost immediately peeling off the paper-thin, cooked layer. Piki could be folded and stored for as long as a week.

Education

Tribal elders were respected for their wisdom. When they became too old for strenuous work, the elderly often joined the town council or became the head of a society. They also assisted in raising the children. They taught the youths about the Pueblo way of life and passed down the tradition of *kachina* dollmaking. (*Kachina* dolls were carved from wood, then covered with white clay and painted in bright colors.)

During the late nineteenth century the U.S. government wanted the Pueblo people to assimilate or "blend in" with mainstream Amer-

ican society. Many Indian children were sent far away from their parents to white-run boarding schools to learn white ways. Throughout the twentieth century, though, the Bureau of Indian Affairs built schools right on the Pueblo reservations, thereby enabling Pueblo youth to maintain a connection to their families and their heritage.

Healing practices

The Pueblo thought that most illnesses had spiritual causes. The most common treatment focused on restoring spiritual harmony between the ailing person and his or her environment. For example, a baby who cried most of the time might be thought to suffer back pain because of the way his father mistreated horses before the child's birth. To cure his child, the father might drive a team of horses hard, then take the horse sweat and rub it onto the baby's back.

Healers, members of the curing society, were sometimes called on to perform special rituals. Some healers were ordinary people who had gained special healing powers in a dramatic way—through the bite of a snake, perhaps, or being struck by lightning.

Plants were also used to treat and prevent illness. Crushed mustard leaves, for instance, were applied to the body as a sunscreen.

ARTS

Pottery and stonework

Pueblo women have been known throughout history for a special kind of pottery featuring black designs painted on a white background. Their polished red and black pottery remains popular today. The Pueblo groups are unique for their high level of craftsmanship in stonework, which allowed them to build houses with as many as 30 floors.

Pueblo Cultural Center

Exhibits on Pueblo history are on display at the Pueblo Cultural Center in Albuquerque, New Mexico. The exhibits trace the origins, traditions, arts, and craftsmanship of the people. The 260-seat theater at the center depicts Pueblo culture through film, drama, and dance. Stage presentations and celebrations are also held on the grounds.

CUSTOMS

Festivals and ceremonies

The Pueblo are sometimes referred to as the "Rain Dance" people. Because water was so important in their desert environment, many of their traditional ceremonies were held to encourage adequate rainfall. Other dances expressed their sadness, told stories of the gods, and celebrated the growth of their crops. Dancers wore fancy costumes and sometimes used masks. They decorated themselves with paint, horns, branches, and feathers.

Both carefully planned and free-style dances were performed in ceremonies that went on for hours. During the Snake Dance, men fearlessly handled rattlesnakes. The rooftop terraces of pueblo homes provided a convenient place for people to sit and watch the ceremonial dances that were held throughout the year.

Prayer feathers were attached to a house under construction to protect it. A "feeding the house" ceremony took place after the walls, roof, and floor were completed. Then crumbs were sprinkled along the rafters to insure the good health of those who would live inside it. Because water, building materials, and firewood had to be transported up and down ladders to the pueblo homes, ceremonies were performed at the foot of the ladders to protect children and adults from accidents.

Modern Pueblo life is steeped in ritual. Pueblo festivals often combine traditional Indian rituals with Christian celebrations. Each pueblo has its own celebrations throughout the year, including one on the feast day of the Catholic saint who serves as patron of the pueblo.

Courtship and marriage

Before a woman married she usually spent three days grinding corn at the groom's home to prove her ability to perform this duty; sometimes she brought samples to prove her breadmaking talents. The groom-to-be and his relatives wove a special wedding garment for the bride. Before the wedding ceremony the bride and groom would have their hair washed by the groom's mother. Then the groom's father would sprinkle a trail of cornmeal from his house to the bride's, where a feast was celebrated. In a final ceremony the couple took a small bit of cornmeal, walked silently to the eastern part of the mesa (a large hill with steep sides and a flat top), breathed upon the cornmeal, threw it toward the rising Sun, prayed, and returned to the village a married couple.

When a Pueblo man married he went to live in the home of his wife's family, bringing along some of his family's carefully preserved seeds for planting.

Childbirth

Various ceremonies surrounded childbirth. To insure a healthy baby, expectant mothers and fathers were supposed to avoid looking at a snake or harming an animal. After a midwife or male healer assisted with a baby's birth, the newborn was washed, sprinkled with juniper ashes, and given an ear of white corn to keep as a reminder of its heritage. For 20 days following childbirth, a new mother drank juniper tea and took sweat baths in steam created by pouring water over a hot stone covered with juniper leaves.

Four to twenty days after birth the baby was taken outside at dawn to be greeted by the Sun. The father, or a healer called a shaman (pronounced *SHAY-mun*), then gave the child its name. After that the baby was strapped to a wooden board, where it would spend its first few months learning the value of stillness.

Funerals

Although death was seen as a sad occasion, the dead were believed to go on living in another, very different, world—a world in which night was day, day was night, and the seasons were switched. Excessive mourning for the dead was discouraged as a waste of time.

Prior to burial a body was cleaned and dressed in fine clothes. Feathers were placed in the corpse's hands. For four days attendants sat by the body; then it was taken outside to be buried, along with food and tools. Dead children, believed to be too little to make the journey to the afterlife, were often buried underneath the family home. It was hoped that their souls would enter new babies yet to be born in the home.

CURRENT TRIBAL ISSUES

Many of the various Pueblo communities are struggling with issues relating to water and land rights, lack of employment opportunities, and adequate health care. In recent years the Indian Health Service has begun to cooperate closely with Native healers to improve the health status of the tribe.

An especially difficult challenge facing the Pueblo groups is the redevelopment of their economy. New methods of farming are being explored and refined. Some pueblos are encouraging tourism and related businesses. Many artists find success selling fine products such as silver and turquoise jewelry, pottery, sculptures, and carved *kachinas*. And several New Mexico pueblos have recently built casino gaming facilities, generating considerable controversy in the process.

In an ongoing effort to hold on to their ancestral lands, the Pueblo people have had to appeal repeatedly to U.S. Congress and the court system. One of the most famous land rights battles was waged by the Taos Pueblo (see entry). The Pueblo are also making continued efforts to maintain their tribal culture and customs in the face of the dominance of modern white culture.

NOTABLE PEOPLE

Joe Simon Sando (1923– ; named Paa Peh in the language of the Pueblo Indians) is a Jemez Pueblo scholar and lecturer who has written four books on the lives, culture, and history of the Pueblo Indians: *The Pueblo Indians, Pueblo Indian Biographies, Nee Hemish: The History of the Jemez Pueblo,* and *Pueblo Nations: Eight Centuries of Pueblo Indian History.*

Popé (c. 1630–c. 1690) was a respected medicine man of New Mexico's San Juan Pueblo. He refused to convert to the Catholic faith and was repeatedly arrested and tortured by the Spanish. Popé organized a Pueblo rebellion, secretly enlisted recruits, and in 1680 oversaw the successful attack on the Spanish that drove them from their headquarters in Santa Fe, New Mexico. But by 1692 the Indian revolt had dissolved in the face of drought and attacks by Apache and Ute bands, and once again the Spanish ruled Santa Fe.

Other notable Pueblo include anthropologist, linguist, author, and educator Edward P. Dozier (1916–1971), who specialized in the study of his own people; Frank C. Dukepoo (1943–), a Hopi-Laguna Pueblo geneticist and founder of the National Native American Honor Society; world-famous Santa Clara Pueblo artist Pablita Velarde (1918–) and her daughter, also an artist, Helen Hardin (1946–1984).

FURTHER READING

Arnold, Pauline. *The Ancient Cliff Dwellers of Mesa Verde.* New York: Clarion Books, 1992.

Burby, Liza N. *The Pueblo Indians.* Broomall, PA: Chelsea Juniors, 1994.

Cory, Steven. *Pueblo Indian.* Minneapolis, MN: Lerner Publications Co., 1996.

D'Apice, Mary. *The Pueblo.* Vero Beach, FL: Rourke Publications, Inc., 1990.

Yue, Charlotte, and David Yue. *The Pueblo.* Boston: Houghton Mifflin Co, 1986.

Acoma Pueblo

See Pueblo entry for more information on the Pueblo peoples.

Name

Acoma Pueblo (pronounced *AH-koh-mah PWEB-loh*). *Acoma* means "people of the white rock." A *pueblo* is a stone and adobe village inhabited by various tribes in the southwestern United States. The Spanish used the word *pueblo* to refer to both the people and their villages. The name of the main Acoma village, *Acu,* may mean "home for many ages" or "place of preparedness."

Location

Traditional Acoma lands may have consisted of some 5 million acres and many villages in present-day New Mexico. The modern-day Acoma Pueblo, a federal reservation, is located 60 miles west of Albuquerque, New Mexico. Most Acoma now live in one of the two more modern towns on the reservation, but some families maintain individual or group homes in the old city.

Population

In 1582, there were an estimated 6,000 Acoma people. In 1776, there were fewer than 600. In a census (count of the population) conducted in 1990 by the U.S. Bureau of the Census, 3,938 people identified themselves as Acoma Pueblo.

Language family

Keresan.

Origins and group affiliations

Modern-day Acoma people have four different groups of ancestors, one of which inhabited the Acoma homeland from prehistoric times. Some Anasazi people (see entry) came and intermingled with them around the year 1200. The other ancestral groups probably migrated to the area from the Cebollita Mesa region of New Mexico.

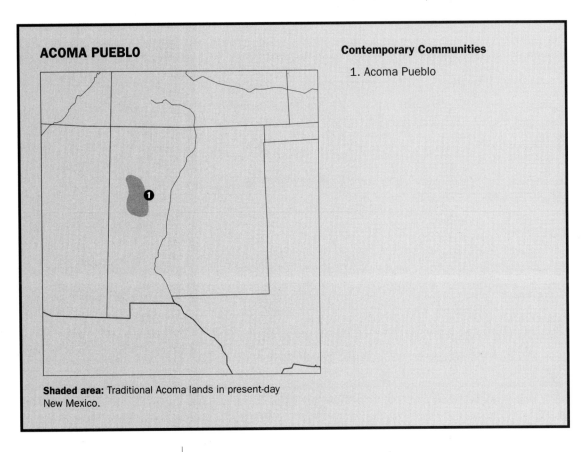

ACOMA PUEBLO

Contemporary Communities

1. Acoma Pueblo

Shaded area: Traditional Acoma lands in present-day New Mexico.

The Acoma people were skilled farmers who grew abundant crops in the fields of what is now the state of New Mexico. While they have since made some necessary adjustments to modern life, they retain many of the old ways. The Acoma Pueblo, sometimes referred to as Sky City, sits like a mighty fortress high above the New Mexico countryside. Some say the Acoma Pueblo is the oldest continuously occupied settlement in the United States. This claim is challenged only by the Hopi Pueblo of Oraibi. (See Hopi entry.)

HISTORY

Contact with the Spanish

The Acoma say that their people have been living in the village of Acu for at least 2,000 years. They were hunter-gatherers and farmers who apparently lived a contented life hunting for game and working their fields. The Acoma people first encountered Europeans in 1540, when Spanish explorer Hernando de Alvarado and his party of 20 soldiers arrived on their land.

Alvarado was impressed by the pueblo, perched atop a large hill with steep sides and a flat top—the kind of terrain the Spanish call a *mesa*. It could only be entered by way of a hand-built stairway of 200 steps, followed by a stretch of about 100 narrower steps. Beyond the steps lay 20-foot high rocks with hand- and toe-holds for climbing to the entrance. The Spanish gave the name "Kingdom of Acu" to this astonishing place and recorded that 5,000 to 10,000 warlike people lived there.

The next major contact with the Spanish came in 1598, when Juan de Oñate, the new governor of the region, toured the pueblo. A year later the governor's nephew visited the Acoma Pueblo, but for some reason his relationship with the Indians disintegrated. The visit ended in violence as the Acoma attacked the Spanish. According to the Acoma, Spanish soldiers had assaulted some women in the village; the Spanish, however, maintained that they did nothing to provoke the murderous assault.

Attack on Acoma

Only four Spanish men survived the attack and were able to escape. Six weeks later the vengeful Spanish stormed the Acoma. With a cannon in tow, a dozen men managed to scale the tribe's mesa wall unseen and launch the bloody, two-day Battle of Acoma (1599). When it ended, the city lay in ruins and 800 of the 6,000 residents had been killed.

More than 500 prisoners were taken to stand trial at the Spanish governor's headquarters. Warriors over the age of 12 were sentenced to 20 years of forced labor; men over the age of 25 also had one foot cut off. This was the beginning of a long and unhappy relationship between the Spanish and the Acoma people.

Acoma rebellion brews

Between 1629 and 1640 Spanish missionary priests forced the Acoma people to build a monumental Catholic church. The building was made of stone and adobe (a sun-dried mud made of a mixture of

IMPORTANT DATES

1150: Acoma Pueblo is a well-established city.

1540: Spanish explorers visit Acoma Pueblo.

1599: Spanish soldiers destroy the pueblo in the Battle of Acoma. The people submit to Spanish rule.

1680: The Acoma people revolt against Spanish rule.

1699: The Acoma people resubmit to Spanish rule.

1848: The Acoma people come under the control of the United States.

1970: A financial settlement with the U.S. government allows the Acoma people to begin purchasing back parts of their traditional lands.

Acoma Pueblo photographed in 1941-42 by Ansel Adams.

clay, sand, and sometimes ashes, rocks, or straw). The materials had to be hauled up to the top of the mesa in buffalo-hide bags and water jars. Indian workers carried massive timbers—some up to 40 feet long—more than 40 miles from Mt. Taylor. The logs apparently could not touch the ground during the backbreaking trip to the building site. Even the soil for a 2,000-square-foot cemetery had to be carried up the steep trail.

The Spanish tried to force all the Pueblo Indians to convert to the Catholic religion. They imposed severe penalties on any Natives found practicing their traditional religion. The Indians grew increasingly hostile over the miserable life imposed on them by the Spanish. The forced labor, the efforts to impose a foreign religion on them, and the burden of keeping the Spanish supplied with food was just too much to take. In 1680 they revolted.

Spanish return to Acoma

Although Acoma was some distance from the other pueblos, its people took part in the Pueblo Revolt of 1680 (see Pueblo entry) by killing the local priest and burning the Catholic church in their home. But they were no match for the superior weapons of the Spanish, and in 1699 the Spanish again asserted their rule. They forced the Acoma to rebuild the church, a magnificent structure 150 feet long, 40 feet wide, and 35 feet tall, with walls 9 feet thick at their base. It is still in use today.

The Acoma faced more hard times during the eighteenth century: their land was raided by the Apache (see entry), and they suffered

from diseases such as smallpox that had been brought from Europe by the whites. By 1776 only 530 Acoma remained alive at the pueblo.

U.S. Congress affirms Acoma rights

Much of Pueblo territory, including Acoma land, was acquired by the United States in 1848 when the United States won the Mexican American War and took over the lands in its southwest area. Ten years later U.S. Congress confirmed that the Acoma, along with other Pueblo tribes, could live on and farm their lands. However, it was not long before an illegal railroad caused the loss of some reservation lands. This left many Acoma unable to support themselves by farming; some left the reservation, finding work as laborers, mechanics, electricians, and painters.

During the twentieth century new laws were enacted that allowed the Acoma to regain ownership of portions of their homeland, including some major religious sites. In 1970 they received a cash settlement of $6.1 million from the U.S. government for the illegal loss of their lands (but none of the land was returned). The money enabled the Acoma to make several purchases during the 1970s and 1980s that added more than 15,000 acres to their tribal land holdings.

For a while in the last quarter of the twentieth century, nearby uranium mines provided employment opportunities for the Acoma people; then the uranium market disappeared. The closing of the Ambrosia Lake Mine meant the loss of jobs for 300 people on the reservation. Well into the mid-1990s the number of Acoma Pueblo who could not find work remained extremely high. The Acoma are searching for ways to expand work opportunities for the residents of their ancient city.

RELIGION

The Acoma have suffered religious persecution because of their beliefs, so they maintain a great deal of secrecy about their spiritual traditions. Their chief gods are Ocatc (the Sun, who is called "Father") and Iatiku (the mother of all Indians).

The Spanish Catholic missionaries were only partly successful in converting the Acoma to their faith. Christianity has never fully replaced the Native religion, but elements of Christianity have blended over the centuries with the tribe's traditional religious beliefs.

LANGUAGE

Acoma Keresan is still the primary language (the one they speak most of the time) of nearly 95 percent of the population on the Acoma reservation. Most of the residents speak English as well, and many of the older Acoma communicate in other Native languages of the region and in Spanish.

GOVERNMENT

Since the time of Spanish rule in the sixteenth and seventeenth centuries, the tribe has maintained a two-part governmental structure. The nonreligious government is led by a governor, his or her assistants, and a tribal council. It is responsible for interactions with the non-Native world. The religious tribal government is an ancient, god-centered system headed by members of the Antelope clan (a group of families who claim a common ancestor). The tribe's first formal court system and written code of law was adopted in 1974.

In 1863 President Abraham Lincoln (1809–1865) presented the Acoma and other Pueblo tribes with silver-headed canes to commemorate their political and legal right to land and self-government. The governors of each pueblo keep the canes during their official terms.

ECONOMY

For centuries the Acoma economy was based on agriculture. Men were expected to take part in work such as planting, harvesting, building irrigation systems, and hunting. Women were in charge of housekeeping, child care, and food preparation, including the grinding of cornmeal. After the fruits and vegetables were harvested, the chief distributed them equally among the tribal members.

In modern times the increasing pollution of the nearby San Jose River has cut down on Acoma farming. Cattle raising is now a major industry. Nearly 125 families work in ranching or farming. However, unemployment remains a serious problem, and some Acoma are leaving their homes to find work elsewhere. The tribal government employs more than half of the Acoma workforce to perform community projects or operate local facilities, but more than 38 percent of tribal members who want to work cannot find jobs.

Tourism is very important to the Acoma economy. Every year at least 80,000 tourists visit Sky City and provide income for the tribe. One popular site at Sky City is the San Esteban del Rey Mission, which was completed in 1640. Potterymaking makes up the single largest private type of employment. More than 120 self-employed potters sell their wares to visitors. The reservation also owns and operates a laundromat, a motel, a restaurant, a truckstop plaza, and a gaming casino. A 17,000-square-foot building is available for rent to manufacturers. In addition, a small portion of trees on the reservation is sold for lumber.

DAILY LIFE

Families

Acoma Pueblo society is matrilineal, meaning descent and inheritances are traced through the mother's side of the family. Aside from his or her inherited clan membership, each person is a member of a *kiva* (a ceremonial society named for the chamber in which the group's meetings are held) and participates in the tribal celebrations.

Buildings

Acoma buildings are aligned side by side in sets of three, forming east-west rows. Most contain kivas (meeting chambers for ceremonial societies). Acoma kivas are rectangular in shape rather than circular, as they are in many pueblos.

Present-day Acoma live in Acomita and McCartys, the reservation's two modern-style villages. But a few families still occupy the old villages, where buildings are maintained for the purposes of tradition, ceremonial gatherings, and tourism. The 250 dwellings in the original

Acoma Pueblo women looking into a pool of water at Acoma.

pueblo have neither running water nor sewer service. The families who choose to live there continue to carry drinking water from natural stone catch basins where water has been stored for a thousand years. The few radios and televisions in the old pueblo operate only on batteries, and all cooking and heating is done with wood.

Clothing and adornment

Acoma clothing is more colorful than the clothing of other pueblo dwellers. Garments are usually made from rectangular cloth strips with bright embroidered designs along the borders.

Food

The Acoma of the late twentieth century enjoyed many traditional foods, some of their favorites being blue corn drink, corn mush, pudding, wheat cake, corn balls, piki or paper bread, peach bark drink, flour bread, wild berries, wild banana, prickly pear fruit, and a chili-spiced stew.

Education

The Acoma Pueblo has two elementary schools and a high school overseen by a tribal school board that was created in 1978. Loan programs help students who wish to attend colleges and universities. The first Acoma-Keresan dictionary was recently developed for use in the schools and in community education programs to help keep the language alive.

Public school education is supplemented by special classes taught by the Acoma men who head various ceremonial societies. They conduct classes on such topics as proper behavior, care of the human spirit and the human body, astrology, child psychology, public speaking, history, music, and dancing. Spiritual teachings are learned mainly through participation in religious activities.

Healing practices

Traditional Acoma had medicine societies that included male healers (men who performed the cures) and female assistants. Healers called shamans (pronounced *SHAH-menz*) were expected to treat anyone who asked for help, and they were given food or other useful items in payment. Shamans were said to receive their abilities from animals—bears, eagles, snakes, or wolves, for example—and would call on their powers with traditional songs and dances. To show off their skills shamans might perform public feats such as sword swallowing, dancing on hot coals without injury, or producing green corn or fresh berries during winter. Three of the Acoma medicine societies remained in operation at the end of the twentieth century.

Modern-day Acoma combine traditional practices with the latest medical techniques. For example, the Acoma hospital, which also serves the Navajo (see entry) and Laguna peoples, is equipped with a ritual curing room as well as alcohol and drug treatment facilities and a ward for treatment of kidney disease.

ARTS

A large percentage of Acoma people are keeping alive traditional crafts such as potterymaking, carving, and the weaving of blankets, belts, dresses, capes, socks, skirts, moccasins, and baskets.

THE STOLEN SQUASHES

The Acoma composed many songs and poems, and some are used for teaching moral lessons. Coyote, an indestructible supernatural spirit with a humanlike mixture of good and evil qualities, is a popular character in their oral literature. He appears in stories like this one about the terrible consequences of stealing:

There is a telling that one day Insect Man went out to weed his squash patch and found that one of his squashes had been eaten.

"Who can the thief be?" he chirped. "I'll think of a way to catch him." So he sat down and thought for a while.

Then he took a sharp stick and went from one squash to another, tasting them all until he found the sweetest one in the whole patch. He chewed a small hole in it and crawled inside.

"Now I shall find out who is stealing my squashes," he said.

Soon Coyote came trotting along. He stopped beside the patch and began tasting each squash. When he came to the sweet one, he ate it up, Insect Man and all.

Down inside Coyote, Insect Man hunted about, singing as usual. Coyote looked first on one side and then on the other. He could not see anyone and was puzzled about that singing.

At last, Insect Man found what he was looking for. He pushed his sharp stick as deep as he could into Coyote's heart, and Coyote fell over dead.

Insect Man crawled out and went back to this weeding and singing.

When Coyote came to life again, he never stole another squash. But that is how it happened that Coyotes have false hearts.

SOURCE: Evelyn Dahl Reed. "The Stolen Squashes." *Coyote Tales from the Indian Pueblos.* Santa Fe, NM: Sunstone Press, 1988.

CUSTOMS

Festivals and ceremonies

The major modern celebrations of the Acoma are the Governor's Feast, the Easter celebration (a Catholic holiday commemorating the resurrection of Jesus Christ), Santa Maria Feast, Fiesta Day, and the Harvest Dance. The tribe gathers every year in the old village atop the mesa to celebrate the Feast of San Estevan, patron saint of Acoma. Both a Catholic mass and a traditional Harvest Dance are held, and fruits of the harvest are randomly distributed to attendees. Animals have always been highly respected by the Acoma, and the pueblo hosts Buffalo, Deer, and Turtle dances, as well as Basket and Turtle dances at Christmastime.

Children

Babies are made full members of the tribe with both Catholic baptism and the traditional presentation to Ocatc, the Pueblo Sun god.

Funerals

Upon the death of a Catholic Acoma, a Roman Catholic mass for the dead is celebrated. Traditional Indian prayers are also said to pave the way for the departed to be received by the Creator.

Acoma rainbow dancers at the Intertribal Indian Ceremonial at Gallup, New Mexico.

CURRENT TRIBAL ISSUES

Alcoholism among Acoma youth has become a matter of great concern to the tribe, not only because of its devastating physical and psychological effects but also because of its link to increased crime. The tribal court and police department seek to function as law enforcement agents, counselors, and educators to this troubled segment of Acoma society.

During the last half of the twentieth century the Acoma have been buying back their original lands. They made land purchases in the 1970s and 1980s that added thousands of acres to their holdings. Later, a new governmental complex was erected. It includes a large visitor's center, a museum, and a cafeteria.

NOTABLE PEOPLE

Simon J. Ortiz (1941–), who grew up in the village of McCartys, overcame alcohol addiction to become a sober and successful professional writer. In 1968 he received a fellowship from the International Writers Program for study at the University of Iowa. Despite having never earned a college degree, he has taught at several universities, held the post of consulting editor with the Pueblo of Acoma Press, and served as an interpreter and first lieutenant governor for his pueblo. Ortiz has written about Native life in essays, award-winning poetry (collected in *Going for the Rain* and *A Good Journey*), and story collections such as *Fightin'* and *Howbah Indians*.

Other notable Acoma Pueblo people include painter and jewelry designer Wolf Robe Hunt (1905–1977); potter Lucy Lewis

(1898–1992), whose painted designs are based on ancient Native patterns; and potter Lilly Salvador (1944–).

FURTHER READING

Cassidy, James J., Jr., ed. *Through Indian Eyes: The Untold Story of Native American Peoples*. Pleasantville, NY: Reader's Digest Association, 1995.

Sando, Joe S. *Pueblo Nations: Eight Centuries of Pueblo Indian History*. Santa Fe, NM: Clear Light Publishers, 1992.

Yue, Charlotte, and David Yue. *The Pueblo*. Boston: Houghton Mifflin Co., 1986.

Jemez Pueblo

See Pueblo entry for more information on the Pueblo peoples.

Name

Jemez Pueblo (pronounced *HAY-mes PWEB-loh*). The Jemez called themselves *Hemes,* which in their language of Towa means "people." The village where most tribal members reside is called Walatowa, which means "this is the place."

Location

The Jemez Pueblo, a federal reservation, includes 90,000 acres of the tribe's former homeland in north-central New Mexico. It is located in the San Diego Canyon on the Jemez River. More than half of the Jemez people currently live in the reservation town of Walatowa. (See map on page 524.)

Population

In 1583, there were an estimated 30,000 Jemez Pueblo people. In 1630, there were only 3,000. In 1706, there were just 300. In a census (count of the population) taken in 1990 by the U.S. Bureau of the Census, 2,238 people identified themselves as Jemez.

Language family

Tanoan.

Origins and group affiliations

Jemez tales trace the tribe's origin to a lagoon near Stone Lake, New Mexico, now the site of the Jicarilla (pronounced *hee-kah-REE-yah*) Apache Reservation. Between 1250 and 1300 C.E. the Jemez moved from that site to the mountains of northern New Mexico in what is now part of the Santa Fe National Forest.

In 1838 the Jemez at the Jemez Pueblo were joined by the people of the Pueblo of Pecos. (*Pueblo* is the Spanish word given to the stone and adobe, or mud-walled, villages inhabited by the various pueblo peoples.)

At the time the Jemez people first made contact with the Spanish, the Jemez Nation was one of the largest and most powerful in the region that is now the state of New Mexico. Their original homes, stone fortresses that sometimes contained more than 2,000 rooms, are some of the largest ruins in the United States. Over the years the people of the Jemez Pueblo have been able to withstand enormous outside pressures and still retain their traditional religion and culture.

HISTORY

Jemez make contact with the Spanish

During the fourteenth century the Jemez made their home in the hills of San Diego Canyon, whose fertile floor is irrigated by the Jemez River. It was in this canyon that the first Spanish explorers of New Mexico came upon the people who identified themselves as Jemez. The meeting took place in 1541, when Francisco Vasquez de Coronado led an expedition into the area. At that time the pueblo had a population of more than thirty thousand.

It was not until 1598 that there was significant interaction between the Jemez and the Spanish. The association lasted for a little more than 80 years and ended in a massive rebellion by the Indians.

Abuse and revolt

The Spanish plan was to convert the Jemez to the Catholic religion, by force if necessary. When the missionary priests first arrived, the Jemez were living either in small pueblos scattered throughout San Diego Canyon or on the surrounding large hills. These large hills had steep sides and flat tops and were called *mesas* (meaning "tables" in Spanish). The mesas offered protection against wandering raiders like the Apache and Comanche (see entries).

To make their own work easier, Spanish priests and soldiers forced the Jemez and other Pueblo peoples down off the mesa tops. They took Jemez homes for themselves and ordered the people to build new villages and churches. The Jemez were made to pay taxes to the king of Spain in the form of crops, blankets, and pottery. They were forbidden to practice their own religion, although many did so in secret. Finally, in 1680, the Jemez could take the mistreatment no longer and agreed to join in the Pueblo Revolt. (See Pueblo entry.) In spite of the superior weapons of the Spanish, the Pueblo peoples succeeded in casting the Spanish out of New Mexico.

Return of the Spanish

But the Spanish were not gone for long. Between 1688 and 1692 they regained their power over Jemez land. The Jemez were ordered to pledge their support to Spain, but most refused to take such a vow. In 1694 the Jemez staged a raid against the Zia and Santa Ana tribes (supporters of the Spanish), taking their livestock and killing four men.

The Spaniards then sent out an expedition to punish the Jemez. In the bloody battle that followed, 381 Jemez women and children were captured, 84 people were killed, and villages were destroyed. Jemez crops and cattle were taken and distributed to Indian allies of the Spaniards. Most of the survivors were later pardoned and released by the Spanish, and in 1696 the Jemez were commanded to leave their homes and live together in the small village of Walatowa.

IMPORTANT DATES

1680: The Pueblo Revolt, in which the Jemez people play a vital role, drives the Spanish from New Mexico.

1694: The Spanish recapture the San Diego Valley, home of the Jemez.

1696: Luis Cunixu, a Jemez war chief, tries to spark another Jemez rebellion but is later executed.

1838: The people of Pecos abandon their pueblo and join the Jemez at Walatowa.

1848: The United States takes control of New Mexico.

1936: The Jemez and Pecos peoples legally become one group.

Return to Jemez Pueblo

But more bloodshed was to follow. In June 1696 a Spanish priest was found dead, and Jemez leader Luis Cunixu (see "Notable People") was accused of his murder. The Jemez, fearing vengeance on the part of the Spanish, left the village and made plans to defend themselves. They requested help from the Acoma, Zuñi, and Navajo peoples (see entries), who obliged by sending some warriors. After a few battles, though, the Indians were forced to surrender. The Jemez scattered and the Indian warriors who were called to help returned home. By the early 1700s matters had quieted down, and the people again began to settle at the Jemez Pueblo.

The Spanish retained control of the region until 1820. During that time Spain's king assured the Jemez people of their rights to more than 17,000 acres of their traditional land. Although the Spanish persisted in trying to convert them and trampled on many sacred shrines and religious centers, the Jemez were able to stay together and preserve much of their culture.

Assured land rights

Pueblo territory passed into Mexican hands in 1820, and the Jemez lost much of their ancestral land. In 1838 the Jemez at Walatowa were joined by Pecos peoples who were fleeing enemy raids and deadly disease epidemics. Nearly 100 years later the two groups would legally become one.

Following America's victory in the Mexican-American War in 1848, the United States took over the Pueblo region from Mexico. The Jemez were assured by the new government that their rights to their land would be protected, but the United States failed to keep its promises. White settlers were allowed to move onto the land illegally. Throughout the twentieth century the Jemez people engaged in ongoing battles with U.S. courts to defend their land and water rights. They did achieve some victories, though, including the 1975 expansion of their land holdings to its present 90,000 acres.

RELIGION

Very little is known about the traditional Jemez religion. Fearing their ceremonies will lose power if they are made public, the Jemez people hold all religious services in secret. It is known that the Jemez try to live in close harmony with nature. Their ceremonies are held to bring rain, help crops grow, and ensure abundant game supplies.

When Jemez people tell tribal stories to outsiders, they sometimes leave out details that would reveal certain secrets about their traditions.

LANGUAGE

The Jemez language, Towa, is still spoken at Walatowa in combination with English and Spanish. Jemez law does not allow the language to be written down because the people wish to keep outsiders from gaining knowledge about the tribe.

GOVERNMENT

The Pueblo of Jemez is a sovereign nation, which means it is not subject to outside laws. Two types of government are in place: traditional and secular (nonreligious). The traditional government has two leaders who hold their positions for life. The most important of these, the *cacique,* is both a spiritual and a societal leader. He is served by the *opng-soma* (war chief), who enforces the religious rules and regulations. The secular government began during the time of the Spanish occupation. It consists of a governor and his staff, who are selected each year by the cacique and a tribal council. (The council is made up of former governors.) The secular government maintains business relations with the outside world.

ECONOMY

The Jemez Pueblo in 1935.

For centuries the Jemez relied on hunting, farming, and gathering to support the tribe. When the Spanish arrived on the scene, the Jemez sold them rabbit fur blankets and simple knee-length dresses called *mantas*. The Spanish introduced to the Jemez Pueblo (1) new crops (chilies, wheat, grapes, and melons) and (2) livestock (horses, donkeys, oxen, cattle, sheep, and goats). In time most Jemez families owned a donkey. Grapes were harvested until World War II (1939–45), when so many Jemez men went off to war that the vines withered from neglect.

Most modern-day Jemez are farmers or ranchers. Corn and chilies are their most important crops. Some Jemez make and sell various arts and crafts such as ring baskets (round yucca-leaf baskets used to store food and wash wheat) and a type of red pottery that was developed in the 1950s. Ponderosa pine and Douglas fir from the reservation is sold for use as timber and fuel wood. The Jemez operate a gas station-convenience store, and since 1989 land on the reservation has been producing oil and gas. The tribe also earns funds by permitting the mining of sand and gravel on its territory.

Some tribal members work at nearby computer firms. Others work for the Bureau of Indian Affairs, the U.S. Forest Service, local law enforcement agencies, and the tribal court system.

Buildings

The pueblo style of architecture (see Pueblo entry) was practiced by the Jemez from around 700 C.E. They constructed and maintained large pueblos containing as many as four levels—each level being smaller by one room than the level below it. The roofs were built by laying whole log beams across two walls. Spaces between the logs were then filled in with grasses and plastered over with adobe (pronounced *uh-DOE-bee*; a sun-dried mud made of a mixture of clay, sand, and sometimes ashes, rocks, or straw.)

The *kiva,* a room where ceremonies and sacred meetings take place, is also central to Jemez culture. One kiva is built for each tribal subdivision in a pueblo village. The kivas are most often built of stone.

Food

The Jemez lived and farmed at a higher elevation than any other Pueblo people. While the men farmed and hunted deer, antelope, elk, sheep, and cattle, the women gathered fruits, cactus, and other wild foods. The cultivation of chilies, melons, grapes, and wheat was adopted from the Spanish. To prepare wheat for grinding, it was first winnowed (separated out), then washed in an irrigation ditch in a ring-basket, and finally spread on canvas to dry. Fields of corn, beans, squash, wheat, and chilies still fill the canyon floor at Walatowa, and agriculture and livestock represent a major source of livelihood on the reservation.

Education

The Jemez Pueblo offers Head Start classes for young children on the reservation. A Bureau of Indian Affairs day school and public elementary and secondary schools have been built there as well. High school students have the option of attending public school in Jemez Springs or boarding school in Santa Fe.

Healing practices

According to Jemez beliefs, supernatural creatures could either heal people or make them ill. The traditional Jemez relied on a curing society rather than a single shaman (pronounced *SHAY-mun*) to do the healing. Healing ceremonies took place before the whole community. To cure an individual or an entire community, the curing society would call forth the supernatural forces—possibly spirits or even a witch within the pueblo—thought to be causing harm. At the end of the twentieth century the Jemez people made use of traditional healing practices in combination with modern methods offered at Walatowa's community medical center.

ARTS

The Jemez traditions of potterymaking and basketweaving date back to about 700 C.E. Aside from their exquisite pottery and basketry, the tribespeople are known for their woven cloth, sculptures, and jewelry. Jemez artworks are sold all around the world and at the Walatowa Visitor Center. The center features photographic exhibits, replicas of Native buildings, and a gift shop.

CUSTOMS

Moieties

The Jemez have two tribal subdivisions, called moieties (pronounced *MOY-uh-teez*): the turquoise and the squash. These are not "clans," that is, groups of people descended from a common ancestor. Rather, they are tribal divisions that determine which group among the Jemez performs certain rites or ceremonies.

From the Spanish the Jemez adopted the idea that the man is the head of the household, and modern families take the last name of father.

Festivals and ceremonies

The Jemez have a very complex organization for ceremonies, with 23 religious societies conducting various rites. Every Jemez male is a member of either the Eagle or Arrow society, but membership in the others is reserved for a select few who show some talent in curing, rainmaking, war, hunting, or other areas.

Dances are central to ceremonial and social life for the Jemez. Many of their ritual dances and ceremonies, like the Corn Dance, are performed to gain the favor of the spirits. Ceremonies and dances are traditionally shared among Pueblo peoples. For example, the Jemez learned the Pecos Bull Ceremony in 1838 after the remaining survivors of the Pecos Pueblo joined their tribe. The Corn Dance and Old Pecos Bull Ceremony at Jemez are still held each August as part of the Saint Persingula Feast Day.

Feast days are a Catholic practice. Many Jemez identify themselves as Catholics and observe ceremonies of the Christian calendar, but they observe them in a traditional Native American way. For example, the celebration of a feast day displays Jemez reverence for the foods—both animal and vegetable—provided by Mother Earth.

Families from different groups within the tribe are selected to host each feast day celebration. They provide a meal for all visitors, and the guests may in turn bring an offering of food to be included with the meal. Part of the food preparation takes place outside in the tall adobe ovens, called "beehives," that are still present behind many Jemez homes. As a feast day progresses, ceremonial dances take place in the town square to give thanks for the bounty, which has been shared.

Other important feast days and festivals include the annual Jemez Red Rocks Arts & Crafts Show in June, Our Lady of Los Angeles Feast Day in August, Fall Arts Fiesta in October, the San Diego Feast Day in November, and Our Lady of Guadalupe Feast Day and the Walatowa Winter Arts & Crafts Show, both in December. The pueblo is open to the public only during selected special events.

Track and field

Running is a longtime tradition at the Jemez Pueblo, which over the years has produced a number of world-class runners.

CURRENT TRIBAL ISSUES

The Jemez, who once inhabited the entire San Diego Canyon, have seen their land holdings dwindle since the Spanish arrived in their territory in the late 1500s. Four hundred years later New Mexico courtrooms were hearing many cases regarding ongoing efforts to protect Jemez land rights.

Water rights are also a problem. With the increasing use of the Jemez River by people north of Walatowa, as well as the frequency of droughts in the area, Jemez farmers find it difficult to secure enough water for the irrigation of their crops.

Tribal elders are concerned about the spread of white cultural practices among the Jemez people. Problems began when the plow replaced the traditional and sacred hoe. The elders thought that the use of modern technology would interfere with the sacred nature of the planting of the corn—and thereby anger the gods. Then the plow was replaced by the tractor and the horse was replaced by the pickup truck. In modern Walatowa, antennas protrude from pueblo rooftops and nearly every household has electricity and appliances. Experts in Native American studies disagree on whether these elements can coexist with traditional life—or someday will replace it altogether.

NOTABLE PEOPLE

Luis Cunixu, a Jemez leader (probably a war captain) who lived during the seventeenth century, refused to accept the return of the Spanish to his land when Spain reclaimed control over New Mexico in 1692. He fought to remove them, then fled to the Pecos Pueblo after being accused of killing a Spanish priest during an uprising in June 1696. Cunixu worked unsuccessfully to gain the support of the Pecos people but was turned over to the Spanish and finally shot to death in Santa Fe in front of the town church.

Other notable Jemez include: painter Jose Rey Toledo (1915–1994); author, historian, and educator Joe Sando (1923– ; see Pueblo entry), who wrote several books about the Pueblo people; and legendary runner Tyila (Pablo Gachupin).

FURTHER READING

"Pueblo Tribes, Eastern." *American Indians.* Vol. 2. Englewood Cliffs, NJ: Salem Press, 1995.

Sando, Joe S. *Nee Hemish: A History of Jemez Pueblo.* Albuquerque: University of New Mexico Press, 1982.

Scully, Vincent. *Pueblo—Mountain, Village, Dance.* Chicago: University of Chicago Press, 1989.

San Juan Pueblo

See Pueblo entry for more information on the Pueblo peoples.

Name

San Juan Pueblo (pronounced *sahn HWAHN PWEB-loh*). The Spanish term "pueblo," which means "town," is used to refer to both the Pueblo people and the pueblos (cities) where they live. In the Tewa language of the San Juan people, their pueblo is called Oke Owinge. In 1598 the Spanish gave it the name San Juan Bautista in honor of St. John the Baptist, a Christian saint.

Location

The San Juan Pueblo, a federal reservation of more than 2,000 acres, is located 30 miles north of Santa Fe in north-central New Mexico, northeast of where the Rio Grande or meets the Rio Chama. (See map on page 524.)

Population

In 1680, there were an estimated 300 San Juan Pueblo. In a census (count of the population) taken in 1990 by the U.S. Bureau of the Census, 1,081 people identified themselves as San Juan Pueblo.

Language family

Tanoan.

Origins and group affiliations

San Juan tales trace the tribe's origin to a land in the North where the first people emerged from beneath a lake. From this place the people migrated to the Rio Grande, the river that separates Mexico from the United States at the Texas border and stretches throughout central New Mexico. There they eventually created seven pueblo communities, of which six still exist. The San Juan Pueblo's closest allies have always been the other Tewa-speaking communities of Santa Clara, San Ildefonso, Nambé, Pojoaque, and Tesuque. The six groups share a common ancestry and similar mythologies and customs. The San Juan also had mostly friendly relations with the other pueblos in New Mexico and with the Jicarilla (pronounced *hee-kah-REE-yah*) Apache (see Apache entry).

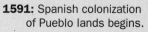
The people of San Juan, the northernmost of the pueblos containing Tewa speakers, called their pueblo the "Mother Village." They have lived and cultivated crops on the reservation's flat farmlands for at least 700 years. The San Juan group has carefully adapted parts of the white culture that are most useful to them while maintaining the most meaningful of their traditional ways.

HISTORY

Spanish persecution

The Tewa-speaking peoples first made contact with Europeans in 1541, when men from the Spanish expedition of Francisco Vásquez de Coronado traveled through the area looking for food. Fearful of these strangers, the people retreated to easily defended villages in the mountains. In 1591 Don Juan de Oñate and his group made their way to the lands of the Tewa-speaking peoples to establish a permanent Spanish settlement.

Throughout the seventeenth century the people of San Juan and other pueblos endured religious persecution at the hands of Spanish Catholics and were forced to work for the benefit of Spanish settlers. This oppressive situation sparked a spirit of revolution among the Natives that fueled the Pueblo Revolt of 1680 (see Pueblo entry). One of the leaders of the rebellion was a San Juan man named Popé.

Alliances with the Spanish

The Pueblo Revolt of 1680 was one of the most dramatic victories against white settlement in Indian history, but it drove the Spanish from the region for only twelve years. The rebellion failed to bring the peace and prosperity sought by the people of the pueblos. Drought, famine, and attacks by the Apache (see entry) compounded problems. In time the alliances among the San Juan and other Natives that had been formed during the revolt were as weak as the people.

The Spanish returned to the area in 1692, but this time some of their leaders took an attitude of greater tolerance and moderation. Because San Juan was centrally located for the Spanish, it became a religious and trade center for the area. Throughout the 1700s the Pueblo peoples and Spanish settlers supported one another in the

face of attacks by Indian raiders like the Apache and the Comanche (see entries). Sometimes the Spanish and the people of the pueblos held joint ceremonies to celebrate their victories in battle, and in this way their friendship was cemented.

A San Juan Pueblo street scene, 1925, photographed by Edward S. Curtis.

Facing U.S. expansion

When Mexico gained its independence from Spain in 1821, members of the San Juan Pueblo were given Mexican citizenship. About 25 years later, following the Mexican-American War (1846-48), the territory of the San Juan was made part of the United States. Like other pueblos, the San Juan had to face the land-greedy settlers in an ever-expanding United States.

The San Juan Pueblo was made a reservation in 1858. The U.S. government claimed it recognized the rights of the San Juan to their homelands, but its behavior over time proved otherwise. For example, the Pueblo Lands Act of 1924 reduced the size of the San Juan reservation from 17,544 acres to 12,234 acres. And over the course of the twentieth century the land and water rights of the San Juan have been the subject of a number of disputes.

RELIGION

Traditional San Juan religious beliefs are linked to all aspects of everyday life. In fact, there is no Tewa word for "religion": the native religious practices are simply known as the "Indian way."

The whole tribe takes part in ceremonial dances, prayer retreats, and games, which are all considered important spiritual events. The San Juan use ceremonies and rituals to thank the Creator for good fortune and to ask for his blessings.

Highly honored groups within the tribe are called sodalities (pronounced *soh-DAL-uh-teez*); members of sodalities organize and carry out the major social and religious rituals of the San Juan people. Tribal members who are accepted into these high-level sodalities are known as the *Pa Towa* or "Made People."

Most modern-day San Juan people are Roman Catholic, but they typically combine their Christian faith with important aspects of the traditional tribal religion. For example, marriage ceremonies and naming/baptism ceremonies have both Catholic and Native elements, and the celebration of the Catholics' San Antonio's Day (St. Anthony's Day; June 13th) features a traditional Corn Dance.

LANGUAGE

The San Juan people speak a dialect (variety) of the Tewa language, part of the Tanoan language family. Tewa speakers originally spoke several languages and could communicate with the other pueblos and neighboring tribes. But when the Spanish took charge of the area, the San Juan began using the Spanish language as their primary means of communication. English later replaced Spanish as the tribe's main language. Some Native children continue to learn Tewa at home, but doing so has become increasingly difficult. The population of Tewa speakers is aging, and most grandparents no longer live in the same house with their grandchildren. The youngest generation of San Juan Indians is therefore not exposed to the Native language on a regular basis.

GOVERNMENT

Unlike most other Native American tribes, the San Juan government operates with no constitution. Three types of government leaders are in place: civil (nonreligious) officers, tribal religious leaders, and officers of the Catholic church.

The civil government dates back to the time of Spanish rule in the early 1600s. It includes a governor, two lieutenant governors, a sheriff, and a tribal council. Officers are appointed to one-year terms by the tribal religious leaders, but they may serve an unlimited number of terms. The tribal council is made up of the serving governor, lieutenant governors, a sheriff, all former governors, and the heads of the religious societies of the village. Active religious leaders select other officers, as well as civil and Catholic officers. A tribal court was established in 1976.

ECONOMY

The emergence of wage labor

For centuries before the outbreak of World War II (1939-45), the San Juan people relied mostly on farming, cattle raising, and trade to make their living. Farming efforts and crops were once shared by all members of the community, but in modern times working for wages has become more common.

In 1965 a tribal program was introduced to help the pueblo gain federal funding for construction projects, including a youth center, a senior center, a tribal office, a tribal court, a warehouse, and a post office. The tribe's bingo facility provides modest profits and employment for tribal members. Among the other facilities owned by the tribe are a service station and the Blue Rock Office Complex. Some mining of sand, gravel, and adobe (pronounced *uh-DOE-bee*; a sun-dried mud made of a mixture of clay, sand, and sometimes ashes, rocks, or straw) building materials adds to the tribe's income.

Growth in arts, tourism, professions

Locally produced art of all kinds is on display at the Oke Owinge Artisan's Cooperative, a business that offers art classes and workshops, as well as a studio, gallery, and shop space. More than sixty Native potters earn at least part of their income from the sales of San Juan pottery, which has earned the praise of art experts. Ceremonial dances attract visitors to the pueblo throughout the year, although the San Juan people also hold dances that are not open to the public.

By the start of the twenty-first century a growing number of San Juan people were graduating from high school, attending college, and working in business, health care, various fields of science, and tribal government.

DAILY LIFE

Buildings

The San Juan Pueblo once consisted of two-story adobe structures that were built around public squares. Individual two- to four-room homes shared common walls to form adjoining "apartments." Because the buildings were made of bricks of mud, the village blended in with its surroundings and was only visible from a few hundred feet away, making it more difficult for enemies to find and attack.

Much of this original pueblo still exists, although the second stories have disappeared. Maintaining the village is an expensive proposition, and many modern-day families live in American-style homes or trailers. During the 1950s and 1960s a relocation program moved some San Juan people to various western cities, but within 20 to 30 years many of these families moved back to San Juan. By the late 1990s a program was launched to renovate (fix up) the adobe homes around the pueblo's central square, and families continued to occupy the old village during ceremonial periods.

Clothing and adornment

Although most San Juan people now wear modern dress, the tribe maintains traditional ceremonial costumes. Large headdresses worn by the men for the Deer Dance are made up of a fan of painted split cane, antlers, and turkey feathers. Cotton leggings complete the outfit. Women wear lavishly embroidered dresses with woven belts.

Food

The tribe's thousands of acres of fertile, well-watered land have been cultivated for centuries. The San Juan people have raised corn, beans, squash, and chilies and made use of wild plant foods such as asparagus, mint, and amaranth, an edible plant with colorful leaves and tassel-like flowers They have also collected pine nuts from the surrounding hills and mountains.

The Spanish introduced many new crops to San Juan—wheat, melons, apricots, apples, and onions among them. At first these crops were grown merely to trade with the Spanish, but in time they became staples of the San Juan Pueblo diet. Likewise, exposure to the Spanish led the San Juan to begin raising livestock such as goats, sheep, cows, horses, chickens, and pigs. These animals provided the tribe with a new source of meat and proved useful for plowing, harvesting, and transportation.

During the 1990s residents and returning retirees began to do more farming at San Juan. Additional crops now raised on the pueblo include a variety of vegetables, alfalfa, and orchard fruit. The tribe owns about 50 head of cattle.

Education

At a very early age San Juan children begin learning the importance of responsible behavior. Formal schooling starts at the preschool level, with three- and four-year-olds attending a Head Start program. There are two grade schools on the reservation: one is a public school and one is operated by the Bureau of Indian Affairs. Junior and senior high school students may attend public schools in nearby Espanola or the boarding school in Santa Fe.

Healing practices

Traditional San Juan believed that illnesses were caused by evil spirits or witches called *chuge*. Charms were often used to protect people from harm and disease.

In early times members of the Bear Medicine Society were responsible for curing the sick. Modern-day tribespeople obtain health care at a hospital in Santa Fe. A community health program on the pueblo offers some limited services, and the New Moon Lodge provides treatment for alcohol abuse.

CUSTOMS

Worldview

Since ancient times the San Juan people have divided the physical world into three parts. The first part is comprised of the village and adjoining areas, which belong to the women and are marked by four sacred objects indicating the directions north, south, east, and west. The second part is made up of the mesas (pronounced *MAY-sas*; a Spanish word meaning "tables"). Mesas are large hills with steep sides and flat tops. They surround San Juan Pueblo and are open to men, women, and children, but they are placed under male authority. The third part of the physical world is the outside world (beyond the mesas). Thought to belong solely to the men of the tribe, the outside world is the place where they hunt, defend their people when necessary, and seek spiritual guidance.

Childhood and adult rites

The San Juan Pueblo observe a series of rituals to bring a child into the community. A "water-giving" rite makes the child a member of a moiety (see "Moieties" below) during the first year of life. A "water-pouring" rite takes place between ages six and nine. An initiation rite officially accepts an adolescent into the Tewa religion. Other rites are associated with sex, marriage, community offices, and membership in various groups.

Moieties

Every San Juan family belongs to one of two social groups known as moieties (pronounced *MOY-uh-teez*). Membership in the Winter and Summer moieties determines the roles played by individuals in religious, political, and economic matters of the pueblo. For example, the annual schedule of religious dances is divided between the moieties. Winter events are usually associated with hunting and trade, while Summer rituals are related to farming and gathering wild plant foods.

Festivals

During the period in the 1700s when the Spanish and the people of San Juan and other pueblos were on friendly terms, festive dances were held to celebrate their victories over raiding tribes of Indians. The dances were called Scalp Dances or Chief Dances. At these events a male dancer dressed up as a chief; a female dancer followed him as he danced. The family of the male dancer gave a variety of gifts to the female dancer, and baskets full of household goods and fruit were tossed into the crowd. Other couples followed them, also dancing and distributing gifts to give thanks for their warriors' safe return.

Buffalo, Animal, and Deer Dances are still held each February in the San Juan Pueblo, and each one is regarded as a significant occasion. The Deer Dance, for example, is performed to assure prosperity for the coming year. Deer dancers often poke fun at Apache-type hunters, stalking the other dancers and pretending to hunt them down with sunflower-stalk arrows. Clowns are major features at other dances held throughout the year.

Additional San Juan celebrations include the June feast days of San Antonio and San Juan, and the Harvest Dances in September. The Turtle Dance is an important winter ceremony, marking the end of one year and the beginning of the next. Some festivities are open only to tribal members, and certain aspects of the celebrations are kept secret.

CURRENT TRIBAL ISSUES

Maintaining the tribe's centuries-old right to water is a critical issue at San Juan. Water is needed for farming and for the development of projects like the San Juan Tribal Lakes Recreation Area, which attracts tourists and provides funds for the tribe. At the end of the twentieth century the state of New Mexico was seeking legal means to limit tribal water rights.

A fiercely proud and honorable people, the San Juan are increasingly concerned about the way their culture has been portrayed by outsiders. Since the late 1800s many scholars have visited the pueblo and then published articles about the tribe's "dying way of life." The San Juan object to the insulting and depressing nature of such commentary and are making efforts to review and approve the content of future articles.

FURTHER READING

Goodman, Linda, J. "San Juan." *Native America in the Twentieth Century.* Ed. Mary B. Davis. New York: Garland Publishing, 1994.

Ortiz, Alfonso. "San Juan Pueblo." *Handbook of North American Indians,* Vol. 9: *Southwest.* Ed. Alfonso Ortiz. Washington, DC: Smithsonian, 1979.

Ortiz, Alfonso. *The Tewa World: Space, Time, Being, and Becoming in a Pueblo Society.* Chicago: University of Chicago Press, 1969.

Sando, Joe S. *Pueblo Nations: Eight Centuries of Pueblo Indian History.* Santa Fe: Clear Light, 1992.

Taos Pueblo

See Pueblo entry for more information on the Pueblo peoples.

Name

Taos Pueblo (pronounced *TAH-ohs PWEB-loh*). The term "Taos" comes from a Spanish word meaning "in the village." The Spanish term "pueblo," which means "town" is used to refer to both the Pueblo peoples and the pueblos in which they live. The Taos referred to themselves as "the people."

Location

The Taos Pueblo, a federal reservation, is located in northeastern New Mexico. It sits on a plateau at the base of Mount Wheeler in the Sangre de Cristo Mountains, approximately 70 miles north of Santa Fe. (See map on page 524.)

Population

In 1680, there were an estimated 2,000 Taos Pueblo. In 1864, there were only 361. In 1930, there were 694. In a census (count of the population) taken in 1990 by to the U.S. Bureau of the Census, 1,875 people identified themselves as Taos Pueblo.

Language family

Tanoan.

Origins and group affiliations

The origin of the Taos people is uncertain but may trace back to the Anasazi (see entry) or Chaco peoples. The Taos have maintained generally good relations with neighboring Pueblo peoples, as well as with the Ute, Apache, and Navajo tribes (see entries).

The Taos Pueblo may be the most photographed and most easily recognized pueblo in the world because of its beauty and
perfectly preserved condition. Since the arrival of the
Spaniards in the sixteenth century, when the Taos people were raising
cattle and doing limited farming, the pueblo has been subject to periods of Spanish, Mexican, and American rule. Its people have been at
the forefront of revolts against outside domination and have twice
rebuilt their city when parts of it were burned by outsiders. The
strong sense of community and interdependence among the Taos
people has helped them to preserve their traditional way of life with
only minor changes through the centuries.

HISTORY

Emerges as trading center

Although little is known about the history of the Taos Pueblo
before the coming of Europeans, their tribal tales tell of a long period
when the tribe roamed the plains near New Mexico's Sangre de Cristo
Mountains. Archaeologists (scientists who study ancient cultures by
examining the things they left behind) estimate the tribe arrived in
the area some 1,000 years ago. The first pueblo may have been built
in the mid-1300s, less than a mile north of its present-day site.

By the time Spanish explorer Francisco de Coronado
(1510–1554) arrived in 1540, Taos was already a thriving trading
center. Coronado wrote then of the wonders he saw. The many-sto-
ried adobe (pronounced *uh-DOE-bee*) buildings, large circular places
of worship, a low adobe wall encircling the original village—all of
these things still exist in Taos. (Adobe is a sun-dried mud made of a
mixture of clay, sand, and sometimes ashes, rocks, or straw.)

Many other Pueblo peoples and members of several different
tribes, including the Comanche (see entry), the Apache, and the
Navajo, traveled to Taos to trade animal hides, meat, blankets, and
vegetables. Long after the Spanish arrived, these trade fairs continued to flourish. In later years non-Native Americans also took part in
the fairs.

The Catholic religion by force

In 1598 Spanish explorer Juan de Oñate arrived in the Pueblo
area, intent on making the Native people part of a Spanish colony.
When he established a headquarters barely 50 miles south of Taos, a
long, difficult, and often violent period in Pueblo history began.

One of Oñate's goals was to convert the Indians to Christianity. Mission San Geronimo was established at Taos and a Catholic priest took up residence there. Anyone caught participating in Native rituals was punished and given a heavy fine. While Taos residents adopted many Catholic rituals, they secretly kept many of their traditional practices as well.

Natives overthrow Spanish for a time

Drawn together by religious oppression and other threats to their ancestral way of life, the various Pueblo tribes began the Pueblo Revolt of 1680. Popé, a medicine man from San Juan Pueblo (see "Notable People" in Pueblo entry), had earlier fled from the Spanish oppressors and sought refuge at Taos, where he planned the revolt. At dawn on August 10, 1680, all of the Pueblo groups struck at once. The mission at Taos was burned and more than 70 settlers were killed, including 2 priests. The Spaniards left the area and did not return for 12 years.

The Spanish began to reestablish their colonies in the Pueblo region in 1692. The Taos Pueblo resisted and staged another revolt in 1696, but the success of 1680 was not to be repeated. The Spanish military quickly forced the Taos to surrender. So began an uneasy peace between the Indians and the colonizers that extended over the next 150 years.

Death and destruction

During that time control of the region passed from Spain to Mexico and then, in 1846 with the beginning of the Mexican-American War, to the United States. The Mexicans were unhappy with this transfer of power and persuaded the Pueblo peoples to help them stage a revolt. The Revolt of 1847, which originated at Taos, led to the assassination of the American territorial governor. The U.S. Army responded swiftly.

Upon learning that the American Army was approaching, more than 700 Taos Pueblo barricaded themselves inside the San Geronimo Mission. U.S. troops, unable to break through the walls of the mission, bombarded it with gunfire and set fire to the roof. In the resulting bloodbath, more than 150 Taos Pueblo lost their lives and the

IMPORTANT DATES

1540: Spanish explorer Francisco de Coronado arrives in Pueblo country.

1598: Juan de Oñate sets up a Spanish colony and builds Mission San Geronimo at Taos Pueblo.

1680: The Pueblo Revolt pushes the Spaniards from the region for 12 years.

1847: Another Pueblo rebellion leads to the assassination of the American territorial governor. In retaliation, U.S. troops destroy the mission at Taos Pueblo, killing 150 Taos Indians.

1970: U.S. returns sacred Blue Lake to Taos Pueblo.

mission was destroyed. The next day Taos surrendered, and the long process of rebuilding the pueblo began.

The battle for Blue Lake

Since that time the battles fought in Taos have been legal, rather than military, ones. The most famous was the battle for Blue Lake, the spiritual home and sacred ceremonial site of the Taos people. In 1906 Congress seized much of the Taos homeland, including Blue Lake, and made it part of Carson National Forest. Tourists visiting the site prevented the Taos people from making their annual pilgrimages to the lake.

The Taos reacted to this threat to their religion with a court battle that lasted for 50 years. It finally ended in 1970 when the U.S. Senate voted to return Blue Lake to the Taos people. The settlement marked the first time that land—not money—was returned to an American Indian tribe upon the completion of a court case over lost territory.

RELIGION

The traditional religion of the Indians continues at Taos Pueblo in modern times, but it is cloaked in secrecy. The Taos Indians forbid

any disclosure of their religious practices, and very little information has been published about them. Scholars say that a lot of the written information about the religion is unreliable.

Most of the pueblo members consider themselves Catholic, and many attend church services regularly. There has been much blending of the Catholic and Native religions over time, but they are still considered separate.

The spiritual leader of the Taos tribe is the *cacique* (pronounced *kuh-SEEK*), who is also a society leader. This lifelong position can only be held by a man. Other important religious leaders are the chiefs of the six *kivas* (circular adobe structures located partially below ground that serve as the center of the Pueblo's spiritual life). Kiva groups are responsible for running ceremonies, dances, and seasonal rituals. Though women may belong to kivas, only men are permitted to participate in their sacred practices.

LANGUAGE

Tiwa is the native language of Taos Pueblo. It is a dialect (variety) of the Tanoan language family. Other pueblos that speak Tiwa are the Picuris Pueblo, Sandia Pueblo, and Isleta Pueblo, but the language varies at each one.

Most pueblo residents spoke English by the end of the twentieth century, but many of the elders still spoke Tiwa, and it was probably also used in Taos ceremonies. Still an unwritten language, Tiwa has been passed down orally for generations. The pueblo's day school is engaged in efforts to teach Tiwa to Taos youth. Classes are conducted by those who still know the language.

GOVERNMENT

Taos Pueblo is an independent, self-governed community. Its government is made up of a tribal council, a governor, and the office of the WarChief. The tribal council, the highest authority, has more than 50 members who serve for life. Council members include major religious leaders and all former governors, lieutenant governors, the WarChief, and the lieutenant WarChief. The governor and the WarChief and their staffs are appointed by the tribal council and serve one-year terms of office. They carry on the day-to-day affairs of the pueblo.

ECONOMY

In early times

The Taos Pueblo sits at a high altitude in the New Mexican mountains and has a short growing season. The tribe's early economy was based primarily on hunting and gathering, with limited farming. Deer, bear, turkey, antelope, elk, and buffalo were hunted regularly, and massive rabbit drives were conducted, which required the participation of every man who knew how to shoot with a bow and arrow.

The Taos reservation boasts 10,000 acres of land that can be irrigated. But the cattle raising and farming of earlier years has mostly been replaced by work for wages and income from government grants and self-help projects.

In modern times

Tourism is now the backbone of the Taos economy. Many people travel from far away to see the pueblo every year. The tribe charges entrance fees and fees for taking photographs, and tribal members serve as paid tour guides. Two restaurants offer traditional and modern foods, and the Taos Indian Horse Ranch provides tours and horseback riding. Dances and other ceremonies are open to the public 12 days each year.

The Taos Pueblo Enterprises, Inc. promotes tribal economic development and manages tribally-owned businesses. Small businesses

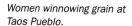
Women winnowing grain at Taos Pueblo.

owned by tribal members produce such handcrafted items as deer horn sculptures, pottery, silver and turquoise jewelry, blankets, tanned buckskin moccasins, and drums. A bingo facility was under development in the late 1990s. Around that time the tribe purchased the 16,000-acre Moreno Ranch and plans were under way to raise bison there.

Although tribal lands are rich in game and forest products, the tribe considers them and the mountains surrounding them as sacred. They do not allow timbering, mining, or grazing there and keep the lands as a religious sanctuary. Because jobs were scarce on the reservation at the end of the twentieth century, many workers had to leave the pueblo to find employment.

DAILY LIFE

Buildings

The buildings that lie on both sides of the Rio Pueblo are classic examples of pueblo architecture, and some families still reside there. But the majority of tribespeople live in single-family homes located outside the pueblo wall. Built with modern materials, these houses have stucco (cement-plastered) exteriors to make them look like traditional adobe buildings.

A man and his granddaughter relax in front of a building in the Taos Pueblo. An adobe oven, used for baking bread, is in the foreground.

Clothing and adornment

While Taos Indian dress has changed considerably since Spanish colonial days, some traditional elements remain. Men still wear the *mantas* (blanketlike cloaks) that were first observed by the Spaniards. Where once the mantas were made from buffalo hide, by the 1900s white cotton was the preferred style. Today, machine-made blankets are commonly worn.

Men used to wear rough cloth leggings fastened to the waist by a cord. They were worn with a cotton loincloth (flaps of material that covered the front and back and were suspended from the waist). When Western-style pants were introduced, Taos men cut out the seat to turn them into "Indian" leggings.

As they still do, Taos men wore their hair in two braids, one behind each ear. Women wore the traditional pueblo dress, consisting of a sleeveless print dress attached at one shoulder and worn over a long-sleeved white cotton garment. A thick woven belt was fastened around the waist. They also wore buckskin boots, often rising to mid-thigh. Many Taos women still wear their hair in the traditional style, long and loose with eyebrow length bangs.

Food

The Taos ate traditional Pueblo foods, but by 1936 their principle crops were corn and wheat, which the men cultivated while the women tended small vegetable gardens. To supplement their food supply, they raised livestock, including chickens, cattle, and pigs.

In the late 1990s the Taos grew beans and pumpkins, tended fruit trees, and raised a small herd of buffalo, but they relied heavily on store-bought groceries as well. The people of the pueblo have, however, maintained the tradition of using small, outdoor adobe ovens called *hornos* to bake bread.

Education

The pueblo has a Head Start Program and an elementary day school operated by the Bureau of Indian Affairs. Students may also attend public and private schools in the nearby town of Taos, New Mexico, or an Indian boarding school in Santa Fe.

Healing practices

Unlike most Pueblo tribes, the Taos did not have curing societies. Instead, they relied on individual healers. Working for four days at the patient's home, the healer sang medicine songs, brushed eagle feathers over the patient, and sucked out disease-causing foreign objects from the body. Since witchcraft was considered the source of sickness, it was part of the healer's job to figure out who sent the sickness and to spit a special type of medicine to ward off witches. Plants and animal blood were used to make medicine. Modern-day Taos receive their medical care at nearby hospitals.

ARTS

The Taos are known for their skilled use of leather in crafting boots, moccasins, clothing, and drums.

Oral literature

The Taos have always enjoyed telling tales during the long winter evenings. They typically begin the stories by naming a character and stating where he lives. Some of the most popular characters are Yellow Corn girl, Blue Corn girl, Magpie-tail boy, and Coyote, the trickster. Tales are passed down orally from generation to generation, and the people often adopt stories from other cultures.

CUSTOMS

Secrecy

The Pueblo people have always been very secretive about the social organization and customs of their tribe, and harsh punishment traditionally resulted from speaking too freely in front of outsiders. Religious ceremonies are closed to outsiders, and photography is not allowed at public dances or in sacred areas. The annual pilgrimages to Blue Lake are private; no non-Native is known to have ever participated.

Naming

Historians say that formal rituals to find the proper name for a child were never observed at Taos. Rather, any friend or relative could suggest a name for an infant. Once the name was determined, a male relative would present the child to the Sun and/or the Moon and pray for good luck and long life for the child. All infants were dedicated to one of the six kivas (places of worship). A short time after the birth, a member of that kiva would arrive to give the child its kiva name. This ceremonial name was only used during the sacred activities of the kiva.

Adolescence

Kiva spiritual training took place when a boy was between 8 and 10 years old. His initiation period lasted for 18 months and ended with a pilgrimage to Blue Lake. During training the boy was required to live within the walls of the kiva.

Although girls were also dedicated to a kiva, they did not undergo initiation. Instead, they participated in an adolescence ritual that began with their first menstrual period. The girl was then confined for four days in the ground-floor room of her home, required to grind corn in silence, and was not allowed to be touched by sunlight. On the fourth day the childhood braid was removed from her hair and her bangs were cut. After this ritual had occurred, the girl—at this point eligible for marriage—could also go to Blue Lake.

Festivals

Various annual festivals and dances are important to the Taos way of life. These community events have continued mostly unchanged for centuries. They include the Deer Dance, held either on Christmas Day or on January 6; the Feast of San Geronimo, held in late September; and the Corn Dances, which take place in the spring and summer. The festivals feature dancing, relay races, and pole climbing

competitions, which visitors are allowed to attend. But the sacred rituals associated with the festivals are open only to participating tribal members.

The tribe's most important ritual is the August pilgrimage to Blue Lake. Blue Lake is believed to be the Earth's navel, from which the Taos people emerged. It is a sacred site that provides more than just water; it has great spiritual meaning as the source of life.

Marriage

Until recent times members of the Taos Pueblo were forbidden from marrying anyone but other pueblo residents, a practice meant to preserve pure bloodlines. Most people who marry outside the tribe choose to reside off the reservation, often many miles away. Marriages are either nonreligious or are performed in accordance with the Roman Catholic church. Divorces, once almost nonexistent, have become easier to obtain in modern times.

Funerals

Traditionally, Taos burials were held the morning after death. Following the burial, family members remained in the house of the deceased for four days to prevent the person's spirit from returning to the home. After the fourth day mourners placed ritual offerings—feathers, food, and moccasins—to the north just beyond the edge of town. A bit of food was offered to the spirits of the dead at mealtimes. As they still are today, the dead were buried at the ruins of the old Taos mission with the head directed toward the south.

CURRENT TRIBAL ISSUES

The people of Taos Pueblo work to preserve the old ways. For example, it was not until 1971 that the Pueblo Council allowed electricity to be installed on the reservation, and electricity and running water are still not used within the old pueblo walls. Every able-bodied adult is expected to perform duties for the community. These include projects such as cleaning irrigation ditches, repairing fences, and plastering buildings, as well as performing ceremonial-linked activities. Activities such as these—and the teaching of the Tiwa language to their children—are community events that reinforce tribal traditions.

The 1970 return of Blue Lake inspired the Taos people and made them even more determined to preserve their traditional religion and culture.

The Taos Pueblo is organized into a wilderness zone, religious and ceremonial zones, housing and cropland zones, commercial zones, recreational zones, and range management zones. The Taos Pueblo Environmental Office trains tribal members to manage Taos environmental lands and helps to protect and preserve the tribe's natural resources.

NOTABLE PEOPLE

Phillip Doren Lujan (c. 1948–), a Kiowa-Taos Pueblo Indian, has served as an attorney for various Native American legal organizations, as director of the Native American Studies Program at New Mexico State University, and as professor of communications at the University of Oklahoma in Norman, where he specialized in intercultural communication and the study of tribal governments. He also has held positions in various tribal court systems.

Other notable Taos Pueblo include painters Albert Looking Elk (1888–1940), Vicente Mirabal (1918–1944), and Pop Chalee (1906–1993).

FURTHER READING

Bodine, John. "Taos Pueblo." *Handbook of North American Indians,* Vol. 9: *Southwest.* Ed. Alfonso Ortiz. Washington DC: Smithsonian Institution, 1979.

Curtis, Edward. "Taos." *The North American Indian (1907–1930).* Vol. 26. Reprint. New York: Johnson Reprint Corporation, 1970.

Dozier, Edward. *The Pueblo Indians of North America.* New York: Holt, Rinehart and Winston, 1970.

Keegan, Marcia. *Taos Pueblo and Its Sacred Blue Lake*. Santa Fe: Clear Light Publishers, 1991.

Mays, Buddy. *Indian Villages of the Southwest*. San Francisco: Chronicle Books, 1985.

Parsons, Elsie Clews. *Pueblo Indian Religion*. Chicago: University of Chicago Press, 1939.

Parsons, Elsie Clews. *Taos Pueblo*. Menasha, WI: George Banta Publishing Company, 1936.

Parsons, Elsie Clews. *Taos Tales*. New York: J. J. Augustin, 1940.

Stubbs, Stanley. *Bird's-Eye View of the Pueblos*. Norman: The University of Oklahoma Press, 1950.

Zuñi Pueblo

See Pueblo entry for more information on the Pueblo peoples.

Name

Zuñi (pronounced *ZOON-yee*) Pueblo. The Zuñi call themselves *A'shiwi,* or "the flesh." They call their pueblo *Itiwana,* or "middle place," because, in the tribe's origin story, it is the place to which their ancestors came after they emerged from the underworld. The Spanish word *pueblo* means "town" and is used to refer to both the Pueblo people and the pueblos (cities) where they live.

Location

The main site of the 408,404-acre Zuñi Pueblo, a federal reservation, is thirty-five miles south of Gallup, in west central New Mexico. The tribe's property consists of four parts: the main portion in west-central New Mexico, which includes five villages and all the tribe's farming and grazing areas, and three relatively small sites in New Mexico and Arizona that are sacred to the tribe.

Population

In 1540, there were an estimated 6,000 Zuñi. In the late 1700s, there were from 1,600 to 1,900. In 1850, there were about 1,300. In a census (count of the population) done in 1990 by the U.S. Bureau of the Census, 8,281 people identified themselves as Zuñi Pueblo.

Language family

Zuñian.

Origins and group affiliations

According to Zuñi tales, their earliest ancestors came into the world with webbed feet, long ears, hairless tails, and moss-covered bodies. They acquired a human form only after bathing in the waters of a sacred spring. The Zuni may be descendants of the Mogollon Indians (see box in Anasazi entry) who, over time, mixed with other groups.

ZUÑI PUEBLO

The Zuñi Reservation

1. Zuñi property consists of the 400,000-acre reservation with five villages in west central New Mexico and three small sacred sites in New Mexico and Arizona.

Shaded area: Traditional Zuñi lands in present-day New Mexico and Arizona.

The Pueblo of Zuñi is now one of the largest of the Pueblo nations, in terms of both population and land ownership. The Zuñi reservation has many attractive features, including a strong sense of community, the availability of good health care on the premises, and a highly developed cultural life. Because of its desirable lifestyle, almost all tribal members have chosen to remain on the reservation, and those who leave to take jobs often return when the employment ends.

HISTORY

Spanish visit trading center

For more than 2,000 years the Zuñi people have occupied the Zuñi and Little Colorado River valleys of the Southwest. By around 1250 C.E., Zuñi was a major trading center for a region that stretched from California to the Great Plains and into Mexico. Items such as corn, salt, turquoise, cotton cloth, and jewelry were exchanged at the pueblo for macaw feathers, seashells, coral, and copper.

In 1539 a man known as Esteban, or Estevanicio, led a party of Spaniards on a quest to find the fabled, gold-paved "Seven Cities of Cíbola," thought to be on Zuñi land. During the trip, Esteban entered the Zuñi village of Hawikuh and rudely demanded gifts of turquoise and women. Some Zuñi men became angry at Esteban's attitude and threats, and killed him so he could not reveal their location to his allies. His companions then retreated without entering the village.

In 1540 a second Spanish group, led by Francisco Vásquez de Coronado, reached Hawikuh. Coronado's timing could not have been worse; he arrived during a sacred ceremony. The bow priests (see "Government"), who were in charge of the pueblo, drew a line on the ground and told Coronado his party could not cross it while the ritual continued. For some unknown reason, the Spaniards proceeded to cross the line. In the bloody battle that followed, twenty Zuñi were killed.

Retreat from invaders

In Hawikuh, Coronado found a well-ordered community rich in tradition but not in gold or treasures. Disappointed, he decided to stay in Hawikuh a while before traveling on in search of riches. The unhappy Zuñi kept their feelings to themselves and encouraged the foreigners to explore other regions. When confrontations with the Spanish seemed unavoidable, the Zuñi retreated to a temporary settlement atop Thunder Mountain, a 1,000-foot-high mesa. A mesa (the Spanish word for "table") is a large hill with steep sides and a flat top.

During the fifteenth and sixteenth centuries, all the villages of the Zuñi were destroyed when Navajos, Apache (see entries), and other tribes overran the area. After the Pueblo Revolt of 1680 (see Pueblo entry), in which the Spanish were expelled from the region, the Zuñi moved to Thunder Mountain. The Spanish returned in 1692 and reclaimed the area for Mexico. Diego de Vargas convinced the Zuñi to accept Spanish authority, and the people came down from Thunder Mountain and began to build a new Zuñi Pueblo atop the abandoned village of Halona.

IMPORTANT DATES

1250: Zuñi Pueblo is an important trading center for Indians from California, Mexico, and the American Southwest.

1540: Spanish expedition forces under Francisco Vásquez de Coronado spend four months at the main Zuñi village of Hawikuh.

1600s: All Zuñi villages are destroyed by raiding tribes.

1692: The Zuñi build a new village atop the old site of Halona.

1846: The United States assumes control of Zuñi lands.

1877: A reservation is established for the Zuñi.

1978: The U.S. government returns ownership of the sacred Zuñi Salt Lake to the tribe.

1984: The U.S. government restores the tribe's ownership of the sacred area known as "Zuñi Heaven" in eastern Arizona.

A Zuñi adobe house in 1879.

The Spanish leave the Zuñi alone

When Catholic missionaries went to Zuñi Pueblo to reestablish the Spanish mission there, they were accompanied by three Spanish officials who were supposed to set up a non-religious government office. But the Zuñi killed the three in 1703 because of their obnoxious behavior. For more than 100 years the Zuñi were largely left alone by the Spanish and lived their lives in their traditional manner.

In 1820 the Spanish missionaries left Zuñi Pueblo for good, unable to overcome tribal resistance to adopting their ways. The Spanish could no longer endure the constant Apache and Navajo raids in the Southwest, and they feared the planned Mexican revolt against Spain. The missionaries left behind little evidence of nearly three centuries of Spanish influence: the use of a few metal tools, the introduction of new crops and animals, and a few religious ideas that were enfolded into the Zuñi belief system.

Taken over by Mexico, then by United States

Mexico's revolt against Spain was successful, but Mexico could not afford to send soldiers to oversee the "northern frontier," which included Zuñi land. The Zuñi began a trading relationship with the United States, and within twenty-five years the United States conquered the region with no opposition.

In accordance with U.S. policy toward all Indians, a reservation was set up for the Zuñi in 1877. From 1879 until 1883, Frank Hamilton Cushing, an American ethnologist (a scholar who studies the cultures of various peoples), lived among the Zuñi and learned their language and customs. He deeply offended them when he later published information about their most sacred ceremonies and spiritual beliefs. The Zuñi people felt their trust had been violated.

Beginning in the 1870s, the influence of non-Native Americans on the pueblo was profound. A railroad was constructed in the region, which made shipping of animals possible. The Zuñi become involved in raising and selling sheep and cattle. By the late 1890s, many whites lived in Zuñi, including teachers, missionaries, traders, and some government officials.

A century of hardships

Whites brought strange diseases, and many Zuñi were killed by a series of smallpox epidemics that swept through their homelands. By the end of the nineteenth century, the Zuñi had lost much of their land to trespassing settlers and railroad barons. The people were no longer able to sustain themselves by raising crops and livestock.

To survive, many Zuñi turned to making silver jewelry, a skill they learned from the Navajo people.

Life improves

By the twentieth century, the Zuñi suffered severe health problems and were preoccupied with land claims and the question of educating their children. Conditions had begun to improve for the Zuñi by the end of the century. With the availability of better health care, the population finally surpassed the level it had reached at the time the tribe first had contact with the Spanish. Since 1978, the tribe has regained ownership of its sacred Zuñi Salt Lake, as well as an area known as "Zuñi Heaven," where the spirits of the Zuñi people are believed to reside after death. In 1980, the reservation established its own public school district, thereby assuming full responsibility for educating its children.

RELIGION

Although the Zuñi recognized many gods, their Supreme Being was the Sun, the source of all life. They admired the keen senses, sharp teeth, claws, talons, cleverness, and quickness of animals, and believed animals were closer to the spirit world than people were.

In modern times, the traditional religion of the Zuñi remains very important, but many of them also belong to one of the various Christian churches located in the Zuñi villages that were established after the Spanish converted many tribe members to Christianity. Today, certain elements of the traditional religion remain secret. For example, outsiders are given no information about *fetishes,* the tiny animals carved from stone that have great spiritual importance to the tribe and are featured in the jewelry they make.

Effigies, which are carvings in the images of war gods made from lightning-struck trees, are worshiped at a special ceremony every year. In 1990, the Zuñi Tribal Council contacted museums and collectors known to possess such Zuñi figures and requested that they be returned to the tribe. Within two months, the Zuñi had received thirty-eight effigies from twenty-four different collections.

LANGUAGE

Although most Zuñi now speak English, the Zuñi language is the basis of their culture and the primary language of most tribal members. It is probably unrelated to any other language family. Programs now exist in the public schools to help teach Zuñi children their language in written form.

GOVERNMENT

For centuries, the Zuñi pueblo was run by men called bow priests, who were in charge of the priestly council. During the 1890s, the United States began putting bow priests in jail in an effort to do away with the tribe's ancient religious and political system. By 1934, the Zuñi could no longer choose their governor and tribal council by traditional means. Over several decades that followed, the switch from a religious to a non-religious democratic government took place. By 1970, the tribe had passed a constitution, and today the Zuñi Tribal Council acts as the governing body for the reservation.

Since 1974, the Zuñi have held elections for the offices of governor, lieutenant governor, and tribal council. In addition to this constitutional government, the tribe maintains the traditional system of matrilineal clans (groups of related families that trace their ancestry through the mother of the family), six kiva (worship) societies, ten medicine societies (groups that cure illnesses), and two priesthoods.

ECONOMY

The decline of agriculture

The economy once depended on farming. After the move to the reservation, the Zuñi population was restricted to a smaller land area than were their ancestors, and it gradually became difficult for them to grow enough crops to sustain themselves.

Hoping to increase farming efficiency, the Bureau of Indian Affairs constructed an irrigation system on the Zuñi reservation in the early 1900s, but the major dam collapsed immediately after it was completed. Over the years, the tradition of community farms became unworkable, so that between 1911 and 1988, the number of acres farmed at the Zuñi pueblo declined by 83 percent. By the late 1990s, only about 1,000 acres were farmed, while 95 percent of the tribal land was used for grazing livestock.

Employment in modern times

Today sheep production is a major source of income on the reservation, and the tribe's herd numbers around 14,000. The Zuñi also tend peach orchards and raise about 2,000 head of cattle, as well as hogs, pigs, fowl, horses, and goats.

The tribal government now administers more than seventy tribal programs and is the major employer on the reservation. Most of the small businesses on the reservation focus on arts and crafts. Crafters work in hundreds of mini-workshops to produce jewelry, fetishes, pottery, paintings, and beadwork. Often families work together to fashion jewelry. Their designs "belong" to them and are passed down from generation to generation. The Zuñi Craftsmen Cooperative Markets sells works by Zuñi artists.

By the 1960s, 90 percent of the tribe's members were reported to be involved in the silver-making craft at least part-time. Today, the Zuñi are also famous as firefighters. They were the first group of Native Americans trained as firefighting experts, and the U.S. Forest Service frequently transports them to extinguish the worst forest fires in the United States.

Since the 1960s, the tribe has received nearly $50 million in the settlement of court cases over land claims. They have used these funds to help increase individual income and educational opportunities, and to improve living conditions on the reservation.

DAILY LIFE

The responsibilities of men and women

According to Zuñi tradition, men were the farmers, herdsmen, and hunters, who provided the food for women to prepare. Men were responsible for keeping the gods happy, while women were responsible for the family and the tribe. Women blessed newborn babies and presented them to the Sun Father, prepared food offerings for the gods, presented food offerings to ancestors at each meal, greeted the sunrise, and prepared bodies for burial. Men made the prayer sticks, carved and painted sticks adorned with feathers and shells, that were offered to the gods. Men also had to organize the annual cycle of ceremonies and impersonate the spirits during ritual dances.

Buildings

As recently as the end of the nineteenth century, most Zuñi lived in typical pueblo "apartment" houses (see Pueblo entry) that stood five stories high. Zuñi is one of the few pueblos that uses rectangular rooms inside their homes as kivas (places of worship), rather than building separate, circular facilities for this purpose.

Today, many Zuñi live in single-family homes. They may be modern in architectural style, but they are often built using the same kind of stone the people have used for centuries. Some structures survive from ancient Halona and are now the ceremonial heart of the pueblo.

Clothing and adornment

Zuñi men wore breechcloths (flaps of material that covered the front and back) with fringed edges and a tassel at each corner, which they tied over the hips. They sometimes added long robes of feathers and the skins of hares or cotton blankets. The women wore the traditional Pueblo *mantas* (pronounced *MAHN-tuhs*), dresses formed by wrapping a dark blue or black rectangular piece of cotton around the body, passing it under the left arm, and tying it above the right shoulder. A sash encircled the waist. After the Spanish introduced sheep herding to the region, wool became a popular material for mantas. Women wore boot-like moccasins that were topped with leggings formed by spiraling strips of deerskin around the leg.

Food

The Zuñi are known for their sophisticated irrigation techniques. For centuries, they constructed small dams and canals that directed rainwater to the crops but protected them from the destructive torrents that often occurred during storms. They even developed a method to protect their crops from birds. They strung cactus leaves on lines crisscrossing the fields. The leaves waved in the wind and frightened scavengers. When this system was not enough, children and elderly people were posted in the fields to make noise and throw stones.

Corn was the major crop; the people thought of it as the flesh of the mystical Corn Maidens. They may have cultivated as many as 10,000 acres of corn at a time. In a good year they produced enough surplus to feed the people for two years in case of a drought or other disaster. The Zuñi supplemented the corn, beans, and various garden vegetables they raised by hunting wild game such as rabbits, deer, and bears, by fishing, and by gathering wild nuts and fruits.

In modern times, the Zuñi are taking steps to protect certain varieties of long-lasting traditional seeds, including corn, beans, squash, melons, chilies, and peaches, so they can be enjoyed by future generations.

Education

Today, the Zuñi manage their own school system. The schools teach language and cultural history, and support tribal customs in various ways. For example, students who are restricted to a special diet because they are undergoing initiation rites are provided with special lunches, and classes are canceled during the important *Shalako* festival (see box on page 600).

Healing practices

Both men and women are permitted to become lifelong members of Zuñi medicine societies, which are groups that help people heal from various ailments. Some societies approach curing from a spiritual standpoint, while others make use of medical methods. Members learn how plants, roots, massage, and healing rituals work.

In earlier times, some Zuñi medicine societies staged displays to show their power and to bring good health to the whole community. These exhibitions featured performers who swallowed fire or swords, or danced unharmed over hot coals. Many ailments were thought to be caused by spirits and witches, either as punishment or out of cruelty. According to Zuñi healers, curing such an ailment might require removing a pebble, feather, or wood particle that had been "shot" inside the body by the supernatural being.

ARTS

The Zuñi love of color is seen in the beautiful jewelry they produce, which is made of turquoise, shell, and jet, and set in silver in

THE CORN RACE

Long ago, when people first came to live in this world, everybody did the same kind of work. When the twin brothers wanted to give the Indians the gift of corn they talked it over. Morning Star said, "It would be better to give the corn to one group—not to all." So they tried to think of a plan. Morning Star said, "I know what we can do. We can have a corn race and see which will be the corn raisers. Let us call all the people."

When all the people had gathered he chose the fastest runner from each tribe—one Zuñi, one Acoma and one Navaho. He took an ear of corn out of his belt and broke it into three parts, the butt being the largest part, the middle piece a little smaller, and the point the smallest of all. He placed them on the ground with the point nearest the runners, the middle part next and the largest piece at the back.

At last all was ready. The signal was given and they were off. They ran as lightly as the deer and as swiftly. The people watched breathlessly. The racers drew apart with the Navaho boy in the lead. As he rushed past the goal he snatched up the first piece of corn which was the point. The Acoma racer came in next and he took the middle piece. The Zuñi boy, coming in last, got the butt end of the ear.

The elder brother shook his head and said, "The Navaho won the race. He should have got the largest piece of corn. Instead he has the smallest." But Evening Star replied, "It is well. The Navaho is the swiftest runner. He will always be moving about from place to place. He will not be able to take care of much corn. The people of Zuñi and Acoma will live in houses. They will stay in one place so they can raise much corn."

And so it has been just as the Evening Star said. The Navaho are always moving. They have their summer homes and their winter homes. But the Zuñi and Acoma are still living in their pueblos and make their living mostly by farming.

SOURCE: Edgar L. Hewett. "The Corn Race." *Ancient Life in the American Southwest.* 1930. Reprint, Indianapolis: Biblo and Tannen, 1968.

---

intricate patterns. Known for their fine beadwork, tribal members make belts, necklaces and even figures out of beads. They also carve animals from translucent shells. The most popular Zuñi pottery is white with a reddish-brown design.

CUSTOMS

Clans

Every Zuñi is born into a clan, a group that traces its ancestry to the same person. An individual's clan membership comes from the mother, but families also retain ties to the father's clan. Zuñi clans are in a constant state of change, as some die out while others grow larger.

Festivals

The most dramatic annual event at the Zuñi Pueblo is the Shalako ceremony (see box on page 600), which is held to celebrate the new year and to bless new houses. It is not open to the public, but several other annual events are. They are the June Rain Dance, various events held at the pueblo in August in conjunction with the McKinley

County Fair, and the Zuñi Tribal Fair, a four-day celebration held over the Labor Day weekend.

Courtship and marriage

Zuñi courtship was a rather complicated undertaking. When a young man became interested in marrying a young woman, he let her know of his admiration and asked if she shared the same feelings for him. If she did, she discussed his suitability as a mate with her mother. If her family approved of the match, the young couple met several times in secret to decide if they wanted to wed. During this time, either party could call off the relationship. If the woman called it off, there were no negative consequences for her. But if the man called it off, he had to pay a "bride price" to her family. If the woman refused the bride price, she could "go public" with her intentions to marry him.

Going public meant that the young woman went to the young man's home during the daylight hours so everyone could see what was happening. She presented his mother with a gift. If the mother liked the young woman she presented the young woman with wedding finery: the traditional black dress, moccasins, shawl, and beads. If at this point the man had a change of heart, he returned to the girl's home with her. If he still would not marry her, she could choose to move into his household and stay until he changed his mind or she became ashamed. At that point, she gave the wedding finery back to his mother and retreated to her family home.

If from the first the couple decided to marry, the woman would grind corn as a gift to her mother-in-law. Then the man presented his wife to his mother, who gave her the wedding finery. The couple went back to the bride's home, and the man spent the night, leaving in daylight so the new relationship was known to all.

Death

A body was buried the day after death, but the spirit was thought to remain in the home for four days. When a person died, he or she was no longer mentioned by name, but silent prayers could be said in his or her memory. In contrast, the people who replaced deceased religious men, called rain priests, prayed to them by name.

The arrival of the Shá-la-k'o at a Zuñi ceremony.

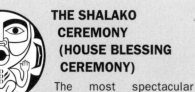

THE SHALAKO CEREMONY (HOUSE BLESSING CEREMONY)

The most spectacular annual Zuñi ceremony involves the Shalakos. They are men dressed as ten- to twelve-foot-tall messenger birds who dramatize the annual visit of the birds to bring blessings to the Zuñi people.

Each year on a late December afternoon, the Zuñi hear the cries of the approaching Shalakos, as they begin their crossing of the small river that runs through the pueblo. Then the crowds of people who have gathered together in the Zuñi village square fall silent. Rhythmic jingles in the distance grow louder, and finally the majestic Shalakos stride into the square.

These commanding, colorful creatures have wide eyes, buffalo horns, and ruffs of raven feathers beneath their domed-shaped, beaked heads. They wear brilliant masks of bright red, turquoise, and black, as well as beautiful jewelry, rattles, ankle bells, and pine boughs.

Some of the most important gods being impersonated are Sayatasha, the rain god of the north; Shulawitsi, the little fire god; and Yamukato, a frightful warrior who swats with green yucca leaves any observers who begin to fall asleep during the all-night celebration.

Through their prayers, the Shalako honor all things in the universe, living and non-living. As the creatures encircle the village square, masked singers chant, and the air rings with the rhythmic sounds of drums, bells, rattles, and the clacking of wooden bird beaks as they open and close. Then the Shalako bend their knees and begin their classic back-and-forth dancing. They dance to awaken the earth and stir the clouds, in hopes of bringing on the rain that is so vital to the parched land of the Zuñi.

Formerly visitors were welcome to watch the Shalako ceremony, but were asked not to record their observations. In recent times, the large crowds of visitors prevented the Zuñi from entering the new houses in the pueblo and carrying out their blessing ritual. As a result, this event has been closed to non-Indians since 1995.

CURRENT TRIBAL ISSUES

"Middle Village" in danger of collapse

Buildings that make up the old "Middle Village" rest on ruins that extend as deep as thirty-six feet below the currently inhabited buildings. Because they have not been maintained for centuries, the old structures are now crumbling, causing walls to crack and floors to slope in the occupied rooms above.

It is in this area of the pueblo that ceremonial dances take place. Hundreds of people climb on walls and sit on rooftops to watch. This adds to the pressures on the decaying foundation. As a result, a number of homes and kivas are in danger of collapsing. Strengthening the foundations will require extensive work. Plans for repair are complicated by the fact that the pueblo is listed on the National Register of Historic Places, an organization that has strict rules for reconstruction. In the late 1990s, the Zuñi tribal council prepared a renovation program and planned to appeal to the U.S. Congress for $2.5 million to carry it out.

The return of religious sites

The Zuñi have achieved the return of two of their major religious sites, Zuñi Salt Lake and Zuñi Heaven. They have also received cash settlements from the federal government for tribal lands that were illegally sold to non-Indians or were damaged by federal mismanagement. The money has allowed the tribe to begin a major project to restore damaged lands.

For twenty years, the Zuñi fought against federal and state approval of a 9,000-acre coal mine that would be located only twelve miles from Zuñi Salt Lake. Despite their argument that the mine would pollute the sacred lake, the project was approved in 1996. Since then, the Zuñi have been trying to figure out how to handle graves and religious sites that will be disturbed by the mine.

NOTABLE PEOPLE

Edmund Ladd (1926–), whose grandfather once served as tribal governor, was the first Zuñi to earn a college degree. In the paper he wrote to get his Ph.D. degree, he explored the roles played by birds and feathers in Zuni mythology and religion. He has worked as an archaeologist for the National Park Service and was an official at the Museum of New Mexico in Santa Fe. He has also published several papers on Hawaiian archaeology.

Other notable Zuñi include: painter Kai Sa (1918–1974), also known as Percy Sandy; jewelry designer Rod Kaskalla (1955–); and

Roger Tsabetsye (1941–), an artist who worked with President Lyndon B. Johnson on his social welfare program called the "War on Poverty" in the 1960s.

FURTHER READING

Bonvillain, Nancy. *The Zuñi*. New York: Chelsea House Publishers, 1995.

Button, Bertha P. *Friendly People: The Zuñi Indians*. Santa Fe, NM: Museum of New Mexico Press, 1963.

Ferguson, T. J., and Cal A. Seciwa. "Zuñi." *Native America in the Twentieth Century: An Encyclopedia*. Ed. Mary B. Davis. New York: Garland Publishing, 1994.

Hirschfelder, Arlene, and Martha Kreipe de Montaño. *The Native American Almanac: A Portrait of Native America Today*. New York: Prentice Hall, 1993.

People of the Desert. Alexandria, VA: Time-Life Books, 1993

Sando, Joe S. *Pueblo Nations: Eight Centuries of Pueblo Indian History*. Santa Fe, NM: Clear Light Publishers, 1992.

Terrell, John Upton. *Pueblos, Gods & Spaniards*. New York: Dial Press, 1973.

Through Indian Eyes: The Untold Story of Native American Peoples. Pleasantville, NY: Reader's Digest Association, 1995.

Trimble, Stephen. *The People: Indians of the American Southwest*. Santa Fe, NM: School of American Research Press, 1993.

Tohono O'odham

Name

The name Tohono O'odham (pronounced *to-HO-no oh-O-tahm*) means "desert people." The tribe was formerly known as the Papago, a name the Spanish called them, that came from a mispronunciation of a Pima word meaning "bean people" or "bean-eaters."

Location

The Tohono O'odham describe their territory as stretching south from the Gila River in Arizona to the Sonora River in the northwestern part of the Mexican province of Sonora, and from the Colorado River in the west to the San Pedro River in the east. They lived in hilly areas away from the rivers occupied by the Pima. Today, most tribal members live in the United States and are members of the Tohono O'odham Nation, which is made up of three reservations located in Arizona. There are a few scattered communities in Sonora, Mexico.

Population

In 1680, there were an estimated 6,000 Tohono O'odham. In a census (count of the population) done in 1990 by the U.S. Bureau of the Census, 16,876 people identified themselves as Tohono O'odham, making them the fifteenth-largest tribe in the United States. About 200 Tohono O'odham live in Caborca, Sonora, Mexico.

Language family

Uto-Aztecan.

Origins and group affiliations

Some historians believe the Tohono O'odham are descendants of the oldest known Native American culture of the area: the Hohokam, whose culture faded by about 1450. The Spanish grouped them with the Pima, but to themselves they were very different people. They were bitter enemies of the Apache (see entry).

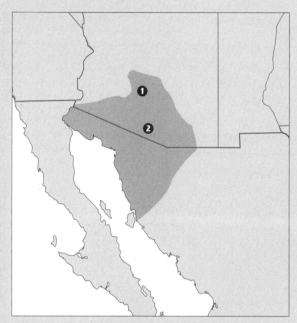

TOHONO O'ODHAM

Contemporary Communities in Arizona

1. Ak Chin Indian Community
2. Tohono O'odham Nation, comprised of four reservations:
   - Tohono O'odham
   - Sells
   - Gila Bend
   - San Xavier

Shaded area: Traditional Tohono O'odham lands in present-day Arizona and the Sonora Desert in Mexico.

The Tohono O'odham were a sociable, desert-dwelling people. Because of the unusual climate and geography of their Arizona-Mexico homeland, they were both farmers and hunter-gatherers. Although they cooperated with the Spanish who overran their territory beginning in the late 1600s, they refused to be dominated by them or by the Americans who came later. Today they maintain a vibrant cultural life incorporating old and new elements, and their numbers have increased dramatically since the days when the Spanish arrived in their territory.

HISTORY

Minimal early contact with the Spanish

For hundreds of years before the Spanish came, the Tohono O'odham divided their time between their winter villages and their summer villages, either growing or searching for food. From time to time they endured severe water shortages, which required them to move in and work with their neighbors, but they adapted to and lived successfully in their desert homeland.

The first Europeans who saw the Tohono O'odham were Spanish explorers, who entered their home territory as early as 1539. The Spanish called the people "Papabotus," which means "bean people"; their diet relied heavily on beans. This name was mispronounced "Papago" by outsiders, and that is the name by which the tribe was known for the next 400 years.

For a time, the Spanish mostly ignored the Tohono O'odham, believing their land was barren and the people were savages. Spanish attitudes toward the land changed when silver was discovered on the San Miguel River in the 1640s. The Spanish began building permanent settlements among the Tohono O'odham, whom they now viewed as perfect candidates to work in their silver mines.

Father Kino's innovations

In 1687 the Catholic missionary priest Eusebio Francisco Kino arrived to work among the Tohono O'odham. Father Kino hoped to win the people as converts to his religion. To do that, he had to win their confidence and their love, which he did by protecting them from the Spanish miners who wanted to make them slaves. Father Kino took great pains to make sure his future converts were not bothered by the miners. He succeeded so well that by 1689 he had performed more than 800 baptisms.

Father Kino introduced the Tohono O'odham to European livestock (horses and cattle), and to crops such as wheat and barley. The Tohono O'odham believed the Spanish missionaries were good men, but their relations with Spanish soldiers and settlers were troubled. Still, the Spanish came to respect the bravery of Tohono O'odham warriors, especially when they cooperated in punishing Apache who raided Spanish settlements. The Tohono O'odham were able to remain on their lands and not be displaced by Spanish settlers because the king of Spain placed them under his protection and granted them legal title to their lands.

IMPORTANT DATES

1687: Father Eusebio Kino begins missionary work among the Tohono O'odham.

1853: The Gadsden Purchase brings Tohono O'odham lands under the control of the United States.

1874: The San Xavier Reservation is established.

1876: The Tohono O'odham make a lasting peace with their traditional enemy, the Apache.

1882: The Gila Bend Reservation is established.

1916: The Sells Reservation (later Papago; now Tohono O'odham), the second-largest Indian reservation in the United States, is established.

1976: The U.S. government awards the Tohono O'odham $26 million for lost lands and restores mineral rights.

1986: The people, until now called Papago, vote to legally adopt their own name for themselves—Tohono O'odham, or "desert people"—to distinguish them from the Pima or "river people."

In 1768 missionary priests launched an ambitious construction program. Father Juan Bautista Velderrain led the Tohono O'odham in the building of San Xavier de Bac, a church that still stands and is considered an architectural and artistic gem. Although the church's architect, painters, and sculptors were Spaniards, the paid laborers who laid the stone foundations, molded and fired the bricks, raised the walls, and constructed the arches and vaulted and domed roof were Tohono O'odham people.

Mexico takes over their land

Mexico gained its independence from Spain in 1821. Without the protection of the king of Spain, the Tohono O'odham found their lands being taken over by Mexican settlers. The hostile relations that developed from these invasions led to open violence and occasional warfare. The fights often involved small battles over water holes. Indians and, occasionally, Mexicans were killed. Fighting of this sort was especially intense in the early 1830s and continued off and on throughout the century. Meanwhile, raiding by the Apache increased, becoming especially heated from the 1830s through the 1850s.

During this time the Natives' relationship with Mexican settlers underwent changes. Some Tohono O'odham began to travel to Mexico to help settlers with the harvest. They took goods and sometimes money back to the homes they still maintained in their traditional villages, far away from their employers. At the same time, however,

Mexican settlers and ranchers moved further and further into Tohono O'odham lands and hostilities increased.

The tense situation between the Tohono O'odham and the Mexicans was relieved with the completion of the Gadsden Purchase (1853). The agreement reached between Mexico and the United States transferred portions of the states of Arizona, California, and New Mexico to the United States and fixed the present borders between the United States and Mexico. Some Tohono O'odham territory came under the authority of the United States but part was left in Mexican hands. Tohono O'odham warriors quickly found employment with the U.S. Army as scouts against Apache raiders. By 1865, the Tohono O'odham had formed a standing army of their own to retaliate against Apache attackers.

In 1871, the Tohono O'odham warriors helped the Arizona settlers carry out the Camp Grant Massacre against long-time enemies, the Aravaipa band of Apaches on the San Pedro River. About 500 members of the Aravaipa band had gone to Camp Grant for protection and to make peace. But on April 30, 1871, a "Public Safety Committe" made up of 140 Anglo-Americans, Mexicans, and Tohono O'odham went into the camp and murdered 125 Aravaipa Apache, mostly women and children, and sold into slavery another 27 children they had kidnaped.

Land disputes begin

The legal title to their lands granted to the Tohono O'odham by the king of Spain had been guaranteed by the U.S. government. This did not stop settlers from trespassing. Finally, the U.S. government stepped in and resolved the land disputes by establishing two reservations for the Tohono O'odham. San Xavier Reservation was established in 1874, and Gila Bend Reservation in 1882. However, the greater part of their homeland was left unprotected from white settlers.

The Tohono O'odham still living in Mexico at the end of the nineteenth century were not in much better condition than their relatives in the United States. The Mexican government proved as unable or unwilling as its northern counterpart to protect Tohono O'odham lands from trespassers. In 1898, the hostility between Tohono O'odham and Mexicans broke out in violence. The Indians made a raid on the mining town of El Ploma in northern Sonora and several of the attackers were killed. After this incident, many Mexican Tohono O'odham voluntarily left their lands and moved to Arizona. The Mexican Army destroyed the homes of many in 1908 and 1927. By 1980, there were fewer than 200 Tohono O'odham living in Sonora.

Another small reservation, Ak-Chin, was established in 1912 for Pima and Tohono O'odham people. A large reservation was finally established in 1916 as the Papago Reservation, but by that time many settlers and business interests were established in the area. Their territory was not fully restored to the Tohono O'odham until 1926. However, the agreement reached at that time did not grant them rights to any minerals that might be on their land. It took another fifty years to resolve that issue. Their rights to their homelands remain an issue today.

RELIGION

The religion practiced by the Tohono O'odham before the Spanish came has been almost entirely lost. Most members of the tribe are Catholics, remaining in the religion brought to them by Father Kino more than 300 years ago. Their Catholicism is so deeply rooted that it has become a major part of their present-day culture. The first of their three reservations was centered on the church of San Xavier de Bac, in part thanks to the efforts of the U.S. government Indian agent R. A. Wilbur. Wilbur declared that it would be a terrible thing "to take them away from the church which their ancestors built . . . and which owes its present state of remarkable preservation to their care and interest alone. . . . They built, and have protected the old mission church, which is now one of the wonders of past ages." Since 1993, Tohono O'odham workers have been engaged in the restoration of the building, learning preservation techniques from masters around the world.

LANGUAGE

The language of the Tohono O'odham has been thoroughly studied because—unlike some other Native American languages—many people still speak it regularly. It is a very complex language. For example, the Tohono O'odham have no tense system—their language cannot indicate the future, present, or past in the same way that English can. Things are not in the future or the past; they are close (in time), or far away (in time) to the speaker. These and other factors in the Tohono O'odham language reveal things about the way their ancestors thought about their world. Based on their language, the ancestors of the Tohono O'odham might have had a non-Western concept of time, or they might have seen time as less important than the great distances they covered in their land.

GOVERNMENT

The Tohono O'odham lived in small, independent communities, where decisions were made by the group as a whole. Each village had a headman or chief, who was the center of public life. He was responsible for making public announcements, keeping the cycle of ceremonies intact, and running public functions in general.

In 1934 the Tohono O'odham voted to form a tribal government. In 1986 a major reorganization occurred when the tribe approved a new constitution and changed its name from Papago to the Tohono O'odham Nation. The new constitution set up a three-branch system of government somewhat like that of the United States, made up of executive, legislative, and judicial branches. Although they call themselves a nation, many Tohono O'odham people continue to think of themselves as members of separate communities.

ECONOMY

The Tohono O'odham had a close relationship with the Pima, and the two tribes exchanged foods from their different environments—wild desert produce in exchange for cultivated crops. In times of drought, when they had little to trade, the Tohono O'odham worked for the Pima and other tribes as farm laborers, earning a share of the crop in exchange for their work. After contact with the Spanish the Tohono O'odham began changing their economy from one based on hunting and gathering to one based on farming.

They still collect food from the desert, but the Tohono O'odham economy is now rooted in the cattle business introduced by Father Kino in 1696. Ranching became really successful after the U.S. government dug deep wells on the Tohono O'odham reservations and water was more easily available. Father Kino also introduced European-style crops, but European produce was sensitive to the lack of rain and sometimes refused to grow in the dry climate.

In the twentieth century, the Tohono O'odham have adopted a money economy. Income derives from the mineral rights to their

DISTRIBUTION OF TOHONO O'ODHAM POPULATION

The four reservations of the Tohono O'odham Nation are (1) the 2.7-million-acre Tohono O'odham Reservation, the second-largest reservation in the United States; (2) San Xavier Reservation near Tucson, Arizona, which has as its center the church of San Xavier del Bac; (3) the Gila Bend Reservation to the west; and (4) Ak-Chin (Maricopa) Reservation, home to a small group of Pima and Tohono O'odham people since 1874.

In 1991 the Tohono O'odham Nation Enrollment Office carried out its own population count. They reported the following figures:

San Xavier Reservation

Living on reservation: 942

Living off reservation: 380

Gila Bend Reservation

Living on reservation: 499

Living off reservation: 463

Tohono O'odham Reservation

Total: 15,295

Total for three reservations: 17,579

SOURCE: Vivian Juan, "Tohono O'odham," in *Native America in the Twentieth Century: An Encyclopedia.* Edited by Mary B. Davis. New York: Garland, 1996, pp. 637-39.

lands (mineral rights were finally granted in 1976), and from work-ing as laborers in mines and on cattle ranches. The Tohono O'odham have also established themselves among the primary producers of extra long staple cotton in Arizona (see box in Pima entry). In 1995, the Ak-Chin Reservation, home to a small number of Tohono O'od-ham and Pimas, became America's first Native American community to open a casino in partnership with the well-known Harrah's casino operations. The casino is expected to attract 1.3 million people annu-ally and employ 700 members of the community.

Members of the tribe who still follow a traditional way of life live in widely scattered villages in southern Arizona and northern Sonora province, Mexico. Their major source of income is through cattle ranching, although they occasionally hire out as agricultural laborers. Most Tohono O'odham, however, live or work in larger Arizona towns or cities.

DAILY LIFE

Education

At the beginning of the twentieth century, government Indian agents sent Tohono O'odham children away to boarding schools far from home, but the Tohono O'odham did not tolerate this policy for long. In 1911 they set aside land for day schools. Today, most children are educated at reservation schools whose foundations were laid by Catholic missionaries in 1912. The Tohono O'odham Nation stresses the value of a Western-style education in improving economic conditions on the reservations. The Nation consults with the University of Arizona to work out ways of supporting higher education efforts.

Buildings

The types of buildings used by the Tohono O'odham have changed greatly over time. The Hohokam, believed to be their ancestors, dug pit houses in the desert soil and built walls and roofs of mud. The Tohono O'odham did not have access to the same water resources as the Hohokam, so mud was not used as a building material. Instead, they made simple shelters from desert materials such as brush. These dwellings, with or without roofs, consisted of a round area enclosed by brush walls. Other buildings in the community included enclosed kitchens; an open-walled sunshade; special buildings for storing food; a corral for livestock; and a brush hut in which menstruating women were isolated.

In every community, there was one house in which no one lived. This was the meeting house, or "smoking house," so-called because "smoking" really meant "to have a meeting." The meetings were actually held outside the building, in an open area covered by a sunshade and containing a fireplace for night meetings. The meeting house was in a central location, so that the announcements of the headman in charge of it could be heard in the most distant house of the village. The headman was also responsible for the material stored in the meeting house, which could include ceremonial wine and other ritual items. In the twentieth century, the meeting house is also called a "o-las ki" (round house), because it is the only building still constructed in the old round style.

Food

The Tohono O'odham were originally a wandering desert people. They got about 75 percent of their food from wild sources, mostly desert plants and animals such as deer, rabbits, elk, and some birds. Their thirteen-month lunar calendar is based on desert cycles; the year begins in June, with the ripening and harvest of saguaro cactus fruits. Other months designate the time when the rains begin (July); the coldest months (the "Inner backbone moon" of December); the "time when animals mate" (January to February); and the time when flowers bloom (April).

The remaining 25 percent of the traditional Tohono O'odham diet came from agricultural produce: corn, squash, and several kinds of beans. Some of this they raised themselves, but the rest they traded for with other tribes.

VILLAGE PEOPLE

The groups of Pima people who shared a common language called themselves *o'odham*, meaning "the people." They distinguished themselves and each other by their three different lifestyles. The Tohono O'odham were "Two Villagers"; they spent half the year in one village, then during the second half they moved to another to exploit the new food resources. In times of extreme drought or famine, they might join the Akimel O'odham (Pima), the "River People," and help them harvest their crops in return for food and water.

The Akimel O'odham lived in river valleys where there was a relatively constant supply of water, and had no need to move to find fresh food supplies. Because they stayed in one place the year around, they were called "One Villagers." The third group was the Hiac'ed O'odham, sometimes called the Sand Papagos. They practiced an entirely nomadic lifestyle, moving from place to place in search of whatever food the desert had to offer. As more and more people moved into southern Arizona at the beginning of the twentieth century, the Hiac'ed O'odham found that they could no longer follow their traditional way of life. They settled down and were absorbed by other Native American populations.

The fruit of the saguaro (pronounced *suh-WHAR-uh*), a very large cactus, was and remains a tribal favorite. Children are taught from an early age to respect the saguaro fruit, because it stores water and provides delicious food even during times of drought. From the saguaro fruit the Tohono O'odham make syrup, jam, and wine for use in ceremonies and prayers for rain. Today, the Tohono O'odham people have harvesting rights in Saguaro National Park.

Corn and desert foods, such as acorns and cactus fruits and flowers, were dried, ground into meal, and stored. They were later made into tortillas (pronounced *tor-TEE-yas*) or *atole* (pronounced *uh-TOW-lay*) a drink made from dried corn and water.

The Spanish introduced pigs, cattle, and the technique of frying food instead of the healthier way of baking or roasting formerly used by the tribe. Living on reservations in the twentieth century, the people grew used to store-bought foods and government handouts of foods high in fat. American teachers in government-run schools taught the people that their traditional diet was primitive and uncivilized. The Tohono O'odham attribute current problems with obesity (being very overweight) to these unhealthy changes in their diet.

Clothing and adornment

The Tohono O'odham wore clothing appropriate for the desert. Men usually wore nothing more than a simple hide loincloth, a garment with front and back flaps that hung from the waist. Women wore skirts or aprons made of a single hide or two hides joined together. With the coming of Catholic missionaries, the tribe adopted European-style dress. Some modern Tohono O'odham women continue to wear the skirts and blouses typical of Mexican peasants of the nineteenth and early twentieth centuries.

Healing practices

Healers called shamans (pronounced *SHAH-munz*) could both cause and cure sickness, and they could put spells on enemies or predict rainfall. In the old days, the Tohono O'odham regarded shamans with some suspicion, and from time to time they killed those they blamed for epidemic sicknesses. The shaman was often a lonely person, shunned because of his powers. Christianity discouraged belief in the power of shamans, but they continue to be treated with a combination of respect and fear.

Tohono O'odham shamans divided disease into two different types: "wandering" sickness and "staying" sickness. The "wandering" sicknesses were infectious diseases like the ones Europeans brought with them into the New World. They were called "wandering" sicknesses because they were brought into Tohono O'odham territory by others, they were infectious and passed from person to person, and they came and went. "Wandering" sicknesses could be treated and cured by Western medicine.

Only the Tohono O'odham came down with "staying" sicknesses. They never spread to other races, and they could never be completely eliminated. "Staying" sicknesses resulted from such things as failure to respect certain animals or plants, lightning, the ocean, or wind. If such a sickness were left untreated for too long, the patient could die. The shaman's job was to diagnose the sickness by blowing smoke over the victim and calling on the spirits to make sure of his diagnosis. The actual process of curing the victim was turned over to specialists in ritual, who knew the songs that were needed to remove the sick-making spirit and make peace with it. The songs acted like prayers and sometimes brought almost immediate relief to the sufferers.

By the 1970s, the rituals and cures of the shamans were falling into disuse, and the only role left to them was that of naming the illness. Curing was left to experts at modern hospitals and clinics. Many Tohono O'odham today value the abilities of shamans, because they provide a connection to the past and make a person think about the way he or she has been living.

ARTS

Basket making

An important Tohono O'odham custom that has survived to be very successful in modern times is the making of their traditional baskets. Except for the storage of food, the Tohono O'odham did not use clay pottery like other southwestern tribes, because it was too heavy to be carried from winter villages to summer villages. Instead, they used baskets made from desert plants, including green yucca, beargrass, devil's claw, and white willow, for food gathering and carrying. Burden baskets were designed to be carried by women, but starting in the 1880s the Tohono O'odham began manufacturing them for the tourist trade.

During the Great Depression of the 1930s, when millions of people were without jobs, the federal government set up the Papago Arts and Crafts Board to help in the marketing (advertising and selling) of these baskets. Many were "novelty" items—baskets in the shape of cacti, dogs, or humans—but others were beautiful works of art, and they helped support the tribe during a long period of drought and poverty.

Popular music

Waila, or chicken scratch music, is popular dance music among the Tohono O'odham people. *Waila* comes from the Spanish word *baile,* meaning "dance," and is a version of country-western dance and music. It probably came across the Mexican border in the mid-1800s and was influenced by the polka music brought to Texas by German settlers. It makes use of guitars, saxophones, and the accordion-like instrument called a concertina.

CUSTOMS

Festivals and ceremonies

Tohono O'odham life was rich with ceremonies, and many of them are still practiced. Among the major ceremonies and celebra-

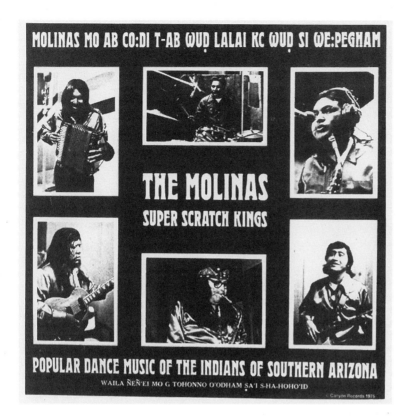

MOLINAS MO AB CO:DI T-AB WUḌ LALAI KC WUḌ SI WE:PEGHAM

THE MOLINAS
SUPER SCRATCH KINGS

POPULAR DANCE MUSIC OF THE INDIANS OF SOUTHERN ARIZONA
WAILA ÑEÑ'EI MO G TOHONNO O'ODHAM ṢA'I S-HA-HOHO'ID

An advertisement for The Molinas, Super Scratch Kings, a Tohono O'odham waila group.

tions are Chelkona, the cleansing ceremony, the Prayerstick Festival, Saguaro Festival, and salt pilgrimages.

The Chelkona ceremony is a dance performed by boys and girls. They ask for rain and fertile fields and carry symbols representing rainbows, lightning, birds, and clouds. The winter hunting season opens with a cleansing ceremony, in which a deer is killed and cooked along with items from the recent harvest. Participants sing, dance, and give speeches. The cleansing ceremony is still performed in Mexico, ten days before the August Prayerstick Festival.

The Prayerstick Festival is a joyous occasion in which the spirits are asked to bring rain and keep the world orderly for another year. As part of the festivities, cornmeal is sprinkled around, corn dancers perform, and there is entertainment by clowns, singers, and musicians. Prayersticks—carved and painted sticks adorned with feathers and shells—are made and passed out to all the participants.

The July Saguaro festival opens the rainy season. All the women of a village gather to make cactus wine and there is much singing and dancing and reciting of poems.

Salt pilgrimages were annual trips made by young men to the Gulf of California. Pilgrims made the trip four years in a row, with little food, water, or sleep allowed on the way. On reaching their destination, the young men made offerings of prayersticks and cornmeal, then ran into the gulf. Sometimes they experienced visions while performing this ritual, and the visions gave them guidance on how to lead their lives.

The Tohono O'odham observe many Catholic feast days. Their celebration honoring the memory of Patron Saint Francis Xavier at San Xavier Mission dates back to the mission's founding in 1692. Such festivities are a way of maintaining contact with other members of the tribe. Other major festivals are San Juan's Day (June 24); a pilgrimage to Magdalena, Sonora (Mexico) on the Feast of St Francis (October 4), and the annual rodeo and craft festival in late October.

CURRENT TRIBAL ISSUES

The issue of primary concern to the Tohono O'odham today is retaining their land and homes. They also suffer from health problems such as obesity and alcoholism. Like the Pima, they have a high rate of diabetes, a serious disorder of the metabolism in which the pancreas fails to secrete an adequate amount of insulin.

NOTABLE PEOPLE

Ofelia Zepeda (1954–) is a language scholar who has done much to preserve O'odham culture. She was one of seven children and the first member of her family to graduate from high school and enter college. Zepeda vividly recalled her two reasons for seeking higher education in an interview for *Notable Native Americans:* "It is sort of a philosophy that we have in O'odham culture . . . a lot of responsibility made sense. My second reason for attending college was to avoid working as a farm laborer. It was hard work, work that children were required to do. More than any of my other siblings, I was disinclined [unwilling] to do farm labor work." Zepeda's highly regarded O'odham language dictionary, *A Papago Grammar* was published in 1983.

Thomas Segundo (1921–1971) was born on the Papago Reservation in southern Arizona, but left as a young man and settled in California. He returned to his homeland in 1946 and found so many in need among his people that he stayed to help. He was elected tribal chairperson in 1951, becoming the youngest Indian chief in the United States. Segundo worked to revive the tribal government and increase tribal income. After seven terms as tribal chairman, Segundo went to the University of Chicago for courses in law and social science and then returned to his home with high hopes of improving conditions there. Segundo introduced the ideas of using conservation measures to increase range land for cattle ranchers and improved irrigation programs for farmers. He believed that no matter how productive the reservation land could be made, though, one-third of the Tohono O'odham people would have to find work off the reservation. He hoped to provide the training and education they needed for these careers on the "outside." Segundo also proposed the construction of boarding schools for children and expanded public health facilities.

Another notable Tohono O'odham is dancer and painter Michael Chiago (1946–).

FURTHER READING

Rosenberg, Ruth, "Ofelia Zepeda," in *Notable Native Americans*. Edited by Sharon Malinowski. Detroit: Gale, 1995.

"The Tohono Today" (2/25/99). [Online] www.heard.org./edu/rain/cultura2/raincul8.html

Bibliography

Books

Abrams, George H. J. *The Seneca People*. Phoenix, AZ: Indian Tribal Series, 1976.

The AFN Report on the Status of Alaska Natives: A Call for Action. Anchorage: Alaska Federation of Natives, 1989.

American Indian Reservations and Trust Areas. Washington, DC: U.S. Department of Commerce, 1996.

The American Indians: Algonquians of the East Coast. New York: Time-Life Books, 1995.

The American Indians: Hunters of the Northern Forest. New York: Time-Life Books, 1995.

Anderson, Gary Clayton. *Kinsmen of Another Kind: Dakota-White Relations in the Upper Mississippi Valley, 1650–1862*. Lincoln: University of Nebraska Press, 1984.

Anderson, Gary Clayton. *Little Crow: Spokesman for the Sioux*. St. Paul: Minnesota Historical Society Press, 1986.

Anderson, Gary Clayton. *Through Dakota Eyes: Narrative Accounts of the Minnesota Indian War of 1862*. St. Paul: Minnesota Historical Society Press, 1988.

Apess, William. *On Our Own Ground: The Complete Writings of William Apess, A Pequot*. Ed. Barry O'Connell. Amherst: University of Massachusetts Press, 1992.

Axtell, James. *The European and the Indian: Essays in the Ethnohistory of Colonial North America*. New York: Oxford University Press, 1981.

Ayer, Eleanor H. *The Anasazi*. New York: Walker Publishing, 1993.

Azelrod, Alan. *Chronicle of the Indian Wars*. New York: Prentice Hall, 1993.

Bahti, Tom. *Southwestern Indian Tribes*. Las Vegas: KC Publications, 1994.

Ballantine, Betty and Ian Ballantine, eds. *The Native Americans: An Illustrated History*. Atlanta: Turner Publishing, 1993.

Bamforth, Douglas B. *Ecology and Human Organization on the Great Plains*. New York: Plenum Press, 1988.

A Basic Call to Consciousness. Rooseveltown, NY: Akwesasne Notes, 1978.

Bataille, Gretchen M. *Native American Women: A Biographical Dictionary*. New York: Garland Publishing, 1993.

Beals, Ralph L. *Material Culture of the Pima, Papago, and Western Apache*. Berkeley, CA: Department of the Interior, National Park Service, 1934.

Bean, Lowell John. *Mukat's People: The Cahuilla Indians of Southern California*. Berkeley: University of California Press, 1972.

Beauchamp, William M. "Notes on Onondaga Dances." *An Iroquois Source Book*, Volume 2. Ed. Elisabeth Tooker. New York: Garland Publishing, 1985.

Beck, W. and Ynez Haas. *Historical Atlas of California*. Norman: University of Oklahoma Press, 1974.

Beckham, Stephen Dow. *Requiem for a People: The Rogue Indians and the Frontiersman*. Norman: University of Oklahoma Press, 1971.

Beckham, Stephen Dow, Kathryn Anne Toepel, and Rick Minor. *Native American Religious Practices and Uses in Western Oregon*. Eugene: University of Oregon Anthropological Papers, 1984.

Benson, Henry C. *Life Among the Choctaw Indians, and Sketches of the Southwest*. Cincinnati, OH: R. P. Thompson, 1860.

Berlainder, Jean Louis. *The Indians of Texas in 1830*. Washington, DC: Smithsonian Institution, 1969.

Berthrong, Donald J. *The Cheyenne and Arapaho Ordeal: Reservation and Agency Life in the Indian Territory*. Norman: University of Oklahoma Press, 1976.

Berthrong, Donald J. *The Southern Cheyennes*. Norman: University of Oklahoma Press, 1963.

Bieder, Robert E. *Native American Communities in Wisconsin, 1600–1960: A Study of Tradition and Change*. Madison: University of Wisconsin Press, 1995.

Biographical Dictionary of Indians of the Americas. Newport Beach, CA: American Indian Publishers, 1991.

Birket-Smith, Kaj and Frederica De Laguna. *The Eyak Indians of the Copper River Delta.* Copenhagen: Levin & Munksgaard, 1938.

Bischoff, William N. *The Indian War Diary of Plympton J. Kelly 1855–1856.* Tacoma: Washington State History Society, 1976.

Blaine, Martha Royce. *Pawnee Passage, 1870–1875.* Norman: University of Oklahoma Press, 1990.

Blaine, Martha Royce. *The Pawnees: A Critical Bibliography.* Bloomington: Indiana University Press for the Newberry Library, 1980.

Boas, Franz. *Chinook Texts.* Washington, DC: Bureau of American Ethnology Bulletin No. 20, 1894.

Boas, Franz. *Kwakiutl Ethnography.* Ed. Helen Codere. Chicago: University of Chicago Press, 1966.

Boas, Franz, ed. *Publications of the American Ethnological Society,* Vol. 1: *Fox Text,* by William Jones. Leyden: E. J. Brill, 1907.

Boas, Franz. *The Social Organization and the Secret Societies of the Kwakiutl Indians.* New York: Johnson Reprint Corporation, 1970.

Bolton, Herbert Eugene. *The Hasinais: Southern Caddoans As Seen by the Earliest Europeans.* Norman: University of Oklahoma Press, 1987.

Bourne, Russell. *Red King's Rebellion: Racial Politics in New England, 1675–1678.* New York: Atheneum Press, 1990.

Boyd, Maurice. *Kiowas Voices,* Vol. 1: *Ceremonial Dance, Ritual and Song.* Fort Worth: Texas Christian University Press, 1981.

Boyd, Maurice. *Kiowas Voices,* Vol. 2: *Myths, Legends, and Folktales.* Fort Worth: Texas Christian University Press, 1983.

Boyd, Robert. *People of the Dalles: The Indians of Wascopam Mission.* Lincoln: University of Nebraska Press, 1996.

Braund, Kathryn E. Holland. *Deerskins & Duffels: The Creek Indian Trade with Anglo-America, 1685–1815.* Lincoln: University of Nebraska Press, 1993.

Bray, Tamara L. and Thomas W. Killion. *Reckoning with the Dead: The Larsen Bay Repatriation and the Smithsonian Institution.* Washington, DC: Smithsonian Institution, 1994.

Brescia, William, Jr. "Choctaw Oral Tradition Relating to Tribal Origin." *The Choctaw Before Removal.* Ed. Carolyn Keller Reeves. Jackson: University Press of Mississippi, 1985.

Bringle, Mary. *Eskimos.* New York: Franklin Watts, 1973.

Brinton, Daniel G. *The Lenape and their Legends.* Philadelphia, 1884. Reprint. St. Clair Shores, MI: Scholarly Press, 1972.

Brown, Mark. *The Flight of the Nez Perce.* Lincoln: University of Nebraska Press, 1967.

Brown, Vinson. "Sioux, Eastern." *Dictionary of Indian Tribes of the Americas,* Vol. 3. Newport Beach, CA: American Indian Publishers, 1980.

Bruchac, Joseph. *New Voices from the Longhouse: An Anthology of Contemporary Iroquois Writing.* Greenfield Center, NY: Greenfield Review Press, 1989.

Bunte, Pamela A. and Robert J. Franklin. *From the Sands to the Mountain: Change and Persistence in a Southern Paiute Community.* Lincoln: University of Nebraska Press, 1987.

Burch, Ernest S. *The Eskimos.* Norman: University of Oklahoma Press, 1988.

Burnham, Dorothy K. *To Please the Caribou: Painted Caribou-skin Coats Worn by the Naskapi, Montagnais, and Cree Hunters of the Quebec Labrador Peninsula.* Toronto: Royal Ontario Museum, 1992.

Bushnell, David I., Jr. "The Choctaw of Bayou Lacomb, St. Tammany Parish, Louisiana (1909)." *A Choctaw Source Book. New York: Garland Publishing, 1985: pp. 1–37.*

Buskirk, Winfred. *The Western Apache.* Norman: University of Oklahoma Press, 1986.

Caduto, Michael J. *Keepers of the Earth.* Golden, CO: Fulcrum, 1988.

Cahokia. Lincoln: University of Nebraska Press, 1997.

Calloway, Colin G. *The Abenaki.* New York: Chelsea House Publishers, 1989.

Calloway, Colin G., ed. *Dawnland Encounters: Indians and Europeans in Northern New England.* Hanover, NH: University Press of New England, 1991.

Calloway, Colin G. *The World Turned Upside Down: Indian Voices from Early America.* Boston: St. Martin's Press, 1994.

Campisi, Jack. *The Mashpee Indians: Tribe on Trial.* Syracuse, NY: Syracuse University Press, 1991.

Carlisle, Richard. *The Illustrated Encyclopedia of Mankind.* New York: Marshall Cavendish, 1984.

Carlo, Poldine. *Nulato: An Indian Life on the Yukon.* Caldwell, ID: Caxton Printers, 1983.

Carlson, Richard G., ed. *Rooted Like the Ash Trees: New England Indians and the Land.* Naugatuck, CT: Eagle Wing Press, 1987.

Carter, Cecile Elkins. *Caddo Indians: Where We Come From.* Norman: University of Oklahoma Press, 1995.

Carter, Sarah. "Chapter 19—'We Must Farm to Enable Us to Live': The Plains Cree and Agriculture to 1900." *Native Peoples: The Canadian Experience.* Toronto: McClellan & Stewart, 1986.

Case, David S. *Alaska Natives and American Laws.* University of Alaska Press, 1984.

Cash, Joseph H. and Gerald W. Wolff. *The Comanche People.* Phoenix, AZ: Indian Tribal Series, 1974.

Castille, George Pierre, ed. *The Indians of Puget Sound.* Seattle: University of Washington Press, 1985.

Castillo, Edward D. and R. Jackson. *Indians, Franciscans, and Spanish Colonization: The Impact of the Mission System on California Indians.* Albuquerque: University of New Mexico Press, 1995.

Catlin, George. *Letters and Notes on the Manners, Customs, and Conditions of North American Indians.* Volume 2 (unabridged republication of the fourth [1844] edition). New York: Dover Publications, 1973.

Catlin, George. *North American Indians.* New York: Viking Press, 1989.

Chamberlain, Von Del. *When Stars Came Down to Earth: Cosmology of the Skidi Pawnee Indians of North America.* Los Altos, CA: Ballena Press and College Park: Center for Archaeoastronomy, University of Maryland, 1982.

Chalfant, William Y. *Without Quarter: The Wichita Expedition and the Fight on Crooked Creek.* Norman: University of Oklahoma Press, 1991.

Champagne, Duane, ed. *Chronology of Native North American History: From Pre-Columbian Times to the Present*. Detroit: Gale Research, 1994.

Champagne, Duane, ed. *Native America: Portrait of the Peoples*. Detroit: Visible Ink Press, 1994.

Champagne, Duane, ed. *The Native North American Almanac*. Detroit: Gale Research Inc., 1994.

Charlebois, Peter. *The Life of Louis Riel*. Toronto: New Canada Press, 1978.

Childers, Robert and Mary Kancewick. "The Gwich'in (Kutchin): Conservation and Cultural Protection in the Arctic Borderlands." Anchorage: Gwich'in Steering Committee, n.d.

Cleland, Charles E. *Rites of Conquest: The History and Culture of Michigan's Native Americans*. Ann Arbor: University of Michigan Press, 1992.

Clifton, James A. *The Prairie People: Continuity and Change in Potawatomi Indian Culture 1665–1965*. Lawrence: The Regents Press of Kansas, 1977.

Clifton, James A., *Star Woman and Other Shawnee Tales*. Lanham, MD: University Press of America, 1984.

Clifton, James A., George L. Cornell, and James M. McClurken. *People of the Three Fires: The Ottawa, Potawatomi and Ojibway of Michigan*. Grand Rapids, MI: Grand Rapids Inter-Tribal Council, 1986.

Cole, D. C. *The Chiricahua Apache 1846–1876: From War to Reservation*. Albuquerque: University of New Mexico Press, 1988.

Cole, Douglas. *Captured Heritage: The Scramble for Northwest Coast Artifacts*. Seattle: University of Washington Press, 1985.

Cook, Sherburne F. *The Conflict between the California Indian and White Civilization*. Berkeley: University of California Press, 1967.

Cordere, Helen, ed. *Kwakiutl Ethnography*. Chicago: University of Chicago Press, 1966.

Corkran, David H. *The Creek Frontier: 1540–1783*. Norman: University of Oklahoma Press, 1967.

Cotterill, R. S. *The Southern Indians: The Story of the Civilized Tribes Before Removal*. Norman: University of Oklahoma Press, 1954.

Covington, James W. *The Seminoles of Florida.* Gainsville: University of Florida Press, 1993.

Cox, Bruce Alden, ed. *Native People, Native Lands: Canadian Indians, Inuit and Métis.* Ottawa: Carleton University Press, 1987.

Crane, Verner W. *The Southern Frontier,* Greenwood, CT: Greenwood Press, 1969.

Crowder, David L. *Tendoy, Chief of the Lemhis.* Caldwell, ID: Caxton Publishers, 1969.

Crum, Steven J. *The Road On Which We Came.* Salt Lake City: University of Utah Press, 1994.

Curtis, Edward S. *The North American Indian.* Reprint. New York: Johnson Reprint Corporation, 1970.

Cushman, H. B. *History of the Choctaw, Chickasaw, and Natchez Indians.* New York: Russell & Russell, 1972.

Cvpvkke, Holátte (C. B. Clark). "'Drove Off Like Dogs'—Creek Removal." *Indians of the Lower South: Past and Present.* Ed. John K. Mahon. Pensacola, FL: Gulf Coast History and Humanities Conference, 1975.

D'Azevedo, Warren L., ed. *The Handbook of North American Indians,* Vol. 11: *Great Basin.* Washington, DC: Smithsonian Institution, 1986.

Dahl, Jens. *Indigenous Peoples of the Arctic.* Copenhagen: The Nordic Council, 1993.

Dauenhauer, Nora Marks and Richard Dauenhauer. *Haa Kusteeyí, Our Culture: Tlingit Life Stories.* Seattle: University of Washington Press; and Juneau, AK: Sealaska Heritage Foundation, 1994.

Dauenhauer, Nora Marks and Richard Dauenhauer. *Haa Tuwunáagu Yís, for Healing Our Spirit: Tlingit Oratory.* Seattle: University of Washington Press; and Juneau, AK: Sealaska Heritage Foundation, 1990.

Davis, Mary B., ed. *Native America in the Twentieth Century: An Encyclopedia.* New York: Garland Publishing, 1994.

Dawson, Dawn P. and Harvey Markowitz, eds. *Ready Reference: American Indians.* Pasadena, CA: Salem Press, 1995.

Deacon, Belle. *Engithidong Xugixudhoy: Their Stories of Long Ago: Told in Deg Hit'an Athabaskan by Belle Deacon.* Fairbanks: Alaska Native Language Center, 1987.

Deans, James. *Tales from the Totems of the Hidery,* Volume 2. Chicago: Archives of the International Folk-Lore Association, 1899.

Debo, Angie. *A History of the Indians of the United States.* Norman: University of Oklahoma Press, 1970.

Debo, Angie. *The Rise and Fall of the Choctaw Republic,* Second edition. Norman: University of Oklahoma Press, 1961.

Denig, Edwin Thompson. *Five Indian Tribes of the Upper Missouri: Sioux, Arikaras, Assiniboines, Crees, Crows.* Ed. John C. Ewers. Norman: University of Oklahoma Press, 1961.

Densmore, Frances. *Chippewa Customs.* St. Paul: Minnesota Historical Society Press, 1929; reprinted, 1979.

Densmore, Frances. *Choctaw Music* (Bulletin 136 of the Bureau of American Ethnology). DaCapo Press, 1936, reprint 1972.

Densmore, Francis. *Papago Music.* New York: Da Capo Press, 1972.

DeRosier, Arthur H. Jr. *The Removal of the Choctaw Indians.* Knoxville: University of Tennessee Press, 1970.

DeWald, Terry. *The Papago Indians and Their Basketry.* Tucson, AZ: DeWald, c. 1979.

Diedrich, Mark, *Dakota Oratory.* Rochester, MN: Coyote Books, 1989.

Dobyns, Henry F. *The Papago People.* Phoenix, Indian Tribal Series, c. 1972.

Dobyns, Henry F. *Papagos in the Cotton Fields, 1950.* Tucson, AZ: University of Arizona, Department of Anthropology, 1951.

Dockstader, Frederick J. *Great Native American Indians, Profiles in Life, and Leadership.* New York: Van Nostrand Runhold, Co., 1977.

Doherty, Robert. *Disputed Waters: Native Americans and the Great Lakes Fishery.* Lexington: University Press of Kentucky, 1990.

Doig, Ivan. *Winter Brothers.* New York: Harcourt Brace Jovanovich, 1980.

Driben, Paul. *We Are Métis.* New York: AMS Press, 1985.

Drucker, Philip and Robert F. Heizer. *To Make My Name Good: A Reexamination of the Southern Kwakiutl Potlatch.* Berkeley: University of California Press, 1967.

Duke, Philip. *Points in Time: Structure and Event in a Late Northern Plains Hunting Society.* Niwot: University Press of Colorado, 1991.

Dutton, Bertha P. *American Indians of the Southwest*. Albuquerque: University of New Mexico Press, 1983.

Dutton, Bertha P. *Indians of the American Southwest*. Englewood Cliffs, NJ: Prentice-Hall, 1975.

Eagle/Walking Turtle (Gary McLain). *Indian America: A Traveler's Companion,* Third edition. Santa Fe, NM: John Muir Publications, 1993.

Eastman, Charles A. *Old Indian Days*. Lincoln: University of Nebraska Press, 1991.

Eastman, Charles A. and Elaine Goodale Eastman. *Wigwam Evenings: Sioux Folk Tales Retold*. Lincoln: University of Nebraska Press, 1990.

Eckert, Allan W., *A Sorrow in Our Heart: The Life of Tecumseh*. New York: Bantam, 1992.

Edmunds, R. David. *The Potawatomi: Keepers of the Fire*. Norman: University of Oklahoma Press, 1978.

Edwards, R. David and Joseph L. Peyser. *The Fox Wars: The Mesquakie Challenge to New France*. Norman: University of Oklahoma Press, 1993.

Eells, Myron. *The Indians of Puget Sound: The Notebooks of Myron Eells*. Ed. George B. Castile. Seattle: University of Washington Press, 1985.

Eggan Fred. *The American Indian: Perspectives for the Study of Social Change*. New York: University of Cambridge Press, 1966.

Elliot, Michael L. *New Mexico State Monument: Jemez*. Santa Fe: Museum of New Mexico Press, 1993.

Elmendorf, W. W. *The Structure of Twana Culture*. Pullman: Washington State University, 1960.

Elmendorf, W. W. *Twana Narratives: Native Historical Accounts of a Coast Salish Culture*. Seattle: University of Washington Press, 1993.

Emmons, George Thornton. *The Tlingit Indians*. Seattle: University of Washington Press, 1991.

Erdoes, Richard. *The Rain Dance People*. New York: Alfred A. Knopf, 1976.

Ewers, John C. *Plains Indian History and Culture*. Norman: University of Oklahoma Press, 1997.

Fairbanks, Charles H. *The Florida Seminole People.* Phoenix: Intertribal Series, 1973.

Fehrenbach, T. R. *Comanches: Destruction of a People.* New York: Alfred A. Knopf, 1974.

Feit, Harvey A. "Chapter 8—Hunting and the Quest for Power: The James Bay Cree and Whitemen in the Twentieth Century." *Native Peoples: The Canadian Experience.* Toronto: McClellan & Stewart, 1986.

Fejes, Claire. *Villagers: Athabaskan Indian Life Along the Yukon.* New York: Random House, 1981.

The First Americans. Richmond, Virginia: Time-Life Books, 1992.

Fitting, James E. *The Archaeology of Michigan: A Guide to the Prehistory of the Great Lakes Region.* New York: Natural History Press for the American Museum of Natural History, 1969.

Fixico, Donald. "Tribal Leaders and the Demand for Natural Energy Resources on Reservation Lands." *The Plains Indians of the Twentieth Century. Ed. Peter Iverson. Norman: University of Oklahoma Press, 1985.*

Fontana, Bernard L. and John Paul Schaefer. *Of Earth and Little Rain: The Papago Indians.* Flagstaff, AZ: Northland Press, c. 1981.

Forbes, Jack D. *Apache, Navajo, and Spaniard.* Norman: University of Oklahoma Press, 1969, 1994.

Ford, Richard, R. *An Ecological Analysis Involving the Population of San Juan Pueblo, New Mexico.* New York: Garland Publishing, 1992.

Foreman, Grant. *The Five Civilized Tribes.* Norman: University of Oklahoma, 1934.

Fowler, Loretta. *Shared Symbols, Contested Meanings: Gros Ventre Culture and History, 1778–1984.* Ithaca, NY: Cornell University Press, 1987.

Franklin, Robert J. and Pamela A. Bunte. *The Paiute.* New York: Chelsea House, 1990.

Fredenberg, Ralph. "Indian Self-Determination." *Hearings before the Committee on Indian Affairs,* United States Senate. 73d Congress, 2d Session. On S. 2755 and S. 3645, Part 2: pp. 110–13, 1934.

Frey, Rodney. *The World of the Crow Indians: As Driftwood Lodges.* Norman: University of Oklahoma Press, 1987.

Fried, Jacob. "Aboriginal Population of Western Washington State." *Coast Salish and Western Washington Indians III*. Ed. David Agee Horr. New York: Garland Publishing, 1974.

Friesen, Gerald. *The Canadian Prairies: A History*. Lincoln: University of Nebraska Press, 1984.

Galens, Judy, Anna Sheets, and Robyn V. Young, editors. *Gale Encyclopedia of Multicultural America*. Detroit: Gale Research, 1995.

Gardener, Lion. "Lieft Lion Gardener: His Relation of the Pequot Warres (1660)." *Massachusetts Historical Society Collections,* third series, Vol. 3 (1833): pp. 131–60.

Garfield, Viola E. and Linn A. Forrest. *The Wolf and The Raven: Totem Poles of Southeastern Alaska*. Seattle: University of Washington Press, 1993.

Gibbs, George. *Indian Tribes of Washington Territory*. Fairfield, WA: Ye Galleon Press, 1972.

Gibson, Arrell M. *The Chickasaws*. Norman: University of Oklahoma, 1971.

Gifford, E. W. "Californian Kinship Terminologies." *University of California Publications in American Archaeology and Ethnology*. Vol. 18, No. 1. Reprint of Berkeley: University of California Press, 1922.

Gill, Sam D. and Irene F. Sullivan. *Dictionary of Native American Mythology*. London: Oxford University Press, 1992.

Giraud, Marcel. *The Métis in the Canadian West*. Translated by George Woodcock. Lincoln: University of Nebraska Press, 1986.

Goc, Michael J. *Land Rich Enough: An Illustrated History of Oshkosh and Winnebago County*. Northbridge, CA: Windsor Publications/Winnebago County Historical and Archaeological Society, 1988.

Goddard, Pliny Earle. "Life and Culture of the Hupa." *American Archaeology and Ethnology,* Vol. 3. Ed. Frederic Ward Putnam. Berkeley: University of California Publications, 1905. Reprint. New York: Kraus Reprint Corporation, 1964.

Goddard, Pliny Earle. "The Morphology of the Hupa Language." *American Archaeology and Ethnology,* Vol. 1. Ed. Frederic Ward Putnam. Berkeley: University of California Publications, 1903–1904. Reprint. New York: Kraus Reprint Corporation, 1964.

Goldman, Irving. *The Mouth of Heaven: An Introduction to Kwakiutl Religious Thought.* New York: John Wiley & Sons, 1975.

Goldschmidt, Walter R. and Harold E. Driver. "The Hupa White Deerskin Dance." *American Archaeology and Ethnology,* Vol. 35. Ed. A. L. Kroeber, et al. Berkeley: University of California Publications, 1943. Reprint. New York: Kraus Reprint Corporation, 1965.

Gonen, Amiram. *The Encyclopedia of the People of the World.* New York: Henry Holt and Company, 1993.

Goodwin, Glenville. *Myths and Tales of the White Mountain Apache.* New York: American Folk-lore Society, 1939.

Goodwin, Glenville. *The Social Organization of the Western Apache.* Chicago: University of Chicago Press, 1942.

Goodwin, Glenville. *Western Apache Raiding and Warfare.* Tucson: University of Arizona Press, 1971.

Grant, Bruce. *American Indians: Yesterday and Today.* New York: Dutton, 1960.

Green, Donald Edward. *The Creek People.* Phoenix: Indian Tribal Series, 1973.

Green, Michael D. *The Politics of Indian Removal.* Lincoln: University of Nebraska Press, 1982.

Gregory, H. F., ed. *The Southern Caddo: An Anthology.* New York: Garland Publishing, 1986.

Grinnell, George Bird. *Pawnee, Blackfoot and Cheyenne: History and Folklore of the Plains.* New York: Charles Scribner's Sons, 1961.

Grumet, Robert Steven. *Native Americans of the Northwest Coast: A Critical Bibliography.* Bloomington: Indiana University Press, 1979.

Haeberlin, Hermann and Erna Gunther. *The Indians of Puget Sound.* Seattle: University of Washington, 1967.

Hagan, Walter T. *The Sac and Fox Indians.* Norman: University of Oklahoma Press, 1958.

Hahn, Elizabeth. *The Creek.* Vero Beach, FL: Rourke Publications, 1992.

Hahn, Elizabeth. *The Pawnee.* Vero Beach, FL: Rourke Publications, 1992.

Haines, Francis. *The Nez Perces.* Norman: University of Oklahoma Press, 1955.

Haines, Francis. *The Plains Indians: Their Origins, Migrations, and Cultural Development*. New York: Thomas Y. Crowell Company, 1976.

Halbert, Henry S. "Courtship and Marriage Among the Choctaws of Mississippi (1882)." *A Choctaw Source Book*. New York: Garland Publishing, 1985.

Hale, Duane K. *Turtle Tales: Oral Traditions of the Delaware Tribe of Western Oklahoma*. Delaware Tribe of Oklahoma Press, 1984.

Harlow, Neal. *California Conquered: War and Peace on the Pacific, 1846–1850*. Berkeley: University of California Press, 1982.

Harrington, M. R. *Religion and Ceremonies of the Lenape*. New York: Museum of the American Indian Heye Foundation, 1921.

Harrison, Julia D. *Métis, People Between Two Worlds*. Vancouver: Glenbow-Alberta Institute, 1985.

Harrod, Howard L. *Becoming and Remaining a People: Native American Religions on the Northern Plains*. Tucson: University of Arizona Press, 1995.

Haugh, Solanus. *Papago, the Desert People*. Washington, DC: Bureau of Catholic Indian Missions, 1958.

Hauptman, Laurence M. *Tribes and Tribulations: Misconceptions About American Indians and Their Histories*. Albuquerque: University of New Mexico Press, 1995.

Hauptman, Laurence M. and James D. Wherry, eds. *The Pequots in Southern New England: The Fall and Rise of an American Indian Nation*. Norman: University of Oklahoma Press, 1990.

Haviland, William A. and Marjory W. Power. *The Original Vermonters: Native Inhabitants, Past and Present*. Hanover, NH: University Press of New England, 1981.

Heath, D. B., ed. *Mourt's Relation: A Journal of the Pilgrims at Plymouth* (1622). Reprint. Cambridge, MA: Applewood Books, 1986.

Heckewelder, John. *History, Manner, and Customs of the Indian Nations Who Once Inhabited Pennsylvania and the Neighbouring States*. Philadelphia: Historical Society of Pennsylvania, 1876.

Heizer, R. F. and M. A. Whipple, *The California Indians: A Source Book*. Berkeley: University of California Press, 1951.

Heizer, R. F. and T. Kroeber, eds. *Ishi the Last Yahi: A Documentary History*. Berkeley: University of California Press, 1979.

Heizer, Robert F., ed. *The Handbook of North American Indians,* Vol. 8: *California.* Washington, DC: Smithsonian Institution, 1978.

Helm, June, ed. *The Handbook of North American Indians,* Vol. 6: *Subarctic.* Washington, DC: Smithsonian Institution, 1981.

Hickerson, Harold. *The Chippewa and Their Neighbors: A Study in Ethnohistory.* New York: Holt, Rinehart and Winston, 1970.

Hines, Donald M. *Magic in the Mountains, the Yakima Shaman: Power & Practice.* Issaquah, WA: Great Eagle Publishing, 1993.

Hippler, Arthur E. and John R. Wood. *The Subarctic Athabascans.* Fairbanks: University of Alaska, 1974.

Hodge, Frederick Webb. *Handbook of American Indians North of Mexico.* New York: Pageant Books, 1959.

Hoig, Stan. *Tribal Wars of the Southern Plains.* Norman: University of Oklahoma Press, 1993.

Hoijer, Harry. *Apachean Culture History and Ethnology.* Eds. Keith H. Basso and Morris E. Opler. Tucson: University of Arizona Press, 1971.

Hoijer, Harry. *Chiricahua and Mescalero Apache Texts.* Chicago: University of Chicago Press, 1938.

Holt, Ronald L. *Beneath These Red Cliffs: An Ethnohistory of the Utah Paiutes.* Albuquerque: University of New Mexico Press, 1992.

Hoover, Herbert T. *The Yankton Sioux.* New York: Chelsea House, 1988.

Hornung, Rick. *One Nation Under the Gun: Inside the Mohawk Civil War.* New York: Pantheon Books, 1992.

Hothem, Lar. *Treasures of the Mound Builders: Adena and Hopewell Artifacts of Ohio.* Lancaster, Ohio: Hothem House Books, 1989.

Howard, James H., *Shawnee! The Ceremonialism of a Native American Tribe and Its Cultural Background.* Athens: Ohio University Press, 1981.

Hoxie, Frederick E. *The Crow.* New York: Chelsea House, 1989.

Hoxie, Frederick E., ed. *Encyclopedia of North American Indians.* Boston: Houghton Mifflin Company, 1996.

Hoyt, Anne Kelley. *The Bibliography of the Chickasaw.* Metuchen, New Jersey: The Scarecrow Press, 1987.

Hrdlicka, Ales. *Physical Anthropology of the Lenape or Delawares, and of the Eastern Indians in General.* Washington, DC: U.S. Government Printing Office, 1916.

Hudson, Charles. *The Southeastern Indians.* Knoxville: University of Tennessee Press, 1976.

Hudson, Peter J. "Choctaw Indian Dishes (1939)." *A Choctaw Source Book.* New York: Garland Publishing, 1985: pp. 333–35.

Hudson, Travis and Ernest Underhay. *Crystals in the Sky: An Intellectual Odyssey Involving Chumash Astronomy, Cosmology and Rock Art.* Socorro, NM: Ballena Press, 1978.

Hyde, George E. *Indians of the Woodlands: From Prehistoric Times to 1725.* Norman: University of Oklahoma Press, 1962.

Ignacio, Amera. "Her Remark Offended Me." *Native Heritage: Personal Accounts by American Indians, 1790 to the Present.* Ed. Arlene Hirschfelder. New York: Macmillan, 1995.

Indian America; A Traveler's Companion. Santa Fe: John Muir Publications, 1989.

Indian Reservations: A State and Federal Handbook. Jefferson, NC: McFarland & Co., 1974.

Iverson, Peter. *The Plains Indians of the Twentieth Century.* Norman: University of Oklahoma Press, 1986.

Ives, John, W. *A Theory of Northern Athapaskan Prehistory.* Boulder, CO: Westview Press, 1990.

Jennings, Francis. *The Invasion of America: Indians, Colonization, and the Cant of Conquest.* Chapel Hill: University of North Carolina Press, 1975.

Joe, Rita and Lynn Henry. *Song of Rita Joe: Autobiography of a Mi'kmaq Poet.* Lincoln: University of Nebraska Press, 1996.

Johansen, Bruce E. *Life and Death in Mohawk Country.* Golden, CO: North American Press, 1993.

Johnson, Elias. *Legends, Traditions and Laws of the Iroquois, or Six Nations, and History of the Tuscarora Indians* (1881). Reprint. New York: AMS Press, 1978.

Johnson, John F. C., ed. *Eyak Legends: Stories and Photographs.* Anchorage: Chugach Heritage Foundation, n.d.

Johnson, Michael G. *The Native Tribes of North America: A Concise Encyclopedia.* New York: Macmillan, 1994.

Johnston, Basil H. *Tales the Elders Told: Ojibway Legends*. Toronto: Royal Ontario Museum, 1981.

Jonaitis, Aldona. *Art of the Northern Tlingit*. Seattle, Washington: University of Washington Press, 1986.

Jonaitis, Aldona, ed. *Chiefly Feasts: The Enduring Kwakiutl Potlatch*. New York: American Museum of Natural History, 1991.

Jorgensen, Joseph G. *Salish Language and Culture*. Bloomington: Indiana University Publications, 1969.

Jorgensen, Joseph G. *The Sun Dance Religion: Power for the Powerless*. Chicago: University of Chicago Press, 1972.

Joseph, Alice, Jane Chesky, and Rosamond B. Spicer. *The Desert People: A Study of the Papago Indians*. Chicago, IL: University of Chicago Press, 1974.

Josephy, Alvin M. Jr. *500 Nations: An Illustrated History of North American Indians*. New York: Alfred A. Knopf, 1994.

Josephy, Alvin M. Jr. *The Indian Heritage of America*. New York: Alfred A. Knopf, 1968.

Josephy, Alvin M. Jr. *The Nez Perce Indians and the Opening of the Northwest*. New Haven, CT: Yale University Press, 1965.

Josephy, Alvin M. Jr. *Now That the Buffalo's Gone: A Study of Today's American Indians*. New York: Alfred A. Knopf, 1982.

Kalifornsky, Peter. *A Dena'ina Legacy: K'tl'egh'i Sukdu: The Collected Writings of Peter Kalifornsky*. Eds. James Kari and Alan Boraas. Fairbanks: Alaska Native Language Center, 1991.

Kappler, Charles J. *Indian Affairs, Laws, and Treaties*, four volumes. Washington, DC: U.S. Government Printing Office, 1929.

Kari, James, ed. *Athabaskan Stories from Anvik: Rev. John W. Chapman's "Ten'a Texts and Tales."* Fairbanks: Alaska Native Language Center, 1981.

Kari, James, translator and editor. "When They Were Killed at 'Lake That Has an Arm' (Kluane Lake)." *Tatl'ahwt'aenn Nenn': The Headwaters Peoples Country: Narratives of the Upper Ahtna Athabaskans*. Fairbanks: Alaska Native Language Center, 1985.

Kasner, Leone Leston. *Siletz: Survival for an Artifact*. Dallas OR: Itemizer-Observer, 1977.

Kennedy, Roger G. *Hidden Cities: The Discovery and Loss of Ancient American Civilization.* New York: Macmillan, 1994.

Kenner, Charles L. *A History of New Mexican-Plains Indian Relations.* Norman: University of Oklahoma Press, 1969, 1994.

Kent, Zachary, *Tecumseh.* Chicago, IL: Children's Press, 1992.

Kidwell, Clara Sue and Charles Roberts. *The Choctaws: A Critical Bibliography.* Bloomington: Indiana University Press for the Newberry Library, 1980.

Kirk, Ruth and Richard D. Daugherty. *Hunter of the Whale.* New York: William Morrow, 1974.

Klein, Barry T. *Reference Encyclopedia of the American Indian,* Seventh edition. West Nyack, NY: Todd Publications, 1995.

Klein, Laura F. and Lillian A. Ackerman. *Women and Power in Native North America.* Norman: University of Oklahoma, 1995.

Kluckhohn, Clyde and Dorothea Leighton. *The Navaho.* 1946. Revised edition. Cambridge, MA: Harvard University Press, 1974.

Korp, Maureen. *The Sacred Geography of the American Mound Builders.* New York: Edwin Mellen Press, 1990.

Kraft, Herbert C. *The Lenape: Archaeology, History, and Ethnography.* Newark: New Jersey Historical Society, 1986.

Kraft, Herbert C. *The Lenape Indians of New Jersey.* South Orange, NJ: Seton Hall University Museum, 1987.

Krech, Shepard III, ed. *Indians, Animals and the Fur Trade.* Athens: University of Georgia Press, 1981.

Kroeber, Alfred L. "The Achomawi and Atsugewi," "The Chilula.," "The Luiseño: Elements of Civilization," "The Luiseño: Organization of Civilization," "The Miwok," and "The Pomo." *Handbook of the Indians of California.* Washington, DC: U.S. Government Printing Office, 1925.

Krupp, E. C. *Beyond the Blue Horizon: Myths & Legends of the Sun, Moon, Stars, & Planets.* New York: Oxford University Press, 1991.

Lacey, Theresa Jensen. *The Pawnee.* New York: Chelsea House Publishers, 1996.

Ladd, Edmund J. "Zuñi Religion and Philosophy." *Zuñi & El Morro.* Santa Fe: SAR Press, 1983.

Langdon, Steve J. *The Native People of Alaska.* Anchorage: Greatland Graphics, 1993.

Laubin, Reginald and Gladys Laubin. *Indian Dances of North America: Their Importance to Indian Life.* Norman: University of Oklahoma Press, 1976.

Laughlin, William S. "The Aleut-Eskimo Community." *The North American Indians: A Sourcebook.* Ed. Roger C. Owen. New York: Macmillan, 1967.

Leach, Douglas E. *Flintlock and Tomahawk: New England in King Philip's War.* New York: Macmillan, 1959.

Leitch, Barbara A. *A Concise Dictionary of Indian Tribes of North America.* Algonac, MI: Reference Publications, 1979.

Lewis, Anna. *Chief Pushmataha, American Patriot: The Story of the Choctaws' Struggle for Survival.* New York: Exposition Press, 1959.

Lewis, David Rich. *Neither Wolf Nor Dog: American Indians, Environment, and Agrarian Change.* Oxford: Oxford University Press, 1994.

Liptak, Karen. *North American Indian Ceremonies.* New York: Franklin Watts, 1992.

Lowie, Robert H. *The Crow Indians.* Lincoln: University of Nebraska Press, 1983.

Lowie, Robert H. *Indians of the Plains.* Garden City, NY: Natural History Press, 1963.

Lucius, William A. and David A. Breternitz. *Northern Anasazi Ceramic Styles: A Fieldguide for Identification.* Center for Indigenous Studies in the Americas Publications in Anthropology, 1992.

Lund, Annabel. *Heartbeat: World Eskimo Indian Olympics: Alaska Native Sport and Dance Traditions.* Juneau: Fairweather Press, 1986.

Lurie, Nancy Oestreich. "Weetamoo, 1638–1676." *North American Indian Lives.* Milwaukee: Milwaukee Public Library, 1985.

MacEwan, Grant. *Métis Makers of History.* Saskatoon: Western Producer Prairie Books, 1981.

Madsen, Brigham D. *The Shoshoni Frontier and the Bear River Massacre.* Salt Lake City: University of Utah Press, 1985.

Mahon, John K. *History of the Second Seminole War 1835–1842.* Gainsville: University of Florida Press, 1967.

Maillard, Antoine Simon and Joseph M. Bellenger. *Grammaire de la Langue Mikmaque.* English translation published as *Grammar of the Mikmaque Language.* New York: AMS Press, 1970.

Mails, Thomas E. *The Cherokee People: The Story of the Cherokees from Earliest Origins to Contemporary Times.* Tulsa, OK: Council Oak Books, 1992.

Mails, Thomas E. *The Mystic Warriors of the Plains: The Culture, Arts, Crafts and Religion of the Plains Indians.* Tulsa: Council Oaks Books, 1991.

Mails, Thomas E. *Peoples of the Plains.* Tulsa, OK: Council Oak Books, 1997.

Mails, Thomas E. *The Pueblo Children of the Earth Mother.* Vol. 2. Garden City, NY: Doubleday, 1983.

Malinowksi, Sharon, ed. *Notable Native Americans.* Detroit: Gale Research, 1995.

Malinowski, Sharon and Simon Glickman, eds. *Native North American Biography.* Detroit: U•X•L, 1996.

Malone, Patrick M. *The Skulking Way of War: Technology and Tactics Among the New England Indians.* Lanham, MA: Madison Books, 1991.

Mandelbaum, David G. *The Plains Cree: An Ethnographic, Historical, and Comparative Study.* Regina, Saskatchewan: Canadian Plains Research Center, 1979.

Markowitz, Harvey, ed. *American Indians,* Pasadena, CA: Salem Press, 1995.

Marquis, Arnold. *A Guide to America's Indians: Ceremonials, Reservations, and Museums.* Norman: University of Oklahoma Press, 1974.

Marriott, Alice L. *The Ten Grandmothers.* Norman: University of Oklahoma Press, 1945.

Marriott, Alice and Carol K. Rachlin. *Plains Indian Mythology.* New York: Thomas Y. Crowell, 1975.

Martin, Calvin. *Keepers of the Game: Indian-Animal Relationships and the Fur Trade.* Berkeley: University of California Press, 1978.

Matthiessen, Peter. *In the Spirit of Crazy Horse*. New York: Viking Penguin, 1980.

Maxwell, James A., ed. *America's Fascinating Indian Heritage*. New York: The Reader's Digest Association, 1978.

Mayhall, Mildred P. *The Kiowas*. Norman: University of Oklahoma Press, 1962.

Mays, Buddy. *Indian Villages of the Southwest*. San Francisco: Chronicle Books, 1985.

McBride, Bunny. *Molly Spotted Elk: A Penobscot in Paris*. Norman and London: University of Oklahoma Press, 1995.

McFadden, Steven. *Profiles in Wisdom: Native Elders Speak About the Earth*. Sante Fe: Bear & Co., 1991.

McFee, Malcolm. *Modern Blackfeet: Montanans on a Reservation*. New York: Holt, Rinehart and Winston, 1972.

McGinnis, Anthony. *Counting Coup and Cutting Horses: Intertribal Warfare on the Northern Plains 1738–1889*. Evergreen, CO: Cordillera Press, 1990.

McKee, Jesse O. and Jon A. Schlenker. *The Choctaws: Cultural Evolution of a Native American Tribe*. Jackson: University Press of Mississippi, 1980.

McKennan, Robert, A. "The Upper Tanana Indians." *Yale University Publications in Anthropology: 55*. New Haven, CT: Yale University, 1959.

Melody, Michael E. *The Apaches: A Critical Bibliography*. Bloomington: Indiana University Press, 1977.

Merriam, C. Hart. "The Luiseño: Observations on Mission Indians." *Studies of California Indians*. Edited by the Staff of the Department of Anthropology of the University of California. Berkeley: University of California Press, 1962.

Meyer, Roy W. *History of the Santee Sioux: United States Indian Policy on Trial*. Lincoln: University of Nebraska Press, 1993.

Miller, Bruce W. *Chumash: A Picture of Their World*. Los Osos, CA: Sand River Press, 1988.

Miller, Jay. *The Delaware*. Chicago: Childrens Press, 1994.

Milliken, Randall. *A Time of Little Choice: The Disintegration of Tribal Culture in the San Francisco Bay Area, 1769–1810*. Menlo Park, CA: Ballena Press, 1995.

Milloy, John S. *The Plains Cree: Trade, Diplomacy and War, 1790 to 1870*. Winnipeg: University of Manitoba Press, 1988.

Minge, Ward Alan. *Acoma: Pueblo in the Sky*. Albuquerque: University of New Mexico Press, 1976.

Minority Rights Group. *Polar Peoples: Self Determination and Development*. London: Minority Rights Publications, 1994.

Mississippian Communities and Households. Tuscaloosa: University of Alabama Press, 1995.

Momaday, N. Scott. *The Way to Rainy Mountain*. Albuquerque: University of New Mexico Press, 1969.

Moore, John H. *The Cheyenne Nation: A Social and Demographic History*. Lincoln: University of Nebraska Press, 1987.

Moorhead, Max L. *The Apache Frontier: Jacobo Ugarte and Spanish-Indian Relations in Northern New Spain, 1769–1791*. Norman: University of Oklahoma Press, 1968.

Moquin, Wayne, ed. *Great Documents in American Indian History*. New York: Da Capo Press, 1973.

Morgan, Lewis H. *League of the Ho-de-no-sau-nee or Iroquois*. New Haven, CT: Human Relations Area Files, 1954: p. 243.

Morrison, R. Bruce and C. Roderick Wilson, eds. *Native Peoples: The Canadian Experience*. Toronto: McClellan & Stewart, 1986.

Murie, James R. *Ceremonies of the Pawnee*. Smithsonian Contributions to Anthropology, No. 27. Washington, DC: Smithsonian Institution, 1981. Reprint. Lincoln: University of Nebraska Press for the American Indian Studies Research Institute, 1989.

Murphy, Robert F. and Yolanda Murphy. "Shoshone-Bannock Subsistence and Society." *Anthropological Records*. 16:7. Berkeley: University of California Press, 1960.

Myers, Arthur. *The Pawnee*. New York: F. Watts, 1993.

Myers, William Starr, ed. *The Story of New Jersey,* Volume 1. Ed. New York: Lewis Historical Publishing Company, 1945.

Mysteries of the Ancient Americas: The New World Before Columbus. Pleasantville, NY: The Reader's Digest Association, 1986.

Nabakov, Peter and Robert Easton. *Native American Architecture.* New York: Oxford University Press, 1989.

Nairne, Thomas. *Nairne's Mushogean Journals: The 1708 Expedition to the Mississippi River.* Jackson: University Press of Mississippi, 1988.

Native Cultures in Alaska. Anchorage: Alaska Geographic Society, 1996.

Newcomb, W. W. Jr. *The Indians of Texas: From Prehistoric to Modern Times.* Austin: University of Texas Press, 1961.

Newkumet, Vynola Beaver and Howard L. Meredith. *Hasinai: A Traditional History of the Caddo Confederacy.* College Station: Texas A & M University Press, 1988.

Noble, David Grant. *Pueblos, Villages, Forts & Trails: A Guide to New Mexico's Past.* Albuquerque: University of New Mexico Press, 1994.

Northway, Walter. *Walter Northway.* Fairbanks: Alaska Native Language Center, 1987.

Norton, Jack. *Genocide in Northwestern California: When Our Worlds Cried.* San Francisco: Indian Historian Press, 1979.

O'Brien, Sharon. *American Indian Tribal Governments.* Norman: University of Oklahoma Press, 1989.

Olmsted, D. L. *Achumawi Dictionary.* Berkeley: University of California Press, 1966.

Olson, Ronald L. *The Quinault Indians.* Seattle: University of Washington Press, 1967.

O'Neill, Laurie A. *The Shawnees: People of the Eastern Woodlands.* Brookfield, CT: The Millbrook Press, 1995.

Opler, Morris Edward. *An Apache Life-Way.* New York: Cooper Square Publishers, 1965.

Orr, Charles, ed. *History of the Pequot War.* Cleveland: Helman-Taylor, 1897.

Ortiz, Alfonso, ed. *The Handbook of North American Indians,* Vol. 10: *Southwest.* Washington, DC: Smithsonian Institution, 1983.

Ortiz, Alfonso. *The Pueblo.* New York: Chelsea House Publishers, 1992.

Osgood, Cornelius. "Ingalik Mental Culture." *Yale University Publications in Anthropology: 56.* New Haven, CT: Yale University, 1959.

Oswalt, Wendell H. "The Crow: Plains Warriors and Bison Hunters." *This Land Was Theirs: A Study of North American Indians.* Mountain View, CA: Mayfield Publishing, 1988.

Owen, Roger C., James J. F. Deetz, and Anthony D. Fisher, eds. *A Guide to Indian Tribes of the Pacific Northwest.* Norman: University of Oklahoma Press, 1986.

Owen, Roger C., James J. F. Deetz, and Anthony D. Fisher, eds. *Indians of the Pacific Northwest: A History.* Norman: University of Oklahoma Press, 1981.

Owen, Roger C., James J. F. Deetz, and Anthony D. Fisher, eds. *The North American Indians: A Sourcebook.* New York: MacMillan, 1967.

Parsons, Elsie Clews. "Notes on the Caddo." *Memoirs of the American Anthropological Association,* No. 57. Menasha, WI: American Anthropological Association, 1941.

Parsons, Elsie Clews. *Pueblo Mothers and Children.* Ed. Barbara A. Babcock. Santa Fe: Ancient City Press, 1991.

Parsons, Elsie Clews. *The Social Organization of the Tewa of New Mexico.* American Anthropological Association Memoirs, Nos. 36–39. Reprint. New York: Kraus, 1964.

Patencio, Francisco. *Stories and Legends of the Palm Springs Indians As Told to Margaret Boynton.* Los Angeles: Times-Mirror Press, 1943.

Paterek, Josephine. *Encyclopedia of American Indian Costume.* Santa Barbara: ABC-CLIO, 1994.

Pauketat, Timothy R. *Temples for Cahokia Lords.* Ann Arbor: University of Michigan, Museum of Anthropology, 1993.

Peat, F. David. *Lighting the Seventh Fire: The Spiritual Ways, Healing, and Science of the Native American.* NY: Carol Publishing Group, 1994.

Penney, David W. *Art of the American Indian Frontier: The Chandler-Pohrt Collection.* Seattle: University of Washington Press, 1992.

Perdue, Theda. *The Cherokee.* New York: Chelsea House Publishers, 1989.

Peroff, N. C. *Menominee Drums: Tribal Termination and Restoration, 1954–1974.* Norman: University of Oklahoma Press, 1982.

Perry, Richard J. *Apache Reservation: Indigenous Peoples and the American State.* Austin: University of Texas Press, 1993.

Perry, Richard J. *Western Apache Heritage: People of the Mountain Corridor.* Austin: University of Texas Press, 1991.

Perttula, Timothy K. "The Caddo Nation." *Archeological and Ethnohistoric Perspectives.* Austin: University of Texas Press, 1992.

Phillips, G.H. *Indians and Indian Agents: The Origins of the Reservation System in California, 1849–1852.* Norman: University of Oklahoma Press, 1997.

Place, Ann Marie. "Putting a Face on Colonization: Factionalism and Gender Politics in the Life History of Awashunkes, the 'Squaw Sachem' of Saconet." *Northeastern Indians Lives.* Ed. Robert S. Grumet. Amherst: University of Massachusetts Press, 1996.

Pond, Samuel. *The Dakota People or Sioux in Minnesota as They Were in 1834.* St. Paul: Minnesota Historical Society Press, 1986.

Pope, Saxton T. "The Medical History of Ishi." *University of California Publications in American Archaeology and Ethnology.* Vol. 13, No. 5. Berkeley: University of California Press, 1920.

Pope, Saxton T. "Yahi Archery." *University of California Publications in American Archaeology and Ethnology,* Vol. 13, No. 3. Berkeley: University of California Press, 1923.

Porter, Frank W. III. *The Coast Salish Peoples.* New York: Chelsea House Publishers, 1989.

Powers, Stephen. "The Achomawi." *Tribes of California.* Berkeley: University of California Press, 1976. Reprinted from *Contributions to North American Ethnology,* Vol. 3. Washington, DC: U.S. Government Printing Office, 1877.

Preacher, Stephen. *Anasazi Sunrise: The Mystery of Sacrifice Rock.* El Cajon, CA: The Rugged Individualist, 1992.

Press, Margaret L. "Chemehuevi: A Grammar and Lexicon." *Linguistics,* Vol. 92. Berkeley: University of California Press, 1979.

Rand, Silas Tertius. *Dictionary of the Language of the Micmac Indians, Who Reside in Nova Scotia, New Brunswick, Prince Edward Island, Cape Breton, and Newfoundland.* Halifax, Nova Scotia: Nova Scotia Print Co., 1888. Reprint. New York, Johnson Reprint Corp., 1972.

Ray, Arthur J. *Indians in the Fur Trade: Their Role as Trappers, Hunters & Middle Man in the Lands Southwest of Hudson Bay, 1660–1860*. Toronto: University of Toronto Press, 1974.

Reddy, Marlita A. *Statistical Record of Native North Americans*. Detroit: Gale Research, 1996.

Rice, Julian, ed. *Deer Women and Elk Men: The Lakota Narratives of Ella Deloria*. Albuquerque: University of New Mexico Press, 1992.

Richardson, Rupert Norval. *The Comanche Barrier to the South Plains Settlement*. Glendale, CA: Arthur H. Clarke, 1955.

Roberts, David. *In Search of the Old Ones*. New York: Simon & Schuster, 1996.

Rockwell, Wilson. *The Utes: A Forgotten People*. Denver, CO: Alan Swallow, 1956.

Rohner, Ronald P. and Evelyn C. Rohner. *The Kwakiutl: Indians of British Columbia*. New York: Holt, Rinehart and Winston, 1970.

Rollings, Willard H. *The Osage: An Ethnohistorical Study of Hegemony on the Prairie-Plains*. Columbia: University of Missouri Press, 1992.

Rountree, Helen C., ed. *Pocahontas's People: The Powhatan Indians of Virginia through Four Centuries*. Norman: University of Oklahoma Press, 1990.

Rountree, Helen C., ed. *Powhatan Foreign Relations, 1500–1722*. Charlottesville: University Press of Virginia, 1993.

Rountree, Helen C., ed. *The Powhatan Indians of Virginia: Their Native Culture*. Norman: University of Oklahoma Press, 1989.

Ruby, Robert H. *The Chinook Indians: Traders of the Lower Columbia River*. Norman: University of Oklahoma Press, 1976.

Ruby, Robert H. and John A. Brown. *A Guide to Indian Tribes of the Pacific Northwest*. Norman: University of Oklahoma Press, 1986.

Russell, Frank. *The Pima Indians*. Tucson: University of Arizona Press, 1975.

Salisbury, Richard F. *A Homeland for the Cree: Regional Development in James Bay 1971–1981*. Kingston & Montreal: McGill-Queen's University Press, 1986.

Salzmann, Zdenek. *The Arapaho Indians: A Research Guide and Bibliography*. New York: Greenwood Press, 1988.

Samuel, Cheryl. *The Chilkat Dancing Blanket*. Seattle: Pacific Search Press, 1982.

Sando, Joe S. *Pueblo Nations: Eight Centuries of Pueblo Indian History*. Santa Fe: Clear Light Publishers, 1992.

Sauter, John and Bruce Johnson. *Tillamook Indians of the Oregon Coast*. Portland OR: Binfords and Mort, 1974.

Sawchuck, Joe. *The Métis of Manitoba: Reformulation of an Ethnic Identity*. Toronto: Peter Martin Associates, 1978.

Schlesier, Karl H. "Introduction," and "Commentary: A History of Ethnic Groups in the Great Plains A.D. 500–1550." *Plains Indians, A.D. 500–1500: The Archaeological Past of Historic Groups*. Ed. Karl H. Schlesier. Norman: University of Oklahoma Press, 1994.

Schultz, Willard James. *Blackfeet and Buffalo: Memories of Life among the Indians*. Norman: University of Oklahoma Press, 1962.

Schuster, Helen. *The Yakimas: A Critical Bibliography*. Bloomington: Indiana University Press, 1982.

Segal, Charles M. and David C. Stineback, eds. *Puritans, Indians and Manifest Destiny*. New York: Putnam, 1977.

Seger, John H. *Early Days among the Cheyenne and Arapaho Indians*. Ed. Stanley Vestal. Norman: University of Oklahoma Press, 1956.

Seiler, Hansjakob. *Cahuilla Texts with an Introduction*. Bloomington: Indiana University, 1970.

Shaffer, Lynda Norene. *Native Americans Before 1492: The Moundbuilding Centers of the Eastern Woodlands*. New York: M. E. Sharpe, 1992.

Shames, Deborah, ed. *Freedom with Reservation: The Menominee Struggle to Save Their Land and People*. Madison: National Committee to Save the Menominee People and Forests/Wisconsin Indian Legal Services, 1972.

Shawano, Marlene Miller. *Native Dress of the Stockbridge Munsee Band Mohican Indians*. Stockbridge Munsee Reservation Library, n.d.

Shipek, Florence. *Pushed into the Rocks: Southern California Indian Land Tenure, 1769–1986*. Lincoln: University of Nebraska Press, 1990.

Silverberg, Robert. *The Mound Builders*. Greenwich, CT: New York Graphic Society, Ltd., 1970.

Siy, Alexandra, *The Eeyou: People of Eastern James Bay*. New York: Dillon Press, 1993.

Slickpoo, Allen P. and Deward E. Walker Jr. *Noon Nee-Me-Poo: We, the Nez Perces*. Lapwai: Nez Perce Tribe of Idaho, 1973.

Smelcer, John. "Dotson'Sa, Great Raven Makes the World." *The Raven and the Totem: Traditional Alaska Native Myths and Tales*. Anchorage: Salmon Run, 1992: pp. 124–25.

Smith, Anne M., ed. *Shoshone Tales*. Salt Lake City: University of Utah Press, 1993.

Smith, F. Todd. *The Caddo Indians: Tribes at the Convergence of Empires, 1542–1854*. College Station: University of Texas A&M Press, 1995.

Smith, Marian W. *Indians of the Urban Northwest*. New York: AMS Press, 1949.

Smith, Marian W. *The Puyallup-Nisqually*. New York: Columbia University Press, 1940.

Snow, Dean R. *The Iroquois*. Cambridge, MA: Blackwell Publishers, 1994.

Speck, Frank G. *Penobscot Man: The Life History of a Forest Tribe in Maine*. Philadelphia: University of Pennsylvania Press, 1940.

Speck, Frank G. *A Study of the Indian Big House Ceremony*. Harrisburg: Pennsylvania Historical Commission, 1931.

Spector, Janet D. *What This Awl Means: Feminist Archaeology at a Wahpeton Dakota Village*. St. Paul: Minnesota Historical Society Press, 1993.

Spicer, Edward H. *Cycles of Conquest: The Impact of Spain, Mexico, and the United States on the Indians of the Southwest, 1533–1960*. Tucson, AZ: University of Arizona Press, 1962.

Spindler, George and Louise Spindler. *Dreamers With Power: The Menomini Indians*. New York: Holt, Rinehart & Winston, 1971.

Spittal, W. G., ed. *Iroquois Women: An Anthology*. Ohsweken, Ontario: Iroqrafts Ltd., 1990.

Spradley, James P. *Guests Never Leave Hungry: The Autobiography of James Sewid, A Kwakiutl Indian*. New Haven: Yale University Press, 1969.

Statistical Data for Planning Stockbridge Munsee Reservation. Billings, MT: U.S. Department of the Interior, Bureau of Indian Affairs, 1975.

Steele, Ian K. *Warpaths: Invasions of North America.* New York: Oxford University Press, 1994.

Steward, Julian H. *Basin-Plateau Aboriginal Sociopolitical Groups.* Washington, DC: Smithsonian Institution. *The Bureau of American Ethnology Bulletin,* No. 120. Washington, DC: U.S. Government Printing Office, 1938.

Stewart, Omer C. *Peyote Religion: A History.* Norman: University of Oklahoma, 1987.

Stevens, Susan McCullough. "Passamaquoddy Economic Development in Cultural and Historical Perspective." *World Anthropology: American Indian Economic Development.* Ed. Sam Stanley. The Hague: Mouton Publishers, 1978.

Stockel, H. Henrietta. "Ceremonies and Celebrations." *Women Of the Apache Nation: Voices of Truth.* Reno: University of Nevada Press, 1991.

Subarctic. Ed. June Helm. Washington, DC: Smithsonian Institution, 1981.

Suttles, Wayne, ed. *The Handbook of North American Indians,* Vol. 7: *Northwest Coast.* Washington, DC: Smithsonian Institution, 1990.

Swanson, Earl H, ed. *Languages and Culture of Western North America.* Pocatello: Idaho State University Press, 1970.

Swanton, John Reed. *Indian Tribes of the Lower Mississippi Valley and Adjacent Coast of the Gulf of Mexico.* Washington, DC: U.S. Government Printing Office, 1911.

Swanton, John Reed. *The Indian Tribes of North America,* Vol. 1: *Northeast.* Washington, DC: Smithsonian Institution. Reprinted from: *The Bureau of American Ethnology Bulletin,* No. 145. Washington, DC: U.S. Government Printing Office, 1953.

Swanton, John Reed. *Source Material for the Social and Ceremonial Life of the Choctaw Indians.* Bulletin No. 103. Washington, DC: U.S. Government Printing Office, 1931.

Symington, Fraser. *The Canadian Indian: The Illustrated History of the Great Tribes of Canada.* Toronto: McClelland & Stewart, 1969.

Tanner, Helen H., ed. *Atlas of Great Lakes Indian History.* Norman: University of Oklahoma Press, 1987.

Tantaquidgeon, Gladys. *Folk Medicine of the Delaware and Related Algonkian Indians*. Harrisburg: Pennsylvania Historical and Museum Commission, Anthropological Series 3, 1972.

Tantaquidgeon, Gladys. *A Study of Delaware Indian Medicine Practice and Folk Beliefs*. Harrisburg: Pennsylvania Historical Commission, 1942.

Teit, James A. "The Salishan Tribes of the Western Plateaus." *Bureau of American Ethnology Annual Report*. No. 45. Ed. Franz Boas. 1927–1928.

Tennberg, Monica, ed. *Unity and Diversity in Arctic Societies*. Rovaniemi, Finland: International Arctic Social Sciences Association, 1996.

Terrell, John Upton. *American Indian Almanac*. New York: World Publishing, 1971.

Thomas, Cyrus. *Report on the Mound Explorations of the Bureau of Ethnology*. Washington, DC: Smithsonian Institution, 1894.

Thomas, David Hurst, ed. *A Great Basin Shoshonean Source Book*. New York: Garland Publishing, 1986.

Thompson, Chad. *Athabaskan Languages and the Schools: A Handbook for Teachers*. Juneau: Alaska Department of Education, 1984.

Thompson, Judy. *From the Land: Two Hundred Years of Dene Clothing*. Hull, Quebec: Canadian Museum of Civilization, 1994.

Through Indian Eyes: The Untold Story of Native American Peoples. Pleasantville, NY: Reader's Digest Association, 1995.

Tilton, Robert S. *Pocahontas: The Evolution of an American Narrative*. New York: Cambridge University Press, 1994.

Tohono O'Odham: History of the Desert People. Arizona: Papago Tribe, c1985.

Tooker, Elisabeth, ed. *An Iroquois Source Book,* Volumes 1 and 2. New York: Garland Publishing, 1985.

"Traditional and Contemporary Ceremonies, Rituals, Festivals, Music, and Dance." *Native America: Portrait of the Peoples*. Ed. Duane Champagne. Detroit: Gale Research, 1994.

Trafzer, Clifford E. *The Chinook*. New York: Chelsea House, 1990.

Trafzer, Clifford E. *Yakima, Palouse, Cayuse, Umatilla, Walla Walla, and Wanapum Indians.* Metuchen, New Jersey: Scarecrow Press, 1992.

Trigger, Bruce G., ed. *The Handbook of North American Indians,* Vol. 15: *Northeast.* Washington, DC: Smithsonian Institution, 1978.

Trigger, Bruce G. *Natives and Newcomers: Canada's "Heroic Age" Reconsidered.* Manchester: McGill-Queen's University Press, 1985.

Trimble, Stephen. *The People: Indians of the American Southwest.* Santa Fe: NM: Sar Press, 1993.

Tyson, Carl N. *The Pawnee People.* Phoenix: Indian Tribal Series, 1976.

Underhill, Ruth. *The Autobiography of a Papago Woman.* Menasha, WI: American Anthropological Memoirs #48, 1936.

Underhill, Ruth. *Life in the Pueblos.* Santa Fe: Ancient City Press, 1991.

Underhill, Ruth. *Singing for Power.* Tucson: University of Arizona Press, 1979.

United American Indians of New England. "National Day of Mourning." *Literature of the American Indian.* Ed. Thomas E. Sanders and Walter W. Peek. Abridged edition. Beverly Hills, CA: Glencoe Press, 1976.

The Vinland Sagas: The Norse Discovery of America. Translated by Magnus Magnusson and Hermann Palsson. Baltimore: Penguin, 1965.

Vogel, Virgil J. *American Indian Medicine.* Norman: University of Oklahoma Press, 1970.

The Wabanakis of Maine and the Maritimes: A Resource Book About Penobscot, Passamaquoddy, Maliseet, Micmac, and Abenaki Indians. Philadelphia: American Friends Service Committee (AFSC), 1989.

Waldman, Carl. *Atlas of the North American Indian.* New York: Facts On File, 1985.

Waldman, Carl. *Encyclopedia of Native American Tribes.* New York: Facts on File, 1988.

Waldman, Carl. *Who Was Who in Native American History: Indians and NonIndians From Early Contacts Through 1900.* New York: Facts on File, 1990.

Waldman, Harry, ed. "Caddo." *Encyclopedia of Indians of the Americas.* St. Clair Shores, MI: Scholarly Press, 1974.

Walens, Stanley. *Feasting with Cannibals: An Essay on Kwakiutl Cosmology*. Princeton, NJ: Princeton University Press, 1981.

Wallace, Anthony F. C. *The Death and Rebirth of the Seneca: The History and Culture of the Great Iroquois Nation, Their Destruction and Demoralization, and Their Cultural Revival at the Hands of the Indian Visionary, Handsome Lake*. New York: Knopf, 1969.

Wallace, Anthony F. C. *King of the Delawares: Teedyuscung 1700–1763*. Philadelphia: University of Pennsylvania Press, 1949.

Walthall, John A. *Moundville: An Introduction to the Archaeology of a Mississippian Chiefdom*. Tuscaloosa: University of Alabama, Alabama Museum of Natural History, 1977.

Warren, William W. *History of the Ojibway People*. St. Paul: Minnesota Historical Society Press, 1885, reprint 1984.

Waterman, Thomas T. "The Yana Indians." *University of California Publications in American Archaeology and Ethnology*, Vol. 13, No. 2. Berkeley: University of California Press, 1918.

Weatherford, Jack. *Native Roots, How the Indians Enriched America*. New York: Ballantine Books, 1991.

Wedel, Waldo R. *An Introduction to Pawnee Archeology*. Bulletin of the Smithsonian Institution, Bureau of American Ethnology, No. 112. Washington, DC: U.S. Government Printing Office, 1936. Reprint. Lincoln, NE: J & L Reprint, 1977.

Wedel, Waldo R. *Prehistoric Man on the Great Plains*. Norman: University of Oklahoma Press, 1961.

Wells, Samuel J. and Roseanna Tubby, eds. *After Removal: The Choctaw in Mississippi*. Jackson: University Press of Mississippi, 1986.

Weltfish, Gene. *The Lost Universe: Pawnee Life and Culture*. Lincoln: University of Nebraska Press, 1977.

Weslager, Clinton A. *The Delaware Indian Westward Migration*. Wallingford, PA: Middle Atlantic Press, 1978.

Weslager, Clinton A. *The Delaware Indians: A History*. New Brunswick, NJ: Rutgers University Press, 1972.

White, Leslie A. *The Acoma Indians, People of the Sky City*. Originally published in *47th Annual Report of the Bureau of American Ethnology*. Washington, DC: Smithsonian Institution, 1932; Glorieta, NM: The Rio Grande Press, 1973.

White, Raymond. "Religion and Its Role Among the Luiseño." *Native Californians: A Theoretical Retrospective*. Eds. Lowell J. Bean and Thomas C. Blackburn. Socorro, NM: Ballena Press, 1976.

White, Richard. *Land Use, Environment, and Social Change*. Seattle: University of Washington Press, 1992.

Wilbur, C. Keith. *The New England Indians*. Old Saybrook, CT: Globe Pequot Press, 1978.

Wilker, Josh. *The Lenape*. New York: Chelsea House Publishers, 1994.

Wilson, Terry P. *The Underground Reservation: Osage Oil*. Lincoln: University of Nebraska Press, 1985.

Wissler, Clark. *Indians of the United States*. New York: Doubleday, 1940.

Witherspoon, Gary. *Language and Art in the Navajo Universe*. Ann Arbor: University of Michigan Press, 1977.

Wolcott, Harry F. *A Kwakiutl Village and School*. Prospect Heights, IL: Waveland Press, 1984.

Wood, Peter H., Gregory A. Waselkov, and M. Thomas Hatley, eds. *Powhatan's Mantle: Indians in the Colonial Southeast*. Lincoln: University of Nebraska Press, 1989.

Wood, W. Raymond. "Plains Trade in Prehistoric and Protohistoric Intertribal Relations." *Anthropology on the Great Plains*. Eds. Raymond Wood and Margot Liberty. Lincoln: University of Nebraska Press, 1980.

Woodward, Grace Steele. *Pocahontas*. Norman: University of Oklahoma Press, 1969.

Woodward, Susan L. and Jerry N. McDonald. *Indian Mounds of the Middle Ohio Valley: A Guide to Adena and Ohio Hopewell Sites*. Newark, OH: McDonald & Woodward Publishing Co., 1986.

Worcester, Donald E. *The Apache*. Norman: University of Oklahoma Press, 1979.

The World of the American Indians. Washington, DC: National Geographic Society, 1974.

Wright, Muriel H. *A Guide to the Indian Tribes of Oklahoma*. Norman: University of Oklahoma Press, 1951, 1986.

Yenne, Bill. *The Encyclopedia of North American Indian Tribes*. New York: Crescent Books, 1986.

Yenne, Bill and Susan Garratt. *North American Indians*. Secaucus, NJ: Chartwell Books, 1984.

Young, Mary Elizabeth. *Redskins, Ruffleshirts, and Rednecks*. Norman: University of Oklahoma Press, 1961.

Periodicals

Alexander, Don. "A First Nation Elder's Perspective on the Environment" (interview with Haida Nation activist Lavina White). *Alternatives* (March/April 1994): p. 12.

Angulo, Jaime de. "The Achumawi Life Force" (Extract, "La psychologie religieuse des Achumawi." *Anthropos* 23, 1928). *Journal of California Anthropology* 2, No. 1 (1974): pp. 60–63.

Arden, Harvey. "Living Iroquois Confederacy." *National Geographic,* Vol. 172, No. 3 (September 1987): pp. 370–403.

Barrett, Samuel A. "The Ethnogeography of the Pomo and Neighboring Indians." *University of California Publications in American Archaeology and Ethnology* 6:1 (1908): pp. 1–332.

Barrett, Samuel A., and Edward W. Gifford. "Miwok Material Culture." *Public Museum of the City of Milwaukee Bulletin* 2:4 (1933): pp. 117–376.

Capron, Lewis. "Florida's Emerging Seminoles." *National Geographic,* Vol. 136, No. 5 (November 1969): pp. 716–34.

Carlson, Paul H. "Indian Agriculture, Changing Subsistence Patterns, and the Environment on the Southern Great Plains." *Agricultural History* 66, No. 2 (1992): pp. 52–60.

Carney, Jim. "Drinking Cut Short Sockalexis' Pro Career." *Beacon Journal* (October 13, 1995).

Crisp, David. "Tribes Make Manufacturing Push: Advocates Use Network to Expand Reach." *Billings Gazette* (February 11, 1996).

Dixon, Roland B. "Achomawi and Atsugewi Tales." *Journal of American Folk-Lore* 21, No. 80 (1908): pp. 159–77.

Dixon, Roland B. "Notes on the Achomawi and Atsugewi Indians of Northern California." *American Anthropologist* 10, No. 2 (1908): pp. 208–20.

DuBois, Constance Goddard. "The Religion of the Luiseño Indians of Southern California." *University of California Publications in American Archaeology and Ethnology* 8, No. 3 (1908): pp. 69–186.

Durham, Michael S. "Mound Country." *American Heritage,* Vol. 46, No. 2 (April 1995): p. 118.

Egan, Timothy. "Tribe Stops Study of Bones That Challenges Its History." *New York Times* (September 30, 1996): A1, A10.

Euler, Robert C. "Southern Paiute Ethnohistory." *Anthropological Papers.* 78:28. University of Utah (April 1966).

Fagan, Brian. "Bison Hunters of the Northern Plains." *Archaeology* 47, No. 3 (1994): pp. 37–41.

Farrell, John Aloysius. "Cheyenne Know Cost, Perils Tied to Energy Development." *Denver Post* (November 21, 1983).

Fischman, Joshua. "California Social Climbers: Low Water Prompts High Status." *Science,* Vol. 272 (May 10, 1996): pp. 811–12.

Fontana, Bernard L. "Restoring San Xavier del Bac, 'Our Church': Tohono O'odham Work to Restore the 200-Year-Old Church Built by Their Ancestors." *Native Peoples* (Summer 1995): pp. 28–35.

French, Bob. "Seminoles: A Collision of Cultures, Independent Indians' Lifestyle Faces Scrutiny," *Sun-Sentinel* (December 24 , 1995).

Garth, Thomas R. "Atsugewi Ethnography." *Anthropological Records* 14, No. 2 (1953): pp. 129–212.

Garth, Thomas R. "Emphasis on Industriousness among the Atsugewi." *American Anthropologist* 47, No. 4 (1945): pp. 554–66.

Gifford, E. W. "Notes on Central Pomo and Northern Yana Society." *American Anthropologist* 30, No. 4 (1928): pp. 675–84.

Gifford, E. W. and A. L. Kroeber. "Culture Element Distributions, IV: Pomo." *University of California Publications in American Archaeology and Ethnology* 37(4): pp. 117–254.

Gildart, Bert. "The Mississippi Band of Choctaw: in the Shadow of Naniw Waiya." *Native Peoples* (Summer 1996): pp. 44–50.

Goddard, Pliny Earle. "Chilula Texts." *University of California Publications in American Archaeology and Ethnology* 10, No. 7 (1914): pp. 289–379.

Halbert, Henry S. "The Choctaw Creation Legend," *Publications of the Mississippi Historical Society* 2 (1901): pp. 223–34.

Halbert, Henry S. "A Choctaw Migration Legend." *American Antiquarian and Oriental Journal,* 16 (1894): pp. 215–26.

Halbert, Henry S. "Nanih Waiya, the Sacred Mound of the Choctaws," *Publications of the Mississippi Historical Society* 2 (1899): pp. 223–34.

Hanks, Christopher C. and David Pokotylo. "The Mackenzie Basin: An Alternative Approach to Dene and Metis Archaeology." *Arctic,* Vol. 42, No. 2 (1989): pp. 139–47.

Heizer, R. F. "Impact of Colonization on Native California Societies." *Journal of San Diego History,* 24:1 (1978): pp. 121–39.

Heizer, R. F. and T. Kroeber, eds. "Indians Myths of South Central California." *University of California Publications in American Archaeology and Ethnology* 4, No. 4 (1907): pp. 167–250.

Hooper, Lucile. "The Cahuilla Indians." *University of California Publications in Archaeology and Ethnology,* 16, No. 6 (April 10, 1920): pp. 315–80.

Horn, Patricia. "Polluting Sacred Ground." *Dollars and Sense* (October 1992): pp. 15–18.

"Incinerator Planned Near Pipe Spring." *National Parks* (July/August 1990).

"Indian Roots of American Democracy." *Northeast Indian Quarterly* (Winter/Spring 1987/1988).

Johnson, Kirk. "An Indian Tribe's Wealth Leads to the Expansion of Tribal Law." *New York Times* (May 22, 1994): p. 1.

Keegan, John. "Warfare on the Plains." *Yale Review 84,* No. 1 (1996): pp. 1–48.

Kelly, Isabel T. "Southern Paiute Ethnography." *Anthropological Papers.* 69:21. University of Utah (May 1964). Reprint. New York: Johnson Reprint Corporation, 1971.

Kniffen, Fred B. "Achomawi Geography." *University of California Publications in American Archaeology and Ethnology* 23, No. 5 (1928): pp. 297–332.

Koppel, Tom. "The Spirit of Haida Gwai." *Canadian Geographic* (March/April 1996): p. 2.

LaDuke, Winona. "Like Tributaries to a River," *Sierra* 81, No. 6 (November/December 1996): pp. 38–45.

LaFrance, Joan. "Essay Review." *Harvard Educational Review* (Fall 1992): pp. 388–95.

Lekson, Stephen H. "Pueblos of the Mesa Verde." *Archaeology,* Vol. 48, No. 5 (September/October 1995): pp. 56–57.

Lepper, Bradley T. "Tracking Ohio's Great Hopewell Road." *Archaeology,* Vol. 48, No. 6 (November–December 1995): p. 52.

Lincecum, Gideon. "Life of Apushimataha." *Publications of the Mississippi Historical Society* 9 (1905–06): pp. 415–85.

Linden, Eugene. "Bury My Heart at James Bay: the World's Most Extensive Hydropower Project Has Disrupted Rivers, Wildlife, and the Traditions of the Quebec Indians. Is It Really Needed?" *Time* Vol. 138, No. 2 (July 15, 1991): p. 60.

Lindgren, Kristy. "Sgt. David H. Mace Shot Wampanoag David Hendricks Eleven Times and Is Still a Free Man." *News From Indian Country,* 7, No. 4 (1993): pp. 1–2.

"Makah Tribe's Net Snares Gray Whale." *Oregonian* (July 18, 1995).

"The Makah's Case for Whale Hunting." *Seattle-Post Intelligencer* (June 8, 1995).

"Menominee Honored at UN Ceremony for Forest Practices." *News From Indian Country,* IX, No. 9 (Mid-May 1995): p. 3.

Menominee Indian Tribe of Wisconsin. "Land of the Menominee" (brochure), c. 1994.

"The Menominee Nation and Its Treaty Rights." *News From Indian Country,* IX, No. 11 (Mid-June 1995): p. 2.

Menominee Nation Treaty Rights, Mining Impact, and Communications Offices. "Protect Menominee Nation Treaty Rights." *News From Indian Country,* X, No. 10 (Late-May 1996): p. 14A.

Millin, Peggy Tabor. "Passing the Torch: Technology Saves a Culture." *Native Peoples,* 9, No. 3 (1996): pp. 48–54.

Momatiuk, Yva and John Eastcott. "*Nunavut* Means Our Land." *Native Peoples* 9, No. 1 (Fall/Winter 1995): p. 42.

Mooney, James. "Calendar History of the Kiowa Indians." *Seventeenth Annual Report of the Bureau of American Ethnology.* Washington, DC: U.S. Government Printing Office, 1898.

Morrison, Joan. "Protect the Earth Gathering Focuses Mining Opposition." *News From Indian Country,* X, No. 5 (Mid-March 1996): p. 2.

Newman, Peter C. "The Beaching of a Great Whale." *Maclean's*. (Vol. 104, No. 37): p. 38.

Norman, Geoffrey. "The Cherokee: Two Nations, One People." *National Geographic* (May 1995): pp. 72–97.

"1,000 Gather to Oppose Exxon." *News From Indian Country,* X, No. 10 (Late-May 1996): pp. 1A, 5A.

Peterson, Lindsay. "Living History: Ruby Tiger Osceola, a 100-Year-Old Seminole Indian, Is Both a Link to the Past and a Leader for the Future." *The Tampa Tribune* (March 12, 1996).

Petit, Charles. "Ishi May Not Have Been the Last Yahi Indian." *San Francisco Chronicle* (February 6, 1996).

Plungis, Jeff. "Administering Environmental Justice." *Empire State Report* (January 1995): pp. 61+.

Roberts, Chris. "Schemitzun: The Pequot People's Feast of Green Corn and Dance." *Native Peoples,* Vol. 7, No. 4 (Summer 1994): pp. 66–70.

Rossiter, William. "CSI Opposes Whaling by the Makah." *Cetacean Society International.* Vol. 5, No. 1 (January, 1996).

Sapir, Edward. "Yana Texts." *University of California Publications in American Archaeology and Ethnology* 9, No. 1 (1910): pp. 1–235.

Sapir, Edward. "The Position of Yana in the Hokan Stock." *University of California Publications in American Archaeology and Ethnology* 13, No. 1 (1917): pp. 1–34.

Sapir, Edward and Leslie Spier. "Notes on the Culture of the Yana." *Anthropological Records* 3, No. 3 (1943): pp. 239–98.

Shaw, Christopher. "A Theft of Spirit?" *New Age Journal* (July/August 1995): pp. 84+.

Sparkman, Philip Stedman. "The Culture of the Luiseño Indians." *University of California Publications in American Archaeology and Ethnology* 8, No. 4 (1908): pp. 187–234.

Spier, Leslie. "The Sun Dance of the Plains Indians: Its Development and Diffusion." *Anthropological Papers of the American Museum of Natural History* 16, No. VII (1921): pp. 459–525.

Stirling, Matthew W. "Indians of the Far West." *National Geographic* (February 1948): pp. 175–200.

Strong, W. D. "The Plains Culture in the Light of Archaeology." *American Anthropologist* 35, No. 2 (1933): pp. 271–87.

Stuart, George E, "Etowah: A Southeast Village in 1491." *National Geographic,* 180, No. 4 (October 1991): pp. 54–67.

Theimer, Sharon. "Menominee Nation Lawsuit Wins Over Motion to Dismiss." *News From Indian Country,* X, No. 5 (Mid-March 1996): p. 3A.

Thompson, Ian. "The Search for Settlements on the Great Sage Plain." *Archaeology,* Vol. 48, No. 5 (September/October 1995): pp. 57–63.

Thurston, Harry and Stephen Homer. "Power in a Land of Remembrance: Their Rivers, Lands." *Audubon.* (Vol. 93, No. 6): p. 52.

Tobias, John L. "Canada's Subjugation of the Plains Cree, 1879–1885." *Canadian Historical Review,* Vol. 64 (December 1983): p. 519.

Todhunter, Andrew. "Digging Into History." *Washington Post Book World* (May 26, 1996): pp. 9, 13.

Turner, Steve and Todd Nachowitz. "The Damming of Native Lands." *Nation,* Vol. 253, No. 13 (October 21, 1991): p. 6.

Van Natta, Don Jr. "Tribe Saw a Promise, but Party Saw a Pledge." *New York Times* (August 12, 1997): A1, C20.

"The Water Famine." *Indigenous Peoples' Literature* (January 7, 1996).

Wedel, Waldo R. "Some Aspects of Human Ecology in the Central Plains." *American Anthropologist* 55, No. 4 (1953): pp. 499–514.

"Welcome to the Land of the Menominee-Forest." *News From Indian Country,* IX, No. 14 (Late-July 1995): p. 6.

White, Raymond. "Luiseño Social Organization." *University of California Publications in American Archaeology and Ethnology* 48, No. 2 (1963): pp. 91–194.

White, Raymond. "The Luiseño Theory of 'Knowledge.'" *American Anthropologist* 59, No. 2 (1957): pp. 1–19.

White, Raymond. "Two Surviving Luiseño Indian Ceremonies." *American Anthropologist* 55, No. 4 (1953): pp. 569–78.

Williams, Lee. "Medicine Man." *New Mexico Magazine* 62 (May 1984): pp. 62–71.

Web Sites

Beckman, Tad. "The Yurok and Hupa of the Northern Coast." [Online] http://www4.hmc.edu:8001/humanities/indian/ca/ch10.htm (accessed on April 22, 1999).

The Cheyenne Indians. [Online] http://www.uwgb.edu/~galta/mrr/ cheyenne (accessed on April 21, 1999).

Lawrence, Elizabeth Atwood, "The Symbolic Role of Animals in the Plains Indian Sun Dance." [Online] http://envirolink.org/ arrs/psyeta/sa/sa.1/lawrence.html (accessed on April 21, 1999).

Magagnini, Stephen. "Indians find 'new buffalo' in casinos." *The Modesto Bee Online.* [Online] http://www.modbee.com/metro/ story/0,1113,4447,00.html (accessed on April 22, 1999).

Powersource Consultants. *Important Dates in Cherokee History.* [Online] http://www.powersource.com:80/nation/dates.html (accessed on April 21, 1999).

Stockbridge-Munsee Home Page. [Online] http://www.pressenter. com/org/tribes/munsee.htm (accessed on April 21, 1999).

CD-ROMs

"Cherokee Language." *Microsoft Encarta 96 Encyclopedia.* Redmond, WA: Microsoft, 1993–95.

Kappler, Charles, ed. *Treaties of American Indians and the United States. Treaties with the Menominees, 1817, 1831 (February 8 and February 17), 1832, 1836, 1848, 1854, 1856. Treaty with the Chippewa, 1833. Treaty with the Stockbridge and Munsee, 1839,* version 1.00. Indianapolis: Objective Computing, 1994.

Schoolcraft, Henry R. "Archives of Aboriginal Knowledge" and "Thirty Years with the Indian Tribes," on *The Indian Question,* version 1.00. Indianapolis: Objective Computing, 1994.

Other Sources

Klasky, Philip M. "An Extreme and Solemn Relationship: Native American Perspectives: Ward Valley Nuclear Dump." A thesis submitted to the faculty of San Francisco State University in partial fulfillment of the requirements of the degree Master of Arts in Geography, May 1997.

Low, Sam. *The Ancient World* (television documentary). QED Communications, Inc./Pennsylvania State University, 1992.

Mashantucket Pequot Nation. "The Fox People." (Leaflet), c. 1994.

Mashantucket Pequot Nation. "The Mashantucket Pequots: A Proud Tradition" and "Foxwoods Resort Casino." (brochures), n.d.

Acknowledgments

G rateful acknowledgment is made to the following sources whose works appear in this volume. Every effort has been made to trace copyright, but if omissions have been made, please contact the publisher.

"Blueberry Pudding." Marx, Pamela. From *Travel-the-World Cookbook* by Pamela A. Marx. Copyright © 1996 by Pamela A. Marx. Reproduced by permission of Addison-Wesley Educational Publishers, Inc.

"The Bluebird and Coyote." *American Indian Myths and Legends* edited by Richard Erdoes and Alfonso Ortiz. Copyright © 1984 by Richard Erdoes and Alfonso Ortiz. Reproduced by permission of Pantheon Books, a division of Random House, Inc.

"Ceremony and Song." Ruoff, A. LaVonne Brown, ed. *Literatures of the American Indian.* Chelsea House Publishers, 1991. Copyright © by Chelsea House Publishers, a division of Main Line Book Co. All rights reserved. Reproduced by permission.

"Cheyenne Bread." Cox, Beverly, and Martin Jacobs. From *Spirit of the Harvest."* Copyright © 1991 Stewart, Tabori & Chang. Reproduced by permission.

"Chippewa Wild Rice." Copyright © 1965 by Yeffe Kimball and Jean Anderson. From *The Art of American Indian Cooking* published by Doubleday. Reproduced by permission of McIntosh & Otis, Inc.

"Choctaw Acorn Biscuits." Cox, Beverly, and Martin Jacobs. From *Spirit of the Harvest.* Copyright © 1991 Stewart, Tabori & Chang. Reproduced by permission.

"Comanche Chickasaw Plum Bars." Kavasch, E. Barrie. From *Enduring Harvests: Native American Foods and Festivals for Every Season.* Copyright © 1995 Globe Pequot Press. Reproduced by permission.

"Coyote in the Cedar Tree." Ramsey, Jarold. From *Coyote Was Going There: Indian Literature in the Oregon Country.* Copyright © 1977 University of Washington Press. Reproduced by permission.

"Coyote Wants To Be Chief." Premo, Anna. From *Shoshone Tales*. Edited by Anne M. Smith. University of Utah Press, 1993. © 1993 by the University of Utah Press. All rights reserved. Reproduced by permission.

"The Death of Wiyót, the Creator." Curtis, Edward S. From *The North American Indian." Edited by Frederick Webb Hodge. Copyright © 1970 Johnson Reprint Corporation.*

"The Emergence." Tithla, Bane. From *Myths and Tales of the White Mountain Apache*. Copyright © 1939 American Folklore Society. Reproduced by permission.

"An Encounter with the Tamciye." Garth, Thomas R. From *Atsugewi Ethnography*. Copyright © 1953 Anthropological Records.

"The Girl and the Devil." Bushnell, David I. From *Choctaw Myths and Legends*. Copyright © 1985 Garland Publishing. Reproduced by permission.

"Glacial Mists Cooler." Kavasch, E. Barrie. From *Enduring Harvests: Native American Foods and Festivals for Every Season*. Copyright © 1995 Globe Pequot Press. Reproduced by permission.

"Of Glooskap and the Sinful Serpent." Leland, Charles G. From *The Alogonquin Legends of New England: or Myths and Folklore of the Micmac, Passamaquoddy, and Penobscot Tribes*. Copyright © 1884 Houghton, Mifflen. Reproduced by permission.

"High Plains Pemmican." Kavasch, E. Barrie. From *Enduring Harvests: Native American Foods and Festivals for Every Season*. Copyright © 1995 Globe Pequot Press. Reproduced by permission.

"The Horrible Bear." Jewell, Donald P. From *Indians of the Feather River: Tales and Legends of Concow Maidu of California*. Copyright © 1987 Ballena Press. Reproduced by permission.

"How the Chumash Came To Be." Blackburn, Thomas C. From *December's Child: A Book of Chumash Oral Narratives*. Copyright © 1975 Berkeley: University of California Press. Reproduced by permission.

"How the Clans Came To Be." From *Creek Lifestyles, Customs and Legends*. Ryal Public School. Reproduced by permission. [Online] http://www.edumaster.net/schools/ryal/creek.html (18 September 1998).

"How the Moon Was Made." Clay, Charles. From *Swampy Cree Legends*. The Macmillan Company of Canada Limited, 1938. Copyright, Canada 1938 by The Macmillan Company of Canada Limited. All rights reserved.

"How Youth Are Instructed by Tribal Elders." Spindler, George, and Louise Spindler. From *Dreamers with Power: The Menomini Indians.* Copyright © 1971 Holt, Rinehart & Winston. Reproduced by permission.

"Jerky." Frank, Lois Ellen. From *Native American Cooking: Foods of the Southwest Indian Nations* by Lois Ellen Frank. Copyright © 1991 by Lois Ellen Frank. Reproduced by permission of Clarkson N. Potter, a division of Crown Publishers, Inc.

"King Philip's Prophecy." William Apess. Reprinted from Barry O'Connell, ed., *On Our Own Ground: The Complete Writings of William Apess, a Pequot.* (Amherst: University of Massachusetts Press, 1992). Copyright © 1992 by the University of Massachusetts Press.

"Mary O'Brien's Apricot Blueberry Cookies." Kavasch, E. Barrie. From *Enduring Harvests: Native American Foods and Festivals for Every Season.* Copyright © 1995 Globe Pequot Press. Reproduced by permission.

"Mohawk Baked Squash." Wolfson, Evelyn. From *The Iroquois: People of the Northeast.* Copyright © 1992 The Millbrook Press. Reproduced by permission.

"The Morning Star." Lacey, Theresa Jensen. From *The Pawnee.* Chelsea House Publishers, 1995. Copyright © 1996 by Chelsea House Publishers, a division of Main Line Book Co. All rights reserved. Reproduced by permission.

"Nanabozho and Winter-Maker." Coleman, Sister Bernard, Ellen Frogner, and Estelle Eich. From *Ojibwa Myths and Legends.* Copyright © 1962 Ross and Haines.

"Navajo Peach Pudding." Frank, Lois Ellen. From *Native American Cooking: Foods of the Southwest Indian Nations* by Lois Ellen Frank. Copyright © 1991 by Lois Ellen Frank. Reproduced by permission of Clarkson N. Potter, a division of Crown Publishers, Inc.

"Pawnee Ground Roast Pound Meat with Pecans." Kavasch, E. Barrie. From *Enduring Harvests: Native American Foods and Festivals for Every Season.* Copyright © 1995 Globe Pequot Press. Reproduced by permission.

"Powhatan Hazelnut Soup" Copyright © 1965 by Yeffe Kimball and Jean Anderson. From *The Art of American Indian Cooking* published by Doubleday. Reproduced by permission of McIntosh & Otis, Inc.

"Puffballs with Wild Rice and Hazelnuts." Kavasch, E. Barrie. From *Enduring Harvests: Native American Foods and Festivals for Every Season.* Copyright © 1995 Globe Pequot Press. Reproduced by permission.

"The Rabbit Dance." Bruchac, Joseph. From *Native American Animal Stories.* Copyright © 1992 Fulcrum Publishing. Reproduced by permission.

"The Race." Grinnell, George Bird. From *Cheyenne Campfires* Copyright © 1926 Yale University Press. Reproduced by permission.

"Simi Chumbo." Kavasch, E. Barrie. From *Enduring Harvests: Native American Foods and Festivals for Every Season.* Copyright © 1995 Globe Pequot Press. Reproduced by permission.

"Sioux Plum Raisin Cakes." Kavasch, E. Barrie. From *Enduring Harvests: Native American Foods and Festivals for Every Season.* Copyright © 1995 Globe Pequot Press. Reproduced by permission.

"Southeast Native American Pecan Soup." Cox, Beverly, and Martin Jacobs. From *Spirit of the Harvest.* Copyright © 1991 Stewart, Tabori & Chang. Reproduced by permission.

"The Stolen Squashes." Reed, Evelyn Dahl. From *Coyote Tales from the Indian Pueblos.* Sunstone Press, 1988. Copyright © 1988 by Evelyn Dahl Reed. Reproduced by permission.

"Succotash." McCullough, Frances, and Barbara Witt. From *Classic American Food Without Fuss* by Barbara Witt and Frances McCullough. Copyright © 1996 by Barbara Witt and Frances McCullough. Reproduced by permission of Random House, Inc.

"The Sun Dance Wheel." Monroe, Jean Guard, and Ray A. Williamson. From *They Dance in the Sky: Native American Star Myths.* Copyright © 1987 Houghton Mifflin. Reproduced by permission.

"Wampanoag Cape Cod Cranberry Pie." Kavasch, E. Barrie. From *Enduring Harvests: Native American Foods and Festivals for Every Season.* Copyright © 1995 Globe Pequot Press. Reproduced by permission.

"Why the Bear Waddles When He Walks." Marriott, Alice, and Carol K. Rachlin. From *American Indian Mythology.* Copyright © 1968 Cromwell. Reproduced by permission.

"Windwalker Pine Nut Cookies." Kavasch, E. Barrie. From *Enduring Harvests: Native American Foods and Festivals for Every Season.* Copyright © 1995 Globe Pequot Press. Reproduced by permission.

The photographs and illustrations appearing in U•X•L Encyclopedia of Native American Tribes were received from the following sources:

Covers Volume 1: tepee, **Library of Congress**; Seminole thatched houses, **P & F Communications. David Phillips, photographer;** Volume 2: Rocky Mountains from Ute Reservation, **North Wind Picture Archives. Reproduced by permission;** Taos Pueblo scene, **Library of Congress**; Volume 3: Inuit mother and child, **National Archives and Records Administration**; Young man at Sioux pow-wow, **Sygma Photo News. Photograph by F. Paolini. Reproduced by permission;** Volume 4: Ramona Lugu, Cahuilla in front of home, **Los Angeles Central Library. Reproduced by permission;** Tlingit longhouse with totem poles, **Corbis. Photograph by Tom Bean. Reproduced by permission.**

© 1998 North Wind Picture Archives. Reproduced by permission: pp. 3, 133, 405; **National Anthropological Archives. Reproduced by permission:** pp. 15, 1066, 1071; **Print by M. J. Burns. North Wind Picture Archives. Reproduced by permission:** p. 21; **University of Pennsylvania Museum. Reproduced by permission:** pp. 23, 1040, 1192; **Photograph by Frank C. Wotm. Library of Congress:** pp. 24, 25; **North Wind Picture Archives. Reproduced by permission:** pp. 32, 42, 51, 90, 109, 121, 141, 160, 172, 246, 247, 290, 317, 319, 329, 346, 373, 379, 381, 400, 418, 419, 443, 463, 468, 476, 498, 527, 534, 599, 637, 687, 693, 722, 756, 766, 785, 792, 796, 814, 827, 884, 897, 975, 1140; **Library of Congress:** pp. 36, 91, 146, 166, 219, 313, 416, 582, 615, 676, 732, 769, 778, 824, 848, 856, 908, 963, 965, 1087, 1117, 1162, 1173; **Bettmann. Reproduced by permission:** pp. 39, 45, 874; **AP/Wide World Photos, Inc. Reproduced by permission:** pp. 53, 84, 118, 138, 271, 305, 424, 458, 503, 750, 841, 1009, 1246; **© 1997 N. Carter/North Wind Picture Archives. Reproduced by permission:** pp. 62, 92, 497, 499; **Photograph by Bruce M. Fritz. *The Capital Times*. Reproduced by permission:** p. 63; **CORBIS/Bettmann. Reproduced by permission:** pp. 67, 108, 188, 356, 533, 828, 832, 877, 925; **Photograph by W. H. Wessa. Library of Congress:** p. 68; **Archive Photos. Reproduced by permission:** pp. 148, 153, 192, 358, 482, 485, 526, 578, 1048; **National Archives and Records Administration:** pp. 152, 178, 296, 348, 436, 464, 538, 546, 592, 635, 641, 643, 645, 748, 793, 810, 960, 1165, 1217, 1235; **Photograph by C. M. Bell. National Archives:** p. 176; **© 1977 North Wind Picture Archives. Reproduced by permission:** p. 202; **© 1994 North Wind Picture Archives. Reproduced by permission:** p. 209; **National Archives:**

pp. 234, 807, 935; **Granger Collection. New York. Reproduced by permission:** p. 249; © **1995. North Wind Picture Archives. Reproduced by permission:** pp. 388, 465, 492, 553, 601, 892; © **1993 North Wind Pictures Archives:** p. 391; **Mesa Verde National Park/National Park Service. Reproduced by permission:** p. 402; **Painting by Waldo Mootzka. Photograph by Seth Rothman. Dick Howard Collection. Reproduced by permission:** p. 460; **Southwest Museum. Reproduced by permission:** pp. 477, 479, 480, 979, 991, 1050; **Photograph by Edward S. Curtis. The Library of Congress:** pp. 512, 567, 694, 1116, 1256, 1259; **Photograph by Edward S. Curtis. CORBIS. Reproduced by permission:** pp. 517, 547; **CORBIS/Arne Hodalic. Reproduced by permission:** p. 519; © **1991 N. Carter/North Wind Picture Archives. Reproduced by permission:** p. 535; **CORBIS/E. O. Hoppe. Reproduced by permission:** p. 550; **Photograph by T. Harmon Parkhurst. Courtesy Museum of New Mexico, negative number 7454:** p. 559; **Photograph by Bluford W. Muir. CORBIS. Reproduced by permission:** p. 579; **Photograph by Orville L. Snider. CORBIS. Reproduced by permission:** p. 581; **CORBIS/Adam Woolfit. Reproduced by permission:** p. 585; **CORBIS/David G. Houser. Reproduced by permission:** pp. 606, 950; **CORBIS/Tom Bean. Reproduced by permission:** p. 610, 1269; **CORBIS. Reproduced by permission:** pp. 670, 672, 768, 922; **CORBIS/Joel Bennett. Reproduced by permission:** p. 675; **Provincial Archives of Manitoba. Reproduced by permission:** p. 714; **Photograph by Wiliam S. Soule. National Archives and Records Administration:** p. 736; **CORBIS/ Brian Vikander. Reproduced by permission:** p. 773; **Photgraph by Alexander Gardner. CORBIS. Reproduced by permission:** pp. 782, 784; **Photograph by William S. Soule. The Library of Congress:** p. 783; **Photograph by William H. Jackson. National Archives and Records Administration:** p. 840; **Buffalo Bill Historical Center, Cody, WY. Gift of Mrs. Cornelius Vanderbilt Whitney. Reproduced by permission:** p. 883; **Photograph by Eadweard Muybridge. National Archives and Records Administration:** p. 934; **Photograph by Larry Philllips. Institute of American Indian Arts Museum, Santa Fe:** p. 952; **Los Angeles Public Library. Reproduced by permission:** p. 992; **California History Section, California State Library. Reproduced by permission:** p. 1018; **CORBIS/David Muench. Reproduced by permission:** p. 1021; **Smithsonian Insititution, Bureau of American Ethnology. Reproduced by permission:** pp. 105, 1036; **CORBIS/Ed Young. Reproduced by permission:** p. 1081; **American Museum of Natural History. Reproduced by permission:** p. 1126; **CORBIS/**

Natalie Fobes. Reproduced by permission: pp. 1142, 1221, 1224; Photograph by Blankenburg Photo. CORBIS/PEMCO—Webster Stevens Collection; Museum of History & Industry, Seattle. Reproduced by permission: p. 1144; Photograph © Thomas Hoepker. Reproduced by permission of Joe Manfredini: p. 1177; Photograph by William McLennan. University of British Columbia Museum of Anthropology. Reproduced by permission: p. 1179; KWA-Gulth Arts Ltd. Reproduced by permission of Richard Hunt: p. 1194; Photograph by Edward S. Curtis. Univerversity of Pennsylvania Museum. Reproduced by permission: p. 1198; Photograph by Anthony Bolante. Reuters/Archive Photos. Reproduced by permission: p. 1207; CORBIS/Museum of History and Industry, Seattle. Reproduced by permission: p. 1210; CORBIS/Seattle Post–Intelligencer Collection. Museum of History and Industry, Seattle. Reproduced by permission: p. 1254; Courtesy Dept. of Library Services American Museum of Natural History, Neg. No. 41184. Reproduced by permission: p. 1268; Reproduced by permission of Preston Singletary: p. 1271; Photograph by Jeff Greenberg. Archive Photos. Reproduced by permission: p. 1272; Photograph by Winter and Pont. CORBIS. Reproduced by permission: p. 1274.

Index

Italic type indicates volume numbers; boldface type indicates entries and their page numbers; (ill.) indicates illustration.

Fish-ins 4: 1218, 1239

Fishing rights 3: 915, 917; 4: 1231
   (ill.), 1254

"Five Civilized Tribes" 1: 244, 251,
   266-268, 273, 294, 309, 313;
   3: 725

"Five Kiowa Artists" 3: 813

Fixico, Donald 1: 325

Flathead 3: 686, 745, 789,
   912-914, 916

"Flight of the Nez Perce" 3: 944

Florida 1: 217, 220, 225, 309, 316

Florida Seminole 1: 315

Flute Society 2: 466

Fonseca, Harry 4: 1075

Forest County band of Potawatomi
   1: 144, 147, 150-151, 155

Forest management 1: 67

Forfeiture Act (1863) 3: 855

Fort Ancient 1: 94

Fort Apache Reservation, Arizona
   2: 443, 449, 451

Fort Astoria 4: 1138

Fort Crevecoeur 3: 762

Fort Defiance 2: 393

Fort Detroit 1: 171

Fort Douglas 2: 356

Fort Gaston 4: 1031-1033

Fort Hall Bannock Reservation
   2: 342, 357

Fort Langley 4: 1229, 1253

Fort Laramie Treaty of 1851 3: 731,
   792, 871

Fort Laramie Treaty of 1868 3: 873

Fort McDermitt Reservation,
   Nevada 2: 351

Fort Mohave Reservation 2: 473

Fort Nisqually 4: 1229, 1253

Fort Randall Casino 3: 893

Fort Rupert 4: 1188

Fort Rupert Band 4: 1198

Fort Sill Apache Tribe 2: 427

Fort Sill, Oklahoma 2: 431-433

Fort Stanwix Treaty 1: 186

Fort Sumner, New Mexico
   2: 393, 492

Fort Victoria 4: 1187

Fort Washakie Historic District
   2: 361

Fort Yukon 3: 662

Four Corners 2: 397,
   398 (map), 455

Fourth of July Encampment 3: 927

Fox 1: 65, 149-50, **169-182,** 170
   (map), 176 (ill.)

Foxwoods Resort Casino, Ledyard,
   Connecticut 1: 135, 137,
   138 (ill.)

Franciscan order 2: 496; 4: 976

Frank, Billy, Jr. 4: 1225

Fraser River 3: 921

Freedman 1: 219, 224, 311

Freedman bands of Seminole
   1: 314

Frémont, John 3: 915; 4: 1123

French and Indian War (1755–63)
   1: 14, 16, 33, 61, 71, 114,
   185, 245

French-Fox War 1: 171

French language 1: 65; 3: 706

Frobisher, Martin 3: 633

Fur seals 4: 1204, 1206

Fur trade 1: 5, 6, 33, 61, 77, 113
   150; 3: 658, 661, 724

G

Gabrieliño 4: 979 (ill.), 1045

Gachupin, Pablo 2: 563

Gadsden Purchase 2: 450, 607

Gaiantwaka (Cornplanter) 1: 34

Gairdner, Meredith, 4: 1158

Gall 3: 873, 886

Gallup, New Mexico 2: 589

Gambling and gaming 1: 68, 118,
   126, 135, 206, 227, 237, 274;
   2: 361, 446, 452, 481, 541,
   549, 569, 610; 3: 916; 4: 982,
   1059, 1245

Ganiodayo (Handsome Lake) 1: 34

Garretson, William 4: 1152

Garza, Jose 2: 426

Gay Head Reservation, Martha's
   Vineyard 1: 204

Gay Head Wampanoag Indians
   1: 200, 205-206

General Allotment Act 1: 226, 297,
   314; 2: 332, 374; 3: 750, 765,
   793, 807, 823, 856, 893, 914;
   4: 980, 988, 1095

Georgia 1: 224, 243, 246, 309-311

Georgia Tribe of Eastern Cherokees
   1: 244

Geronimo 2: 414, 430, 431 (ill.),
   434, 450

Ghost Dance 1: 235, 272; 2: 341,
   344, 352, 359; 3: 734, 808,
   826, 875, 876, 878; 4: 980,
   1067, 1083, 1097, 1098, 1112,
   1126, 1245

Gibson, Isaac 3: 823

Gila River 2: 443

Gila River Reservation 2: 509

Girard, Corine 3: 835

Girard, Leona 3: 835

Gitksan 4: 1136

Glacial Mists Cooler (recipe)
   4: 1234

Glacier National Park 3: 743,
   747, 758

Gladstone, James 3: 750 (ill.), 759

Glooskap 1: 20, 75, 80

Gold rush 2: 341, 356, 372,
   373 (ill.), 512; 3: 726; 4: 987,
   1243, 1244

Goodwill, Jean Cutland 3: 701

Gorman, Carl Nelson 2: 494, 507

Gorman, R.C. 2: 507

Goshute 2: 330, 359

S